URBAN TRANSFORMATIONS

From Liberalism to Corporatism in Greater Berlin, 1871–1933

German and European Studies

General Editor: Jennifer J. Jenkins

Urban Transformations

From Liberalism to Corporatism in Greater Berlin, 1871–1933

PARKER DALY EVERETT

UNIVERSITY OF TORONTO PRESS
Toronto Buffalo London

Toronto Buffalo London
utorontopress.com

ISBN 978-1-4426-5053-4

(German and European Studies)

Library and Archives Canada Cataloguing in Publication

Everett, Parker Daly, 1978–, author
Urban transformations : from liberalism to corporatism
in greater Berlin, 1871–1933 / Parker Daly Everett.
(German and European studies ; 33)

Includes bibliographical references and index.
ISBN 978-1-4426-5053-4 (hardcover)

1. City planning – Germany – Berlin – History – 19th century. 2. City planning – Germany – Berlin – History – 20th century. 3. Urbanization – Germany – Berlin – History – 19th century. 4. Urbanization – Germany – Berlin – History – 20th century. 5. Berlin (Germany) – History – 19th century. 6. Berlin (Germany) – History – 20th century. I. Title. II. Series: German and European studies ; 33

HT169.G32E94 2019 307.1′2160943155 C2018-906312-2

University of Toronto Press acknowledges the financial assistance to its publishing program of the Canada Council for the Arts and the Ontario Arts Council, an agency of the Government of Ontario.

Canada Council for the Arts
Conseil des Arts du Canada

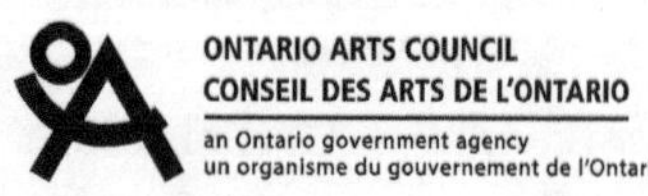

Funded by the Government of Canada
Financé par le gouvernement du Canada

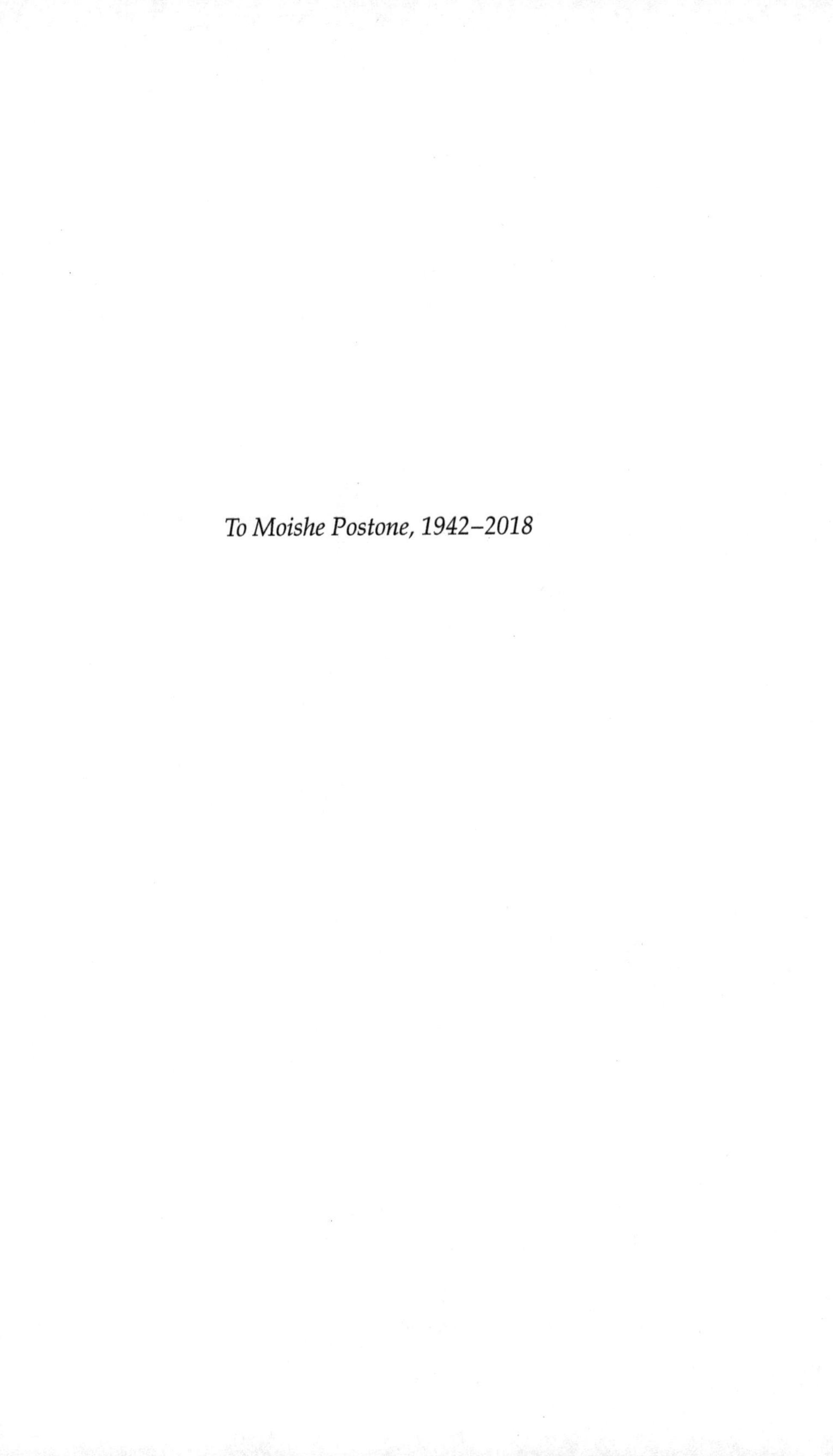

To Moishe Postone, 1942–2018

Contents

Figures

Acknowledgments

I would like to thank the many people who helped this project come to fruition. Richard Ratzlaff and Stephen Shapiro at the University of Toronto Press shepherded this book from proposal to revised submission. My anonymous readers who challenged me to elaborate, expand, and tighten my arguments. Moishe Postone, as a teacher and scholar, inspired me to think in new ways and to question rigorously my own assumptions and those of the prevailing historiography. I would also like to thank Michael Geyer, Leora Auslander, and Neil Brenner. While at the University of Chicago, my academic home was the Social Theory Workshop. This workshop modelled intellectual rigor, constructive criticism, and amity. I made many close friends there, and I would like to thank Mark Loeffler, Jason Dawsey, Andrew Sloin, Robert Stern, and Andrew Sartori, as well as the friends I made in my cohort: Thomas Dodman, Sean Dunwoody, Carlos Bravo Regidor, Alexia Yates, and Heather Welland. In particular, Tom has been a close friend, confidant, and intellectual collaborator.

I did not have the good fortune of having my research supported by grant-giving institutions, but I would like to thank the University of Chicago, my wife, Nancy Everett, and my parents for their financial support. I would also like to thank the librarians and archivists at the Landesarchiv Berlin, Geheimes Staatsarchiv, the Baukunstarchiv of the Akademie der Kunst, the Staatsbibliothek zu Berlin, the Bauhaus-Archiv, and the Ryerson and Burnham Libraries at the Art Institute of Chicago. I want especially to thank the Interlibrary Loan Office at the Regenstein Library at the University of Chicago. I am grateful to the staff of the history department, especially David Goodwine, for all the questions they have answered and the work they have done on my behalf.

Finally, thank you to my wife, Nancy for the many ways that you supported my morale as I worked on this project, and to my children, Henry, George, Alice, and Cormac Everett for keeping my priorities in order and my spirits high. I am indebted to my parents, my brothers, and their wives for the ways that they contributed to this project. I love you all.

URBAN TRANSFORMATIONS

From Liberalism to Corporatism in Greater Berlin, 1871–1933

Introduction

Towards a Critical Historical Study of Greater Berlin

"Architecture or Revolution?"

Le Corbusier (Charles-Edouard Jeanneret), 1924[1]

In the midst of the 1848 Revolution, Rudolf von Gneist, a young legal scholar at the University of Berlin, wrote that in creating the Berlin City Council, the revolutionaries broke fundamentally from previous forms of municipal government. He argued that the emergence of a middle class challenged both the city fathers and the Prussian state.[2] He believed that "even a child of the revolution could not deny that the city council was his mother," and he encouraged "the community of citizens" to make this new council, with the Magistrat, the lone municipal authority and the expression of the Berliners' general will. For Gneist, the city council represented the "basic conditions of a constitutional monarchy."[3] Legal historian Andreas Heusler argued in 1872 that municipal administration generated the "free *Bürgertum*" and "civic liberty," which were "the basis of the modern nature of the state."[4]

A similar liberal world view shaped areas distant from politics and economics. The city planner Gustav von Rössler wrote in 1874 that abstract legal norms in city planning – such as the height of buildings and the width of streets – created the foundation for freedom: a gridwork of roads would "preserve the freedom [of the owner] to use his property" and create reliable, consistent size and shape of plots of land.[5] Under these conditions, real estate was measured against every other plot on the market or potentially on the market, so, Rössler contended, when a property owner sought to develop his or her property, and "without any intervention of the city or state," building plots could be brought to market, and "unrestricted competition" could regulate land prices.[6] In both municipal administration and city planning in the mid-nineteenth century, liberal assumptions and world views pervaded the understanding of urban life. Furthermore, contemporaries believed that this liberalism was merely an expression of a natural state of affairs, of nature freed from the fetters of privilege and superstition.

By the 1920s this liberal world view was gone. In its place one finds a corporatist outlook that fused organic and mechanistic metaphors to grasp urban life and that focused on coordinating the totality of the population. Comparing social theorist and Berliner Georg Simmel's descriptions of urban bustle in 1903 to the visions of urban life put forward in films such as Walter Ruttmann's *Berlin: Die Sinfonie der Großstadt* and Fritz Lang's *Metropolis,* both from 1927, clarifies this vision.[7] Simmel wrote, "Thus the metropolitan type – which naturally takes on a thousand individual modifications – creates a protective organ for itself against the profound disruption with which the fluctuations and discontinuities of the external milieu threaten it."[8] The depiction of a bustling and industrial Berlin in Ruttmann's film, however, is symphonic, in that while it certainly is complex, it is highly organized and carefully structured. The extensive imagery of machines in the first act gives one a strong sense that Ruttmann viewed the movement of Berliners in the same way, as parts in one vast and complex but ultimately orderly machine. In the metropolis of Lang's film, the city has no money, market, or civil society, all of which are traditional components of a more abstract vision of a city and are key to liberal understandings of the city. (They played a central role in the mental life of a metropolitan, for example.) Lang's vision of a future city comprised only oppressed workers, parasitic and indulgent factory owners, and the unpredictable and potentially corrupting engineer. Lang's city is a massive factory, but it produces no commodities for the market; it just keeps the rest of the city functioning.

This book is an urban-environmental and intellectual history of the appearance, function, and perceptions of Greater Berlin that examines how historical actors understood and responded to challenges of the built environment and regional government of Greater Berlin between 1871 and 1933. Its central focus, however, is the period between roughly 1900 and 1933, to which the nineteenth century provides a necessary prehistory. For many, the metropolitan region of Greater Berlin drew together modern social and cultural problems, creating an intensified crisis: rapid industrialization, working-class radicalism, dramatic population growth, poor-quality housing, and regional administrative incoherence. This book focuses on Greater Berlin because the transformations that occurred in the late-nineteenth and early twentieth-century Greater Berlin were acute. This book argues that a significant change in the appearance, function, and perception of Greater Berlin occurred in this period. This change took place across many ostensibly separate disciplines, including forest preservation, city planning, jurisprudence, and municipal administration. Nonetheless, a pattern appears in the way these disciplines shifted. In the 1870s they were largely liberal, but by the 1930s they had become corporatist. The changes in Greater Berlin share many common elements with other industrial cities throughout the world. However, a more traditional empiricist study or discourse analysis will not fully grasp this transformation. Therefore, this book offers both a new, synthetic methodology and a theory for understanding urban transformations in the period that is the central focus of the book, but also in other periods as well. This book holds that a methodology and a theory should be developed simultaneously and through an examination of the research object. Both the method and the theory will be introduced in what follows and unfolded in full in the body of the book. This book will contribute as much if not more to theories of urbanism as it will to the history of Greater Berlin.

From the beginning of the Kaiserreich in 1871 to the end of the Weimar Republic in 1933, the form, function, and perception of the city of Greater Berlin were transformed in discourses on city planning and municipal administration. This transformation from a city constituted through liberal social forms to one organized along "corporatist" social forms was dialectical and, as such, it was not smooth or teleological. At the level of the metropolitan region, during this period, the condition of Greater Berlin structured the theory and practice of city planners, municipal administrators, and concerned citizens, giving rise to a wide variety of attitudes from the sanguine to the pessimistic. The regional social transformations, such as rapid urbanization, population growth, inadequate housing, working-class radicalism, and administrative incoherence, gave rise to a variety of cultural responses, which, in turn, shaped the social transformation. This transformation, in its regional form, was also mediated by national processes that were the dialectical consequence of the shift from liberal to corporatist social forms. These processes include the failure of liberalism, the rise of socialism, the First World War, the November 1918 Revolution, the hyperinflation of 1921–3, the Great Depression, and the rise of fascism.

During the nineteenth century, German municipal administration expanded its autonomy and expanded its liberal political structure, notwithstanding the persistence of the conservative Prussian bureaucracy. Across this period, industrialization slowly undermined the basis of this autonomy. Social conflict, expanding welfare services, and geographic-economic influence and integration all became focused on cities. These urban issues attracted the attention of the higher levels of government. In this same period, a form of city planning developed that was structured around basic ideas of liberal political economy and politics. The planners understood the principles of liberalism to be the natural and rational response to the demands of the city developing these ideas, even though they were not necessarily liberal in an overtly political sense.

This liberal city-planning framework was undermined by industrialization and urbanization in Greater Berlin. The ideas about abstract equality so central to a liberal understanding of the world were challenged by the concrete consequences of liberal city planning, politics, and economics. Liberals had predicted that the freedom of the market and of the private property holder would create the conditions of possibility in the built environment for a just society; however, that did not happen. Liberals were forced by the poor-quality housing, monopoly of real-estate property ownership, inefficient (from the point of view of capitalism) layout of the city, poor hygienic conditions, and the absence of green space to reconsider their previous ideals. They began to advocate addressing the spatial consequences of capitalism through intervention in the functioning of the market and private property.

Liberal city planning and municipal self-administration were weakened by these conditions, but these liberal social forms were metamorphosed by the First World War and the November 1918 Revolution. Tendencies inherent in the Kaiserreich were accentuated by the war and revolution, but the war and revolution altered these tendencies. In the war economy, the market and liberalism more generally appeared to capitalists to be impediments to efficiency. A new ideology forced city planning and municipal administration to emphasize a new cohesive character of the society and on expanding the territory of planning. The social transformation brought about by revolution shifted to emphasize a planned, unified, productive society, especially with regard to housing. Finally, the war economy demanded new institutions, which, in turn, created new possibilities for the unification of Greater Berlin into a single city. While the liberal mode of planning and administration valued individual autonomy, abstract law, private property, and rational self-interest, this new corporatist mode of planning emphasized the integration of the individual into the collective, rule by decree, expropriation of private property, and planning for the social totality.

By the 1920s new theories and practices of city planning and municipal administration were established that valued social integration and greater state intervention in urban administration and the economy. During the Weimar Republic, Berlin's city planning and municipal administration was shaped by an expanded territory for planning, a shortage of capital, the politics of birth rates and living space, and a new aesthetic that emphasized form that followed function and productivity. In the discourses of city planning and municipal administration, Germany's well-being and power were connected to the productivity of the nation and the productive dimensions of capitalism. In particular, these discourses emphasized a belief that new spatial arrangements could remove the perceived fetters on production.

While particularly articulated in city planning, architecture, and municipal administration, this shift in social forms pervaded the society. It extended beyond obviously political or economic realms, to the law (e.g., it affected the legal definition of a municipality), the social relevance of city parks, architectural aesthetics, and the function of working-class homes. This transformation in social patterns is linked to larger changes in the nature of capitalist modernity.

The sections of this introduction that follow have several goals: The book will develop a critical analysis of the ways that others have understood the key categories of this history, such as liberalism and corporatism. It will provide context for the relationships between society, politics, culture, and capitalism in the era that this book analyses. It will engage critically with the historiography in order to demonstrate its shortcomings, but more importantly, to justify the turn to social theory that this book makes, and it will expose the ways that the prevailing literature is structured by a series of antinomies. It will then begin to propose a way of considering changing forms of urbanization and the perception of urbanization that sees these practical and ideological dimensions as intrinsically related and root the changes in a theory of capitalist modernity. Finally, it seeks, retrospectively, to suggest the ways that the prevailing literature itself is shaped by the historically specific logic of capitalism.

Liberalism and Corporatism

A shift from a liberal to a corporatist appearance, function, and perception of Greater Berlin occurred between 1871 and 1933. To develop adequate concepts of liberalism and corporatism, this introduction will examine the dominant ways of understanding these categories. Furthermore, understanding liberalism and corporatism as social forms and the transition from one set of forms to the other requires a more abstract, theoretical lens than is common in the historiography. In his classic essay on German urban liberalism, James Sheehan argues that in 1850, liberalism shaped urban life from politics, to economics, to the public sphere.[9] However, by the 1870s the liberal advance was halted, and liberal reforms inadvertently created right- and left-wing radicals and a society where liberal ideas no longer seemed adequate.[10] In response, liberals found refuge in local politics, where they defended undemocratic measures that assured their privileges.[11] Liberal ideas were taken for granted to such an extent that a liberal urban policy could be seen as unpolitical.[12] Sheehan's concern for social relations and political economy, on the one hand, and the conditions of possibility of liberal politics, on the other hand, is valuable, though Sheehan does not sufficiently mediate between levels of abstraction. Responding to this inadequacy in Sheehan's work and believing that Sheehan regarded German urban liberals as unpolitical, Jan Palmowski sets out to debunk the idea that liberals in Frankfurt were apolitical. Seeking to avoid the problems of mediation that affected Sheehan and deeming that synthetic analysis of the form or timing of those politics in other cities and general arguments about urban liberalism mask key differentiating details, Palmowski rejects the feasibility of such efforts.[13] This book, however, will argue that a synthetic analysis that works at a higher level of abstraction and generality, but that does not lose the fine-grained detail that Palmowski emphasizes, is possible, and for certain key insights, necessary.

The *Sonderweg* or German "special path" historiography of liberalism, of which Sheehan is an example, made a valuable contribution to addressing social relations and political economy, on the one hand, and the conditions of possibility of liberal politics, on the other hand. This literature is often dismissed as teleological by the historiography of German liberalism. However, it does attempt to connect politics and ideology more broadly to the social relations and political economy within which those ideas function. Furthermore, it attempts to develop an analysis of why liberalism stopped being an effective ideology whose explanation reaches beyond a series of contingent events. According to the *Sonderweg*, after 1873 the grounds for the existence of liberalism were eroding. The *Sonderweg* attempts to explain this growth of governmental responsibilities and their relationship to transformations in capitalism. Importantly, it emphasizes that, while liberals regarded their market-based social order as an "inevitable result of quasi-natural laws," in fact liberalism was a historically specific phase of capitalism. Furthermore, according to this approach, the state and the economy constituted and changed each other as the state responded to economic turbulence with counter-cyclical measures.[14] For *Sonderweg* historians, the inner dynamic of liberalism concentrated ownership and undermined the social basis for that liberalism, as businesses pressured the state to increase state economic regulations and used liberal social forms such as contracts and private-sphere associations to develop illiberal defensive cartels and syndicates.[15] In the place of liberalism, "organized capitalism" developed, wherein the increasing concentration of capital, especially into the hands of the large banks, and the interventions of the state made it possible to pacify business cycles and social unrest.[16] According to Hans Ulrich Wehler, this state intervention angered orthodox liberals but benefited "the preindustrial agrarian elite" and the "new lords of heavy industry," who constituted "a cartel of anxiety."[17] This new social alliance between the agrarian aristocracy and the big-business elite was powerful in Greater Berlin, which had a large number of industrial elites as well as aristocrats who served in military, royal, imperial, and bureaucratic capacities.

Beginning in the late 1970s, the lack of mediation between the more abstract claims made by the *Sonderweg* and the self-understanding of historical actors became a focal point of critique. Geoff Eley and David Blackbourn were the lead proponents of this critique, which will be more fully discussed in chapter 1, and a brief summary will have to suffice for now. Eley and Blackbourn argue against the *Sonderweg* and the way it attributed the weakness of German liberalism to the failed revolution of 1848. Eley and Blackbourn contend that liberalism triumphed over the ancien régime, not through one swift blow, but through a long, reconstitution of social forms to fit the needs of capitalism.[18] This transformation of society appeared to be natural, but this apparent naturalness in the face of a significant break in social history is a testament to the power of capitalist social relations and their ability to adapt to local history and geography.[19] Their central criticism of the *Sonderweg* was that it did not mediate sufficiently between the structure of the society and economy on the one hand and political or cultural ideas on the other hand. However, this approach, in the hands of Eley and Blackbourn's followers, treated cultural and political social forms idealistically, as separate from the social world they inhabit.

Criticizing the same lack of mediation that Eley and Blackbourn addressed in the *Sonderweg* literature, though in a later historical period, Charles Maier introduces the category of corporatism in response to the weaknesses of "organized capitalism" as a category. While the *Sonderweg* historians argued that the social relations and political economy of the Kaiserreich and the Weimar Republic were essentially the same, Charles Maier introduces the category of "corporatism" to grasp the historical specificity of the Weimar Republic as a period distinct from German society during both the First World War and the Great Depression. As this study is interested in grasping a historical shift in the appearance, function, and perception of Greater Berlin, Maier's attention to historical specificity and to understanding the uniquely modern features of the corporatism are invaluable. He argues that, during the Weimar Republic, the state continued to transform the political economy of Germany, now under peacetime conditions, from a market economy into "a predictable and planned capitalist economy." He contends that capitalism and the state transformed the traditional liberal boundaries between public and private and between the state and business.[20] Unlike the *Sonderweg* historians, Maier contends that big-business interests and agrarian interests did not always coincide. Of particular importance for this book, he argues that these powerful interests mis-recognized their world and took steps that resulted in situations quite contrary to their original intent.[21] For example, German liberals and conservatives achieved a "bourgeois victory" but did so "only by resorting to the corporatist settlements that undermined the basic anchoring conceptions of the bourgeoisie."[22] The idea of misrecognition that Maier introduces is more than just a question of unintended consequences; rather, it is a tendency of the society to produce systemic misrecognitions. This idea should not just be posited, as Maier does. Rather, in this book, it will be rooted in a theory of society that can account for the other features of the society.

Demonstrating the overly broad claims of *Sonderweg* historiography and the weakness of accounts of industrial paternalism that treat it as pre-modern, Dennis Sweeney insightfully shows that proponents of a corporatist society regarded that society as a progressive, scientifically based advance from nineteenth-century liberalism. Furthermore, he shows that the transition from liberalism to corporatism began earlier than Maier claims; it began before the First World War. At the 1905 meeting of the Verein für Socialpolitik, a shift in the discourse about labour conflict and large-scale industry crystallized, constituting a new form of corporatism. In a speech at the meeting, Max Weber attacked paternalist industrial policies of owners of modern steel factories from a liberal perspective that saw the owners' policies as antiquated.[23] However, when the employers defended themselves, they criticized Weber's liberal perspective from what they regarded as a more modern, economic, scientific, and even biological position.[24] They believed that global economic competition made their corporatist approach to their employees necessary.[25] Sweeney asserts that this moment exemplified a corporatist restructuring occurring in the society.[26] This shift supports the contention of this book that a significant transformation in the structure of German society began in the early twentieth century towards a more corporatist society. Such an ideological shift from an industrial paternalism that liberals could regard as antiquated into a corporatism that regards itself as more advanced than liberalism can be and should be accounted for by an approach that sees social forces and ideologies as intrinsically related. However, such an approach demands that one consider society at a higher level of abstraction than the typical, discourse-analytical historiography can sustain.

However, the rise of this corporatist thinking was broader than ideas about the workplace and political economy. Similar theories about the organic cohesion of society and the social character of nature developed at roughly the same time. For example, Ferdinand Tönnies's idea of *Gemeinschaft* and *Gesellschaft* contrasted "'order and freedom' or 'relations based on obligation,' on one side (*Gemeinschaft*, or community), and those based on 'exchange,' on the other (*Gesellschaft*, or society)." Lynn Nyhart places Tönnies's organicist understanding of community in the context of zoologist Karl August Möbius's ideas of "'*Biologische Gesellschaft*' (biological society)'... [and] *Lebensgemeinschaft*, or living community," which "viewed the organism as a living being embedded in nature."[27] Both Sweeney and Nyhart provide important insights and pose a question about the relationship between corporatism and culture; however, their analyses of discourse and intellectual networks are inadequate. To explain the rise of this organicist and corporate vision of society, historians must turn to a theory of social mediation and capitalism, such as those offered by David Harvey and especially Moishe Postone.

The Antinomies of Contemporary Urban Historiography

This book brings together an analysis of a transformation of liberal to corporatist social forms through the critical engagement with the work of *Sonderweg* historians, Eley and Blackbourn, and historians of corporatism with a study of urban history and geography. The historiography of Berlin is vast and covers many features of Berlin's variegated history. This book will address those more particular historiographies as the topics they address arise in the body of the text. Therefore, this section will contend with paradigmatic examples of four important modes of historiography on Berlin and on cities more generally: urban politics, urban society, urban culture, and urban governmentality. The history of Greater Berlin, and of urban history in Germany more generally, began with urban biographies that trace the political history of the city since its founding, such as late nineteenth- and early twentieth-century studies of Berlin by Wolfgang von Oettingen and Oscar Schwebel.[28] This literature describes the large-scale development of city politics and government, and, in the case of more specialized studies, the subtle vacillation of local politics amidst key political events, such as the Revolution of 1848 or the fortunes of smaller social groups, such as the Jews.[29] This politically focused approach to the history of Greater Berlin, however, assumed that social processes such as industrialization and urbanization were quasi-natural forces and, as such, could not adequately come to terms with political responses to industrialization and urbanization.

Beginning in the 1950s, in response to the weaknesses of the existing political historiography, historians took a social science–oriented approach to German urbanization and industrialization. This social historiography is valuable for the ways that it demonstrates the existence and constitutive power of social processes that are beyond the control of individual agency. This research interrogated historical developments that the political historiography had regarded as parts of the natural evolution of civilization, such as the location of cities, the character of their urbanization, the relationship between industrialization and urbanization, neighbourhood and industrial network formation, social mobility, and mass migration. However, these developments are not natural; they are the consequence of historically specific social relations. Understanding these developments is key to grasping the political as well as the social and cultural dynamics that underpinned changing appearance, function, and perception of Greater Berlin. This social science–oriented literature argued that quantitative measures could accurately describe social forces in urban history. The work of Lothar Baar and of Ingrid Thienel marked the high point of this literature's exploration of Greater Berlin.[30] However, critics correctly argued that this literature did not mediate effectively between the social forces it described and the self-understanding of the individuals experiencing these social forces. Historians also demonstrated that the statistics gatherers held the political, social, and cultural presumptions and revealed that the "hard facts" on which social-science history was built could create a weak or skewed foundation, because of the historically specific cultural ideas that shaped the counting and categorization of the statisticians.[31] However, in their rejection of social history, these cultural historians sacrificed and forgot important insights from social history.

In the 1970s a cultural historiography responded to this lack of mediation between the self-understanding of historical actors and social forces in the social history. It peaked in the 1990s and remains the prevailing mode of historical scholarship. The work of Andrew Lees and Peter Fritzsche represents some of the best of this cultural history. Lees uses the reaction to the rapid urbanization of Greater Berlin as a way to understand attitudes towards modernity.[32] Lees does an excellent job of grasping a wide variety of ideas about Berlin and cities more generally and demonstrating "not only the paradigmatic centrality but also the complexity and the variability of the often heated conversation that revolved around the Prussian-German capital."[33] According to Lees, the response also had an influence "on patterns of thought and feeling" and "generated a vast outpouring of inquiry, research, reflection, and debate."[34] While Lees's work demonstrates a multiplicity of "thoughts and feelings," this book will seek to understand the "patterns" that shape this multiplicity, why they exist, why they take their particular form, and why they change over time. Peter Fritzsche analyses the "'word city,' the accumulation of small bits and rich streams of text that saturated the twentieth-century city, guided and misguided its inhabitants, and in large measure fashioned the nature of metropolitan experience." True to this culturalist approach to cities, he seeks to examine "the terms of mediation between city and text." Fritzsche regards the city through a textual lens: "reading and writing in the city invited as well as contained public movements through the city." He hopes to demonstrate this textuality through maintaining "the broad strokes of narrational order," but also "bring[ing] in the sharp counter-strokes of interpretative disorder, both of which emerge out of the relations between readers and texts and contexts." Fritzsche contends that this "word city" can mislead inhabitants.[35] The possibility that urbanites can be misled and misrecognize their world suggests that a social world exists that is beyond the intertextual realm that Fritzsche lays out. For Fritzsche, the city is a site of circulation and consumption and a locus of critical indeterminacy and resistance. He celebrates the metropolis as city, which he associates with market anarchy, and compares to the metropolis as capital, which he associates with "regimentation and discipline."[36] In other words, for Fritzsche, the market and the state stand opposed to each other. In Fritzsche's vision, Berlin is a dynamic social chaos, yet it is also capable of creating forms of misrecognition. Explaining the possibility of such misrecognition demands a theorization of society that is not possible within the standard discourse-analysis or empiricist approach to history. This book attempts to explain the misrecognitions that Fritzsche and Maier describe and the patterns of urban consciousness that Lees outlines with reference to the dynamic structural forces that the quantitative historiography delineates while mediating between the self-understanding of historical actors and these structural forces, as Eley and Blackbourn encourage.

The cutting-edge contemporary literature picks up the same opposition that Fritzsche expresses between the power of the state and a purported natural anarchy of social life, often associated with the market. This most recent literature employs Michel Foucault's idea of "governmentality" to grasp the ways that modern society is structured by abstract forms of mediation such that a society ostensibly built on freedom and rationality could be dominating.[37] This literature has important insights into this peculiar, modern form of abstract domination and finds the cause of abstract domination in concrete social practices. Leif Jerram treats massive and rapid urbanization as the consequence of individual choices, rejecting the insights gained by the social-science-oriented historiography, which grasped urbanization abstractly and quantitatively.[38] Jerram ascribes significant cultural changes such as new notions of selfhood, of the interiority of psychic life, and of privacy to concrete changes in urban social space, such as the separation of work and home and the division of the home into rooms. He notices an important shift in the appearance, function, and perception of the city in the early twentieth century: "The nineteenth-century obsession with the superficial appearance of buildings was displaced by a revolutionary obsession on the part of 'experts' and states with what went on inside of buildings." Jerram asserts that intervention and social planning necessarily led to domination, even mass murder.[39] Here Jerram reveals a common problem with discursive and governmentality-focused accounts of social change. His approach cannot account for the new power of experts or the shift in the population from desiring privacy to seeking intervention "in the minutest details of people's everyday lives."[40] Jerram cannot explain how experts, who were subjected to this same liberal, privacy-oriented ideology, could step outside of this ideology and transform it. This book develops an approach that is adequate to the research problem that Jerram raises and can explain this shift in both expert and popular subjectivity.

The pioneering text of this urban governmentality historiography is James Scott's *Seeing like a State*. It focuses on the abstract rationality of the state, which it roots in the Enlightenment. Scott claims that this abstract rationality drives the state's purported desire to make cities visible and legible and is the view of the foreigner, and prefers "a repetitive, abstract logic that would allow a newcomer to orient herself."[41] He sides with the locals against the "outside elites" and celebrates illegible spaces as defensive fortresses and refuges.[42] Like Jerram, Scott associates the horrors of the late nineteenth and twentieth centuries with a desire to plan.[43] This literature claims that planning necessarily leads at best to tragic failure and at worst to mass murder. This literature is important for the ways that it reveals that certain abstract, dominating modes of thought can constitute social life; however, it is limited, because it sees this mode of thought as imposed from the outside, as separate from and prior to social relations, and as driven by an ontological will-to-power of the state. This governmentality-influenced scholarship opposes the abstract, superficial, and rational character of state actions to the concrete, chaotic, authentic, and unplannable character of social life.[44] This literature is valuable for the ways that it describes forms of abstract domination embodied in concrete social practices. However, the theoretical approach it employs cannot explain why the abstract domination exists, why it has this concrete embodiment, and how and why this domination changes. This urban governmentality literature reifies the dominating structure of knowledge out of its social context, that is, out of capitalism. The approach developed in this book will attempt to account for the historical specificity of this abstract domination and its concrete form.

The discourse of the dominating state and the free, authentic, and anarchic local market that is evident in Fritzsche, Jerram, and Scott is a very common ideology in the present era – and is employed in far more areas than this specific context of late nineteenth- and early twentieth-century city planning. Jan van Ballegooijen and Roberto Rocco insightfully criticize this ideology in the context of the contemporary celebration of informal urbanization, revealing the ubiquity of these ideas and suggesting that intellectual networks and influences cannot explain their proliferation. They demonstrate the centrality of a celebratory vision of informal urbanization in contemporary discourses about cities and housing that emphasizes the creativity, anarchism, and authenticity in informal urbanization and that attacks the dominating, abstract, uniform manner of state-supported planning. They show the way that this opposition between the local, unregulated market and the overweening state reflects neoliberal visions of the world and reveals the historical specificity of this critique of the state. They argue that this celebration of informal urbanization lost its critical valance with the end of Fordist-Keynesian state regulations, and informality became idealized. They argue that this celebration amounts to "the aestheticization of poverty" and reifies it from its political and economic context.[45] The authors demonstrate how what began as an "anarchist or liberal leftist" discourse became a neoliberal critique of the remnants of the Fordist-Keynesian state.[46]

The point here is not to condemn the form of city planning, architecture, or historiography for reflecting the prevailing, in this case neoliberal, vision of the world. Rather, the problem arises that when authors regard this discourse as *critical*, when, in fact, it *affirms* the status quo. Moishe Postone cautions that just as "in an earlier global transition of capitalism, Marxists frequently opposed general rational planning to the anarchic irrationality of the market" in a way that "legitimate[d] a subsequent state-centric capitalism," this celebration of a natural chaos in human society in opposition to state planning and intervention "can serve to veil and legitimate a new global form that combines decentralization and heterogeneity of production and consumption with increasing centralization of control and underlying homogeneity."[47] The literature on urban governmentality is still battling with the state of the mid-twentieth century and doing so in a neoliberal or conservative fashion.

The City and Culture

If scholars are to move beyond the idealism that characterizes discourse analysis and the concretism that delineates the historiography of the spread of an idea or of the constitution of urban liberal subjects, they need to begin to relate the practical world of modern capitalism to the ideas about that world. This is not an immediate relation; rather, it is mediated by a wide variety of social and cultural ideas and forces, but theory and practice are nonetheless connected in fundamental ways. Grasping the transformation of ideas about Berlin (as well as other cities) between 1871 and 1933 demands an understanding of how Berlin, as a geographic and economic process, was itself being transformed. This book relates the dual transformation of theory and practice to broader changes in the character of capitalism. However, this book has no model to follow. It cannot apply this or that theory or use this or that historiographical method, because such a theory or urban historiography does not exist. Therefore this book attempts to develop a new approach through a critical engagement with primary sources, historiography, and social theory.

Incorporating the work of Neil Brenner, this book suggests that a reterritorialization of urban economic geography, territory, and scale occurred in the early twentieth century.[48] It attempts to respond to Henri Lefebvre's provocation in *The Production of Space*, "The fact is that around 1910 a certain space was shattered."[49] While Lefebvre moves on without substantively addressing this comment, David Harvey answers Lefebvre with an eclectic list of new ideas about space coming around 1910, revealing lack of theorization of the relationship between culture and capitalism.[50] To account for this simultaneous shift in culture, economy, and geography, this book draws on Brenner's idea that the "second industrial revolution" led to cities that were "engines of Fordist mass production," and a global, liberal economic system became "compartmentalized into distinct territorial states" in which "a relatively tight fit was established between urban dynamism and national economic growth," though transnational connections between cities did remain important.[51] An era of relatively vibrant global capitalism and financialization ended, and in its place arose a more nationally based and autarkic system.[52] This book will offer an account, on a more concrete level, of this change in the theory and practice of urban space.

An approach adequate to the transformation in the appearance, function, and perception of Greater Berlin from ones structured by liberal social forms to ones structured by corporatist social forms needs to be able to bring politics, social forces, and culture into a dynamic relation. Furthermore, it must be capable of understanding the historical specificity of politics, social forces, and culture and explain a shift at various levels from a liberal society and culture to a corporatist society and culture. This book builds upon David Harvey's concept of a regime of accumulation that periodizes modern history according to the relationship between historically specific global social, political, cultural, and economic configurations that are generated by and facilitate the continued accumulation of capital. However, this book attempts to account for the subjective dimension of a regime of accumulation and a transition between regimes.[53] Harvey's concept is helpful for the ways that it grasps the fact that the form of appearance of capitalism can change while remaining, fundamentally, capitalism. This book seeks to move beyond Harvey by seeing capitalism and culture as intrinsically related and graspable by the same set of categories.[54]

Grasping this transformation in the appearance, function, and perception of Greater Berlin and other cities, as this introduction has argued, requires considering these transformations at a higher level of abstraction and theoretical considerations of social processes. Urban space did change fundamentally around 1910, and, through the example of Berlin, this book will examine that change in the character of modern, capitalist, urban space. As Max Horkheimer argued, "The fortunes of the individual have always been bound up with the development of urban society. The city dweller is the individual *par excellence*.... The antagonism between individuality and the economic and social conditions of its existence ... is an essential element in individuality itself. Today, this antagonism is supplanted in the conscious minds of individuals by a desire to adapt themselves to reality. This process is symptomatic of the present crisis of the individual, which in turn reflects the breakdown of the traditional idea of the city."[55] Employing the work of Max Horkheimer and his colleagues in the Institute for Social Research, this book argues that a specific form of individuality and selfhood is closely related to a specific form of urban space.[56] In the early twentieth century, concepts of individuality, selfhood, and urban space began to change and change in the same way, such that integration and adaptation were valued over individuality and liberalism.

Engineers guided the city planning of Greater Berlin, but by the late nineteenth century, aesthetic planners, who were often also architects, sought to introduce beauty into urban design. After the First World War the dominant mode of planning came from functionalist architects who argued that form followed function but also tried to make functionality beautiful. Debates about what constitutes a beautiful city and what about urban life is culturally deleterious or edifying run throughout the sources for this book. Furthermore, the perception and reality of the functionality of cities – and their relationship to beauty – drive significant changes both in the aesthetics and the policy of urban government and city planning. Drawing on "The Affirmative Character of Culture" by Herbert Marcuse, this book argues that this form of the opposition between the functional and the beautiful is distinctly modern. While feudal society ensured the undesirable practical existence of most people and the beautiful existence of a few, with the advent of capitalism the good and the beautiful were viewed as available, applicable, and obligatory values for the lives of all people. While capitalism deems practical life not directed at continued accumulation of capital to be superfluous, from the perspective of these affirmative cultural values, the beautiful can transform social life.[57] This affirmative form of culture removes ideas of beauty from their specific moment in social history and assumes, incorrectly, that they are universal and an end in themselves capable of transforming individuals while leaving the prevailing society intact.[58] Freed from the constraints, protections, and responsibilities of feudal society, liberal subjects provide for their own needs and satisfaction through mass-produced commodities available on the market. However, this equal access to happiness is abstract only; the concrete inequality of capitalist society meant that for much of the society, such happiness is unattainable, but acknowledging that this abstract equality was insufficient for most people would surrender liberalism's claim to universality.[59] However, Marcuse points out, this idea of culture is double-sided: "It contains not only the justification of the established form of existence but also the pain of its establishment: not only quiescence about what is but also remembrance of what could be."[60]

In the movement from a city organized by liberal social forms into a city organized by corporatist social forms, this book argues, the First World War marks a significant crux point. Furthermore, this shift is evident not just in the functioning of the city, but also in the ideas about what does or could make a city beautiful and culturally edifying. Marcuse suggests that under the pressure of total mobilization during the First World War, the form of affirmative culture changed, undermining the progressive dimensions of individuality, though not changing the content of affirmative culture. This new form of affirmative culture was transformed from focusing on an "abstract internal community" to demanding that the individual is integrated and integrate himself into "a false collectivity (race, folk, blood, and soil)." However, in both cases, this ideology of culture perpetuates capitalism and demands "renunciation and subjection to the status quo, made bearable by the real appearance of gratification."[61] In this new form, affirmative culture celebrates "humility, sacrifice, poverty, and dutifulness on the one hand, and extreme will to power, impulse to expansion, and technical and military perfection on the other."[62] The form of culture underwent a significant change between liberal and corporatist ideas of culture, but they remained capitalist ideas of culture and were thus affirmative.

Liberalism and Corporatism as Historically Specific Social Forms

This transformation in the appearance, function, and perception of Greater Berlin from ones structured by liberal social forms to one structured by corporatist social forms constitutes and reconstitutes political, social, and cultural dynamics, all while remaining essentially capitalist. The approach to this problem needs to understand the historical specificity of politics, social forces, and culture and to explain a shift from liberal to corporatist social forms. Drawing on the arguments of Georg Lukacs, this book regards social forms as constituted and reconstituted in and through processes of social history. Social forms appear ontological but are part of a social process called reification, which is historically specific to capitalism.[63] To grasp this process of reification, this book relies on a historically specific category of theory and practice: the commodity form. Using the commodity form, this book endeavours to understand the embeddedness of culture in its historical moment, and in particular the transition out of liberal politics and political economy and into mid-twentieth-century capitalism. This book argues that the commodity form enables the historian to mediate between the deep structure of the capitalist dynamic and its historically specific forms of appearance. The problem of this transformation in the form, function, and perception of Greater Berlin from one mediated by liberal social forms into one mediated by corporatist social forms demands a theory that can address, with the same apparatus, both social relations and cultural ideas in capitalism.

As already suggested, the visions of the capitalist dynamic take on a dualistic form. This dualism is constituted by the commodity form, which is a historically specific form of mediation linked to capitalism that brings together and shapes all of the subjective and objective dimensions of capitalist society.[64] The commodity is both the consequence of labouring activity in the form of an object, and the objectification of the social relations that went into the creation of the commodity. These social relations are both expressed and veiled socially in this commodity, and they have no expression independent from this commodity.

This notion of the commodity form suggests that fundamental dualisms characterize capitalism and attempt to ground those dualisms socially and historically. As Moishe Postone explains, the commodity has "an abstract, general, homogeneous dimension ('value') – including a system of abstract domination and compulsion which, although social is impersonal and 'objective' – and concrete particular, material dimension ('use-value'). Moreover, because they are mediated 'objectively,' both dimensions appear to be natural rather than social." The abstract dimension appears in the form of abstract and "objective" natural laws, and the concrete dimension manifests itself as pure "thingly" nature.[65] With this approach, one can offer a more compelling account of the historical specificity of this dualistic thinking in general and of the systematic forms of misrecognition described by Fritzsche and Maier. One can also suggest the further historical specificity of each side of the duality. Furthermore, it can provide social historical grounding for the forms of abstract domination and their concrete carriers that the governmentality-oriented historians describe, and because it is linked to a theory of social dynamics, it can explain the changing character of these abstract forms of domination.

The visions of the city, which contemporaries often conflated with capitalist modernity and with capitalism itself, underwent a significant shift from "liberal" to "corporatist" frames of reference. This book accounts for this historical change as an effect of the way the commodity form mediated social relations. Following Postone, this book argues that as capitalism develops, it sheds the dominant mechanistic vision of the world characteristic of the early modern period and "the naturalization immanent to the commodity fetish becomes increasingly biologized.... Society, as well as historical process[es], becomes increasingly understood in biological terms." As Postone explains, the "double character" of the commodity form "allows concrete labor to appear as a purely material, creative process, separable from capitalist social relations, and allows the commodity to appear as a purely material entity rather than as the objectification of mediated social relations." This brings about a dichotomy between industrial production, "as a purely material, creative process, separable from capital," and finance capital as "parasitic." The "biological interpretation" facilitates a "glorification of industrial capital and technology" in that "both are on the 'thingly' side of the antinomy."[66] Such a dichotomy exists in the discourse on Greater Berlin. Over the course of this study, contemporaries changed the side of that dichotomy that they privileged, but the dichotomy persists. Capitalism appeared in this discourse as a duality, one concrete and the other abstract, because of the peculiar and historically specific character of labour in capitalism. Especially in developed capitalist societies, the economy as a whole appears divided in two, with the abstract dimensions of capitalism – finance, liberalism, the market, and speculation – expanded so that they are perceived to be the totality of capitalist relations, while production, labour, technology, and other more "concrete" social forms appear as outside of capitalism and thus natural. This dualistic vision of the world often leads people to criticize the abstract aspect of capitalism as distinguished from the concrete dimension. Planners and administrators understood the concrete as a unified, deeply rooted, perhaps racially particular organism beset by the rootless, parasitic, unproductive abstract.[67]

The Plan of This Argument

Chapter 1 addresses the growth and development of Greater Berlin in the nineteenth and early twentieth centuries. It explores the growing sense that Berlin represented a social and cultural crisis and then attempts to address this crisis through the means of municipal administration. Chapter 1 explores the political and economic development of liberalism in Berlin and in Germany, with the goal of showing that liberalism is best understood not as just an ideology of economy and politics; rather, liberalism is best understood as the formal structure of culture and society during a historically specific period. The dynamics of capitalism shaped and reshaped the political and social history of Greater Berlin.

Chapter 2 focuses on the sense of crisis in the built environment and analyses liberal forms of city planning. This chapter proposes the existence of a distinctly liberal form of city planning and then examines liberal city planning and its subsequent crisis of both theory and practice. It provides context for liberal planning within prevailing territorialization of the economic region, municipality, state, and Reich, arguing that they are historically specific to a liberal regime of capital accumulation.

Chapter 3 examines two major efforts to create a single city – administratively and as an urban space – to address the historical development of capitalism and the contemporary historical reterritorialization. The first part analyses a city-planning contest held to organize the rapidly agglomerating urban space of Greater Berlin. The second section interrogates the creation of a new regional administration – the Verband

Groß-Berlin – and the ideology that it brought to its specific tasks and its practical efforts. Both of these efforts illustrate the limits of liberal city planning and municipal administration and offer up a new direction. It is here, around 1910, that one can begin to see liberal space shatter.

Chapter 4 argues that while the transformation from liberal to corporatist social forms took roughly sixty years between 1871 and 1933, the First World War and the November 1918 Revolution represent a crucial point. The chapter contends that the social conditions of the First World War restructured the relationships among the state, civil society, the economy, and the military, changing how the urban region was understood and functioned, and eroded the conditions of possibility for liberal capitalism, introducing the expectation of significant levels of planning.

Chapter 5 contextualizes the struggles of municipalities in the Weimar Republic within the broader socioeconomic conditions of the period. This chapter proposes that a coercive political economic dynamic developed between the state, banks, industry, and municipalities and the housing industry. It argues that there was a significant shift in the scale of city government and in the living space necessary for a healthy community and a dynamic economy and that the crisis of the Great Depression deepened the commitment, on all levels of government, to a corporatist state.

Chapter 6 follows the development of city planning and architecture in the Weimar Republic. In particular it focuses on the perceived connections between access to living spaces, nature, modern city planning, and a healthy, productive society. As was the case with the expansion of the scale of city government, city planning significantly increased its scale and pressed for more intensive and extensive planning.

This book examines a transformation from liberal to corporatist in the form of the discourses and practices that shaped the appearance, function, and perception of Greater Berlin. I show that around 1871, city planners and municipal administrators emphasized free markets, the rule of law, and trade. By the early 1930s, however, they emphasized an integrative, corporate, and productivist vision. I argue that this change was a broad transformation in the social forms that shaped popular understanding of Greater Berlin and relate this change to contemporaneous shifts in the cultural and social history of global capitalism. The volume engages city planning, municipal administration, architecture, political economy, and jurisprudence sources held in the Landesarchiv Berlin, Geheimes Staatsarchiv, and Archiv der Akademie der Künste, as well as digitized and hard-copy published sources.

Chapter One

The Rise of Industrial Berlin

Introduction: The Limits of Liberalism

Berlin was "an infinitely expanding image of crisis" that "still could be five times larger," claimed Karl Scheffler in 1910.[1] This common perception grew out of the social, political, geographic, and cultural conditions of capitalist industrialization and the way those circumstances transformed the form and content of German cities and in turn changed their administrations.[2] This transformation also reconstituted spheres of urban life that were not immediately connected to either politics or economics.

The sense of crisis arose from a conflict between the prevailing view of society, which was liberal, and the trajectory of both capitalism and the state. Carl Schorske frames a similar sense of crisis among Viennese liberals as turning away from a celebration of rationality to a romantic glorification of irrationality and intuition due to a political defeat.[3] Schorske's account, however, underestimates the social complexity of this sense of crisis. At one time a liberal world view seemed in tune with capitalism and government and to exemplify the achievements and aspirations of modernity, such that it appeared that liberal political and social revolutions were stripping away a history of innocence and superstition to reveal the essence of humans and their society. By 1900, however, capitalism was transforming itself away from structures that coincided with liberal principles and fabricating a new social framework, a new regime of accumulation.[4]

Around 1910, the form, function, and perception of Berlin shifted away from ones structured by a liberal world view and practices to ones structured by a corporatist world view and practices. To understand this shift, it is necessary to understand this liberal structuring of Greater Berlin and to grasp the tendencies in liberalism that gave rise to this shift. This shift was a global change in the character of capitalism that had local consequences in Germany and in Berlin. This change affected the character of political and economic relations and of governmental structure, part of a "reterritorialization" of the municipality, the province, the state, and the empire (though this book will focus on the municipal level).[5] This shift transformed the prevailing ideological assumptions about the world and especially about cities. It extended beyond stereotypically liberal realms of economics, state structure, or jurisdiction; rather, it reconstituted social and cultural perceptions of the world, including of Berlin. The sense of crisis and the disjunction between a liberal world view and the society and culture it attempted to comprehend, however, arose from the contradictions within liberalism itself.

This chapter will chart the political, social, and economic development of liberalism in Germany, and in Berlin in particular, to then demonstrate that liberalism cannot be understood merely as one among many modes of the economics and politics. Rather, liberalism is best understood as the formal structure of culture and society during a historically specific period. This chapter will argue that capitalism fundamentally transformed German society and cities, but this transformation appeared natural and silent as if guided by the natural laws that govern society. Despite this appearance, this new structure was radically different from what had come before. Though institutions from earlier historical epochs endured, formally, such as the aristocracy, their content changed. Historians, at times, miss the change in content and thus misinterpret this endurance of older institutions as evidence that the society in question was caught in a pre-modern social structure and miss the ways that the content of that institution had been reconstituted to seek modern ends.

The chapter will explore an example of such changes: the changing legal justification of municipal self-administration, a pre-modern institution, which survived into the nineteenth century. To historians, the structure of municipal administration seems to be a legal question distinct from capitalism; in fact, capitalism shaped and reshaped this legal institution. Municipal administration attempted to address the problems and opportunities generated by industrial capitalism.

The form, function, and perception of Greater Berlin were transformed from entities based on liberal principles into one built along corporatist principles, a shift reflected in capitalism itself. This change in capitalism also entailed a "reterritorialization" of the municipality, the state, and the Reich. This chapter will examine the social forms of liberal capitalism in the urban context of Berlin and then trace the growing contradiction between the urban social order in Berlin and liberal ideas. Finally, it will address attempts by liberal thinkers to understand and account for the failure of liberalism to effectively grasp this increasingly post-liberal world. In so doing, the chapter establishes the condition of possibility for a crisis of liberal social forms in the context of Greater Berlin.

The Social and Political Transformation of Nineteenth-Century Germany and Its Cities

As the liberal era of capitalism was constituting itself, it reorganized social relations – including municipal administration and city planning – according to abstract principles that seemed to express the essence of social relations. In the nineteenth century, industrialization, intensified interconnection of the global economy, and rapid urbanization transformed societies globally and, though many locales had their own iteration of this new society, capitalism subsumed existing societies into itself. Capitalism, in overcoming the ancien régime, expressed itself as liberalism and structured society according to abstract principles that liberals believed expressed the essence of society. Geoff Eley and David Blackbourn argue that the "bourgeois society" arose slowly through a *longue durée* reconstitution of social forms.[6] For Eley, liberalism was the manifest politics and the revolutionary edge of this process: it meant eliminating impediments to private enterprise, a free market for all commodities including land, the equality before the law for citizens, a separation between church and state, commercial law, meritocracy, and some representative government. This social transformation affected the form, content, and perception of social relations. The formal changes Eley enumerates coincided with a society increasingly organized by capitalism and a capitalism increasingly able to reconstitute the content of social relations to fit its needs.[7]

Liberals believed that their economic and governmental reforms revealed an essence of social relations, which tradition had obscured. As capitalism transformed society, Blackbourn argues, the victories of this liberal social revolution appeared "natural," a testament to how fundamentally it changed both the activities of social life and how society understood these activities.[8] The global revolution, Eley explains, took a form in Germany that was specific to the country's history and culture, to Germany's mid-nineteenth-century industrialization, and to the specific form of absolutist society that capitalism was transforming.[9] The essence, which liberals believed they were revealing, was abstract. Liberal economic and legal reforms began in the late eighteenth century with the development of abstract social categories of the citizen, the law-based state, the private individual, private property, and distinct systems of "public and private law." They broke radically from the pre-modern corporate state and society. During the Napoleonic era in German-speaking states, liberals instituted reforms including emancipating peasants, eliminating guilds, and secularizing charitable foundations.[10] This legal and economic vision guided the North German Confederation of 1867 and the German Reich of 1871 and made the bureaucracy subject to the law in the 1870s. Blackbourn suggests that these reforms, along with rights to free speech and petition, made citizens formally equal before the law.[11] Furthermore, the nineteenth-century penal and civil code was based on the rights of private citizens.[12] Even those who were ambivalent or opposed to liberalism implemented liberal reforms, illustrating the apparent naturalness of this revolution.[13] Through these reforms, liberalism constituted society and did so on a distinctly abstract basis.[14]

In Germany, as in Britain, liberals believed that expanding the franchise would constitute individuals and citizens. They trusted that this abstract form of representation would counteract concrete and pre-modern corporate relations. Elaine Hadley's argument about mid-nineteenth-century British liberalism is also valid for Germany: liberalism offered a private and "abstracted individuality," freeing people from their particular, concrete bodies and social spaces.[15] This market-centred revolution replaced corporate mores and rights with openness and formal equality. Furthermore, as Blackbourn notes, members of society met most of their needs through a market, shared a legal system, and, as abstract individuals, constituted "the 'public.'"[16] These individuals were freely associating as abstractly equal citizens, and the market mediated their production and consumption.

This transformation of social relations according to the abstract principles of liberal capitalism appeared "natural," not simply because it was slow or silent, but because key categories of capitalism – like time, money, and labour – appear commonplace, despite their radically new form. If this transformation of legal and economic relations was not the agentive project of the bourgeoisie or of liberals, one must ask what caused this change and why it appeared so organic. The liberal revolution that Blackbourn describes is peculiarly abstract and universalist, and its slow pace is insufficient to explain the relative silence and apparent naturalness of this radical transformation. Blackbourn relates this process to capitalism but pursues that issue – beyond concerns for legal protections for property – no further.

Liberal assumptions about social relations having an abstract, law-like essence have shaped the reforms of municipal government after the French Revolution. These reforms introduced a key legal and political category: municipal self-administration. When German-speaking Länder were under Napoleonic control, Karl Freiherr vom Stein, a Franconian aristocrat with a family estate in Nassau who briefly served as minister of the economy and finance but went into exile for his anti-Napoleonic views, orchestrated reforms that opened municipal and provincial government to property owners, to harness their talents to the public good.[17] Stein proposed new representative institutions to counteract the Hohenzollern civil service and hereditary nobility. Edicts in 1807 and 1808 abolished serfdom in Prussia, opened up the professions, made private property a commodity, and created local self-administration.[18] The new institutions established an elected city council, the Stadtverordnetenversammlung, which in turn elected an executive branch, the Magistrat, which included the *Oberbürgermeister* (Lord Mayor). The council had budgetary powers and supervised the executive branch of the municipal administration, which was staffed by salaried employees elected to six- or twelve-year terms, and worked with unpaid city fathers, whose number depended on the size of the city. Geographically determined wards elected the councils, and estates and guilds held no special power. Only citizens could vote, but the city could not deny citizenship to residents of "reputable character," including unmarried women. Business people were required to become citizens and had the franchise, as did owners of property of a certain size; all others needed to demonstrate that they received a modest income. Aspiring citizens needed to apply and pay a fee. Citizenship did not guarantee suffrage, and residence did not guarantee citizenship: wives, children, servants, and apprentices, and those without permanent residence, including soldiers, were excluded. Women and Magistrat members could not vote. The numbers with the franchise remained remarkably small.[19]

While the 1848 Revolution challenged the illiberal aspects of municipal government and advanced a liberal municipal agenda, the counter-revolution retrenched the Prussian elites and incorporated new capitalist elites. However, the Prussian elite power was no longer based on aristocratic privilege, but on their role as large-scale capitalist farmers.[20] The counter-revolution curtailed municipal self-administration, making it a liberal goal. The Städteordnung of 1853 opened citizenship to all men over twenty-five years of age residing within the city boundaries, grounded the roles of the Magistrat and the city council, and set up the municipality as a legal corporation.[21] The ordinance also reduced the fraction of city councillors who needed to own residential buildings from two-thirds in Stein's ordinance to one-half.[22] However, the 1853 Städteordnung also tightened state control over municipal affairs in the six eastern provinces (which included Brandenburg, home to Berlin) and maintained the property restrictions on who could hold office.[23] The ordinance banned discussion of general political questions in the city council, and if such questions arose, the state could immediately dissolve the council and hold new elections. In addition, the 1853 Städteordnung established a three-class voting system in Prussian city elections.[24] The power of votes was determined accordingly: the full range of direct tax payments was divided into thirds, and each of those thirds elected a third of the representatives. Because of rapid urbanization and proletarianization, this division roughly translated into less than 5 per cent of the population in the first tier, less than 15 per cent in the second, and more than 80 per cent in the third. By the 1890s wages had increased enough so that workers could qualify for citizenship and membership in the third tier, placing 90–94 per cent of the electorate in that third tier.[25] In Berlin, in 1900, 1,446 first-class voters elected the same number of representatives as 304,418 third-class voters.[26]

When Otto von Bismarck created a German nation state in 1871, liberals achieved a central political goal; however, as the result of Bismarck's role it had a conservative, bureaucratic, and Prussian character. With this goal achieved and Bismarck turning away from liberal allies, liberal politics began to retreat. Two Prussian laws in the 1870s addressing municipal self-administration registered the liberal acquiescence to a capitalist modernity that brought together liberal and aristocratic social orders. After 1871, Bismarck turned to protectionist economic policies in response to the Depression of 1873–96, and a revolutionary workers' movement was founded. These pressures from the right and left made liberals more comfortable in their retreat. The first Prussian law addressing municipal self-administration, in 1874, gave cities the power to expropriate land to build streets. The second, in 1875, and known as the Fluchtliniengesetz, "clarified and expanded" the municipality's right to set street and building lines and to assess property owners for the cost of streets and sewers, and to prohibit building in areas without street layouts.[27]

This constitution of society in the image of liberalism, a testament to the ways that the transformation worked behind the backs of those carrying it out, was often undertaken by people who were ambivalent or even opposed to liberalism. Though the state established a more genuine self-administration for municipalities in the 1870s, it retained police powers, including control over building inspection. In most major Prussian cities, the police force was a state institution, and the Polizeipräsident was appointed by and responsible to state authorities.[28] However, the existing society was fundamentally transformed, and while liberals were forced to acquiesce to the continued existence of the aristocracy, aristocrats had become capitalists.

The Particularity of Municipal Administration in Greater Berlin

The national- and state-level liberal politics and the consequences of capitalism on legal and administrative structures had important, though varied, consequences for local politics. The capitalist transformation and reform of administrative structures of Greater Berlin spurred rapid industrialization, working-class radicalism, dramatic population growth, poor-quality housing, and regional administrative incoherence. These social changes spurred cultural concerns among Germans about modernity, but the first urban historiography of Greater Berlin treats this transformation as a political question; for example, the important work of Hans Herzfeld and Otto Büsch focused on parties and personalities in the city council, the Magistrat, the police, and the state.[29] Their research was part of the early period of urban historiography in Germany, the United States, Britain, and France.[30]

Berlin's municipal self-administration was unique for a variety of reasons. It had unusual local voting laws and had uniquely fractious local politics. The municipal administration's autonomy was newer and weaker than in most German cities. The Berlin municipal self-administration was directly subordinate to the will of the minister of the interior and to the Kaiser and king. And finally, Berlin was a massive centre of military power.

When liberals confronted the conservative Prussian state, universal male suffrage had been a central goal of liberal politics, in the belief that this would register the general will and empower liberal politics. However, with the combination of industrialization, the expansion of the franchise, and the growth of working-class politics, liberal responses to working-class electoral power reveal a fissure in a society structured by liberal norms. Berlin's municipal government and its role in higher levels of German government were structured by the systematic undermining of the power of Berliners' votes. Changes in municipal voting laws in 1850 led to the municipal legislative body in Berlin shrinking to a third of its former size, with the conservatives winning 76 per cent of the seats. Despite an electorate that nearly quadrupled between 1850 and 1870, the voting turnout for the city council fell from 70 per cent in 1850 to 18 per cent in 1870.[31] Meanwhile, the three-tier system prevailed in Berlin communal elections. In 1867 the state divided Berlin into six geographical wards, which remained unchanged until 1918. As the population ballooned, especially in working-class districts, these wards remained the same. In 1871 the wards varied from 16,000 voters at the smallest to 22,000 voters at the largest; however, by 1912 – the year of the greatest electoral success for the Socialists in the Kaiserreich – the smallest ward had 13,000 voters and the largest counted 220,000 voters. The state denied workers a true franchise in order to block the growth of opposition parties, especially the Social Democrats (SPD), in the Reichstag. However, in 1912 the SPD garnered more than 34 per cent of the vote nationally and five out of the six seats representing Berlin, as well as four more seats from Greater Berlin. A left-liberal politician had represented most wards by 1881, but by 1884 the Socialists were able to win the vote in two wards. Beginning in 1903 the Socialists held growing majorities in five of the six wards.[32] The rise of the socialists as an urban electoral power challenged the liberal view of the world. The responses to this socialist power contributed significantly to the transformation of liberalism into something else.

The politics in Berlin were fractious because, in addition to the military and the sizable bureaucratic presence, Berlin was also the home to significant right-wing populist, liberal, and Socialist politics. When the state allowed local politics to exist in Berlin, it tended to have a strong petit bourgeois leaning. Even though the city was a major centre of industry, commerce, and banking, "artisans and shopkeepers (and often the property owners association) set the tone of city government."[33]

One example of this tilt towards the petit bourgeois was the success of Adolf Stöcker's anti-Semitic Berlin Movement.[34] This tendency was one that Berlin shared with Vienna.[35]

Prussia and the Reich constrained Berlin's municipal self-administration more than in most German cities. Both the Polizeipräsident and the Oberbürgermeister were directly subordinate to the Ministry of the Interior and to the kaiser and king himself. This, combined with the left-leaning politics of the city, meant that governing Berlin was "a question of domestic power of the first rank," provoking special constitutional regulations – breaks from liberal legal norms.[36] Berlin never gained the right to police powers during the Kaiserreich.[37] As city councillor Heinrich Dove argued about Berlin in a 1906 Verein für Sozialpolitik project on city government, Berlin retained "only a small measure of its allotted independent activity," and Berlin's "rapid development ... went hand in hand with the expansion from above of the structure of the state itself and with the rise of Hohenzollern princely power."[38]

The changes wrought in Berlin through the rise and collapse of liberal politics and the industrialization of the city shaped and were shaped by the major political forces and how they interacted with the municipal administration. In many circumstances, the results of voting in Berlin were of little consequence, because the municipal administration was not under the control of elected bodies. Rather, its authority lay with the chief of police, who reported to the Prussian minister of the interior, and with the Prussian military and ministerial building commission.[39] In the aftermath of 1848, Karl Ludwig Friedrich von Hinckeldey, the Polizeipräsident, had his power massively expanded; he militarized the police and created a secret police. The chief of the Berlin police was also the chief of all Prussian police.[40]

As Berlin concentrated liberal civil society and cultural power, liberals worked to reform Berlin politics. Prominent left-liberal reformers included the physician Rudolf Virchow, founder of the Progressive Party, opponent of Bismarck, and member of the city council and of the Prussian Abgeordnetenhaus, and Theodor Mommsen, a jurist and historian, a Prussian legislator from 1873 to 1882, and a member of the Reichstag from 1881 to 1882. Berlin also had a number of prominent liberal Oberbürgermeisters: Karl Theodor Seydel, who served from 1862 to 1873; Arthur Hobrecht, a National Liberal in office from 1873 to 1878; and Max von Forckenbeck, a member of various splitting and joining left-liberal parties, who served for fourteen years after Hobrecht.

Robert Zelle, Martin Kirschner, and Adolf Wermuth, the first mayors of the twentieth century, were also cut from this same left-liberal cloth. In addition, Berlin was home to the liberal anti-Bismarck press, which included Rudolf Mosse's *Vossische Zeitung*, Peter Langmann's *Berliner Tageblatt*, Eugene Richter's *Tribune*, Leopold Ullstein's *Berliner Morgenpost* and *Berliner Zeitung*, and Maximillian Harden's *Zukünft*.[41]

The Socialists considered Berlin to be theirs and the capital of the German labour movement both politically and culturally, even if this was meaningless electorally under the prevailing political structure. Despite Berlin's prominent role in the working-class movement, the historiography of the politics of the local working-class movement is relatively short. It narrates the numerical growth of the working class as well as the banning and subsequent legalization of the Social Democratic Party (SPD), its rapidly growing membership, and its success in labour conflicts and in the ballot box.[42] Once Kaiser Wilhelm II lifted the ban on the Social Democratic Party (SPD) participation in elections in 1890, the SPD was increasingly able to overcome the three-tier voting system and vote their members onto city councils. Moreover, even though the party representatives were illegal, they managed to get their members onto the ballot as independents.

Berlin was a major industrial centre – closer to Chicago in character than to London or Paris – and so had a large working class. The political and organizational leaders of the party included Berliners like the party founder August Bebel; head of the Socialist unions, Carl Legien; and the millionaire party financial backer and the first representative in both the Reichstag and the city council, Paul Singer. The revisionist Eduard Bernstein was a Berliner, as were the revolutionaries Karl Liebknecht and Rosa Luxemburg. Finally, the main press organ of the Socialists, *Vorwärts*, was centred in Berlin.[43] The expanding social diversity of the councils closely coincided with the wealthiest families removing themselves from local politics in response to both the changing character of the councils and the demands of their businesses.[44] However, the concerted entry of the SPD into local politics, by its own assessment, came relatively late. In 1902, for example, Hugo Lindemann, a Socialist municipal expert, argued that the historical conditions that made the state and the Reich the centre of power, and thus of agitation, had begun to change: the growth of the union movement, the Social Democratic Party, and industrialization in Greater Berlin challenged municipal electoral representation as well as the municipal, state, and Reich welfare apparatus, and in important ways put liberals on the defensive.

Between 1894 and 1905 the number of unionized food workers in Berlin nearly quadrupled, unionized service workers grew more than six times, unionized building workers more than eleven times, metalworkers more than seven times, woodworkers more than three times, clothing and leather workers four times, and workers in the paper and publishing industry more than three times. Together the unionized workers in Berlin expanded by nearly 485 per cent, from 38,152 to 223,077.[45] Because of the growth of the municipal welfare system, the city had become a key battleground for Socialists. Lindemann's main concern was the full autonomy of the municipality from the state and from there, reforms in voting laws and social welfare.[46]

Finally, Berlin was a massive centre of military authority. The capital of a rapidly ascending world power, Berlin had a martial tradition older than its metropolitan character. In many ways Berlin was an armed camp, and the state focused the military's attention domestically, as the working-class population grew and became radicalized. Military parades played an important role in the culture of the capital, and at the start of the First World War, Greater Berlin could be considered the largest military base in central Europe.[47] Before 1860 the military so dominated the municipal bodies that it could circumvent most liberal reforms. After the 1860s the military was integrated into the built environment of Berlin, dotted with armament factories and depots, barracks, uniform factories, and administrative buildings.[48]

The military played a central and exalted role in the culture of civil society in Berlin. In the tourist literature for the Berlin Business Exhibition of 1896, for instance, an article claimed, "The Berliner, in general, loves the military and grants it a preferential position … in civilian life." Furthermore, "Each offence against this special position strikes the Berliner … unpleasantly and brings censure." This state of affairs, the booster explained, was "presumed by soldiers and non-commissioned officers" and only increased in degree with higher ranks. If a soldier were to act "rapidly and independently under private responsibility" and out of "a strongly developed expression of self-confidence," no one could possibly object. The booster continued, "On the other hand, a strict condemnation in the public will meet a person who conducts himself inappropriately toward a military figure." Even in the "low classes of the population," one would find "unexpected appreciation" of the military, and an officer who would "nearly never meet a hostile … action in the public."[49]

This statement was both descriptive and proscriptive. The Prussian state deployed the military to quell social conflicts with Socialists, Poles, Catholics, and, early on, liberals. However, the 1889 national miners' strike and the legalization of the SPD forced the military to reconsider the practicality of the use of the military to quell popular protest. (The military and upper levels of the state planned for a violent and general repression of Social Democracy until 1918.)[50] Like liberals before them, Socialists knew that Prussian militarism was not only about fighting an external enemy, but also about repressing internal foes.[51] As Karl Liebknecht commented in 1907 in a lecture that led to an eighteen-month prison sentence for treason, any police action against the striking working class implied a military threat, where, behind the police and gendarmerie, the military was "always ready to help even with the everyday work."[52] The Berlin Garrison remained directed towards internal security, despite the extension of civil authority, especially when Berlin became the Reich capital. Guards constantly protected royal, military, and major civil office buildings, residences, and individuals.[53] As Alexander Schwab noted, the military located the barracks in the city strategically throughout working-class districts to project military power so that "the city centre with its political and commercial office buildings, with government, banks, business houses and newspaper districts, [could be quickly walled off] against actions in the outskirts" where workers lived, isolating rioting workers.[54]

The problem of municipal administration was politically contentious during the nineteenth century, and in Berlin it took specific forms because of that city's position as capital, as a city with a large and radical working class, and as one with a large and integrated military presence. The form and content of municipal administration and municipal politics became a key point of disputation for liberal politics in Germany in general and in Berlin in particular. Although liberal activists or Prussian bureaucrats could carry out liberal reforms as a revolutionary project or as an ameliorative undertaking, they envisioned a separation of powers between legislative and executive powers and a constitutional legal structure where the "law [was] king," not to mention adequately abstract and general. It presupposed that property-holding citizens, at first, and later all citizens, created the sovereignty of the government and guided its politics. Furthermore, these legal conditions were intended to make free and equal exchange possible, to open all occupations to all people, and to defend private property.

Municipal Administration and Industrial Capitalism

The intensive and extensive industrialization in Berlin contributed to the crisis of liberalism and the transformation in the form, function, and perception of Greater Berlin from ones structured by liberal assumptions about the world to ones structured by corporatist principles. During the nineteenth century, capitalism changed cities and subsequently their government, introducing large-scale industry, socioeconomic disparities, migrant farmer-peasants, and problems of the built environment. Social forces, like industrialization and proletarianization of neighbourhoods and towns, played a fundamental role in constituting the problems of Greater Berlin. The politics of Greater Berlin both facilitated the growth of these problems and responded to them. This development transfigured municipal government, the territory of the municipality, and urban space.

Berlin's urbanization belongs in the context of global urbanization and industrialization, as well as their historiography. This section of the chapter will argue that this industrialization transformed the economic geography of the region in a manner that was similar to the ways it transformed other large cities of the period: it created new responsibilities for the municipality, and ultimately it pressured administrations to reterritorialize the municipality, the state, and the Reich.

In the 1950s, urban history, as part of a broader project to understand society as a totality, relied on statistics and, with social history, qualitatively changed historiography. In the United States, Arthur Schlesinger Sr, Oscar Handlin, and Blake McKelvey practise a synthetic historiography that aimed at studying urban society rather than urban politicians.[55] McKelvey seeks to grasp "multiple urban developments" that appear as elements in a total historical process through analysis of demographic transformations. He suggests that the modern city was organized by a number of antitheses: "diffusion versus centralization, heterogeneity versus standardization, expressionism versus planning, to mention only a few."[56] This tendency to understand urban questions through antitheses was and is not specific to an American context, and as we shall see, many of these same antitheses structure German urbanism.

Political historiography and social historiography both, though to differing degrees, assumed a relationship between urbanization, industrialization, and modernization that they did not explain. This category, "modernization," groups together a variety of social processes, such as bureaucratization, democratization, industrialization, and urbanization and posits a connection between these processes but does not explain the relationships among them. Modernization has acquired several contradictory meanings over the course of the twentieth century: from increasing state intervention in the economy in the 1960s to removing the state from the economy in the 1980s. In the realm of urban questions, increasing population density and industrial concentration were considered processes of "modernization" until roughly the eve of the Second World War. After about 1945, the suburbanization of industry and population were considered processes of "modernization." Since the 1980s, a de-industrialized re-concentration of population in cities is considered "modernization." Many historians criticize "modernization" by attacking the teleological assumption that supposedly all societies develop along the same path in favour of the idea of multiple modernities. However, the idea of multiple modernities does not address the relationships among the different social processes gathered under the heading "modernization." This has important implications for this book, which examines a transformation from one vision of what a modern city should be into quite a different vision. This book argues, that capitalism, understood as a set of social relations and processes that constitute a historically specific form of society and culture, can address the contradictory shifts in the meaning of modernity.

While the political history-oriented city biographies assume that industrialization and urbanization proceeded hand-in-hand as part of a natural process of modernization, the social history of the city investigates this relationship more deeply, though still regarding them as separate processes. For example, Wolfgang Köllmann details the ways that they combined and intimately reinforced each other, fundamentally transforming the social and economic life of both the city and the country.[57] Eric Lampard and Oscar Handlin, both historians of the United States, similarly argue that urbanization and industrialization concentrated productive activity in cities, drew masses of workers into the cities, and facilitated economic growth by creating systems for the division of labour.[58] Lampard argues that to understand the empirical details, the complexity of the modern city and its dynamics demanded a level of theorization and abstraction that was not necessary for political history.[59]

Berlin rapidly and intensively urbanized and industrialized, making the crisis of liberalism especially acute. Population growth began to accelerate in 1841 in Berlin and its Brandenburg hinterland, but it remained a fortress and garrison city with a limited industrial sphere, which was focused on military needs. Road systems and canals connected mercantile Berlin to its hinterland, over which Berlin had influence. Industrialization increased and intensified the connections between Berlin and other areas of Prussia.[60] The Spree River and the system of canals extending out from Berlin facilitated the industrial agglomeration of the city. Like the Spree, the Danube, its tributaries, and its canal systems played a similar role in the development of Vienna.[61] The River Lea also played a central role in the industrialization of the eastern periphery of nineteenth-century London.[62]

Writing about the United States, Handlin argues that transit networks were fundamental to urban and economic growth. Furthermore, capitalist production exceeded the needs of the local market, required significant capital investment and risk, and created administrative challenges. Success in this system depended on correctly anticipating the right ratio between production costs and market price, and on an ability to assure long-term access to supplies and markets. This firm-level capitalist planning created systems of accounting and credit, which were facilitated by increasingly extensive and accelerating radiating communications and transportation networks. This dynamic, however, "deprived [the city] of autonomy and integrated it into a larger economic and social whole."[63] In Berlin, Lothar Baar explained, in the 1840s early industry moved beyond publishing, basic manufacturing, and calico printing to the production of necessities, with steam-powered mills as well as water and windmills. By 1861 Berlin had eight industrialized factories with twelve steam engines. Though breweries and distilleries used older forms of production, they too grew from thirty to sixty-eight in the decade before 1871. But the industries that ignited the transformation of Berlin were engineering and the metal industry, in particular, tool and machine tool production. The construction of the railway rapidly increased their production beginning in the 1830s, and by the 1860s there were 137 machine plants employing 8,500 people. By 1861 more than 60 per cent of the employed population of Berlin – roughly 150,000 people – worked in industry or the crafts. Berlin was no longer just a political centre; it was also a core of the Industrial Revolution and the economic heart of Germany.[64]

Expanding Municipal Responsibilities

Industrialization and urbanization altered regional geography and challenged liberal notions of municipal self-administration and governmental responsibilities. This change also generated pressures that contributed to a crisis of liberalism and the transformation in the form, function, and perception of Greater Berlin from ones structured by liberal assumptions about the world to ones structured by corporatist principles. Capitalist urbanization inspired a significant expansion of the local welfare state. Liberals attempted to ameliorate the worst conditions of modern urban capitalist life while not challenging fundamentally those circumstances by creating what they called "municipal socialism." As one speaker at the 1907 general assembly of the Verein für Socialpolitik argued, this policy was motivated by equal parts humanitarian concern, anxiety over the spread of disease, and the desire to undercut the recruiting grounds for Social Democracy.[65] According to Socialist statisticians at the time, most urbanites lived "in extremely poor conditions, often even in bitterest poverty." In Berlin in 1890, 159,639 people, or 14 per cent of the population, inhabited dwellings with six or more people in one room or ten or more in two rooms. In industrial areas one could recognize "the consequences of excessive work, insufficient wages and unsatisfactory nutrition."[66] Left-liberal municipal administrators pressed municipalities, as Frankfurt a. M. Oberbürgermeister Franz Adickes did at the Deutsche Städte-Ausstellung in Dresden in 1903, to mitigate the effects of the market and private property, demarcate public and private interests in the municipal economies, intervene in the economy on behalf of the poor, and promote a "healthy social body."[67] As Ernst Scholz, Oberbürgermeister of Charlottenburg, put it, "Abolishing or at least alleviating unemployment and social discontent is ... among the most important and most beautiful tasks of the modern city administration."[68] To be clear, this expansion of the role of the city, state, and federal government in assuring the welfare of citizens and this significant scepticism about the capacity to the market to create an equitable and fulfilled life represent an abandonment of the principles of classical liberalism.

Industrialization and urbanization precipitated a similar crisis of liberalism in Britain with the significant expansion of municipal responsibilities and abandonment of definitional liberal principles. Infrastructure expansion increased two and a half times between 1870 and 1900 in Britain and accounted for 40 per cent of United Kingdom investment, a sum that was nearly as large, if one left out housing, as the capital invested in manufacturing in Britain.[69] Like the left-leaning Liberal Party in Manchester, German liberals transformed the meaning of liberalism so that by the end of the nineteenth century it meant giving the working class the social advantages of the rich man, removing barriers to the worker's self-improvement, and creating conditions where each person had an equal opportunity for success.[70] As Scholz expressed in 1913, "It is hardly an exaggeration if one notes that [the modern city] will satisfy all the entire spiritual and material interests of citizenship if they are not fulfilled by the private business."[71]

As municipal welfare expanded, so did municipal ownership of utilities and facilities, such as gas, sewerage, water, bathing, and lighting. These municipally owned utilities challenged a liberal principle of private property, contributing to this crisis of liberalism and the transformation in the form, function, and perception of Greater Berlin from ones structured by liberal assumptions about the world to ones structured by corporatist principles in Berlin. These utilities often began as multiple competing private businesses, which over time became monopolies, with municipal residents a captive customer base. In response, the municipality either tightly regulated or took over these interests. When a project was too large and too unprofitable for private industry to undertake, governments would invest in creating public works. While these municipal utilities improved living conditions in cities, human needs – and thus deprivations – are historically specific and socially constituted. (When sewer systems did not exist, it was not unjust to be left out of the system, but once they existed, it became so.) Thus, these new municipal systems, because they were created in a society fraught with social and cultural conflict, incorporated that heteronomy.[72] Christoph Bernhardt points to a contradiction between liberal laissez-faire economics and these significant interventions in Berlin and other German cities.[73] However, on this specific issue of large, unprofitable projects, classical liberals like Adam Smith thought state intervention was necessary to further growth.[74] Writing about British cities, Chris Otter argues that the environmental protections, such as sewerization, clean air regulation, regulation of trash disposal and of animals within the city, and efforts to allow more light into the built environment were a form of domination. They established the "hegemony of vision" and liberal governmentality over other sensory experiences.[75] However, as previously discussed, such accounts misapprehend the abstract forms of domination characteristic of a modern capitalist society as features of concrete, state "technologies."

These municipally owned utilities further undermined liberal principles, contributing to this crisis of liberalism, because cities that owned and operated utilities began to have labour concerns. Municipalities hired large numbers of working-class employees and attempted to mediate between capital and labour.[76] Doing so, municipalities took on the role of a corporate state. City workers could count on long-term employment and high wages, but these conditions, according to commentators, required submission to a "patriarchal" relationship between employer and employee.[77] Left-liberal jurist and local politician Hugo Preuß argued that urban social life was entering a new epoch in 1906: municipal social services contradicted private economic enterprise and transformed not only the owner but also the nature of the enterprise, and that the free market was eliminating competitive capitalism. Municipal services forced laissez-faire liberals to choose between private monopolies and public enterprises.[78] The Socialist municipal expert Lindemann suggested in 1909 that these municipal utilities facilitated the social life of the city and that they created a "larger economic unity."[79] Industrialization and urbanization transformed regional geography, undermining liberal concepts municipal self-administration and beliefs in the limits of governmental responsibility. These changes also contributed to a crisis of liberalism and the transformation in the form, function, and perception of Greater Berlin from ones organized according to liberal understandings of the world into ones shaped by a corporatist vision of society.

Suburbanization of Industry

The liberal vision of municipal self-administration and of the role of government was undermined by the suburbanization of industry, the expansion of transit networks, and the rise of working-class suburbs, which pressured for a reterritorialization of the municipality, the state, and the Reich. This geographic change helped to precipitate a crisis of liberalism and the transformation in the form, function, and perception of Greater Berlin from liberal ones into corporatist ones. Significant firms moving towards the urban periphery during the nineteenth century transformed the economic geography of Greater Berlin. As Sam Bass Warner argues in an article about Philadelphia, examining the spatial distribution of businesses, homes, and public services, the "social organization of labor" and urban space can reveal important features of the society, because of the way that labour creates new social networks and a new culture.[80] Industrial engineering firms, including Egell (founded 1830), Borsig (1837), Pflug (1837/8), Wohlert (1842), and Schwarzkopff (1852), all played important roles in the city's growth. Between 1830 and 1860 the Berlin suburb and then the district of Moabit became the preferred industrial site along the Spree. This move from the city centre to Moabit was the first step in a larger process of the suburbanization of industry.[81] The successful approval and construction of freight harbours at the eastern and western periphery of the city responded to and facilitated the growth of this phenomenon.

Examining similar suburbanization of industry, the expansion of transit networks, and the rise of working-class suburbs in North America, Richard Walker, Richard Harris, and Robert Lewis argue that suburban industrial and residential growth moved hand-in-hand, beginning in the middle of the nineteenth century, and they cite the examples of New York, the San Francisco Bay area, Boston, Baltimore, Montreal, Toronto, Los Angeles, and Chicago. Furthermore, they demonstrate that this outward movement was a relatively coordinated project of private industry, real estate, and merchants as well as of government. The expanding metropolis absorbed these peripheral areas, and so they appeared to be at the city centre.[82] By 1900 in Paris, the working-class population had shifted to the suburbs. The Department of the Seine, home to Paris, grew from two million to five million people between 1871 and 1931. The bulk of this growth occurred in the suburbs, where peripheral heavy industrial growth attracted both urban and rural job seekers, an inner-city housing shortage drove out renters, and the development of a municipal transit system facilitated the workers' commutes. In 1896 there were twice as many factories with 100 or more employees in the suburbs than there were in Paris proper.[83]

This transformation of the population and the economy challenged the pre-industrial municipal administrative structure and forced the incorporation of smaller administrative spaces into larger and larger municipal units, and this development created a contradiction with liberal understandings of municipal self-administration. Though the dichotomy between poor and industrial city centres, on the one hand, and wealthy and bucolic suburbs, on the other, is an oversimplification, flight by the wealthy from the city centres in response to social conditions did commonly occur in industrializing cities in Europe and North America.[84] After a certain critical mass of wealthy people had fled the city, an impetus for incorporations became building tax revenue and limiting outlays. Similar and contemporaneous developments in the British industrial city of Leeds, as well as its suburbs, Hunslet and Holbeck, which were almost exclusively working class, resulted from the flight of wealthier residents.[85] As mentioned above, Greater Paris had suburbs that were almost exclusively working-class.[86] As Horst Matzerath noted, changes in jurisdiction and territory were as essential to urbanization as population growth and migration. Beginning in the 1840s, one can see a highpoint between 1871 and 1919 and a decline after 1919.[87] In 1908 one statistician argued that incorporation had almost immediate negative consequences for birth rates in the newly incorporated area.[88] This movement of population created a territorial and jurisdictional conflict between Greater Berlin as an economic region and Berlin as an administrative entity.

As the transformations wrought by capitalist industrialization stratified population spatially and drove population outward from the city centre, it also focused social life on the city and its social relations. This change challenged liberal theory and practice of municipal government and jurisdictional territory. Berlin was considered uncontainable. Capitalism integrated Greater Berlin, drawing the suburbs into the city's orbit.[89] This development convinced one observer in 1909 that the same modern economic forces that "concentrat[ed] industry, trade and monetary transaction" pressured municipalities and metropolitan regions to expand their connections commensurate with industrial expansion.[90] Rapid urbanization reached across once-distant borders and made life "intercommunal."[91] As Lindemann commented in 1906, small towns became exurbs bound to the city through industry, which looked for cheap land and in turn sought out and attracted workers. Rising property values drove workers and industry to the periphery while expanding traffic, which remained focused on the old city but necessitated increasing radial connections between suburbs. The streets of the city centre could no longer bear the load. The flight of business and industry from the city centre pressured the authorities there to adapt the inner-city streets to attract and accommodate the concentration of commerce and financial businesses in order to balance the loss of industry. Road breakthroughs in the city centre reduced the supply of housing and increased property value.[92]

Capitalism was transforming urban geography and forcing government to reterritorialize itself. In the process, it was undermining the basis of liberal ideology and practice of local government. Two simultaneous spatial pressures resulted: one drew economic, social, and cultural life into Berlin, and the other cast influence and capitalist social and cultural relations out. Labour and industrial capital were pushed to the periphery in search of cheaper land rent, greater space, access to transportation, industrial linkages, and a different labour pool – perhaps larger, perhaps with specific skills, or perhaps with different politics. At the same time the flow of businesses, especially banks and merchants,

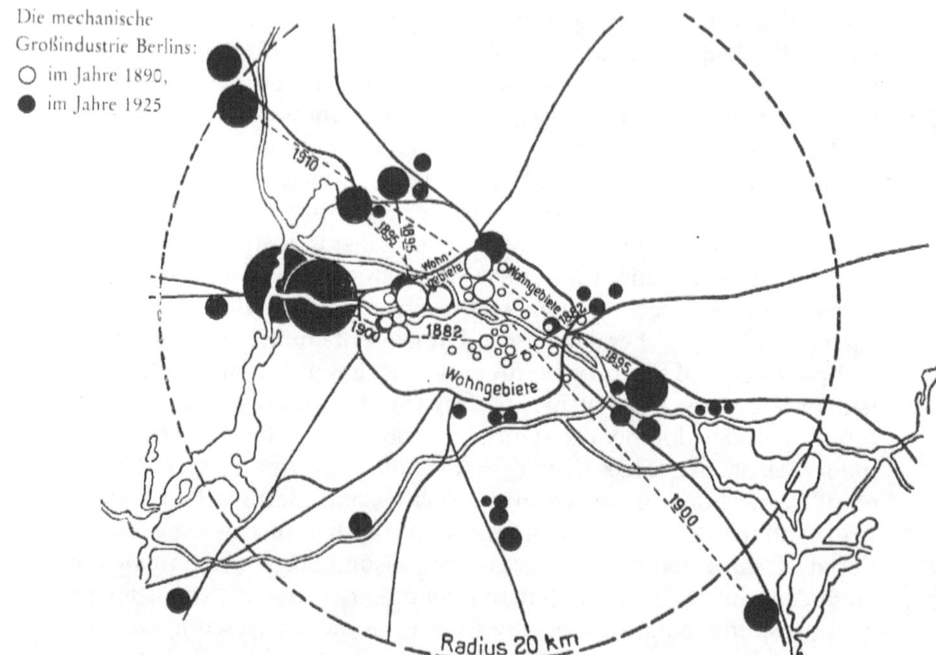

Die Randwanderung der Berliner Industrie orientierte sich an den Wasserstraßen und am Eisenbahnnetz.

1 "The edge migration of the Berlin industry oriented itself on the waterways and the rail network." The mechanical large-scale industry of Berlin: the white circle represents industry in 1890 and the black circle in 1925. Michael Erbe, "Berlin im Kaiserreich (1871–1918)," in *Geschichte Berlins: Von der Märzrevolution bis zur Gegenwart*, ed. Wolfgang Ribbe (Munich: C.H. Beck, 1987), 729.

brought traffic back into the city centre or to centralizing nodes of business activity, such as Kurfürstendamm. These two opposing pressures – centrifugal and centripetal forces as the statistician and pioneer in the social-spatial analysis of Berlin, Ernst Hirschberg, called them in 1905 – subsumed the suburbs into the city. The centrifugal force drove the de-centralization of industry and of the working class, while the centripetal concentrated business leadership and finance as well as the population in the city, with transportation mediating practical limits of the economic region.[93] Hirschberg warned that failing to heed this dynamic, one created by human activities but beyond the control of individuals, could have grave consequences. He thought the failure to incorporate Greater Berlin into a single city meant that the two forces were out of balance. The centrifugal pressure "hurled" the population to the periphery, but municipal and state administrative attention did not attend to the centripetal pressure. Even if one did not "want to merge already organically commensurate parts into an organism," then one had to "nevertheless give it some form, that can guarantee continuous common function." Otherwise, Hirschberg believed, one risked "atrophy of the central organ and hypertrophy of the limbs," using an organic metaphor to describe the urban totality.[94] According to the city councillor and real estate entrepreneur Georg Haberland in 1913, private capital concentration created the conditions of possibility for such a consideration of the city as a totality.[95] Ernest Burgess noted similar phenomena in Chicago.[96] And Henri Lefebvre referred to this dynamic of centripetal and centrifugal development as implosion-explosion.[97] Neil Brenner uses Lefebvre's term to grasp simultaneous, "wide-ranging territorial transformations that have ensued at various spatial scales during the longue durée history of capitalist urbanization. As cities are extended outwards into their surrounding territories and are woven together via thickening long-distance logistics networks, these erstwhile non-city zones are more tightly integrated into large-scale spatial divisions of labor. With the intensification, acceleration and territorial expansion of capitalist forms of growth, precapitalist and mercantile cities and towns are either peripheralized or remade into strategic locations within heavily industrialized landscapes."[98] Despite the efforts of some social actors, Greater Berlin was being transformed, pressuring municipal administrations to integrate and function at a greater economy of scale.

These spatial pressures forced government at each level to rethink territory and jurisdiction: about the expansion of municipal welfare and utility responsibilities and regarding the geographic transformation and locational dynamics of the growing city, which created problems for municipal tax revenues and fiscal responsibilities. The municipality needed to pay for this expansion, but while the economic region integrated, the administrative region did not. The contradiction between the geographic transformation of the region and the administrative stasis allowed entire cities and towns to become islands of a single class, creating tax revenue shortages for working-class locales. Between 1850 and 1913 the expenditures of the German municipal governments increased by 2,230 per cent because of new tasks.[99] According to Haberland in 1913, fiscal pressure explained the sixfold increase in incorporations in Prussia between 1897 and 1907 over the previous decade.[100] In the first decade of the twentieth century, the flight of the wealthy to certain suburbs was particularly acute in Berlin and meant that the city had difficulty raising tax revenue.[101] As one observer noted at the time, "The city centre remains a mainly business centre." The "calmer" and "freer" suburbs drew the wealthy, while the poor "preferred" areas with cheaper housing costs, often near the city centre. As a result, wealthy suburbs could exceed their economic and communal obligations, while poor areas could only partially fulfil them.[102] Regions used incorporations and Zweckverbände, (ad hoc associations), which formalized practical cooperation, to economize care for the poor and provide for the maintenance of schools and the construction of roads. When communities of different social character fused, they reconciled their interests and redistributed the fiscal burdens.[103] Cities sought to incorporate both "a suburb consisting of industrial plants" to "accommodate and maintain the workers," and a rich suburb to increase tax revenues.[104]

These changes in municipal responsibility and economic geography reterritorialized the social and economic life of Greater Berlin, forcing the hand of the regional administration. This pressure, in turn, challenged the amalgam of victorious liberal politics and successful tactical retreats of the Prussian bureaucracy that characterized nineteenth- and early twentieth-century German municipal administration. By the turn of the twentieth century, the municipal administration of Greater Berlin had reached a crisis point.

Municipal Self-Administration as a Legal and Political Category

These transformations in the character of municipalities also affected the concept of municipal self-administration in German jurisprudence. Across the second half of the nineteenth century, the administrative and liberal law, which had been an active political project – of which self-administration was a central category – began to appear to be a rote system, applied from outside of social relations. It became reified and alienated from those who created it.[105] It became a system distinct from human action, and jurists and politicians became little more than minders of a legal apparatus.

After Stein's early nineteenth-century reforms, the left-liberal participant in the 1848 Revolution and National Liberal politician Rudolf von Gneist did the most to think through self-administration. Gneist attempted to create a self-administering municipality in Berlin whose political structure formally separated the legislative and executive powers. Gneist wrote that the revolution had created a new Berlin city council and that the "rebirth" of a "political middle class" challenged both the city fathers and the Prussian state. He noted, "Even a child of the revolution could not deny that the city council was his mother." Gneist encouraged "the community of citizens" to make this new council, with the Magistrat, the lone municipal authority and the expression of Berliners' general will, thereby creating the "basic conditions of a constitutional monarchy and the true people's freedom." With the subsequent counter-revolution, however, Gneist reconciled himself to a municipal government of an undemocratically small electorate and subordination to the conservative bureaucracy.[106] Like the rest of liberal politics, Gneist began as revolutionary in 1848, but with the defeat of liberals, he had to adapt his goals to the modified, aristocrat-dominated government.

After 1848, writers muted the break from the past that municipal self-administration represented and emphasized in its place the slow, many-generational evolution of the legal structure. In 1864, for example, Ernst von Möller argued that Prussian law analogized the municipality to the citizen. Municipalities, as enduring, concrete administrative structures, functioned as the object through which the abstract category of the citizenry was realized. Like citizens, municipalities could reach private law agreements, were corporations with property rights and obligations, and were subject to private law. He argued that the division of labour created conflicting interests, which necessitated establishing complex systems of administration that would balance and aggregate individual interests.[107] In 1869, Gneist emphasized the limitations on municipal autonomy in Germany and its subservience to the state.[108] He contrasted the term "self-government" with *Selbstverwaltung* (self-administration) to reveal the absence of autonomy and democracy.[109]

The dominant liberal mode of jurisprudence, known as legal positivism, regarded law and of administration as apolitical, which in turn structured the self-understanding of the municipal administrators and the creation of the Bürgerliches Gesetzbuch (BGB), the legal code of the Kaiserreich. Central to legal positivism and to liberal political aims was the project to create the *Rechtstaat* system of general laws, created all at once in a constitutional convention. However, the BGB, which was introduced in 1881 and effective as of January 1, 1900, was formed through a conservative codification of laws that already existed. The administrators drew on laws as old as the 1794 Prussian Allgemeine

Landrecht. In 1900 legal positivism was defensive; it appealed to state power and existing law to defend the law's "apolitical" character, and the legal bureaucrats of a variety of political persuasions creating the BGB avoided political questions.[110] Whether historians characterize this apolitical self-understanding as quietism or as an affect, they agree on its centrality to municipal liberals' self-understanding.[111] Legal positivism, as David Blackbourn has put it, marked a bourgeois retreat that was fearful of and sealed off from social conflict and that used "a highly formalized notion of the law" to defend the status quo. The law ceased to be a weapon against the ancien régime.[112] In this moment, frustrated and defeated by social conflicts in national politics, liberals turned their attention to municipal concerns.[113] For example, by the 1870s Gneist regarded the Rechtsstaat as an impossibility because of social conflict.[114] He even lamented the loss of the "beloved bounds and proprietary rights" of feudal corporate society.[115] Expressing the alienation of the law from politics, Gneist declared that the law had its own dynamic logic, and all citizens could draw on its "self-active" execution.[116] This independent, "self-active," dynamic logic was unassailable by both political action and everyday activity.

The positivists treated BGB as a complete and nearly "history-less" system, and they diminished questions of historical development or precedent that legal history appeared as a chain of present moments wherein a judge applied the appropriate statute. This ahistorical interpretation of the legal code diminished the political project that was necessary to create the code and instead treated it as if it were simply the natural order. The leading jurist of legal positivism, Paul Laband, endeavoured to create a single dogmatic system based on what he regarded as seamless, systematic, and ontological legal principles.[117] This closed, self-active system of abstract principles, as the political scientist, lawyer, and critical theorist Franz Neumann put it, took all intellectual, decisional labour away from the judge, who merely had to apply the law.[118] Thus, as political scientist and critical theorist Otto Kirchheimer argued in 1928, the judge became a minder of the "self-active" legal structure, merely giving voice to its machine-like application.[119]

In this context, the unfulfilled potential of liberal law, expressed in Gneist's 1848 vision of self-administration, became "inverted and protected," with liberals defending the failed dimensions of their project because their success would fundamentally threaten the status quo.[120] This change in the character of liberal jurisprudence is symptomatic of a deeper crisis in the liberal social order. Representatives of wealthy suburbs used municipal self-administration to shield "intimate" municipal administration from progressive features of the state.[121] This resulted in the development of two interpretations of municipal self-administration. First, right-leaning liberals and conservatives, especially in wealthy suburbs, used claims of municipal self-administration to combat the progressive state measures or Socialist municipal politics. Thus the once-revolutionary claim of municipal self-administration became a tool of counter-revolution and reaction. Second, the dominant legal positivist interpretation of the law stuck to the letter of the law and denied that the municipality was independent at all; instead, it was merely devolution of state authority. Liberals obfuscated the unfulfilled revolutionary politics of municipal self-administration and dismissed the politics, which appealed to an unfulfilled potential, as relapses into natural law.[122]

In the place of Gneist's actual liberal radicalism, liberals began to tell themselves a conservative story of the origins of this liberal system of municipal self-administration and liberal politics that viewed the two as the consequence of the slow evolution of an ontological germ in German cities. For example, cultural historian Andreas Heusler, in 1872, celebrated cities as generating the "free *Bürgertum*" and "civic liberty" that brought to life "the basis of the modern nature of the state, above all the modern idea of the state and of the civil society as contrary to the feudal principle." He claimed that liberal principles shaped society by "slowly maturing fruit of a germ lying in the nature of cities ... a rejuvenation of the old Frankish freedom, the urban constitution and the free *Bürgertum*," *not* "by usurpation and revolution on the part of the *Bürgerschaft*."[123] Heusler made liberal social relations, which were actually radically new, appear natural and denied the role of politics in their creation, espousing this because of the threatening and unfulfilled character of bourgeois radicalism in 1848 and its inheritors, the SPD. This vision of municipal self-administration made what was once a political project into an eternal, ontological condition, further reifying law and administration. In other words, municipal self-administration was removed from its historical context and treated as if its concerns were eternal.

Legal positivism, with its formalist, largely ahistorical, and abstract interpretation of the law and of municipal self-administration, was a one-sided jurisprudential tradition, and the reaction against it revealed the deeper crisis in liberal ideology and practice. The one-sidedness was strongly criticized, most notably by Otto von Gierke, from an equally one-sided, though inverted jurisprudential convention that focused on the content of the law, its historical development, and its connection to a concrete community.[124] Gierke, a monarchist with National Liberal leanings, led the Germanist school of historical jurisprudence. A professor at the University of Berlin, Gierke attacked the BGB for supposedly adding inauthentic and foreign legal code.[125] He assailed the Anglophilic, "abstract, individualistic, and 'soulless legal person'" in the name of the "real personality of the collectivity."[126] He viewed municipal legal corporations as part of the organic body of the state.[127] He attacked legal positivism's ahistorical character, its analogies between public and private law, and its ossification of the law to "retain" the law's apolitical character.[128] Further, Gierke attacked Laband, who was Jewish, for the rootlessness, "empty formalism," mechanical character, and "denatured positivism" of his jurisprudence.[129] He and his school attempted to overcome the abstraction and ahistorical character of legal positivism by basing their view of jurisprudence on purportedly concrete social life. In so doing, it trafficked in its own abstractions, while denying that a certain level of abstraction was necessary for modern capitalism.

The most prominent jurist of Gierke's school to focus on municipal self-administration was the municipal politician and jurist Hugo Preuß. He diagnosed the developing contradiction between the social organization of German municipalities, like his home Berlin, and the liberal ideology that organized political life. Preuß attempted to understand self-administration in a two-sided way. As a Jew, he suffered from significant discrimination and did not take on the nationalist and anti-Semitic strains of Gierke's thought, but he did adopt Gierke's focus on history and political power. However, while Gierke viewed this history affirmatively, Preuß did so critically.[130] Preuß argued that legal ideas were historically constituted in a dynamic interrelationship between state and civil society in the Rechtsstaat.[131] Furthermore, he wrote that economic needs drove the history of jurisprudence.[132] Preuß criticized the positivist concept of the state for individuating then immediately aggregating citizens and municipalities into the state will, thereby obfuscating individuals' social relationships.[133] For Preuß, apparent legal and social constancy masked infinite small changes shaped by economic needs and the consequences of the failed bourgeois revolution, which allowed the anachronistic German legal institutions such as the Allgemeine Landrechts to survive.[134] Unlike both the positivist and the German schools, Preuß attempted to move through and beyond the dualistic thinking that characterized those schools. He contended that self-administration had "a political soul and a legal soul" and that logically one could neither determine a "true soul, which reveals the other as a phantom" nor juxtapose the unreconciled souls.[135] The first "soul" was *"bürgerlich"* and emphasized political autonomy and "self-government," and the second "soul" was *"körperschaftlich"* and recognized the integration of administrative bodies into the state.[136] In light of the history of German municipal administration, its interaction with industrial capitalism, the history of this legal category, and the particular manifestation in Berlin, we can understand the attempts to solve the problems of Greater Berlin through administrative means.

As the jurisprudence of Preuß suggested, a certain mutually constitutive opposition seemed to develop in the area of jurisprudence, especially in the opposition between legal positivism and Gierke's school of thought. These jurisprudential schools revealed an unconscious opposition between the abstract, rational, all-encompassing, and ahistorical on the part of positivism and the (purportedly) concrete, "rooted," particularist, and historically constituted on the part of the Germanist school. But this was not an opposition between liberal rational modernism and romantic anti-modernism; rather, both sides were fundamentally new, modern social forms. Furthermore, the liberal alienation of the law from politics and its removal from its context into a closed, abstract system outside of human activity was related to the above-mentioned oppositions and equally modern. The apolitical stance of liberal positivist jurisprudence reveals a key dimension of the alienation of the state and law and the way that the state and law were removed from their historical context and treated as eternal features.[137] This submission of the jurist's or bureaucrat's subjectivity to an abstract and quasi-objective system, the tendency towards oppositions between abstract and concrete, and the romantic response to reification, I argue, following Lukacs, are all intimately related to the peculiar character of modern capitalism. Further, the dynamic character of capitalism, I contend, was very closely related to both the emancipatory dimensions of revolutionary liberalism and to the never-ripe, yet overripe character that liberalism took on by the turn of the twentieth century

Conclusion: Liberalism Transformed

This chapter has argued that changes in the social, political, geographic, and cultural conditions of capitalist industrialization transformed the form and content of German cities and in turn changed their administrations. In the process, this transformation also reformed spheres of urban life that appear distant from politics or economics, such as jurisprudence. This chapter has maintained that the sense of crisis manifested itself in response to a split between the prevailing liberal understandings of the world and of Berlin and the functioning of that world and of Berlin. Liberalism, which once appeared to be the natural expression of the essence of society, was now increasingly unable to explain society. This change was a global shift in the character of capitalism, but it had local permutations in Germany and in Berlin. It affected the political economy and governmental structure but was also part of a reterritorialization of the municipality, the state, and the Reich. This chapter posits that liberalism was not just a mode of economics or politics but also rather the formal structure of culture and society during this historically specific period. This chapter has traced the history of liberalism and capitalism in Germany and in Berlin, the history of the industrialization of Berlin, as well as the spatial, social, and political consequences of industrialization. Finally, the transformation of liberalism has been explored through an analysis of the discourse of municipal self-administration.

This understanding of liberalism at the municipal level, especially in Berlin, will be explored further in chapter 2, which examines liberal understandings of urban space and city planning. Together, these chapters will lay the groundwork for explaining a shift in the social forms that shaped the appearance, function, and perception of Greater Berlin from social forms organized along liberal principles to social forms constituted by corporatist conventions, a change that was part of a broader shift from liberal capitalism to corporatist capitalism.

Chapter Two

The Decline of Liberal City Planning

The wanderer, who approaches … in the evening light of the metropolis, experiences the descent into this region. Once he crosses the atmosphere of the effluents before him opens the darken rows of teeth of the housing cubicles [*Wohnkästen*] and blocks out the sky. The green flames hem the street. Illuminated iron ships grind [*schleifen*] their human freight over the flattened unfortunate soil. In a naughty light, the lathe machines and chutes of a riotous place sound and thunder: this is a place of joy; and thousands stand, black thronged, with flickering eyes before the posters of the fenced wilderness. Out of the courtyards, overtired men and women pour, filling up the space behind the windowpanes, whose labels twitch in white-blue arc light. "Great Distillation," "Hair-Dressing Salon," "Bonbon Source," "Boot Paradise," "Cinema," "Repayment Business," "World Bazaar": those are places of acquisition … That is the nightscape of those cities, which are praised and applauded as places of luck, longing, intoxication, and spirit, which depopulate the country, which kindle the desire of those excluded to the point of criminality.

Walter Rathenau, 1913[1]

Introduction: The Built Environment in Crisis

In 1910 Karl Scheffler referred to Berlin as an "infinitely expanding crisis," which included the built environment and inspired Walther Rathenau to illustrate what he termed "the place of soullessness" with a stroll in Berlin. Rathenau was the head of Allgemeine Elektricitäts Gesellschaft (AEG), a banker, and an author who would play an important role in the First World War and the Weimar Republic. Elsewhere, Rathenau portrayed Berlin's built environment positively, as a site of production at the "centre of a spider web of rails," waterways, wires, and roads, creating "visible and invisible networks" that "pump twice-daily human bodies from the extremities to the heart."[2] Rathenau's comments about the built environment captured a dualism in the received perception of Berlin: on the one hand, the city's consumer economy and its absence of green space were signs of moral decadence and cultural decline; on the other, Berlin's technical and industrial capacity was celebrated as part of a massive, dynamic organism.

The built environment of Berlin seemed to crystallize a sense of sociostructural crisis. The inadequacy of older, liberal forms of city planning for the needs of a city as dynamic as Berlin in 1900 gave rise to this sense of crisis. Rathenau and Scheffler are symptomatic of this shift in the form, function, and perception of Greater Berlin from ones structured by liberal social relations and ideologies to ones structured by corporate social relations and ideologies. Contemporaries recognized changes occurring around them but did so only partially. They tended to fixate on particular changes and miss the society-level changes. This chapter traces the formation of that liberal city planning, its hegemony, and its subsequent crisis. The chapter places this new mode of planning in the context of the prevailing territorialization of the economic region, municipality, state, and Reich. It argues that both the mode of planning and the form of territorialization are historically specific to this liberal regime of capital accumulation.[3] In so doing, this chapter considers the theory and practice of liberalism in a realm often considered distinctly illiberal – city planning. Liberalism is an ideology in a broad sense, a general mode of thought or a world view. City planning in its form and content during the nineteenth century was distinctly liberal in character. The transformation of socioeconomic relations brought about by capitalism gave rise, through mediations, to liberalism and made liberalism appear, again through mediations, to express what seemed to be essential to society. As capitalism similarly transformed itself into a post-liberal form, this model of city planning became inadequate to deal with the world that it had helped to create, the industrial metropolis.

This chapter will explore a debate about urban real estate speculation, which shaped the built environment of the city by supplying the stock to accommodate the population growth and creating the derelict conditions of most of the working-class housing. As the chapter will show, this discourse about speculation also exposes a crisis in liberal ideology. This example, like the example of municipal self-administration in the previous chapter, reveals a social form that underlies most urban ideologies: an opposition between social institutions and processes that seem abstract, such as the market, finance, and the regulatory or "law-like" behaviour of capitalism, and social institutions and processes that appear to be concrete, such as the conditions of working-class housing, practical social politics, and capitalist production.

Liberal Planning in Europe

Like the liberal municipal administration, the liberal form of city planning included both the theory of city planning and its practice, and liberal city planning was shaped by liberal understandings of the order of the society, and of cities in particular. Likewise, planners acted as agents, but under conditions not of their choosing. They shaped urban historical socio-dynamics and were shaped by them. This dialectical approach is uncommon in the study of urban history and city planning. The prevailing historiography of architecture and city planning varies according to the role it attributes in constituting the urban form ascribed, on the one hand, to individuals, and, on the other, to social dynamics.

Understood as a field as a whole, the historiography of architecture and city planning is structured by a dualism that opposes individual planners or architects against society. Those who view the history of architecture and city planning through the lens of individual planners or architects understand the individual as capable of significant, wilful transformation of urban space. While the iconic figure of this vision of planning and architectural history is Baron Georges-Eugène Haussmann of Paris, historians employ this narrative in circumstances beyond that of Paris. In nineteenth-century Berlin, the key figure is James Hobrecht. Hobrecht took the master builder exam twice – in 1856 and in 1858 – after an eleven-year course of practical training, and accepted a job planning and constructing railways in the province of Brandenburg. After just a few months in this position, the Polizeipräsident of Berlin offered him the job of developing a plan for Berlin and its surrounding towns. Hobrecht led a team that had been working on questions of urban development for a few years already when he took over in February 1859. Hobrecht held this position until December 1861.[4] For this short stint, he has received credit for massive transformations in Greater Berlin's built environment. Claus Bernet characterizes Hobrecht's design for Berlin from 1862 as the "foundation of modern Berlin."[5] Hobrecht's plan established the layout of streets but then let the market determine what followed. The planners themselves expressed this view of the power of the iconic planner and blamed Hobrecht for creating the problems of Greater Berlin. Christoph Bernhardt argues that Hobrecht combined a laissez-faire city plan and significant state intervention that included sewerization.[6] Neither the planners nor the historians, however, explain why Hobrecht's approach seemed adequate to solving urban questions, at one point, and then later was cited as the cause of the urban problems that resulted. This chapter argues that the urban society and its built environment had transformed itself such that ideas that appeared adequate at one point could appear as fetters to progress and as socially and aesthetically malignant at a later point.

A historian can also address the relationship between the planner or architect and the society from the perspective of an analysis of social forces. John Robert Mullin claims that city-planning theory "reflects existing societal values, culture, technology, economic and demographic trends, ideas for future changes and planning practice."[7] Similarly, Anthony Sutcliffe argues that city planning arose in a moment of recognition that the social forces registered through the market did not necessarily serve all the needs of urban development, forcing the planners and architects to act.[8] While, at one level, Sutcliffe argues that figures like James Hobrecht, who relied on the market to determine the character of the city, were not involved in city planning, at another level, he asserts that social forces coerce architects and planners to respond in a particular way. Wolfgang Sonne contends that one could see that creating a general plan for Greater Berlin as the working out of the conflict between the conservative Prussian state and German Reich bureaucrats, on the one hand, and the Social Democrats, on the other hand. However, he continues, an explanation at this particularistic, local level does not address the international dimensions of urbanization and urban planning.[9] Sonne argues that an international ideological turn towards understanding the metropolitan region, in its totality, as an object of aesthetic contemplation, socioeconomic planning, and potential transformation occurred at the beginning of the twentieth century.[10]

While strong in Germany, the ideological turn described by Mullin and Sonne towards considering the urban region as a whole was too consistent across both regimes and nations to be attributed to a particular state or form of government.[11] Contemporaneous examples abound. In 1909 Daniel Burnham created his plan for Chicago, while the Cook County Forest Preserve was established by Illinois in 1913; Boston set up the Boston Metropolitan Parks Plan in 1893 and subsequently undertook a six-year regional planning project known as Boston 1915. Vienna developed a general plan for the region in 1893, while London and Liverpool undertook projects of slum clearance periodically from the 1860s onward.[12] Mullin notes a shift in the ideology of planning around the time of the First World War, away from a focus on very local issues to complex, regional challenges wherein, it was hoped, good design could address both the built environment and the social structure.[13] Brian Ladd regards the development of planning as part of a broader bourgeois discourse on reformism, irreducible to the economic interest of the planners, one that reveals bourgeois attitudes towards workers, civic pride, and urban geography.[14] Ladd argues that municipalities used the terms *public interest* and *general welfare* to justify economic, ethical, cultural, and social actions by the municipality when it became clear that the market and private charities alone could not resolve urban problems.[15] He argues that a larger process of Weberian bureaucratization and the development of a professional technocracy at the city level subsumed the commitments of liberal municipal leaders to private ownership and the free market.[16]

This approach sees individuals' actions as the consequence of social forces. Ironically, those arguments emphasize the power of social forces over individuals, but to explain a shift in the social forces, they set one part of society – "elites," "experts," "technocrats," etc. – as superior to society and capable of changing it. However, they cannot explain who or what educates these "educators." The historiography of architecture and planning that privileges the wills of individuals risks becoming a history of great men, while the historiography that emphasizes the supremacy of society risks becoming teleological. This dualistic historiography persists because it reflects a dichotomy in the historical reality that survives through the sources. Furthermore, it is not enough to see ideas about the social world, like this opposition between the auteur and social forces, as merely a projection of that social world into the realm of ideas – one must explain what aspects of that social world cause individuals to think that way. The approach offered in this book sees modern society as riven with contradiction and creating the conditions of possibility for social transformation.[17]

Berlin in the 1850s began to rapidly transform. At this point the form, function, and perception of the city are shifting from one organized according to pre-industrial and relatively pre-modern social forms into one organized by liberal social forms. In this period an old built environment not yet adapted to modern capitalism created urban problems, including tangled streets and city walls that inhibited trade, the need to incorporate a train station into the city, the imperative to house the waves of migrants in search of work, the increasing demands for space for industrial production, and the revolutionary activities in the newly formed working-class districts. A number of urban administrators and reformers tried to adapt the pre-modern space of European cities to the demands of a modern society and removed the city walls, many of the tangled streets, and the unhygienic sewer systems. They sought to facilitate circulation of people and commodities, clear slums, and connect rail stations to centres of civic life.[18] These liberal planners did not choose these goals randomly or because of a tautological appeal to modernity and progress. They made these changes because if the businesses and the city were to survive the transition to a capitalist society, they needed to retrofit the built environment to the needs of capitalism. This reorganization of the city broke through buildings to create wide, straight roads, centralized the city structure around monuments, isolated those monuments from the rest of the built environment, and established a unified form of building facades.[19]

Not only is the historiography of city planning and architecture structured by a dualism between the auteur and social forces, but it is also structured by an opposition between the concrete and communal, on the one hand, and the abstract and social, on the other hand. This dichotomy does not persist because of the misguided thinking of one side or the other, but because it reflects a dichotomy in the historical reality that survives through the sources. Often the literature about city planning projects that destroy working-class homes celebrates the old district for its concrete community and sociality and contrasts it to the abstract and individualized development that replaces them. In many cases, though, this new development has elements that are worth celebrating. This literature often urbanizes Ferdinand Tönnies's idea of *Gemeinschaft*, creates "urban villagers," and romanticizes communal life.[20] As Alain Faure argues, this academic discourse often glosses over the oppressive conditions of these neighbourhoods and the desire of the residents to escape from the community that was enforced by the density and poverty to attain a level of privacy.[21] This celebration of neighbourhood *Gemeinschaft* also attacks displacement of residents and uprooting of communities; the literature presumes a "placed-ness" and rooted-ness that are at odds with the actual churn of residential working-class districts and take on a conservative rhetoric about the relationship between space, place, and culture. This book does not celebrate one side of this urban *Gesellschaft* and *Gemeinschaft* opposition; rather, it sees both sides as mutually constituted and as historically specific to *modern* capitalist society.

In Paris in the 1850s, as was soon to be the case in Berlin, a process of transformation in the form, function, and perception of the city accelerated. It shifted from the urban environment from one organized according to pre-industrial and relatively pre-modern social forms into one organized by liberal social forms. In Paris, Haussmann destroyed inconvenient parts of the city, scrapped uncoordinated local development plans, and fought neighbourhood parochialism in the name of the higher, abstract unity of the municipality. Haussmann did "rationalize" space and proceed according to abstract plans; however, not all projects of urban rationalization and not all forms of abstraction are the same. Haussmann's form of abstraction and its assumptions were historically specific to the liberal period of capitalism. He sought to promote the movement of commodities, to make business smooth and predictable, to physically facilitate the freedom of the market and of civil society, and to contain proletarian revolution. By means of a general plan he fused particular neighbourhoods through a network of boulevards into a Parisian totality. Freedom of movement, commerce, and transportation constituted this totality.

Liberalism guided Haussmann's building. Like the liberal concepts of the abstract equality of citizens, he emphasized the centrality of symmetry and rationality among individual buildings. Like the liberal concept of the nation, he tried to create a type of cohesion that joined many particularities into a single, politically mediated totality. The aesthetic ideal of his Paris was movement and free exchange, and Haussmann designed the city to be an equalizing, rational, symmetrical accompaniment to that movement. The whole city, he believed, should free itself from its medieval built environment and accord with the logic of this commercially constituted totality. Nonetheless, this transformation of inner Paris was not simply the vision of one man. Haussmann was committed to improving transportation, but he incorporated other people's projects, such as moving traffic routes from along the Seine to multiple railroad heads.[22] The demands of the system as a whole, that is, of capital, reconstituted the city and not the particular interests of that or this capitalist. While this was a state-ordered process, private firms on municipal concessions conducted all of Haussmann's construction.[23] Despite his authoritarian style, Haussmann was overcoming feudal tradition and setting the ground, like a liberal constitution writer, for liberal capitalism.

A liberal social imagination also reshaped the form of Vienna, as Carl Schorske notes. In the place of the old walls, the city built a wide, ring-shaped boulevard lined with grand imperial, municipal, civil, and private structures. All of these buildings took on a homogeneous style and scale. Administrators coupled them with new hygienic regulations for the development of city space.[24] Geometric organization of urban space, the development of areas for martial parades and bourgeois strolling, and the smooth, uninterrupted flow of commodities and people represented guiding principles. Cities planned in this manner became the rational space for realizing the potentials of the bourgeois public sphere. The width of the streets, created to facilitate large flows of traffic, pedestrians, horse riders, and carriages, enabled collective activities like military parades but hampered other collective functions, such as the building of barricades. As Walter Benjamin and William Sewell Jr point out, the experience and perception of the individual bourgeois stroller taking in the crowds and examining the wares in the shops constituted the liberal vision of urban space and an early cultural consequence of capitalism transforming social life.[25] In general, in this transformation in the form, function, and perception of the city from one organized according to pre-industrial and relatively pre-modern social forms into one organized by liberal social forms, city planning endeavoured to overcome the feudal and early modern urban environment. Liberal public health– and exchange–oriented public works projects often required state executive, administrative, or fiscal effort and are often seen as illiberal. However, as Adam Smith recognized, the state needed to take on expensive and unprofitable tasks to further the growth of the wealth of the nation.[26] As Franz Neumann noted, liberalism regarded the state's "nonexistence as the highest virtue of the state" and "according to this ideology, the state must function unperceivably and must really be negative." Historians, however, should not confuse this "negativity" with "weakness." The state certainly asserted itself when threatened (internally and externally) and to facilitate further economic growth.[27] Liberal city planning sought to organize the city in such a way that the space facilitated exchange, commodity circulation, and the market. Furthermore, it sought to realize a bourgeois liberal habitus but did not rule out state intervention to protect private property and the state or to set the conditions of possibility, in spatial terms, for liberal civic and economic social life.

Liberal Planning in Berlin

The form, function, and perception of Greater Berlin were transformed from ones organized according to pre-industrial and relatively premodern social forms into one organized by liberal social forms. A liberal vision of urban life and modernity similar to that of Paris and Vienna guided the creation of city plans in Berlin in the middle of the nineteenth century. An amalgam of liberalism and state bureaucracy characterized city planning. Conflicting jurisdictions overlaid Greater Berlin, and property holders strenuously fought against any attempt to clarify those jurisdictions or threats to property rights and privileges. Small property holders, in particular, used their property rights to differentiate themselves from the working class.

The ideological power of these liberal social forms is evident, as was the case with the reforms to the administrative structure of Greater Berlin, in the fact that city planners who carried out liberalizing reforms were not necessarily avowed liberals. At this point what was believed to be the rational, adequate response to problems of urban space proceeded with liberal assumptions. As Kristin Poling notes, in the late eighteenth century, some fifty years before Berlin saw significant industrialization, critics worried that Berlin was growing too quickly and, in the terms of this book, in a constitutionless manner. They did not like the small size of the urban core of Berlin, relative to other European capitals. Neither did they admire the congested, medieval streets. They preferred the open, unplanned space for building outside of the old city. Nonetheless, they were concerned about the dense inner city and the rapid, disconnected, and chaotic development of buildings beyond the old city walls. They felt that a certain balance had been lost and worried this would impede economic growth.[28]

The reformation of the built legacy of the feudal and early modern city in Berlin according to liberal norms began before Hobrecht's plan took effect in 1862. From the 1820s to the 1860s, planners created a series of parks in the north, south, and east of Berlin and converted the Tiergarten from a royal hunting ground into a park. All followed an English garden model that focused on the interaction between the individual bourgeois stroller and the distilled, accentuated naturalness of the park.[29] The geographic area of Berlin was small in comparison to that of other European cities, at only 35.11 square kilometres. Berlin remained within its old tariff walls, with the exception of an 1841 incorporation of land to the north of the city. Those who wanted to enter or leave the city had to use one of the fourteen gates. However, the city council opposed any further expansion because of the costs of developing roads and establishing poverty relief systems.

More consciously liberal reformers battled with the Prussian bureaucracy to remove the wall, because it limited trade, and the small city core translated into inadequate housing for the poor.[30] While the bureaucracy was committed to maintaining the wall, critics believed that an open, expanding city would resolve housing issues. This liberal discourse unified working-class and bourgeois politics in opposition to the aristocratic and bureaucratic pre-modern police state. The liberal press regarded the wall's continued existence as an embarrassment, especially because the short and thin wall had been subsumed by tall rental barracks. Citizens and those living in the lands outside the walls broke new holes in the city wall. As Poling explains, commentators preferred this illegal activity to the housing riots that had erupted in response to evictions in 1863 and treated dismantling as "natural, inevitable, and an expression of the city's collective spirit" and as "invisible, stealthy, and 'wonderfully secret,'" carried out by mysterious actors.[31] The business press invoked Adam Smith's invisible hand to describe this destruction and the spirit of the metropolis. In 1861 Moabit and Wedding, as well as the northern sections of Schöneberg and Teltow, were joined to Berlin, increasing the size of the city by nearly 70 per cent, to 59.23 square kilometres. The state tore down the wall in 1865–6[32] and removed all city gates except the Brandenburg Gate.[33]

In 1862 the abstract liberal principles that set the stage for the future development of Berlin were laid down in a plan – a sort of spatial constitution-writing process. In 1855 the Berlin Polizeipräsident Karl von Hinckeldey ordered the creation of a plan to regulate urban development, and in 1859–61 the Polizeipräsident commissioned James Hobrecht to produce a compilation of all existing laws and plans for Berlin. His work went into effect in 1862.[34] Hobrecht's plan outlined the form of building and the system of sewers at the borders of Berlin as well as in Wilmersdorf, Charlottenburg, Rixdorf, Reinickendorf, Weißensee, and Lichtenburg.[35] In the 1870s and 1880s liberals, led by medical professor and politician Rudolf Virchow, convinced city officials to expand the sewer system in wealthy areas and create a centralized sewer system.[36] Hobrecht focused on traffic flow and orderly development and created "a vast grid of large regular blocks," accommodating "existing roads and property lines wherever possible." The owner and the builder alone determined the form and content of the building on the property. New state ordinances enabled the purchase of land along planned streets but forbade construction until the streets existed. This legal measure encouraged speculative land purchases and the rise in land value as a housing shortage set in. The escalating value of land discouraged building the street, because the shorter the supply of housing was the more valuable the undeveloped land.[37] Building codes limited the freedom of business and challenged the liberal doctrines of free trade; however, this infringement of liberal rights furthered another liberal right: not to have your life and well-being infringed upon by another.[38] The Hobrecht plan enabled the real estate

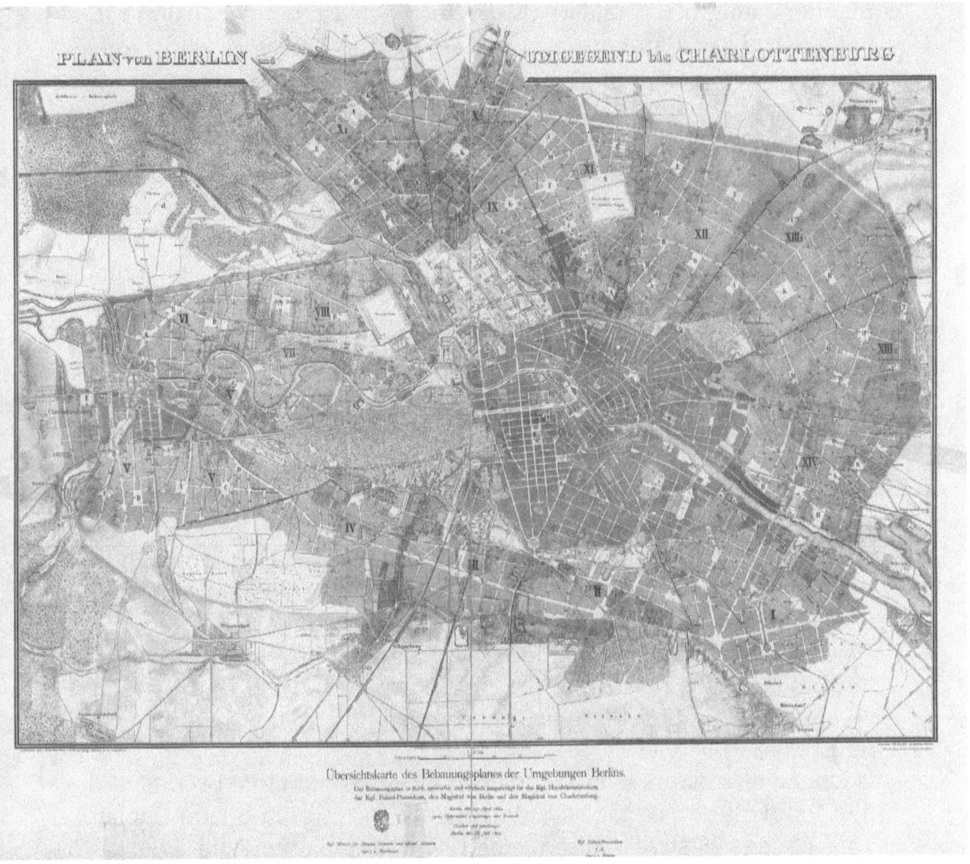

2 Hobrecht's plan for Berlin and Its Environs. Ferdinand Boehm, "Plan von Berlin und Umgegend bis Charlottenburg" (Berlin: Keller, 1862).

development and business to occur in a predictable and quantifiable manner and ensured that each citizen was abstractly equal as he or she conducted business.

A liberal approach to political economy facilitated the agglomeration of industry in German cities, and especially Berlin, creating centripetal coercive power drawing population and economic activity to the city. This development generated new pressures towards a reterritorialization of the municipality, state, and Reich. The city planners sought to manage this industry-mediated expansion rationally. Reinhard Baumeister, a professor of engineering and pioneer of city planning, attempted to address the unplanned, speculative building and shantytowns at the urban periphery, and the expensive, dense city centre. Baumeister argued that suburban developments for the wealthy would not solve crowded, derelict housing, because their customers were too few. He also believed that the planning, including Hobrecht's, did not take class into account and did not resolve problems of high property values in the old city centre, which made expensive and unhygienic rental barracks likely. Baumeister argued that the inflated value of real estate pressured builders to construct expensive homes under significant debt to recover their costs. Planners sought free-market solutions to these problems by promoting urban expansions in order to glut the market with housing and drive the price down. This approach seemed to challenge the building and real estate speculators, but construction occurred only for expensive homes – a market that was quickly saturated – and housing for the poor offered an insufficient return on investment. The approach that Baumeister preferred was to build working-class housing on cheap land at the urban periphery, where the factories were moving for more space for less money and better access to transportation systems. This movement of the poor from the city centre meant that the city would no longer be supposedly unsafe and unhealthy, so the wealthy would return.[39]

Liberal city planners in Vienna had a similar plan that promoted the development of a cottage system, akin to the ones in liberal England. This cottage system caused small working-class-owned homes to sprawl across the urban periphery.[40] While the Crown did intervene into a market, much of the contemporary literature hoped that members of the working class, the "urban nomads in their stone tents," would settle on property they owned. However, this wandering was common to many working-class people, including, as David Ward has shown, in the British industrial city of Leeds.[41]

As the liberal form, function, and perception of Greater Berlin became dominant, the contradictory features of this set of social forms also became more apparent. Just as was the case for criticisms of liberal jurisprudence and ideas about municipal self-administration, critics of liberal cities focused their attack on the role of abstract principles in shaping the development of the city. Progressive and reactionary critics of modern cities drew on anti-urban views to explain their critique of urban life, especially of cities such as Berlin, which lacked deep historical roots and grew rapidly.[42] For example, in 1856 Wilhelm Riehl, a pioneering and controversial folklorist and a nationalist, favoured "organically" developing cities whose "slow growth and maturation developed out from 'natural conditions.'"[43] Riehl argued that in the eighteenth century German cities aspired to be Versailles, but in the nineteenth century cities sought to be London and Paris. He believed that all cities were creating unnatural symptoms, including "a precocious and extremely agitated intellectual life." Riehl proclaimed, "Europe is sick at the monstrosity of its major cities," and he criticized the application of abstract cosmopolitan enlightenment and liberal principles to all situations, because they eliminated particularity, making every city a "world city, that is, identical to all other major cities." In these world cities, the "natural differences between the groups in society" disappear and "'bourgeoisie' and 'society'" are presupposed to be synonyms. Riehl was troubled that migrant laborers and not birth rates drove urban growth and that universal suffrage could mean that big cities could dominate the country politically. He attacked what he saw as the individualism of the city, contrasting it with the family-oriented structure of rural communities. He worried that in Berlin, the housing shortage and population growth could focus anger over rents into a version of the social question, and that the city would need to create proletarian barracks, like those in Britain.[44] Ironically, given the way that conservatives conflated Jewishness with the urbanity and modernity that Riehl attacked, discourses within the Jewish community had similar dichotomies and blamed cities like Berlin for the assimilation of Jews and for the loss of cultural particularity and tradition.[45] By contrast, the hope of liberal city planning was to become part of a global community built on universal laws and commodity exchange among abstractly equal citizens that would overcome these purported "natural differences."

Liberal Planning Theory

The city-planning theory based on the liberal form, function, and perception of cities was built on a set of liberal assumptions about society. It sought to enable the city to function as smoothly and with the greatest freedom and equality possible and was developed largely in the 1870s, with the exception of Joseph Stübben's 1890 synthesis of its principles. With increased trade and population growth, the old city walls limited urban economic growth and public health as well as a civil rights and freedoms. The state removed these walls.[46] Overcoming this limitation on citizenship in addition to expanding occupational freedoms and eliminating guild barriers would allow "complete freedom from trade barriers" and liberal planners to expand citizenship and foster free trade.[47] Liberal city planners placed exchange at the centre of their understanding of society. The urban growth that they attempted to manage and focus was understood as a natural consequence of the division of labour and mutual exchange.[48]

Private property and the free exchange of commodities were central principles of liberal political economy, and they formed the basis of liberal ideas of politics. Liberal planners believed that facilitating exchange in the built environment demanded a rationalization of transportation. Joseph Stübben, author of the major synthesis of liberal planning principles and designer of Cologne's Neustadt, argued that major public buildings such as railway stations, post offices, city hall, and market halls increasingly took on an aesthetic of transportation. Intercity roads slowly transformed building types from small homes to factories and apartment houses to large commercial buildings as the traveller moved to the city centre. This urban growth transformed residential streets into economic thoroughfares.[49] Moreover, as Baumeister argued, trade grew through technical advances, facilitating direct shipments of commodities by rail and water.[50]

Liberal city planners like Stübben argued that a spatial, local or regional, division of labour and liberal political economic relations began to reconstitute pre-industrial urban space. The streets that created city blocks were further partitioned into thoroughfares and residential streets. To avert fires spreading through large blocks, the streets were subsequently subdivided. Adequate plans required careful attention to the "division of labour" in spatial terms between factories, which required "large undivided land"; workers' housing blocks, which required shallow blocks; business districts, which required "large fronts and direct (even diagonal) sight lines" – including acute-angled corner buildings; and residential, which required garden areas and roughly rectangular blocks.[51] Baumeister and others organized the city in such a way that each sector – industrialists, merchants, and rentiers – could expand without affecting the others.[52] First, Liberal city planners like Baumeister established a business area that included large-scale industry, wholesale trade, factories, and storage, likely also encompassing the flats there for workers and even factory owners. Second, they created an area for those who made their living through exchange with the factory workers and factory owners, such as small stores and industrial suppliers. Third, they designed an area for those who lived on fortunes – rentiers, officials, merchants, factory owners, and private business bureaucrats. For the first sector, the goal would be "lowering production costs ... [and] costs of transportation." The second sector would "naturally [lie] in an early extension of the city centre." The third sector was increasingly concentrated in the bucolic western suburbs.[53] "The droves of labour and industry," meanwhile, grouped together in the east. Akin to the liberal idea that the economy is guided by quasi-objective, seemingly natural laws, Ernst Bruch went so far as to call this geography of class one of the modern "laws of motion."[54] Bruch wanted to eliminate from Hobrecht's plan all streets that had not yet been built and allow for a still more laissez-faire approach to the layout of the city.[55]

Liberal planners regarded a grid-like layout to be the best means to protect private property and achieve a free market in real estate. They believed that a free market would naturally meet the apartment needs of all social classes "in the right balance" without state intervention.[56] The extension of this grid into undeveloped land taxation created valuable new characteristics of real estate property that demanded legal protection. Area, fertility, and accessibility did not determine value any longer; rather, value depended on future frontage and the likelihood of encroaching development. Frontage needed to remain "completely intact and never changed" to obtain the difficult-to-find "continuity and solidity" of property ownership.[57] They believed that a grid-like street layout and the real estate market preserved "the freedom [of the owner] to use his property" and provided abstractly commensurable plots of "consistent size and shape" to the developer.[58] With grid-like plans the city or state regulated the roads and the distance between them; entrepreneurs created new streets and determined the size of the plot. Once this was established, the planners believed it allowed urban development to regulate itself. Competition among plots, so the argument went, meant that the property owner's interest lay in developing the property with all of the appropriate utilities.[59] A level of constitution writing was necessary for organic, natural development to take place in a mutually beneficial way. Liberal city planning was seen as creating "not only the ground and the framework for the development of the built environment but [also] ... a comprehensive, caring service to the physical and mental well-being of the citizens" that brought the totality of "private and public activity" into a "higher unity" for the benefit of all classes.[60] Liberal city planners viewed the grid-work city plan as the logical built-environmental manifestation of liberal social, cultural, and economic principles.

The result, liberals believed, was a rational expansion of the city, of general social wealth, and of general social well-being. However, as Peter Marcuse argues, city layouts have been grid-like for millennia, but ancient urban spaces were not developed as speculative commodities.[61] Marcuse clarifies and problematizes the historical specificity of the modern city grid. The nineteenth-century planners cited above insightfully diagnosed a change in the evaluation of urban land, but then inverted the relationship between cause and effect. They argued that a change in the organization of space – the creation of a grid-like structure – led to a change in the way a property was valued. A plot was, in this new era, valued both for its exchange value to the seller and for the use value to the buyer. Planners commonly blamed a spatial, concrete form for the abstract activity that occurs in that space. In this case, the grid caused speculation. Nevertheless, the abstract processes involved with the production and circulation of capital reconstituted social relations, including their concrete form in the built environment. The city grid, like money, time, and labour, predated capitalism, but capitalism transformed it into something historically new and specific to capitalism. Capitalism, which is a historically specific set of social relations, can appear to be an eternal feature of human nature.[62]

Even those who opposed the particular development of the Hobrecht plan endorsed a laissez-faire liberal response to urban development. Ernst Bruch and Gustav von Rössler were more open to an approach that did not attempt to shape the road network.[63] However, they believed that granting complete freedom to the builder without the development of a grid-like plan, i.e., without a constitutional congress, "systematically suppressed an entirely legitimate expression of the life of a city" and tangled streets adversely affecting transportation and other property owners.[64] It was "positively hostile" to urban development and forced the city to "condense within itself."[65] This mode of completely unfettered building tended to sprawl along existing roads, since developers were unwilling to invest in public utilities, creating "no organic connection" among buildings.[66] A constitutional congress-like moment was necessary, they believed, to establish the conditions of possible long-term capitalist urban development and liberal principles, including a laissez-faire model of urban development.

Not all city planners created equally skilful planning "constitutions," and liberal planners such as Bruch criticized the way Berlin's urbanization led to supposedly homogenous buildings of lower quality.[67] Berlin's plan was regarded as an irresistible "secret horror" that created "numberless and soulless housing blocks" and tolerated "no independent life."[68] The large plots were believed to lead to the "sad advantage, which Berlin [had] above all cities": increasingly large and unhygienic buildings constructed to maximize profitability.[69] The critique of Berlin's general plan was ultimately one of the weakness of Berlin's municipal administration and Prussian regulation.[70] Therefore, for liberal city planners, the problems of the built environment of Berlin resulted from a city plan that was too authoritarian and insufficiently liberal.

Even as the liberal version of the form, function, and perception of Berlin became dominant, and liberal city planning guided the basic decisions about urban space, the tendencies that would precipitate a crisis in liberal city planning were beginning to appear. According to liberal planners like Baumeister, the Industrial Revolution had created new urban populations, especially the proletariat, which created social conflict and caused moral decline. The planners argued that industrial technology reduced the cost of production, simplified labour, and drove down wages, creating a large, industrial proletariat largely comprising new migrants, especially in Berlin. The rapidly growing, "artificial" cities established festivals as "coarser or finer ways to attract foreign money," but they were "based on immoral beliefs and a population … [in] moral decline."[71] Workers' low wages meant they were forced to find only the most meagre housing, and liberal city planners believed that this called upon the community to act, because "each person should be considered as an equal member of the society."[72] Planners believed that the "only correct solution" to socio-economic structures, caused by "'immutable' natural laws" of political economy, was a "moral principle … [in] all human affairs, especially in social issues."[73] In response to problems ostensibly created by what liberals regarded as the natural laws of economics and society, liberal planners offered only morality – charity from the rich and better choices by the poor.

Even as the liberal model of city planning was showing its cracks, liberals insisted on liberal solutions to the problems that liberalism created. For liberal city planners, the cause of this set of social problems was the absence of property ownership, and thus the solution was greater property ownership. Liberal city planners like Baumeister attributed this supposed decline of morals in largely proletarian cities to rental apartments, which did not allow "safe and intimate relationships."[74] They did not inspire "a love of home and hearth," so poor people spent their money on "the vice of pubs" and scarcely knew "a domestic, orderly, clean family life."[75] These environmental conditions led to a simultaneous "degeneration of the body" and "of morals."[76] Apartments affronted liberal sensibilities in two ways: On the part of the landlord, property ownership created no new value and generated profits that supported people who did not work, consequently, as Stübben put it, the landlord had "no confidential, ... spiritual relationships with the residents." Among the working class, it limited access to homeownership, and apartments were homogenizing and inspired no love from the residents.[77]

The response to the inadequate housing created by liberal political economy revealed the contradictions in this vision of the form, function, and perception of the city. Liberal planners like Baumeister protested that "spiritual and physical well-being" demanded that one not "treat housing as a commodity."[78] This attitude is ironic, because treating real estate as a commodity is central to liberal city planning. This commitment to a laissez-faire housing market, combined with significant population growth, created pressure on the supply, distorted the value of the land, and made landlords deeply in debt so that they needed to exploit their land as much as possible.[79] Liberal planners like Gustav Assmann ascribed the housing shortage to the old city walls.[80] Despite liberals' reverence for the purported "natural laws" of society, Baumeister and others attacked state and local authorities for their passivity in the face of the socially destabilizing force of high rents.[81]

For liberal city planners, treating housing and land as commodities was, on the one hand, the key to the adequate and just development of housing and of urban space, and, on the other hand, the source of the disintegration of cultural values among proletarians. Between 1850 and 1875 real estate had become exchangeable like any other commodity, and private developers monopolized suburban land. As Brian Ladd notes, given the general acceptance of a liberal economic view, neither the state nor municipal authority had an interest in hindering their profits, as they created wealthy neighbourhoods exemplified by

West End and Lichterfelde. The crash of 1873 bankrupted many of these real-estate businesses, just as contemporaneous crashes in the housing market had struck developers in suburban Chicago.[82] The 1875 Fluchtliniengesetz (flight line law) took the right to determine streets and building lines and to assess the cost of public works for property owners from the Polizeipräsident and gave it to the municipal government, in an important victory for local autonomy.[83] Liberal planners recognized social problems generated by a liberal political economy, yet possessed a romantic desire to place purportedly essential aspects of social life outside of political economic relations.

For liberal city planners the spatial consequences of social transformation should be addressed within a liberal world view. For example, for Baumeister the goal of balancing the "revolutionary labour unions" and the "reactionary" Reichstag could go only so far, because "according to economic theory, perfect freedom of the individual should prevail and the community should not meddle in the natural laws of the market." Planners believed that the state should sponsor "self-help" so that the poor could own small single-family homes.[84] Property ownership supposedly solved these problems, because it freed individuals from miserable conditions, and even "modest property" would bring "more joy and advantage than the most beautiful rented apartment" as well as "a number of virtues" then missing in the lower classes. In owning property, "the worker became a capitalist," who acted with "thrift and diligence" in his own "self-interest" to "preserve and defend public order," to "care for the family life" and to desire "salvation through education, friendship, and neighbourhood."[85] Planners believed that Berlin's population growth was "normal and inevitable" and that the housing shortage could be resolved by increasing the developed land and roads so that building companies could "compete effectively" and encourage "construction of small and medium-sized homes."[86] Writing about British cities in the same period, Robert Home argues that that discourse also regarded homeownership as a key measure of self-help, acculturation, and economic advancement.[87] The second main means of solving social disorder was through abstract regulations of the city grid, such as the relationship between the dimensions of the house and that of the building lot.[88] However, planners believed that this regulation should not impinge on the free market.[89] Liberalism created the basic social forms that structured the ideas about cities like Berlin and shaped the basic assumptions that guided the development of a liberal planning canon.

Source of the Ideological Crisis

The liberal version of the form, function, and perception of Berlin and other cities, even at its height, had begun to reveal contradictions. However, with the further development of industrialization and urbanization, these contradictions were pushed to the point of an ideological crisis. The development of Berlin, especially from 1890 to 1910, challenged liberal city planning principles and their supporters. Population growth and erratic building generated a crowded city and immediate suburbs, and an enduring housing shortage. As the working class and industry moved to the suburbs, the suburbs themselves grew rapidly, fusing with Berlin architectonically, turning open suburban land directly into urban land.[90] The related rise in land values, as well as the demand for space and better access to canals and rail lines, drove major industries such as AEG and Siemens & Halske to the periphery of Greater Berlin. This movement pressured the mass transit system to move more people across greater distances.[91] In 1890 one writer described the urban growth at the northern border of Berlin as unsanitary and unaesthetic, littered with piles of trash of various origins, smoking and flaming factories without a trace of greenery.[92] The development of Greater Berlin as an integrated economy was forcing planners to reconsider how and where to address housing and transit questions. But city planning also increasingly took on the task of dealing with social issues.

As was already evident in liberal city planning theory, the role of housing and real estate as commodities and spaces of working-class dwelling formed the key question in this crisis in the form, function, and perception of Berlin. For planners, the social problems of turn-of-the-century Greater Berlin revolved around the predominant form of housing: the *Mietkasernen* or rental barrack. The state offered the army barracks left empty after the Prussian defeat in 1806 to the poor as housing. Beginning in the 1820s, private developers used these "rental barracks" as the model for working-class housing, and then the term came to refer to all working-class housing. But by the 1860s and 1870s new sketches for inexpensive housing by Assmann formed the basis of the buildings known as rental barracks. In 1890 the prominent Berlin city planner, housing reformer, and founder of the planning journal *Der Städtebau,* Theodor Goecke, defined the true rental barrack as a rectangular building of from three to six stories, with a central corridor beginning from the stairs lined with small rooms and kitchens. The second form of rental barrack became more common around 1900; it had multiple staircases that led to apartments, but without corridors.[93] The typical rental barrack apartment had a room and a kitchen and rarely included a toilet. In the largest rental barracks, toilets were between floors in the stairwell.[94] The courtyard of the rental barrack needed to be at least 5.6 metres by 5.6 metres, so that a fire wagon could be turned around inside. The regulations determined the height of the building by the width of the street, typically somewhere between 12 and 22 metres.[95] To maximize profits on the land, landlords filled the courtyards with other rental properties, closing off apartments from fresh air and from natural light and creating problematic public-health conditions.[96]

The sense of crisis inspired by these housing conditions led to two large studies by the Verein für Socialpolitik, first in 1886 and again in 1901. These studies reported that in Berlin the number of rental barracks – apartments with four or more floors plus a ground floor – grew by 750 per cent between 1864 and 1895 and nearly doubled between 1885 and 1895, while the gross number of all other inhabited types of buildings decreased. The number of people living in rental barracks buildings grew from about 18,500 to 314,494, or by more than 1,700 per cent between 1864 and 1890, and increased by 250 per cent from 1880 to 1890. The number of buildings with eleven or more people grew by 375 per cent, with more than twenty people by 960 per cent from 1861 to 1895, and with more than fifty people by 170 per cent between 1875 and 1895.[97] However, these statistics could be misleading, because the number of inhabitants per building did not necessarily translate to population density, and Berlin's density and sanitary conditions were comparable with Düsseldorf and London, and according to some visitors Berlin did not have slums like London, Paris, and New York.[98]

Similarly, in Vienna, between the construction of the Ringstraße and the First World War, the city's population grew and the city industrialized. Vienna's territory expanded, and a single municipal government for the metropolitan region was created. However, the Ringstraße encouraged a densely populated and densely constructed city centre and slower growth at the periphery. The 1893 plan for all of Vienna promoted wealthy housing in the west by the Wienerwald, and industrial development and working-class housing to the south and east. Vienna was more compact than Berlin, because there was less suburbanization of industry, and Vienna did not have a park comparable to Berlin's Tiergarten or the "poly-centric" form characteristic of Greater Berlin.[99]

The sense of crisis inspired by these housing conditions created rifts within the liberal city-planning theory. In the 1860s and 1870s, the liberal city-planning theory seemed to adequately address the problems of cities. However, the conditions in the cities changed, while the theory stayed the same. This created a contradiction between the conditions in the cities and the principles of liberal city-planning theory. For planners, this contradiction undermined the legitimacy and adequacy of liberal city-planning theory. It was widely believed that a new mode of planning was necessary. Despite this sense of transformation, the critiques of the principles of liberal city planning did challenge its central axioms.

Perceptions of Crisis

The further industrialization and urbanization of Greater Berlin accentuated these poor housing conditions and sharpened the contradiction between housing and real estate, as commodities and as spaces of working-class dwelling, posing a new set of problems for city planning in Greater Berlin. This contradiction gave rise to an acute sense of crisis. The impression of a crisis and the propositions to resolve it among city planners and the public took a number of forms.

The responses to this perceived crisis in the built environment were shaped by a dichotomy between abstract and concrete social forms. The sense of crisis pervaded the cultural responses to Berlin, either lambasting its poor condition as Rathenau did, cited at the beginning of this chapter; celebrating its decadence and decrepitude; or attempting to solve its problems pragmatically. Right-wing critics saw Berlin as a place of rootless, finance-driven, aesthetic chaos. In 1909, Paul Schultze-Naumburg – a Heimat activist (of the Bund Heimatschutz, or Association for the protection of National Heritage) staunchly opposed to architectural modernism and later a member of the National Socialist Party – deplored Berlin's "sad uniformity" and proclaimed the metropolis the "Moloch of our time."[100] Karl Scheffler, who was a proponent of modernist art before the First World War, but who became critical as the art became more abstract, argued in 1910 that the relationship between the city and the country had reversed and now the country existed only for the metropolis, changing the entire social structure. He argued that this caused a metamorphosis from a "natural patriarchal culture" into an "artificial industrial culture." This change, "alongside an enormous expansion of labour," had "an infinitely more problematic and ugly result": the modern city.[101] Scheffler blamed this development on "the general [social] democratization" and an "unavoidable compulsion to the world economy," particularly the "money economy."[102] He believed that greed and "the passion of the lawyer" formed Berlin and that Berlin's absence of deep historical roots allowed it to become the first European city to "Americanize" and succumb to metropolitan "economic materialism." He argued that "the international spirit of trade and industry" was hostile to particularity and was especially able to sink roots in Berlin.[103] For Scheffler, Berlin lacked clear centralization or decentralization, and the plazas were merely "a larger or smaller opening" through which six to a dozen roads and traffic intersected. It was a modern metropolis characterized by wide roads, decorative squares, boulevards with rows of trees, gardenlike facilities, a metropolitan park, and pompous buildings in abundance."[104] Thus, for Scheffler, the built environment was the consequence of a particularly abstract culture that emphasized abstract law, economic materialism, superficial Americanism, finance, and international trade.

The more positive responses to the built environment were also shaped by this dichotomy between abstract and concrete. Boosters celebrated what they understood to be the concrete and productive elements of society and the rapid, dynamic, and industrial character of Berlin. Mark Twain argued in 1892 that Berlin made Chicago look old and venerable.[105] Egon Friedell, a prominent Jewish and Viennese cabaret performer and cultural critic, celebrated Berlin in 1912 as a forward-leaning and American-style city. He believed that the city was an adequate German capital, becoming "a centre of the modern civilization," and compared Berlin to a "wonderful modern machine-hall, an enormous electric motor" characterized by "precision, speed, and energy." This machine was a soulless, virtuoso *homme-machine*, he argued, and Berlin's "tastelessness was preferable to the most tasteful unmodernity," because it contained future possibilities.[106]

Others celebrated the concrete by focusing on the ephemeral, immediate experience of urban life and nonetheless were shaped this same a dichotomy between abstract and concrete. August Endell, who studied philosophy in Tübingen and taught himself the aesthetic theory of architecture, praised Berlin's chaotic, ephemeral beauty that lent itself to flânerie. According to Endell's 1908 view, Berlin, and metropolises generally, held the whole economy together and "naturally" attracted "excessive attacks" from anti-urbanists. However, Endell noted, this idyllic vision of the country and the ghoulish vision of the city were the daydreams of the urbanite.[107] Therefore he sought to appreciate and foster the particular beauty of the metropolis.[108] Hans Ostwald and his collaborators set out to find beauty in modern Berlin and developed a sort of urban gothic travel literature for flâneurs. For example, in his pioneering 1905 urban ethnography of Berlin coffeehouses, he described the various characters with a fascination on the enervated and indulgent. Ostwald, who spent time as an itinerant craftsman, returned in the 1890s to Berlin, where he was born. He wrote a novel about his travels and then undertook the project of editing and writing some of the fifty volumes of the *Großstadt Dokumente*.[109] Richard Dietrich's 1907 study of Berlin nightlife commented on prostitution near major train stations: "The boundlessness in the intemperateness has increased so that the vice accelerates yearly massively, and that also no prospect exists that a change could occur here in the foreseeable future. Berlin became the Dorado of an international rabble, which the other large cities of Europe have expectorated. As if the city on the Spree would not have enough on its own, it also still willingly opened its mother arms to foreign vices."[110]

Another of Ostwald's colleagues used a corporal and concrete metaphor, describing the Berlin of 1908 as an overgrown but sickly child.[111] Ostwald's emphasis in his volumes on the non-bourgeois social and cultural spaces bore some resemblance to what we know as the practice of slumming. As Chris Heap describes slumming in New York and Chicago, slumming and the *Großstadt Dokumente* offered a safe way for the bourgeois to walk on the wild side.[112] This emphasis on concrete experience focused on seeking and finding an immediate engagement with the city.

Pragmatic Responses to Crisis

Confronted with this crisis in the liberal form, function, and perception of Greater Berlin and in other cities, the first group of planners, the pragmatists, who were committed to liberal solutions to planning problems, treated urban problems somewhat like a positivist jurist would, as situations where the planner needed to simply apply the appropriate principle. However, in their work there was also a desire to understand this crisis in Berlin and shape this complex urban system as a totality and not as an agglomeration of individuals, interests, and firms. This system was a product of human activity but seemed to be beyond human control.

Pragmatic planning, instead of trying to set the conditions for capitalism to flourish in the city and then leaving it alone, tried to direct urban capitalism towards a better way of life. These planners no longer viewed capitalism as the rational order of nature hidden beneath feudal and absolutist irrationality; now they saw capitalism as a system that could and should be shaped. Joseph Brix, who pioneered in Germany the drainage and purification of water on a city scale in Wiesbaden, established city planning as an academic discipline at the Imperial Technical College in Berlin.[113] He wrote in 1912 that industrial capitalism had become the compulsion and objective prerequisite for urban development and location. Capitalist corporations, he claimed, became place-determined, even for those outside the direct sphere of interest of the capitalist economy, like bureaucrats, rentiers, and pensioners.[114] City planners simultaneously pointed to what they saw as an inadequacy of liberal city planning, suggested ways of moving beyond this problem, and reasserted other liberal city-planning norms.

This pragmatic approach remained within the liberal city-planning ideology, even as they criticized the way it precipitated the current crisis, in that its proponents sought to create adequate city-planning laws. Addressing legal regimes of building ordinances and urban development in 1908, Conrad Bornhak – who was a strong and insistent advocate for transforming Germany into a more fully parliamentary state, in which the majority party and not the head of state determine the cabinet – argued that with the fall of the absolutist police state, its arbitrariness from above fell too. He asserted that under the new conditions, which reached a peak in the 1850s, individual power and the free play of individual tastes became the guiding principle of society. These new conditions, he contended, created arbitrariness from below. This led to both a loss of concern for long-term planning and an increase in urban property values and real estate speculation. This individualistic anarchy of laissez-faire, according to Bornhak, resulted in the levelling of beautiful buildings for traffic efficiency.[115] Like the liberal planners already discussed, Bornhak believed that laissez-faire, without a system of abstract laws to focus behaviour, generated problems, but an abstract legal code for urban development that would apply to everyone equally could solve urban problems.

At the same time, this pragmatic approach had begun to push beyond liberal city planning by addressing the city as a cohesive totality. In 1908 Brix sought to use technical and artistic tools to develop general plans, creating the best possible dwelling conditions.[116] Theodor Goecke argued that planners had teased out the connections among housing problems, building regulations, urban development plans, and the cityscape, and in so doing had unmasked the connection between the economic and social conditions of the city, the built environment, and the laws that regulated it. This realization, he continued, made artistic city planning possible, and he hoped his magazine, *Der Städtebau*, could help to facilitate "cooperation from the community and private citizen, from the owner and tenant, from the bourgeois and worker."[117] These planners argued that liberal planning had made steady progress since its foundations. Felix Genzmer, Brix's co-coordinator of the city-planning curriculum, had worked as a city planner for the cities of Strasbourg, Cologne, Hagen, Wiesbaden, and Berlin.[118] In 1909 he contended that the city should be considered a work of art.[119] Furthermore, a planner seeks the harmony in streets and plazas, like an interior designer does with home furniture.[120] Art historian Max Georg Zimmermann, who specialized in Italian and early Renaissance art, suggested in 1909 that planners and architects could give new working-class, small-business, factory, shopping, and mansion quarters a distinctive style and could artistically arrange gardens, kiosks, electrical lighting, fountains, long roads, and large plazas to both dissipate air pollution and beautify the city.[121] This approach both left the liberal planning approach largely intact and put forward the increasingly common vision of the city as a total work of art, which could be shaped for the betterment of all.[122]

This pragmatic approach to liberal city planning did not regard the past nostalgically, but it did try to mobilize the past to serve the present and create a more aesthetically pleasing city. These planners accepted the notion that the continued expansion of the urban economy conditioned the possibility of a "city beautiful." As Genzmer maintained, the rapid changes in style on the long, straight roads created a sense of domination, but these roads were responses to an imminent demand of the traffic itself.[123] Zimmermann agreed, arguing that many of the past picturesque effects used in city planning were no longer adequate for the needs of modern German cities.[124] In 1908 Hans Mackowsky, an art historian of the Renaissance, suggested that urban dynamism took precedence and that capitalism had accelerated the life of cities.[125] This made the slow, careful city planning from the past inadequate, idealized, and nostalgic.[126] The recognition of a break since the height of liberal city planning and of new, capitalism-determined urban conditions distinguishes the pragmatic planners. Yet they did not seriously challenge liberal city-planning norms or address large-scale problems, with the exception of their rhetoric of the city as a work of art; instead, the pragmatic approach applied liberal principles in local ways.

Aesthetic Responses

Confronted with the crisis in the liberal form, function, and perception of Greater Berlin and in other German cities, other city planners addressed urban social problems through preservation and application of predominantly nostalgic pre-modern aesthetics. These aesthetic planners believed that the monotony of the city and the effects of an excessively abstract and engineered reality caused urban problems. They believed that greater intimacy, artistry, and particularity in the built environment could solve these concerns.

Just as was the case with other ideologies of urban space discussed above, a dichotomy between abstract and concrete social forms structured the response of aesthetic planners to this perceived crisis in the built environment. Aesthetic planners attacked homogenization of the cityscape – in particular, abstract planning and geometric solutions – and saw this planning, particularly that of Hobrecht, as foreign and imposed.[127] Peter Marcuse notes that the timing of the grid's construction often shaped the aesthetic perception of the city. Pre-capitalist grid cities supposedly had a pleasing symmetry, were convenient, and had intimate quarters. City grids constructed after the inception of capitalism, however, were described as endless and distractingly regular. Marcuse suggests that this change in perception is the consequence of capitalism, because it cannot be attributed to the form itself.[128] For example, according to Rudolf Eberstadt in 1909, Hobrecht's plan represented the "half-absolutist, half-liberal" Prussian state and was "a foreign element which had been forced onto the public."[129] Camillo Sitte, a Viennese architect, planner, and a founding editor of *Der Städtebau*, catalysed this approach to city planning. He criticized the abstract character of city plans and development for destroying the joy of life in neighbourhoods. In 1889 Sitte described what he saw as the modern system of planning:

> To approach everything in a strictly methodical manner and not to waver a hair's breadth from preconceived notions, until genius has been strangled to death and *joie de vivre* stifled by the system – that is the sign of our time. We have at our disposal three major methods of city planning, and several subsidiary types. The major ones are the *gridiron system*, the *radial*

> *system*, and the *triangular system* ... Artistically speaking, not one of them is of any interest, for in their veins pulses not a single drop of artistic blood. All three are concerned exclusively with the arrangement of *street patterns*, and hence their intention is from the very start a purely technical one. A network of streets always serves only the purposes of communication, never of art, since it can never be grasped as a whole except in a plan of it.[130]

In addressing this crisis in the liberal form, function, and perception of Greater Berlin and in other German cities, aesthetic planners attacked the abstract side and celebrated the concrete side of the dichotomy that structured this perceived crisis in the built environment. To counter the abstraction that Sitte believed was suffocating the joy of life in modern cities, he argued for an emphasis on local particularity, asymmetry, and intimate urban spaces. Frederick Law Olmsted, the American pioneer of landscape design, offered a similar critique in 1876 of New York City's grid and its rigidly uniform and abstractly equal plots, which make no differentiation between a church, a blast furnace, a tenement, or a stately mansion.[131] The discourse of aesthetic city planning bears similarities with the discourse of public city art museums in working-class cities, such as Manchester, Birmingham, and Liverpool. Philanthropists and aesthetic theorists believed that the art museum could counteract the urban experience and the deprivations caused by poverty through an encounter with nature and beauty.[132] Ironically, Sitte's ideas of the city evolved out of an abstract and liberal theory of perception of architecture and urban space but became a desire to preserve the quirky and intimate parts of a city and change the individual experience of the city.[133]

This dichotomy between abstraction and particularity organized the discussion of aesthetic urban planning. In 1891 Karl Henrici, a convert from liberal city planning to Sitte's ideas and a former colleague of Stübben, criticized the abstract, mathematical, and axiomatic way that liberal planners laid out urban streets, creating unnatural and arbitrary street plans filled with busy intersections. Henrici objected to the idea that street patterns, developed over a thousand years, were arbitrary, but mathematically determined streets were well grounded.[134] As with Eberstadt's comment quoted above, abstraction was associated with foreign, particularly French and Italian, forms of planning, and with commerce-based traffic patterns. The prevailing literature connected this critique of abstraction to a larger national interest and imperialist-inflected discourses of *Zivilisation* and *Kultur*.[135] In certain respects, this argument is convincing; however, it shifts the question to why the abstract is foreign and the concrete is essentially German. It also avoids the role of capitalism in forming ideas of culture and beauty that are abstracted out of everyday life raised by Herbert Marcuse's critique of "affirmative culture" discussed in the introduction. This book will address why this dichotomy appears when it does and why it is so central to the discourse.

Karl Henrici and Joseph Stübben argued about the goals of planning, representing aesthetic planning and liberal planning respectively. This argument illustrates the crisis in the liberal form, function, and perception of urbanism, each voicing one side of the dichotomy between abstract and concrete social forms that structured this crisis in the built environment. Karl Henrici criticized Joseph Stübben because he had argued that pre-modern city squares were poor models for contemporary squares because the modern people who inhabit cities have fundamentally different needs and because medieval buildings were sited according to a logic historically specific to their time of construction.[136] Henrici objected to destroying romantic, gothic structures in the name of traffic efficiency and to replacing them with what he saw as French and Italian styles, though he acknowledged that straight efficient streets met modern needs. However, he contended that planning with compasses and rulers was non-German and found treating city streets primarily as paths for traffic and trade, and secondarily as sites for dwelling, reprehensible.[137] Stübben responded with many examples from history of straight roads and right-angle intersections.[138] Stübben's response raises again the argument made with the help of Peter Marcuse above.

This crisis in the liberal form, function, and perception of urbanism inspired aesthetic planners to celebrate the concrete side of this dichotomy. Aesthetically inclined planners sought a more intimate, concrete, organic, and ultimately curvaceous aesthetic. This ideology advanced the view that humans were a more accessible, harmonious, and organic measure than the rigid mathematical model of organization.[139] This aesthetic approach shared many features of liberal city planning, such as deference to the market and to private property, but did away with all abstraction. It celebrated the concrete, intimate, and particular, and attacked the abstract, the general, and the planned.

This crisis in the liberal form, function, and perception of urbanism was indeed international, and the proffering of aesthetic solutions that attacked the abstract side and celebrated the concrete side of this dichotomy was too. The turn to considering urban aesthetics and the usefulness of that urban aesthetic was not limited to German and Austrian urbanists. This moment, as Wolfgang Sonne argues, inspired a host of plans and reforms: "the Arts and Crafts movement with their village garden city ideal in the UK, the picturesque town planning by Camillo Sitte in Austria and Germany, the City Beautiful movement in the U.S. or the Beaux-Arts urban planning in France."[140] As Mark Jarzombek contends, those who turned to aesthetics recognized that classical liberal political forms were inadequate to the new politics of mass parties and social conflict of the turn of the twentieth century. It represented a belief that an aestheticization of politics and of social life could placate and avoid political and social conflict generated by capitalism in a way that older, liberal forms of politics could not. However, he notes, this entailed "a radical expansion of the notion of aesthetics."[141] This critique focused on the abstract, reified character of modern architecture and city planning in the name of local particularity, indeterminacy, and popular self-understanding. The proponents of this critique viewed the abstraction of the modern as a form of domination. However, it is not yet entirely clear why aesthetic planners viewed abstraction as dominating and the concrete as outside of this domination.

Producerist Responses

A third response to the crisis in the liberal form, function, and perception of urbanism and of city planning embraced the new forms of social organization of the early twentieth century, such as monopolies and cartels, and saw them as a means for creating a beautiful city through economies of scale. Walter Curt Behrendt posited that one should consider the city as an artwork, embracing a certain form of abstraction. Behrendt diminished the role that great buildings or monumental groupings of buildings played in the cityscape; he claimed that the uniformity of apartment buildings constituted the cityscape.[142] He acknowledged that historically a consistent (and abstract) aesthetic centralization of the city and architecturally uniform formation of the facades of a block tended to signal concentrated power in one planner, who "champions the artistic interests of the total system," but, he argued, this uniformity could also be an "aesthetic need demanded by social conditions."[143] Behrendt blamed "boundless individualism" for the chaotic facades of residential districts. He argued that planners and architects needed to understand housing blocks as a basic architectural unit and believed that a well-planned organization of housing could succeed if a "generous sense of community" could subordinate subjective special interests to modern urban conceptions of style.[144] Behrendt believed that entrepreneurs could create this uniformity without state intervention by monopolizing urban expansion land.[145] Despite his conviction that his ideas would work – moreover, they were already working – he worried that critics would reject his ideas as utopian because of their emphasis on laissez-aller.[146]

In addressing this crisis, producerist planners attacked the concrete side and celebrated the abstract side of the dichotomy that structured the built environment. Behrendt, in other words, rejected particularity, intimacy, and the concrete as the problems and argued for greater size, generality, and abstraction. In addition, contrary to the aesthetic planners, he did not pretend that it was possible to return to a pre-modern form of urban development; rather, he embraced the most modern forms of urban development – monopolies, cartels, and economies of scale. Unlike the pragmatists, who puttered along espousing the liberal city-planning world view, making small changes, and small progress, Behrendt argued for a new approach to cities that used concentration of capital and modern technology to its advantage in order to address the city as a totality. Interestingly, the abstract totality that Behrendt embraced was not that of abstractly equal citizen commodity buyers and sellers, but instead, the abstraction of a monopolistic, integrated housing producer. This difference separates him from liberal city planners, but Behrendt remained explicitly committed to laissez-faire, laissez-aller principles.

The response to this crisis expressed by Behrendt is part of a larger discourse that criticized the abstract and often liberal dimensions of capitalist modernity – such as the market – in the name of the more apparently concrete dimensions of capitalist modernity – such as mass production and technology. As such, it remained within the dichotomy that structured this perceived crisis in the built environment. One site where this discourse flourished was within the Werkbund, a civil society association made up of architects, artists, craftsmen, and manufacturers that advocated for "Germany's cultural renewal through a synthetic approach to economic, aesthetic, social, and technological questions."[147] As John Maciuika explains, across Europe, "closer integration of the fine and applied arts not only became an aesthetic end in itself but also came to be understood as a means of encouraging social unity and economic development."[148] The Werkbund rapidly became a site of this integration and the spokespersons for modernism in Germany before the First World War.[149]

The form of this dichotomy between the concrete and the abstract in the context of architecture created significant antagonism between those in the Werkbund who saw themselves as promoting a "made-in-Germany" brand and those who saw themselves as defending individuality, as members worked through the crisis in the liberal form, function, and perception of urbanism. The discourse framed this choice in terms of *Zivilisation* and *Kultur*, respectively.[150] Both sides joined their aesthetic ideas to a social theory that posited the capacity of artists and aesthetics to fundamentally alter social conditions for the better.[151] The first group, like Behrendt, celebrated the potential of mass production and the modern business.[152] It embraced, according to Alan Colquhoun, Tönnies's vision of *Gesellschaft* and saw the "relation between artist and material" as "mediated, impersonal and intellectual."[153] The second group in the Werkbund attempting to address this crisis in liberal ideology, those who focused on the concrete, individual, and artistic side of this dichotomy between the concrete and the abstract, sought to use modern industrial techniques to reintroduce individual, artisan-like mastery of the tools and material for developing an individual style. This approach combined new artistic forms with a longing to return to un-alienated pre-industrial social life.[154] This group, Colquhoun explains, was committed to the preservation of Ferdinand Tönnies's *Gemeinschaft* and preferred "a direct, personal and intuitive connection between the artist and the material to be transformed." They understood Enlightenment rationalism as "the precursor of a materialistic positivism."[155] This conflict came to a head at the Werkbund's 1914 Congress but the details of that institutional struggle are beyond the purview of this book.

This dichotomy between the concrete and the abstract played an important role in the work of Adolf Loos as he confronted the crisis in the liberal form, function, and perception of urbanism. A Viennese architect and modernist forerunner, Loos, like Behrendt and both Hermann Muthesius and Henry van der Velde, who represented the respective opposed sides above, sought to make architecture adequate to the present and free it from the limitations of its history. Like Behrendt, he embraced new forms of social organization of the early twentieth century and saw them as a means for creating a beautiful city. In 1908 Loos satirically argued that decorating walls was a sign of degeneracy, and removal of ornamentation was evidence of further social evolution.[156] For Loos, ornament slowed what he saw as the inexorable progressive advancement of humanity, because it wasted "human labor, money and materials," and "that is damage that time cannot repair."[157] According to Theodor Adorno, Loos misunderstood modern capitalism, and even as he was critical of some dimensions of capitalism, he celebrated others and did so as if they were not capitalist. For Adorno, Loos revealed this in his attitude towards work and capital: workers and capitalists must not waste them and they must be reduced to their bare minimum. The former comes from the desire to maintain profitability and the latter comes from a desire for a society that overcomes work and profit.[158] Adorno pairs Loos with the Chicagoan Thorsten Veblen as figures symptomatic of their times.[159] For Veblen and Loos, according to Adorno, man must accommodate himself to modern industrial capitalist technology.[160]

In their responses to the crisis in the liberal form, function, and perception of urbanism, the members of the Werkbund and Loos shared a number of important assumptions about modern capitalism with the critics of the abstract and liberal character of the prevailing form of city planning. As Frederic Schwartz has argued, the artists, architects, city planners, critics, economists, and politicians who were members of the Werkbund did not attack all of capitalism. Instead, they remained within this dichotomy that has characterized their other statements on modern cities and focused their ire on what they regarded as superfluous and those engaged in abstract profit taking, such as speculators, bankers, and merchants. However, they affirmed mass production, celebrating those connected to it, such as workers and industrialists. They saw the merchant as "'the true carrier of the theory of the free play of forces'; in other words as the incarnation of economic laissez-faire." According to this view, the merchant, who does not care about quality, forces the industrialist, who would rather create something of concrete quality, to create products with a high price but limited usefulness and quality. Supposedly, the merchant middlemen, "those furthest from production, … create the distorted physiognomy of modern trade."[161] This ideology often conflated the merchant with Jewish people, most famously by Werkbund member Werner Sombart.[162] In 1907 Sombart applied a similar opposition between the superficial, quantifiable, and market-oriented, on the one hand, and deep cultural history, quality, and authentic production, on the other. With Berlin representing the former and Vienna the latter, he saw Berlin as an impoverished version of German culture as best represented by Vienna. Berlin, he argued, was a "suburb of New York," and New York was a desert and a "huge cultural cemetery" that had confused quantity over quality and the technical over "ultimate and true values."[163]

This dualistic attack on the abstract and celebration of the concrete and productive was not limited to questions of architectural aesthetics or jurisprudence – ideas addressed in the previous chapter. This complex opposition between the concrete and the abstract shaped discussions of real estate speculation.

Ideologies of Speculation

Analysis of the discourse on real estate speculation in Berlin helps to reveal the crisis within liberal ideology. Social reformers blamed the built environment for a host of social ills, from low birth rates and infant mortality, to infectious disease, to alienation from the nation, to Socialism like their American contemporaries.[164] Many blamed speculation for the poor condition of the Berlin working-class housing stock. In housing speculation, on the one hand, there were the rational actions of individuals pursuing profit through the mediation of the market and, on the other hand, individuals accumulating property and capital without labour. The freedoms of the market came into conflict with a labour theory of property and value that was formative for liberals. Both John Locke and Adam Smith argued in favour of it.[165] The ability to buy and sell land, especially Crown lands, meant significant liberal progress in the countryside, but, as Hirschberg saw it, these reforms had "fatal" consequences in Berlin.[166] Around 1910, addressing housing was often understood as a means to fortify martial strength and to increase birth rates. Reformers supported tighter laws for Berlin's urbanized suburbs, because "if an armed struggle for the fatherland against the world was necessary, most of the fighting men would be drawn from the weak and sickly metropolitan population." The Socialists, the perceived domestic enemy, haunted these discussions: "In the background resound the footsteps of the million-strong socialist army, for whom only the opportunity for victories is missing, because the carriers of education and property did not fulfil and still do not fulfil their obligation to the economically weak."[167] Despite this martial tone and the anti-Socialism, the discourse on building regulations deferred, in a typically liberal manner, to the power of the legislative branch and to the *Rechtstaat*.[168] For most observers, though, the existing laws remained inadequately general, so that powerful, self-interested parties were able to use them to their advantage.[169]

As was common in many contemporaneous cities, real estate and construction in Greater Berlin was cyclical, causing some liberals to question the logic of the market and other liberals to question the ability of the working class to make rational choices. Drawn by the demand for credit, large Berlin banks saw land and building speculation as profitable.[170] Speculation was commonly associated with "American" styles of urban development, and in the United States, land speculation was indeed popular both on undeveloped land in the West and in Florida, as well as on land in rapidly growing cities.[171] In Chicago, for example, failures of speculative housing developments in the suburbs in 1873 and 1877 led to the collapse of two of the city's major banks.[172] Similar waves of building transformed the older city of Paris between 1877 and 1885, speculative developers erected 11,000 apartments, and the rental stock expanded by 25 per cent.[173]

As liberal political economy contributed to the industrial growth of Berlin, it also increased the percentage of the population who were property-less and the concentration of the control over the housing stock. In Berlin the percentage of the population who were homeowners fell from 5 per cent in 1871 to 2 per cent in 1905. According to contemporary statistical studies, between 80 and 90 per cent of Berliners were renters, and in 1900, 39 per cent of housing in Berlin comprised one-room apartments, 39 per cent two-room apartments, and 14 per cent three-room apartments. The preferences of landlords often forced families with many children to rent the smallest dwellings.[174] In 1868 the Berlin Mortgage Bond Office was established and was obliged to offer credit and mortgage insurance. But the prevailing stigma against state involvement in the economy from the 1860s into the beginning of the twentieth century meant that property owners looked with contempt on any involvement with this institution. As land and building prices rose, the ability of the city to provide credit dwindled, leading to various informal, often non-contractual, agreements. Rental property owners in the 1890s were small-scale and often only barely survived on the income from rents. The capital for investment in properties was scarce, and lenders demanded high interest rates, and in order to pay the interest, the rents remained high.[175] According to Lujo Brentano in 1909, large dwellings were not produced that poor people could afford, forcing landlords to rent to poorer tenants and subdivide the apartments with a curtain or chalk line to ensure that he could collect enough rent. But often the renters could not pay the rent, so they would sublet a room or offer shifts in a bed, though those who rented a room or a bed overnight often could only find living space in a pub.[176]

Liberals affirmed other dimensions of liberal capitalism, such as its natural-law-like appearance and a labour theory of value. The transit entrepreneur Richard Petersen, in 1911, questioned whether the increase in urban land value was "based on unalterable laws of nature" or on "artificial" legal or administrative channels. Petersen believed that the high property values meant an indebted "working population" benefited "the non-working real estate property owner" and an unproductive increase in the fixed capital increased the cost of production and hurt Berlin's export economy.[177] A second transit entrepreneur, Otto Blum in 1908, argued that building uncrowded, hygienic, and peripheral flats for the working class would instil the "ethical and political" advantage of homeownership.[178]

Social reformist critics of real estate speculation regarded society dualistically, attacking "unproductive" real estate and financial capitalists, while they defended "productive" workers and industrial and merchant capitalists. The Deutscher Bund für Bodenreform, followers of the American theorist Henry George, blamed rent increases on land speculation, including by large banks. Their ideology can be categorized as anti-speculation and anti-finance, leading to anti-urban positions. They believed that banks dominated urban land and raised the "tribute" that "producers," i.e., capital and labour, had to pay. This "tribute" was a component of the value of a piece of land that was unaccounted for in the relationship between the investments necessary to make the land profitable and the actual profits received. Land reformers believed that this new value belonged to the people born into that community and that the state should nationalize land and only land.[179] Banks supposedly knew that the "producers'" activity indirectly created that value, but the banks tried to confiscate it and "artificially" increased land value and rent.[180] For their leader, Adolf Damaschke, in 1913, conditions caused by a housing shortage and high rents threatened "the most fundamental basis of the living cells of our German social body" and made moral family life impossible.[181] In 1910 Karl von Mangoldt, the leader of the Housing Reform Movement, also believed a plutocratic minority chose their individual profits over a better Greater Berlin.[182] According to Rudolf Eberstadt, the most prominent reformist theorist of speculation, in 1905, land value could increase in two ways: by useful investment of capital and "by price rigging or 'speculation.'"[183] For Eberstadt, monopoly ownership of the land and speculative investment made the cost of urban decentralization exorbitant, creating a wall around the city more impenetrable than the old fortresses.[184] Eberstadt posited that speculative investment and state withholding of lands had distorted the natural functioning of supply and demand. His ideas made note of the failure of liberalism in Germany, but his ideal remained a liberal housing economy.

In 1905 the laissez-faire opponents of the reformers defended the "natural laws" of the market, forbade state intervention in the market for any reason, and denied the existence of real estate speculation or monopolies.[185] Adolf Weber in 1908 attacked the reformers' "arduous search into the dark sides of the private speculation."[186] In 1905 Ludwig Pohle mocked the reformists' vision of land speculators as possessing "a nearly uncanny power to drive up the price of land."[187] Weber criticized reformists for their moralistic condemnations of "business-like trade in land."[188] He claimed that increased urban land values were a natural effect of competition and rose in proportion to building density.[189] Furthermore, according to Pohle, any state efforts to balance the housing market would fail and distort the natural workings of the market.[190] According to Andreas Voigt and Paul Geldner, urbanization was a natural necessity of "modern economic culture" and the geographic consequence of the division of labour on the location of homes, businesses, and government. In a city, production was cheaper and productivity greater; metropolitan consumption was mass consumption.[191] These laissez-faire economists in 1908 were, however, concerned with the social and moral effects of high rents, especially on children, who, they believed, were guiltless and victims of their parents' poor choices or lack of industriousness.[192] This vision of the problems of the metropolis found the market innocent and morality, personal determination, and luck guilty for the social conditions in Greater Berlin.

On the basis of their political and social theoretical analysis of rent in capitalism, the Socialists dismissed speculation and the housing shortage as superficial social problems. Friedrich Engels in 1872 argued that there was nothing particular to capitalism about the oppressed living in inadequate dwellings, therefore the outsized responsibility attributed to housing ought to be treated as an ideology. For him, inadequate housing was not "a direct result of the exploitation of the worker as a worker by the capitalists" in capitalist production, where value and surplus value are created. Rather, noted Engels, the problem of housing was over the distribution of this value, and a landlord cheating a worker who, in this situation, was a buyer, that is, the owner of money or credit, and hence not a seller of labour power. This exchange was an "ordinary commodity transaction between two citizens."[193] Engels criticized wealthy bourgeois philanthropists who became concerned with poor neighbourhoods for epidemiological reasons only when these epidemics spread to the wealthier areas.[194] However, according to Engels, these philanthropists wanted both to continue "'iron laws' of bourgeois economics," which created classes and poverty, and to elevate the poor to the cultural and economic level of the rich.[195] Consequently, the philanthropists wanted the working class to change its culture and the landlords to choose not to speculate or cheat their tenants.[196] Engels and Karl Marx alike regarded housing reformers as followers of Pierre-Joseph Proudhon and other left Ricardians.[197] Proudhonian socialists, according to Marx, left "wage labor and therefore capitalist production in existence" while arguing that "if ground rent were transformed into a state tax all the evils of capitalist production would disappear." This form of Socialism, he argued, was "simply an attempt ... to save capitalist domination and indeed to establish it afresh on an even wider basis than its present one."[198] According to Marx, once capitalism developed to a certain point, landed property could *appear* "superfluous and harmful ... from the point of view of the capitalist mode of production."[199] Marx argued that this antagonism between industrial and landed capital came about because landed property creates a structural barrier to the continued industrial accumulation of value and the distribution of that value after production.[200] Marx contended that rent became possible only once capitalist industry was established in the cities and began to transform society so that the landowner was forced to treat landed property as a site of capital production.[201] Socialist municipal expert Hugo Lindemann argued in 1905 that in the arguments against speculation one could find "enmity against our current economic system" invested in the "figure of high finance" and "puppy love" for medieval guilds. Speculation appeared as the universal answer to the downwardly mobile, and Lindemann explained, "just as anti-Semitism makes the Jews responsible for all bad states of our current social order.[202]

On the basis of these theoretical arguments, the Socialists called into question the assumptions of both the land reformers and the laissez-faire liberals. The Socialists were able to demonstrate that both the apologetic affirmation of the natural laws of capitalism and the attacks on the "excrescence" of speculation were merely the working out of liberal responses to the changing conditions of capitalism. On one side, a group professed that the abstract laws of capitalism ultimately, in a realm beyond human control though constituted by human interaction, resolved social problems and mediated conflicting interests. On the other side, another group appealed to purported concrete "producers" against abstract rentiers, landlords, and bankers, and against concrete conditions made unhealthy by abstract laws of the market run amok. Ironically, both laissez-faire liberals and reformers maintained their faith in the laws of the market despite its problems, but for reformers private rent seekers, monopolists, and speculators had unfortunately distorted the market.

Conclusion: The Future of Liberal City Planning

This chapter has argued that beginning in the 1850s a new form of city planning developed, one that took for granted the key categories of liberal political economy and of liberal politics. It assumed the abstract equality of citizens and/or buyers and sellers; the sanctity of private property; the value of regular, legal, calculable exchange; the importance of the bourgeois stroller and the public sphere; and the ease of free circulation of commodities and people, among other concerns. Initially those who were taking the steps to recreate the city were not politically liberal. Rather, they undertook a project that they believed would free the natural and ontological character of the city as a site of free exchange, civil society, and rule of law from the superstition and arbitrariness of previous forms of government and political economy. In transforming the city, they trusted that they were making it adequate to its own essential character, which had always been there, even if masked by the detritus of history. The second generation of planners, who were perhaps more politically liberal, sought to finally strip the effects of absolutist bureaucracy from the planning of the built environment. These liberal city planners saw themselves as merely trying to make the city equal to the natural conditions that had only recently begun to flourish. Their critique of the administrative planners who preceded them focused on the slant of their politics and not on the form of their planning. Liberal city-planning advocates strayed from the tenets of administrative city planning only to the extent that they relied on the private sphere – after a moment of "constitution writing" to create the groundwork – and they reacted to the aesthetics of the administrative planners with "yes, but more so."

The further development of urbanization in Berlin fundamentally called the assumptions of liberal city planning into question, and this led to three basic perspectives and a great deal of polemical vitriol. The first ignored the problem and built Whiggishly on past success. The second responded critically to all modern forms of city planning, which they conflated with liberal city planning and viewed as abstract, generalizing, reified, and inorganic, and sought, romantically, a more concrete, particular, and organically historical form of city planning informed by the past. The third point of view, the one represented by Behrendt, embraced those abstract features that the more romantic planners rejected and attacked exactly those concrete features they celebrated. However, unlike classical liberal city planners, their embrace of abstraction, generality, and mathematical regularity was not that of relatively equal and competing entrepreneurs, but rather linked to features of a monopoly trying to organize efficient production in the absence of competition. They emphasized and recognized a privately generated, socioeconomic cohesion of society. Many who did not perceive of themselves as liberals initiated the principles of liberal city planning. Furthermore, often those planners who enacted liberal modes of planning were attempting to stamp out the more radically liberal strains of the Revolution of 1848 through their design plans. Finally, even those who considered themselves to be radically challenging and superseding liberal city planning then perpetuated these liberal city-planning principles. The liberal form of planning was more than a purposeful political and economic project. Historians cannot understand only the hegemony of this planning functionally – as the most effective way for municipal administrations to preserve Prussian bureaucratic dominance. Rather, we must be able to explain why this planning took a liberal form. Political self-interest seems an insufficient explanation. Finally, this transformation of liberalism is explored through an analysis of discourses of real estate speculation.

A remarkable formal similarity arose in the ideas of the city planners. It was shaped by an opposition between the abstract, general, and calculable on the one hand and the concrete, particular, and ineffable on the other. These similarities recurred in the ideologies of municipal administration, liberal jurisprudence, and speculation. This formal similarity between disparate areas suggests that something structural was at work behind the backs of rational actors. Furthermore, the form and content of city planning's response to the perceived crisis of Berlin were not random. The timing and the formal consistency of these changes suggest a systemic cause. This change in city-planning ideology, much like the system of liberal municipal administration, followed closely the rise and self-generated crisis of liberal political economic relations with the collapse of free-trade regimes and the growth of monopolies and cartels. There are many layers of mediation between political economy and social perception of the city. Nonetheless, this similarity is not random.

The realm of liberal political economic relations and commodity circulation constitutes, through much mediation, the ideologies of liberal city planning as well as of liberal municipal administration. In everyday exchange, two people of their own free will meet in the marketplace as both buyer and seller of commodities. They agree to contracts that govern that buying and selling and thereby create a legal expression of their commitment. In this exchange they come together as equals and exchange objects of equal value. Similarly, people give and take only what is their own private property. Finally, they act to rationally maximize their own utility for their own gain and, in so doing, inadvertently contribute to a general social coordination of needs and resources. These social relations create the grounds for a wide variety of visions of social life and social possibility.[203] The practice of exchange, so elemental to modern life, generates new ideologies that are not limited to the realm of political economy and politics but also constitute a new conception of the world that includes attitudes towards the city and a new aesthetics of city planning. But because this exchange relationship is part of a dynamic whole, it is subject to transformation and thus is historically specific. This social transformation undermined the basis of exchange and the ideologies connected to it.

An opposition between the abstract and the concrete fundamentally shapes the various discourses of city planning and municipal administration. In the early periods, social actors viewed the abstract side of this opposition positively and the concrete side negatively. However, over the course of this period, one can see the valuation of the sides of this opposition become inverted, so that by the 1930s the abstract side was viewed negatively and the concrete side was seen positively. This opposition is constituted by and through the ways that capitalist social forms mediate our social world. This inversion of the opposition is related to large-scale changes in the history of modern capitalism that gave rise to a biologization and ontologization of the productive dimensions of the capitalist economy.

Chapter Three

Creating Greater Berlin

We also notice enormous displacements taking place within national boundaries. We observe that certain regions rapidly grow poor in human beings and capital, while others become saturated. We see in metropolitan centers great masses conglomerate, seemingly without end. We philosophize about these matters, talk about the advantages and disadvantages [that] result, about *Asphaltkultur*, or "decline of morals." Of course, we have long since become partisan in these matters. To some of us it seems that the populace "runs" to the big cities only for "pleasure's" sake – to the ultimate ruin of itself and its posterity; to others it appears that these people follow inevitable laws, as for example the flow toward the place of lowest pressure socially, etc. Much thought has been spent upon the "rush to the city" (not only upon its consequences, but also upon its causes), but is it possible for us to arrive at any conclusion about its causes when we do not possess as yet any real knowledge of the general rules determining the location of economic processes – when the purely economic laws which without any doubt somehow influence location are not discovered?

Everybody who moves into a large city goes there, among other purposes, in order to follow some economic pursuit. Is it sensible for us to argue about cultural and social motives when perchance we are simply fettered by the iron chains of hard economic forces? It may be that the enormous agglomerations of today are nothing but inevitable results of a certain stage of economic and technical development; or perhaps they are the consequence of the social organization of our economic system. Concerning this we really ought to have some exact knowledge. At any rate we cannot very well go ahead assuming that there are no rules of economic location at all, or that people are guided by "pleasure" and other irrational motives when choosing the location of their economic pursuits, although we know them to be controlled by hard-and-fast rules in every other economic situation.

Alfred Weber, 1909[1]

Introduction: Spatial Solutions to Social Problems

In the midst of the crisis of the liberal form, function, and perception of urban life, the first serious attempt to reterritorialize Greater Berlin and to respond to the changing urban geography of Greater Berlin came in the early years of the twentieth century. These took the form of a city-planning contest for the design of the entire economic region and the creation of a new administrative body that would address regional questions brought on by Berlin's rapid urbanization and industrialization. This crisis shaped both the theory and the practice of urban government and planning in the late nineteenth and early twentieth centuries in Greater Berlin and other urbanizing areas. Social actors responded to this crisis both deliberately and unintentionally, attempting to shape capitalism as it reconstituted and reterritorialized itself. In the opening passages of the first-of-its-kind study of industrial location, from 1909, Alfred Weber noted that the transformation of contemporary society demanded new modes of analysis.[2] This chapter will argue that city planners and municipal administrators also addressed Weber's question, though in a more pragmatic way. Neil Brenner describes a dialectical transformation in how capitalist societies at different scales – from the neighbourhood, to the city, to the province, to the nation, to global systems – mark out their territory. This transformation was characterized by a "contradictory dynamic of de- and reterritorialisation." Capitalism transforms spatial relations on all scales to fit its changing needs. As the older spatial order collapses, a new one takes shape to meet the needs of capitalism. However, the contradictions in the new spatial order begin to undermine its conditions of possibility.[3] This process often worked without the knowledge of the social actors, who battled over the form that this reconstituted city would take and misjudged the forces at work.

Berliners attempted to address this reterritorialization by proposing new city plans for Greater Berlin and by creating a new governmental institution dedicated to regional problems. The first section of this chapter argues that the inauguration of a city planning contest to organize the rapidly agglomerating urban space was an attempt to reterritorialize the area. Although the contest sought to balance the pragmatic and aesthetic forms of planning discussed in chapter 2, the contest organizers were constrained by this dichotomy between the practical and the beautiful. The second section argues that the contestants' plans sought to express and direct the spatial consequences of industrial agglomeration in Berlin and Berlin's role as a capital of a rising international power. The third section contends that the organizers and contestants, whose work was displayed at the Greater Berlin General City Planning Exhibition, believed that they were part of an international project to renovate the mode of human settlement for the betterment of humanity. They regarded capitalism as both the source of the problem and the means for improvement. The fourth section of this chapter argues that the effort to create a unified administrative body for all of Greater Berlin represents a governmental response to the reterritorialization of capitalism, and the fifth section maintains that the new regional administrative body, the Verband Groß-Berlin, pointed beyond liberal modes of local government while remaining trapped within liberal assumptions about the world. The final sections of the chapter contend that in the three areas over which the new administrative authority was given jurisdiction (transportation, forest, and housing policy), the same ideological conditions – recognition of social problems, partial attempts to overcome those problems, and the constraints of liberal ideology ultimately blocking the ability to address the problems – that shaped city planning and municipal administration prevail here.

Unifying Greater Berlin before 1908

The crisis of the liberal form, function, and perception of urban life significantly challenged the inherited understandings of the urban region; however, despite the changing urban geography of Greater Berlin, powerful local and state interests had thwarted attempts to respond to this transformation, such as a single municipal government. Previous efforts to plan the region were either schematic and antiquated, like the Hobrecht plan, or failed private initiatives, like Johann Anton Wilhelm von Carstenn-Lichterfelde's ideas for Berlin and Potsdam.[4] Carstenn, a real estate developer in Hamburg and then in Berlin, worked in the south and southwest of the city and contributed to the development of Grunwald. Known as the "Napoleon of real estate speculators," he lobbied authorities steadily from 1866 to 1892 for the right to build in Grunwald, especially on the waterfront to the west of the forest. Seeking to counteract land speculation and the laissez-faire attitude of the municipal leaders, he monopolized the development of the land. Carstenn believed that the Hobrecht plan and the free market created poor living conditions, high rents, and high labour costs. Worried about a Paris Commune–like event occurring in Berlin, in 1872 he proposed building villa suburbs and new state buildings in Grunwald, from Charlottenburg to Potsdam, isolating the working class in the east and on the other side of the Landwehr Canal and Spree River. However, the government preferred to retain this land for recreation, as collateral for state debt, as a hunting ground, and as speculative real estate. As Jeffrey Wilson notes, the Prussian officials sought to imitate Carstenn's entrepreneurialism in their real estate transactions.[5] This point demonstrates how liberal capitalism transformed behaviour, even of those who were often stridently opposed to liberal capitalism and modernity. As Lefebvre might suggest, in 1910 cracks appeared that threatened the stability of the liberal city.[6] The reterritorialization of Greater Berlin involved a reconceptualization of the space of Greater Berlin and the means for integrating the metropolitan region into a whole.

Launching the Greater Berlin Contest

This crisis in liberal urban life and the changing urban geography of Greater Berlin inspired serious effort to reterritorialize Greater Berlin between 1908 and 1910. Berlin and the neighbouring communities in the metropolitan region sponsored a contest to design a plan for this rapidly agglomerating urban space. In classic liberal fashion, this project was driven by a civil-society organization of professionals wielding their influence in the hope that the state would address the area's complex socio-spatial problems. This project was one of a number of prominent international efforts to reconsider the territory of a municipality. The contest sought to find a balance between the pragmatic form of planning and the aesthetic approach. Try as they might, the contest organizers could not escape this opposition between the practical and the beautiful, in part because it was rooted in basic conceptions about beauty and more prosaic concerns structured around modern capitalist social relations not specific to planning.

The Greater Berlin City Planning Contest sought to reterritorialize the space of Greater Berlin in response to the crisis brought on by the changes in economic and cultural geography during the liberal period.[7] The contestants were charged with designing the space in a twenty-five-kilometre radius of Berlin's Potsdamer Platz to address the problems of Greater Berlin's built environment. This contest and the plans its contestants produced pointed beyond the prevailing liberal perceptions of the city and manifested features of the crisis in liberal city planning. The contest sought an integrated, comprehensive plan to address the housing, transit, aesthetic, and green-space problems of Greater Berlin and was part of a broader international movement to develop *Gesamtplan* or total plans for cities.[8] This international movement expressed the ideals of liberal city planning and attempted to push beyond them, in particular through the massive expansion of scale.

In a liberal fashion, the contest began as the project of two civil-society professional associations, which hoped to use their influence to make the state address socio-spatial questions. The Architects Association of Berlin and the Association of Berlin Architects formed the Committee for Greater Berlin and tried to convince state and municipal authorities to participate in a city-planning contest. Theodor Köhn, the project's instigator, claimed that this planning effort could form the basis of a Zweckverband for Greater Berlin, an ad hoc association dedicated to particular regional tasks.[9] To begin, the commission established guidelines for the planning contest.[10] It claimed that everything within twenty-five kilometres of Potsdamer Platz had become an economic unity, but that state interests and local communities defending their self-administration had thwarted the administrative integration of the region. The commission believed that conceiving of Greater Berlin as a single unit and creating a single municipal administration and legal code was indispensable to any solution to the area's problems. The committee argued that the particular laws and the parochialism of local communities constrained development.[11] The committee set guidelines for a general plan that would:

1. Regulate undeveloped areas and propose improvements to existing developments;
2. Pursue these two basic goals by the most progressive technical, hygienic, and economic means of modern city planning and according to the highest aesthetic principles;
3. Address the social problems of housing and create satisfactory housing for the different social classes, as well as help to locate large and small businesses according to the particular features of each of the subregions of Greater Berlin;
4. Create a network of main streets for large vehicles, local high-speed transit systems, and a canal network, as well as expanded parklands, sports fields, playgrounds, and parkways, and, finally, spaces for new public buildings; and
5. Be judged to be well conceived and artistic by the way it regulated city development, protected the water sources and Markish landscape, and accomplished technical and aesthetic unity, which was considered typical of a powerful twentieth-century metropolis.

Remaining within liberal ideas of municipal self-administration while also trying to organize urban space on a scale that exceeded liberal norms, the organizers envisioned all of the involved communities adopting the plan that best fulfilled these aims.[12] The contest principles brought together concerns for the movement of commodities, labourers, and consumers through the city; for bourgeois strollers; for the physical and moral education of the working class; and for the aesthetic experience of Berlin's particular historically formed space. The Committee for Greater Berlin, soon called the Committee for the Structural Development of Greater Berlin, sought to wield its civil society power and become more official and influential with the municipal and state bodies. On 30 May 1907 the committee expanded to include members of the City Planning Inspection Commission, the Magistrat's Office, and the Magistrat's Building Office. It sent a program to Oberbürgermeister Martin Kirschner.[13] On 24 January 1908 Otto March, the head of the committee, whose architecture focused on villas and churches, submitted a funding proposal.[14] The committee members found a sympathetic ear in Kirschner, a National Liberal and later a member of the Deutsche Freisinnige Partei.[15] Although the planning principles remained within a liberal vision of the city, they expanded the scale and asked that the planners integrate all of the elements into a cohesive totality, which pushed beyond liberal planning.

The Greater Berlin contest, like contemporaneous efforts in Greater Boston and Chicago, attempted to address the city as a unified totality in response to the crisis in liberal urban life and changes in urban geography and to reterritorialize metropolitan regions. The Boston plan of 1915 was a six-year project that began in 1909, initiated by the department-store entrepreneur Edward Albert Filene (whose store in downtown Boston was designed by Daniel Burnham), and led by prominent regional businessmen. It involved thirty-seven communities surrounding Boston and endeavoured to create a unified Greater Boston. Werner Hegemann, who would play a role in the planning of Berlin, was also part of this Boston project.[16] In Chicago, Daniel Burnham and Edward H. Bennett developed a plan, which, as Samuel Kling explains, "proposed a comprehensive and carefully integrated network of landscaped boulevards and broad avenues to undergird an economically thriving, physically healthy, and aesthetically appealing commercial metropolis."[17] As Margaret Garb argues, the Plan for Chicago achieved the Progressive goal of expanding governmental authority and using this authority to transform the lives of the citizens, a key first step in creating the Fordist-Keynesian welfare state in the United States.[18] The schemes for Chicago, Greater Boston, and Greater Berlin began to push beyond liberal planning norms in some areas but were constrained by them in others.

The organizers tried to balance the post-liberal regional demands that the economic geography placed on planning with liberal ideas of municipal self-administration, as well as pragmatic, aesthetic, and producerist planning. They encouraged contestants to respect existing plans and neighbourhood economic activity but not to be bound by them; to plan not only Berlin and its immediate suburbs but also more distant areas; and to develop a regional rapid-transit rail network connecting existing and newly conceived communities with the inner city. Like the Plan for Chicago, the contest sought to centralize and rationalize the various passenger, freight, long-distance, and commuter rail lines as well as the canal and road systems.[19] Finally, contestants were encouraged to preserve some remaining vacant land for parks. The committee presented the idea to the city council on 19 March 1908, and the council approved it on 9 April.[20] On 15 October Berlin, Charlottenburg, Schöneberg, Rixdorf, Wilmersdorf, Lichtenberg, Spandau, and Potsdam, as well as the administrative districts of Teltow and Niederbarnim, made the contest materials available.[21] The planners then set to work re-envisioning the economic region.

The crisis in the liberal form, function, and perception of urbanism generated conflicts between the pragmatic planners and the aesthetic planners, despite the organizers' attempts at peacemaking. Joseph Stübben made a number of suggestions of people to include in the prize committee and those to exclude, especially Karl Henrici.[22] The editors of the *Tägliche Rundschau*, a conservative, anti-Semitic, anti-Catholic, and anti-Socialist newspaper that advocated for colonial expansion, criticized the committee's lean towards the liberal status quo and away from aesthetic city-planning ideals that the exclusion of Henrici implied. Though the newspaper does not make this explicit, it is not surprising that these two found common cause, given the newspaper's politics and the stances that Henrici took and that were discussed in the previous chapter.[23] *Berliner Architekturwelt*, which was inclined towards Jugendstil and aesthetic city planning, quoted the *Rundschau*'s disapproval at length and contended that if these experts did not return on a voluntary basis, then the scope of the results might be foreshortened, because the local government representatives would have to answer questions better suited to expert planners.[24] The conflict, however, was not resolved, because it was part of a broader contradiction that characterized social conceptions of beauty and functionality in modern capitalist society, as Herbert Marcuse theorized.[25]

The Greater Berlin Contest was an attempt to take up the complex socio-spatial problems of the metropolitan region and to deal with it as a single territory. This project was championed by a liberal civil-society organization and was part of a broader international project to reconsider urban space. Although the contest struggled to balance questions of aesthetics and pragmatics, conflicts such as this one proved difficult to escape.

The Contest Results

In the midst of this crisis of liberal urban life, the contestants sought to reterritorialize Greater Berlin response to the metropolitan region's changing urban geography. They tried to address the spatial consequences of rapid industrial agglomeration in Berlin and Berlin's role as a capital of a rising international power. The first of the two winning plans, submitted by the Hochbahngesellschaft and Joseph Brix and Felix Genzmer, assumed that Berlin would continue to grow at its then current rate and used pragmatic means and a vision of a grand national capital to plan Greater Berlin. Hermann Jansen's plan, the other first-place winner, took a more aesthetic and restrained approach. Rudolf Eberstadt, Bruno Möhring, and Richard Petersen's third-place plan tried to address social problems spatially by creating working-class housing and monumental military structures, in the hope of creating national unity. The fourth-place plan, by Havestadt & Contag, Otto Blum, and Bruno Schmitz, was grand in its vision of Berlin as a national capital, but not in the imperial sense; they expressed their monumental vision through works that valued the *Bildungsbürger* world view. Each of the contestants attempted to address the problems that capitalist industrialization and urbanization forced on liberal city planning and grappled with the problems of liberal city planning. In keeping with the ideals of liberal city planning, their central concerns focused on efficient traffic management; the experience of the flâneur; and the circulation of capital, commodities, and labour in, within, out of, and through the city.

In certain respects the contest results pointed beyond liberalism, but in other respects they reaffirmed assumptions of organized liberal city planning. The contest judges and reviewers in the architectural and city-planning press were split between aesthetic city planners and transportation engineers. Architects resented the centrality of transportation to the final products, because the program sought "the artistic transformation of Greater Berlin," which would express the "meaning of the city as capital of the German Reich and as a world city" through monumental buildings. For example, Walter Lehweß hoped for a set of buildings, like a capitol or an Acropolis. However, engineers and traffic technicians thought that the program had understood the problem of transportation in a way that the plans themselves did not.[26] Albert Hofmann argued that neither side offered a fusion of the technical and the artistic.[27] Both Hofmann and Lehweß believed that the contest's reterritorialization of geographic scale and concerns for aesthetics marked an epochal shift in planning.[28] However, all of the plans fell short of one or another aspect of these lofty aspirations.

The first-place plan was designed by the founders of the city-planning curriculum at the Imperial Technical College, Joseph Brix and Felix Genzmer, as well as by a mass-transit business, Siemens & Halske's daughter firm, the Hochbahngesellschaft. Their plan exhibited a contradiction in liberal city planning in that they believed that the city would continue to grow at its current rapid pace, but that this quantitative change did not require a qualitative change in the planning, and piecemeal liberal city planning would be sufficient to address the needs of the metropolitan region. "Think of the Future," as it was titled, combined technocratic pragmatism with imperial grandeur and assumed that Berlin would grow at its then-current rate for ninety years.[29] Guided by Paul Wittig, the chief of the Hochbahngesellschaft, this plan focused on mass transit. Wittig had worked as an architect, including on the Reichstag, but in 1897 Hochbahngesellschaft's founders, Deutsche Bank and Siemens, appointed him to be the director of the firm, and he turned his attention to both practical and theoretical transportation questions.[30]

Like many liberal planners, these planners focused on the transportation of commodities through the city. They regarded transit as the prerequisite for urban development, prioritizing a north-to-south long-distance train line through the city with a central train station near the Brandenburg Gate.[31] Brix, Genzmer, and the Hochbahngesellschaft planned a number of intersections between suburban lines and the Ringbahn, and a new north-south local line to follow the proposed long-distance train line, and then envisioned a number of lines that crossed central Berlin from the southeast to the northwest. The judges praised the planners' organization of freight transit and their development and widening of a canal to the northwest of the city, which would improve the connection of the industry there to the lakes to the west and the Spree to the southeast.[32] However, as Wolfgang Sonne argues, the planners created a patchwork

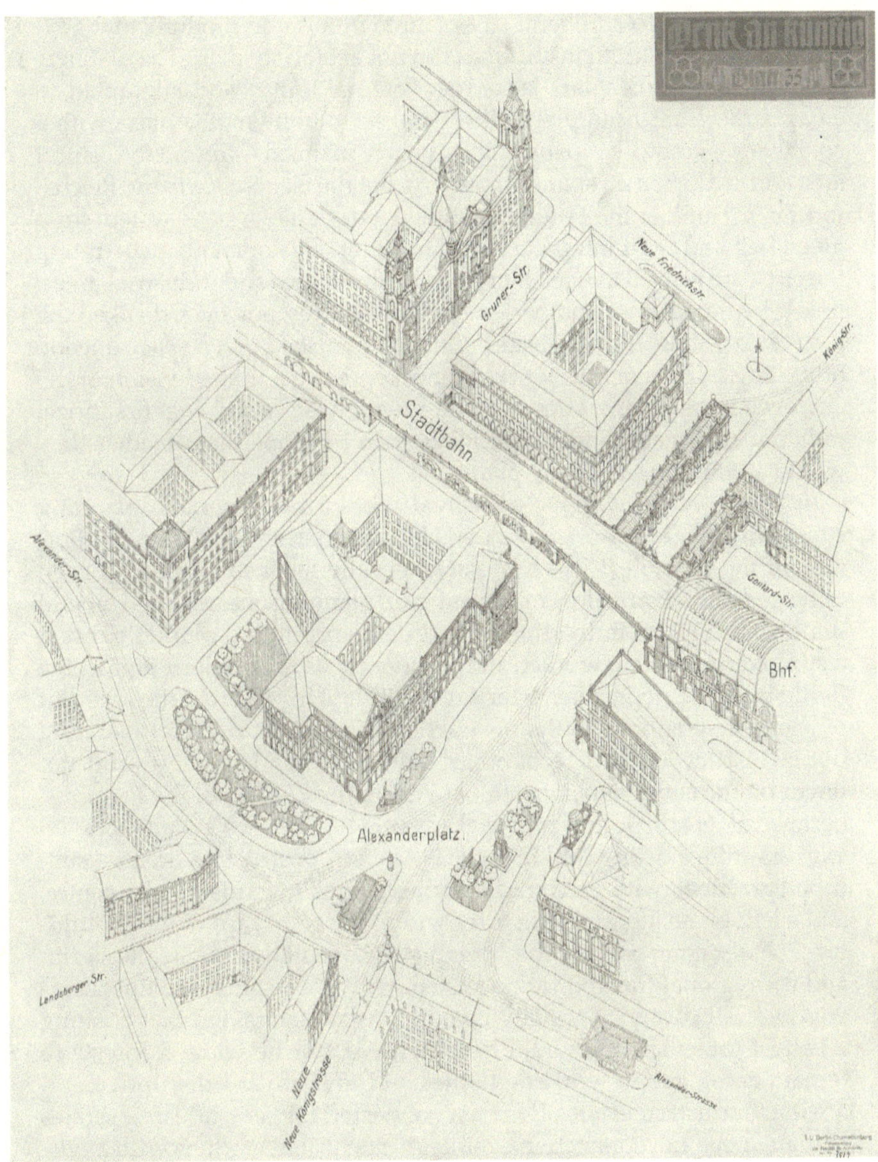

3 Brix and Genzmer's Plan for Alexanderplatz. "Umgestaltung des Alexanderplatzes und Umgebung unter Beibehaltung der Königs-Kolonaden," from Brix, Joseph, Genzmer, and Hochbahngesellschaft in Berlin. "Preisgekrönt mit der Hälfte des Zusammengelegten I. und II. Preises: Kennwort: 'Denk an Künftig.'" In Wettbewerb Groß-Berlin, 1910: Die preisgekrönten Entwürfe mit Erläuterungsberichten (Berlin: Ernst Wasmuth A.-G., 1911).

of strategically placed liberal city-planning tools and monumental governmental and cultural institutions but not a total city plan. The planners believed that Königsplatz lacked an "eternal unity" and attempted to create a more balanced plaza. They suggested unifying the plaza with a colonnade – according to the judges, poorly planned – around the central area and creating a monumental street from the Siegesallee to the Reichsforum.[33] "Think of the Future" included a design of a park system for a green belt and radii integrated with housing developments penetrating the city core as well as socially mixed communities and industrial areas, linked by transit lines and parkways.[34] The judges, however, disliked the way twenty new industrial sites in the plan pushed green space outside of the city.[35] To them, this work did not represent a unified vision of the city, even if the planners designed on a massive scale and won first prize; rather, it aggregated individual features in the hope that together they would amount to a cohesive plan.

If "Think of the Future" remained within the pragmatic planning rubric, the other first-prize winner, Hermann Jansen's "Within the Borders of the Possible," was more aesthetically inclined. Though Jansen criticized the abstraction of liberal city planning, he retained liberal understandings of individuality and deference to the market. Jansen, a student of Henrici, worked independently as an architect and in the Berlin building department starting in 1897.[36] He preferred the restraint of aesthetic planning to the abstraction of pragmatic liberal planning out of respect for laws, economics, and history.[37] The judges did not linger on the constrained vision of "Within the Borders of the Possible" because of its artistic and practical advantages.[38] Jansen's plan included waivers from existing building codes, zoned construction areas, a suburban greenbelt with green radial strips headed towards the city centre, and a ban on residential structures within the courtyard of other buildings.[39] He tried to balance the "organic" incorporation of Greater Berlin and the regional transportation system with "restor[ing] the unconsidered placid beauty" of the city layout. Jansen maintained that creating a belt of green spaces would be expensive, but he wanted forests to remain accessible to workers' homes and to surround disruptive and noxious industrial estates.[40] Jansen connected his new housing estates to high-speed rail connections, reintegrating urban workers with a purportedly pre-modern nature. He placed industry within proximity of freight lines, and he expanded existing railway networks and waterways serving businesses that had moved to the northwestern periphery of the city.[41] Lehweß criticized the execution of a number of Jansen's ideas, and Albert Hofmann regarded Jansen's plan as overly technical, while the judges praised its clear, beautiful, and thorough answers to all the questions.[42] Instead of designing new monumental structures, Jansen followed Henrici and created beautiful experiences; however, he did so through uniform blocks without breaks between plots of land.[43] The building facades were plain and curved slightly with the road. His empirical research concluded that accents every 400 to 600 metres or four to seven minutes of walking were appropriate and thus punctuated these roads with periodic municipal structures. Unlike Sitte and Henrici, Jansen considered artistic city planning from the perspective of a moving observer.[44] Jansen's limited goals reflected his commitment to aesthetic planning.

The judges felt that the third-place plan, from Rudolf Eberstadt, Bruno Möhring, and Richard Petersen (a housing economist, an architect, and a transportation engineer, respectively), "Et Terra in Pax," hoped to use the built environment to address social issues and create a more cohesive citizenry. Sharing the social politics that Eberstadt expressed in his critiques of real estate speculation discussed in chapter 2, this group pointed beyond the liberal era, because it tried to combine a producerist regard for working-class housing conditions with a celebration of imperial power. Nonetheless, while this group criticized the abstraction of liberal city planning, their combination of concrete pragmatic and aesthetic planning remained within the liberal vision of city planning.[45] They based their design in historically existent aesthetic features, combining state regulations with incentives for the private sphere. The planners believed class conflicts among Berliners profoundly influenced national life.[46] The judges and Lehweß praised the planned peripheral workers' housing developments near the heavy-industry region of northwest Greater Berlin near Tegel, Wittenau, and Reinickendorf.[47] "Et Terra in Pax" envisioned a new central train station north of the Spree and northwest of the Reichstag that would connect the east-west and north-south lines through the city as well as the exhibition grounds and barracks in the working-class district of Moabit. For the southeast of the Tiergarten, they designed a new opera house, justice ministry, and interior ministry.[48] "Et Terra in Pax" agreed with "Think of the Future" that cities developed radially and that a green girdle could function like a city wall; thus, this plan developed – and the judges and Lehweß loved – green radii.[49] The planners convinced Lehweß that the lack of suburban lines contributed to urban density, but that density did follow the radii.[50]

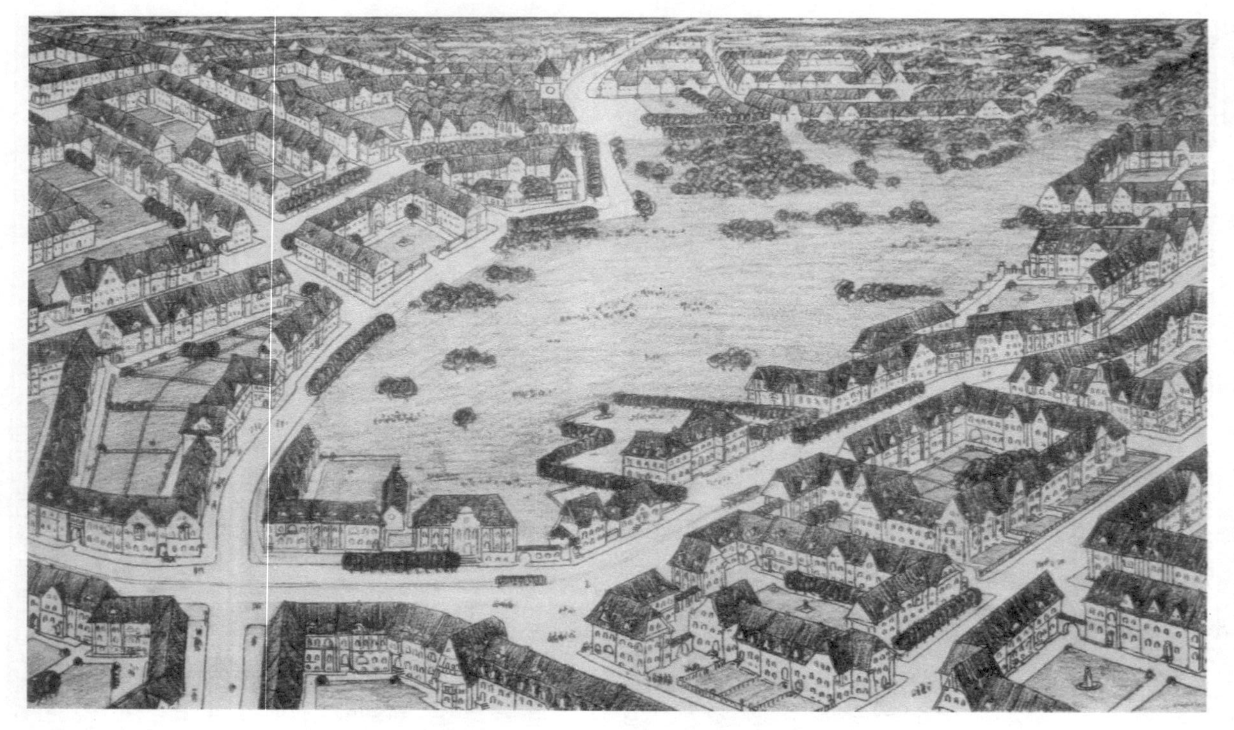

4 Jansen's Plan for a Small Home Settlement. "Kleinwohnungssiedlung (Tafel 4)" from Jansen, Hermann. "Preisgekrönt mit der Hälfte des Zusammengelegten I. und II. Preises: Kennwort: 'In den Grenzen der Möglichkeit.'" In Wettbewerb Groß-Berlin, 1910; die preisgekrönten entwürfe mit erläuterungsberichten (Berlin: Ernst Wasmuth A.-G., 1911).

5 Eberstadt, Möhring, and Petersen's Plan for a New Opera Plaza. "Neuer Opernplatz (Tafel 4)" from Rudolf Eberstadt, Bruno Möhring, and Richard Petersen. "Preisgekrönt mit dem III. Preise: Kennwort: 'Et in Terra Pax.'" In Wettbewerb Groß-Berlin, 1910: Die preisgekrönten Entwürfe mit Erläuterungsberichten (Berlin: Ernst Wasmuth A.-G., 1911).

The planners' vision of a militarized Königsplatz, including a new war ministry across Königsplatz from the Reichstag and a new Reichsmarine building to the north, a new colonial office and a new military cabinet building to the northeast corner of Königsplatz, makes clear the imperial dimension of "Et Terra in Pax." These planners believed that this grand new military and cultural space would resonate with visitors and Germans alike, unifying the working class with the state.[51] This military monumental space – when compared to the civic monumental space in the Plan for Chicago – demonstrates Berlin's role as a national capital and a military encampment.[52] As the judges noted, Eberstadt, the opponent of speculation, proposed speculative sale of state treasury land to pay for the construction of new buildings.[53] "Et Terra in Pax" regarded Berlin's architectural heritage as powerful but believed that modern capitalism challenged the city beyond its capacity.[54]

This plan drew on the formal principles of aesthetic city planning, and remained, in certain respects, liberal, but expanded the scale and the territory of the planner, moving beyond liberal norms of planning and municipal self-administration.[55] Möhring believed that Berlin could become a capital adequate to Germany's global role by integrating the urban totality as a *Gesamtkunstwerk* (total work of art).[56] Lehweß praised Möhring's carefully conceived and "artistically masterfully accomplished proposals" and claimed that the reorganized Königsplatz created a sense of tranquillity and a worthy conclusion to the Siegsallee. The new opera house, Ministry of Justice, and a ministerial garden had the "wise and mature restraint" of "splendid old Berlin."[57] This plan exhibited a vision of the city as an integrated, productive, and militarily powerful city that was post-liberal.

The plan that offered the grandest reterritorialization and challenge to liberal municipal self-administration came from Havestadt & Contag, Otto Blum, and Bruno Schmitz. Their plan, "Where There Is a Will There Is a Way," rejected abstract city planning in favour of a combination of pragmatic and aesthetic design, but on a massive scale.[58] The judges believed that this vision of Berlin would inspire future generations and focused its monumentality on education and civilian government, including a plan for a new university on the shores of the Havel and moving nearly all the garrisons to the exterior of the city.[59] Like Burnham's plan for Chicago, they emphasized civic spaces and social integration, hoping these would create a newly engaged citizenry.[60] The Havestadt & Contag group planned a "Forum of Labour" for the Havel lakeshore, a grand boulevard stretching from the Potsdamer Station to the "Central

Southwest Station," and a "Monumental City" around Lehrter Station, including a new "Forum of the Arts" and a grand boulevard connecting Friedrichsstadt and the Tiergarten.[61] While the judges criticized the economy of its ideas, they agreed with Lehweß, who believed these monumental features were "wonderfully implemented in enormous charcoal sketches [that] gave an intoxicating picture to the future metropolis."[62] Like the other planners, Havestadt & Contag, Otto Blum, and Bruno Schmitz endorsed radial parks along train lines and in cemeteries, large peripheral parks, and parks for organized physical activity.[63] They worried that surrounding industrial and housing development with forests would concentrate industry and the working class, sharpening social stratification. Instead, they favoured mixed-income neighbourhoods to ameliorate social differences, form social solidarity, empower members of the working class to help themselves, and provide jobs for poor women and children in service.[64] Fritz Eiselen praised Havestadt & Contag, Blum, and Schmitz for their plans for rail and water transportation to serve the distribution and interconnectedness of industry within the metropolitan region.[65] These planners argued that as businesses grow, they push from the inner city to the suburbs in search of more and cheaper land and transportation. This relocation, they claimed, would also entail a relocation of workers to these external regions, providing the working class with more space and better living conditions. They sought to coordinate this change "to create an organic whole."[66]

Each of these plans attempted to resolve the problems of late-liberal city planning on a regional scale. They reorganized forests, transportation, housing, and monumental structures to make the city adequate to its early twentieth-century needs. While the planners recognized the deficiency of the liberal city-planning ideology to solve the problems that Berlin presented, none of them strayed far from it. This disjuncture between the world and the intellectual tools used to grasp that world is evidence of the crisis of liberal city planning. Principally, the emphasis on the concrete, on integration, and on social production would form the basis of a new planning ideology, but it would take, as we will see in the next chapter, the First World War and a revolution to bring this about.

The General City Planning Exhibition of 1910

Those involved with the Greater Berlin contest believed that they were changing the world by fundamentally altering human settlement and that their efforts were international and humanitarian. This self-confidence as they tried to set the terms for future capitalist urbanization reveals that the organizers too believed that the liberal form, function, and perception of capitalist urbanism was at odds with the world as it now existed. Throughout their discourse, as in other discourses examined in this book, an opposition between the concrete and the abstract undergirded their analysis of the social world.

The contestants and the exhibition organizers who presented the contest plans sensed that they were on the cusp of a very different form of city. They believed that the right ideas and presentations of those ideas could set the terms for the new form, function, and perception of cities. They did change the social structure and the trajectory of history through their actions, just not always in on the terms and in the direction they wanted. The prize committee planned an international exhibition to present the contest winners and like-minded planning from other cities. On 5 January 1910 the contest deadline passed, and on 19 March they announced the results.[67] Despite the press attention and the international scope of the contest, it attracted only twenty-seven plans, the majority of which were only fragments.[68] In January 1910, Oberbürgermeister Kirschner and Otto March, representing the General City-Planning Exhibition of 1910, told the Prussian Minister of the Interior Moltke, Minister of Works Breitenbach, Minister of Education Trott zu Solz, and Minister of Agriculture, Crown Lands, and Forests Arnim that they intended to create an exhibition in May and June.[69]

The organizers understood, if only partially, that the form, function, and perception of cities were shifting around them and hoped that the exhibition would demonstrate a fundamental break from earlier planning methods, marking a socio-political event in German, even world, history.[70] Eberstadt argued that the ideas in this first-of-its-kind exhibition would influence not only architects, civil servants, and social reformers, but the whole population. He worried, however, that the public did not understand city planning and would dismiss the exhibition as a collection of models, maps, and palaces, because the idea of building something on the scale of a city was new. He hoped the exhibition would inspire people to consider the city in its totality but also to restore to modern cities the balance of architectural scale of medieval cities.[71] Eberstadt believed that the exhibition could address housing and that class conflict was "abiding and well-founded," but the bad housing policy that created socio-spatial oppositions could and needed to be changed, because it threatened industry with inefficiencies and "led to the alienation of urban people from the state."[72] Eberstadt shared this focus on housing with social reformers in cities like Chicago, New York, Boston, and London.[73] Eberstadt hoped to fix problems of social conflict and capital accumulation with spatial solutions.

The city planners who organized the exhibition and their international colleagues believed they were part of a new period of urban development. In addition to the contest plans, the exhibition featured a statistical exhibit about the population density of Berlin, London, Munich, Paris, Schöneberg, and Vienna; and demonstrations on workers' housing from Krupp in Essen am Ruhr; on garden cities from Hellerau outside Dresden; on people's parks from Berlin, Düsseldorf, and Hamburg; on soil parcelling and city block formation from Breslau and the Berlin suburb of Rixdorf; on plaza arrangement such as Theatre Plaza in Dresden and Stuttgart, Friedrich Plaza in Mannheim, Karl Plaza in Vienna; and on the division of festival grounds in Königsberg and Posen. It also featured examples of large building groups and street organization: from the seniors home in Buch outside Berlin, slaughterhouses in Dresden, schools in Frankfurt a. M., and a communal forum in Weißensee outside Berlin. Finally, a section addressed the completion of difficult projects, such as a palace bridge in Karlsbad; city high-speed rail networks in Berlin, Boston, Chicago, London, and Paris; and bridges in Berlin and Munich. The exhibition welcomed foreign exhibits, including entries from Copenhagen, as well as presentations from Robert Unwin, the British city planner, with exhibits on Hampstead and Liverpool; displays from Eugène Hénard from the Ministry of Fine Arts of France; and from representatives from Budapest, Brünn, and Vienna in Austro-Hungary. Also featured were exhibits from John Nolen of Harvard University's Museum for Social Ethics, and from representatives of Gothenburg, Helsingborg, and Stockholm in Sweden.[74] The diversity of origins of the contributions to this exhibition, combined with the sense of a shared, international project, spoke to the visionary scale of the planners' scheme.

The organizers saw the shift in the form, function, and perception of cities from liberal to something new and their intervention into city planning processes as part of an international movement. For example, London, Liverpool, and Hamburg tore down slums and rebuilt the neighbourhoods. Boston and Vienna created greenbelts surrounding their cities. Chicago developed a general plan for development of the city.[75] The Plan for Chicago envisioned massive civic structures on the grounds of what were, at the time, West Side slums, pushing industry and working-class housing to the urban periphery.[76] The Plan for

Chicago attempted to "remake the industrial city according to the models of imperial Rome or Second Empire Paris."[77] But Imperial Rome was not an industrial city; Haussmann's plan for Paris drove industry and working-class housing to the suburbs; and Paris was not an industrial city on the scale of Chicago. Lehweß thought the exhibition for making city-planning ideas accessible, but subordinating individual urban interests to a general city plan would be a great challenge.[78] This style of engagement with urban questions suggests the international form that urbanization and city planning would flower after the First World War.

The organizers, in their attempts to demonstrate their new ideas and this shift in the form, function, and perception of cities, created an extensive exhibition program guide. The program attempted to understand capitalism and its culture and their spatial consequences. Werner Hegemann, the general secretary of the exhibition, was a German social reformer who received his PhD in economics from the University of Pennsylvania. He had become involved in urban-planning and social-reform circles in the northeastern part of the United States before returning to head this exhibition, at the request of his uncle Otto March.[79] Hegemann's introduction to the program accentuated the relationships among liberalism, the Prussian state, abstract planning, space, class struggle, and capitalism. Hegemann quoted Otto March, arguing that "blood and iron" politics were necessary to create "medicinal openings" between buildings with a pickaxe to accommodate the surge of traffic, despite its dictatorial character and the many inadvertent victims.[80] By embracing this aggressive, destructive, and modernizing yet conservative approach, March and Hegemann demonstrated a willingness to pursue liberal economic goals in politically illiberal ways.

Hegemann believed that dramatic state measures were necessary to address these urban changes in the context of turn-of-the-twentieth-century capitalism and its spatial consequences. He commented that measures more radical than the ones March suggested for traffic were necessary to resolve housing shortages. He believed that the social, economic, and demographic conditions of Berlin were comparable only to the poor condition of American cities.[81] Hegemann argued that half a million residents lived in apartments with between four and thirteen people per heated room and that a quarter of a million children, many from these same buildings, suffered from withered limbs and bodies and had no place to play or rest except for the street itself. According to Hegemann, the children raised in such conditions were destined for the public welfare service, but since they had nothing, even prison appeared healthy, expansive, and preferable. These conditions formed "an army of desperados, a social explosive, whose dangers grow with its agglomeration," expanding exponentially, "like dynamite."[82] Like Eberstadt and other housing reformers, Hegemann's concern about the radicalization of the working class provided the foundation for his concern about housing policy. He argued that industrial automation meant that humans serve machines during a large part of their lives, so they must recover for time that exceeds their labour time and do so in a way that renews their strength: recover, sleep, and, "in the broadest sense of the word, dwell, according to a probably irrefutable law of nature."[83] His rhetoric on housing was consistent with both social reformist and conservative discourses on housing in Berlin, but his concern for automation and its consequences on housing and recreation was new.

Hegemann embedded the development of city planning in the economic, social, technological, and political developments of the second half of the nineteenth century. For Hegemann, urban problems were part of a larger historical struggle and transformation, a "struggle of order against chaos" that was unleashed in a "cultural collapse" caused by a "distinctive break from the great tradition." This was a complicated battle between what Hegemann called an elder, exhausted form of power on the one hand, and on the other, a dynamic opposition of uprooted creative power and "a form destroying, yet formally insubstantial economic power." The transformative yet destructive power of the new could be both beneficent and brutal. This power of the new both created society and rent it asunder.[84] Hegemann did not refer to this new set of social and cultural relations, with its dynamic of destruction and construction, as capitalism. However, given this book's consideration of the transformative character of capitalism, it is clear that this uniquely dynamic and abstract form of social mediation that Hegemann described was indeed capitalism. Nonetheless, he misunderstood it as modernity or a consequence of laissez-faire policies, which were historically specific forms that one dimension of capitalism – the circulation of capital – took.

The critique of abstraction already discussed in this book in the context of the housing and land reform movements and in liberal city planning and economics also structured Hegemann's understanding of his world. His explanation of the history of planning in Berlin exemplified the complicated history of liberalism, city planning, and the Prussian bureaucracy. Hegemann attacked Hobrecht's city plan and the Prussian bureaucracy for carrying it out with "Manchesterian" indifference through "the remnants of the absolutist administrative machine."

Hegemann concluded that the Prussian autocracy and Hobrecht's liberal plan had defeated a vanguard of city planners, but what people once regarded as radical ideas had become prerequisites of adequate city planning. Nonetheless, while city planning was "the social-political activity area par excellence," as he wrote, it was "still governed by the most fatal of laissez-faire policies."[85] Hegemann blamed the abstraction of the plan, the absolutism of the bureaucracy, and laissez-faire policies for causing the problems of Berlin and argued that though people had begun to realize the city's socio-political potential, it was still constrained by liberal economics.

In the exhibition, participants believed a fundamental break had taken place in models of city planning. The planners themselves thought that because of a growing reservoir of knowledge and judicious use of past examples, they were creating a new form of city planning. Yet fundamental tenets of liberal city planning – private property, calculability of exchange, abstract equality of parcels of land, and abstract notions of equal access to land ownership – remained unchanged.

Verband Groß-Berlin

In the crisis of the liberal form, function, and perception of urban life, administrators tasked with governing Greater Berlin sought to reterritorialize the region in response to the transformation of its urban geography. This effort tried to overcome the limitations of the liberal understandings of the urban region and municipal self-administration. However, even as they tried, they could not break free from liberal social forms. Roughly contemporaneous with the planning contest and exhibition, authorities attempted to address regional administrative failings by creating a new form of administrative territory. Berlin was one of many cities, internationally, engaged in similar projects of reconfiguration of their territories. Local authorities increasingly believed that the administrative structure of Greater Berlin could not deal with the most pressing problems, and while this view was gaining momentum, anti-Socialist politics thwarted its further progress.

This second major effort to reterritorialize Greater Berlin created a regional authority that superseded municipal self-administration on a specific set of issues: the Verband Groß-Berlin, an ad hoc association, or *Zweckverband*, was intended to preserve regional forests, reform housing law, and develop and rationalize mass transit. Among other goals, the contest and the exhibition had sought to create a single city out of the Greater Berlin region. Though various administrative authorities, since the 1890s, had attempted to create a single administrative region out of Greater Berlin, not until the 1910s did it become a genuine possibility. Elek Takáts, a student of world economics in Vienna with a PhD in economics, business, and economic geography at the University of Cologne, wrote his 1932 dissertation on the Verband Groß-Berlin. In it he argued that rapid agglomeration of industry and population beginning in the 1870s in Greater Berlin made clear the consequences of a "lack of a unified municipal organization for the first time" and demanded a coordinated effort to address "traffic, aesthetic city planning, open-space, education and poor relief," because the social welfare responsibilities for poor cities "had long outgrown the narrow limits of the municipalities."[86] In 1875 and again in 1876, the Prussian Landtag voted down a bill to create a province out of Berlin that included Old Berlin, Charlottenburg, and the area within the Ringbahn that was not part of these two cities, including undeveloped areas. A directly representative government would have led to an overwhelming majority for (poor) Berlin, so the state maintained the three-tier system and a scheme for city council members to select the members of this provincial government.[87] According to the Greater Berlin Zweckverband legislation from 1911, incorporation had failed in the 1890s because of Berlin's concerns about supporting the poorer suburbs fiscally.[88]

Greater Berlin was not alone in facing a crisis created by the contradiction between urban geography and liberal modes of municipal government. In 1888, London, a city that was similarly socially riven and expanding in population and territory, established the London County Council (LCC) as a regional government. However, arguments between local political interests and progressive administrators in the LCC in 1898 compelled the conservative central government to decentralize power and divide it between the LCC and the local borough governments.[89] In the case of Greater New York City, the coexisting utility infrastructure made several peripheral towns (Morrisania, West Farms, and Kingsbridge) accept annexation, but the existence of this utility infrastructure in Yonkers enabled that town to refuse annexation and retain local autonomy. Similarly, Oakland saw San Francisco's consideration of creating the Hetch Hetchy Aqueduct as a threat to its autonomy, after initially expressing interest in San Francisco's ideas of consolidation of water interests.[90]

By 1900 both the state bureaucracy and the Greater Berlin municipalities believed that the administrative structure had become inadequate.

Socialists and left liberals advocated for creating a single regional municipality to create an economy of scale. Local administrators wanted to fix current conditions, although they feared that such a change would also create a Red voting bloc. In 1903 a Berlin Magistrat member argued that Greater Berlin already formed a single urban economic unit and that local administration should be a single unit too.[91] Conservative-leaning liberals and the conservative Prussian state bureaucracy resisted creating a single Greater Berlin municipality, sacrificing administrative efficiency for short-term political interests.

While liberal defences of municipal self-administration and concerns about creating a Socialist voting bloc predisposed liberals and conservatives against reterritorializing Greater Berlin, the development of the urban geography and its consequences for economic and administrative efficiency pushed liberals to consider reterritorialization seriously. Supporters of incorporation had difficulty convincing the city council to expand Berlin. In September 1903 Hugo Preuß proposed a bill to the Berlin City Council that called for "an organic reorganization" of Greater Berlin, because in those municipalities "whose entire economic and social life has its heart in Berlin," "the public suffers most acutely" under the current administration. He endorsed a voluntary association of municipalities as a pragmatic first step to creating a "total municipality" (*Gesamtgemeinde*).[92] Others, even if sympathetic to Preuß's goals, considered the local politics impracticable and the tax burden on Berlin too great.[93] The SPD sought full autonomy and unification for Greater Berlin to free the municipality from what it regarded as the reactionary control of the state administration and to ameliorate social problems.[94] Socialist city councillor Paul Singer praised Preuß's proposal and mocked the "great loyalty and patriotic industry" of the wealthy who fled to the suburbs in search of lower taxes. While the tax revenue from the rich exited Berlin, Singer argued, the city's fiscal burden for poverty, health service, and schools expanded, and a sufficient tax base was essential to expanding protections for workers.[95] The expansion of the municipal utility and welfare responsibilities clashed with the fiscal consequences of the flight of wealthy people from Berlin and drove the push to incorporate the suburbs into Berlin.

The powerful conservative forces in the city council, however, defeated the liberals attempts to reterritorialize the region. On 26 April 1904 an investigative committee rejected Preuß's proposal. Singer subsequently offered a similar plan, but the council rejected this too.[96] On 21 November 1905, the Prussian minister of the interior, Theobald von

Bethmann Hollweg, asked Oberbürgermeister Kirschner to silence the discussion of incorporation but also to research a possible solution.[97] Kirschner composed a memorandum arguing that the borders of Berlin were inadequate: that Greater Berlin formed a single interconnected city and its administration simultaneously demanded centralization and decentralization, but neither the state nor the municipalities adapted to this reality, constraining Berlin's development.[98] Kirschner wanted to untangle the conflicting communal bureaucracies and overlapping jurisdictions.[99] Nevertheless, the state ruled out an incorporation of Greater Berlin and instead proposed an association that focused on regional tasks.

The Creation of the Zweckverband: A New Administrative System

The rapid industrial agglomeration of Greater Berlin posed new problems and posed old ones in a more acute form to administrators who were committed to liberal modes of municipal government. Two new laws attempted to address this problem – one creating the administrative entity of a Zweckverband and the other establishing one in Greater Berlin. The new laws called into question liberal assumptions about municipal self-administration in a way that pointed towards a post-liberal society.

Capitalism had transformed the urban geography of the region since the state first proposed incorporation of the regional governments, both politically and in terms of the built environment, but important aspects of the politics of incorporation remained the same. Bethmann-Hollweg's replacement as minister of the interior, Friedrich von Moltke, ruled out incorporation but suggested the development of a Zweckverband to Kirschner in February 1909.[100] Like the contest, the Zweckverband would focus on forest preservation, housing regulation, and transit rationalization.[101] The business community pressed municipalities to connect their cities to Berlin nominally by adding Berlin to town names.[102] This attempt to reterritorialize Greater Berlin became law in July 1911, when the Landtag passed and the state approved a general law for creating Zweckverbände, and in April 1912 the Landtag passed and approved a specific Zweckverband law for Greater Berlin.[103] The general law enabled municipalities to link themselves through a resolution of the county committee, district committee, or (if those did not exist) the *Oberpräsident* of the province. Existing governmental structures remained in place, even as the law gave the Zweckverband the legal rights and obligations of a corporation.[104] The specific Zweckverband law created "a communal federation autonomous in its affairs, with the rights of a corporation," to be known as "Verband Groß Berlin."[105] The Zweckverband was a weak institution and meant a defeat for the proponents of a more robust incorporation. The Social Democrats considered the Zweckverband an attempt to solve the problems of Greater Berlin without empowering their party.[106] They believed that it would not be able to fulfil its tasks, because it had no power relative to the state government and to the Landtag.[107] While the state and the metropolitan region were attempting to create a new scale of local government, they were unwilling to take the steps necessary to make it succeed.[108] As Takáts and Wilson have argued, while the sale of forests around Berlin failed, it generated a new collectivist approach to city forests.[109] The Oberbürgermeister of Charlottenburg, Ernst Scholz, described the Zweckverband as an institution inserted between the isolation and the expansion of interleaved individual administrative corporations, like the municipality, the province, and the state. The Zweckverband law, he continued, was an "important and unusual intervention ... by the state into the right of municipal self-administration."[110] However, he doubted self-administration had meaning, given the new responsibilities of government.[111] The Zweckverband challenged the assumptions of liberal municipal government, like self-administration and general laws, in the effort to address a new urban scale.

Liberal ideas of municipal self-administration had lost their original revolutionary meaning, and now the state depended on them to thwart incorporation and to protect the wealthy suburbs. The "partial flowering" of suburban "independent local administrations" rendered "a comprehensive incorporation" impossible. However, the state recognized, as the law itself explained, that "the economic standardization process of Greater Berlin could no longer lack a common local legal organization."[112] The structure of the Zweckverband mimicked the municipal structure, with a hundred-member Zweckverband assembly, a committee, and a director, though the law barred the Oberbürgermeister of Berlin from membership in the assembly. It divided the assembly among member cities according to population: each had at least one member and none had more than forty – limiting the power of large cities like Berlin over smaller communities. However, the Zweckverband committee included the Oberbürgermeister of Berlin and another member of the Berlin Magistrat; the Oberbürgermeister of each of the six largest municipalities; the chairmen of the county committees;

eight members from the assembly; and the director.[113] Karl Steiniger was elected the first director of the Zweckverband in February 1912; later, he was elected to the Reichstag during the Weimar Republic as a member of the German National People's Party.[114]

The social and economic transformation of Greater Berlin's urban geography presented significant challenges to nineteenth-century liberal forms of municipal government and territory. Prussian leaders hoped that a Zweckverband dedicated to forests, traffic, and housing would address these challenges. However, this new institution also changed municipal self-administration in significant ways.

Ideologies of Transportation

The Prussian state attempted to address this new regional reality that grew out of the crisis in liberal city planning and liberal municipal administration by creating a new level of government: the Verband Groß-Berlin. This Zweckverband was responsible for regional transit, housing, and green-space reform. It took over the negotiations and ultimately the ownership of local rapid-transit corporations. The reach and speed of the transportation system mediated the location of both industry and working-class housing, as well as the expansion of Greater Berlin. City planners, municipal leaders, and economists saw the transit system and securing a nodal position in the world economy as fundamental to the historical, present, and future demographic, cultural, and economic growth of Berlin. Furthermore, mass transit to the suburbs both opened up access to green space and made it economically feasible to level the forest and create housing.[115] Richard Petersen argued that the suburban rail lines "grasped only a fraction" of the available land, and communities needed to move beyond self-interest to consider the regional development by opening new territories to development.[116] Petersen and Otto Blum both saw speculative real-estate investment as contributing to an imbalance between supply and demand and to monopolies; as discouraging housing improvements; and as limiting suburban growth. However, they agreed, expanded transit could address these conditions.[117] Hugo Preuß agreed that the Zweckverband could use mass transit to address social problems spatially.[118] Urban reformers in the United States also believed that the fast electric streetcar presented a way of overcoming poor conditions, population density, and social strife. American cities like Boston, New York, and Pittsburgh used rapid transit as a spatial fix when the real-estate value of downtown land became an impediment to new building.[119] The Socialists in Berlin agreed that expansion of mass transit could ameliorate working-class housing conditions and that municipalization could solve problems of mass transit, but they did not believe this would resolve social conflict.[120]

In a manner consistent with liberal modes of city planning, contemporaries believed that expanding Berlin's role in the movement of commodities and raw materials was fundamental to the social and economic health of the metropolitan region. Long-distance transportation enabled the city's central position in both a national and a world economy.[121] As the liberal city planner Ernst Bruch noted, Berlin was the east-to-west hub of the Prussian rail system, and locomotive factories triggered industrialization in Berlin.[122] Blum argued that metropolises were "only possible [with] efficient, punctual, cheap, fast means of transport" and occurred not only because of physical geography, but more commonly because of "conscious or unconscious promotion of transportation."[123] While the state did determine the path of the railway through Berlin in the 1860s, private initiative determined the uniformity of the Prussian state railway system.[124]

The liberal focus on the transportation of commodities, consumers, and labour through the urban environment was challenged by the movement of industry to the suburbs in search of less expensive land, a particular labour force, and/or more land. Businesses located in the city centre and businesses moving to the periphery, as well as housing, city planning, and the fixed capital in the built environment, such as buildings, streets, railways, and depots, had a complex and dynamic relationship. For example, the capital investments in freight rail depots intended to facilitate economic growth. The depots were initially on the periphery of the city but soon were enveloped by the urban growth.[125] In 1913 the Architects Committee of Greater Berlin investigated moving to the periphery and expanding freight train depots.[126] Urban agglomeration and pressure from increasing industrialization and capital accumulation in Berlin meant that once-peripheral sites were now in the city centre and inhibiting growth.[127] The Architects Committee argued that these depots created serious obstacles to city planners, because of the difficulty of crossing their width and the large swathes of land on either side that developers could not use.[128] However, the Architects Committee determined that the regional diffusion of industry made the concentration of freight traffic, similar to what Chicago did, impossible.[129]

In addition to the rise of a desire for a coordinated plan for the city, including for the freight train depots, there also arose a wish to improve the water-based freight transportation system for the whole region. According to Friedrich Krause, before 1913 the barges would be landed along the Spree and be unloaded by hand or wheelbarrow, not taking full advantage of new labour-saving technology, like cranes or grain silos. Between 1891 and 1906 the water-based movement of commodities increased from roughly 426,000 to 10.4 million tons in and out of Berlin.[130] The state constructed the old facilities in 1876, but by 1885 Ältesten der Kaufmannschaft and the Ministry for Trade and Commerce were pushing for a new central storage facility with access to rail connections and water transport. During the 1890s several efforts, each with limited or no success, were made to expand Berlin's industrial harbour capacity.[131] In 1898 Krause, who was *Stadtbaurat* at the time, convinced the Magistrat of Berlin to build ports, beginning with the Osthafen at Oberspree, which served the upper and middle Oder. However, conflicts between municipal and state authorities delayed construction, and the harbour ultimately opened on 1 October 1913, with the latest technology and warehouses. This harbour proved key to the mobilization and food distribution effort during the First World War.[132] The slower-developing Westhafen served the lower Oder and the Elbe, including Stettin, Magdeburg, Hamburg, and Lübeck, and was envisioned as part of the future Mittellandkanal with the Ruhr and the Rhine. Between 1905 and 1913 various local authorities debated the location of the harbour, but on 16 March 1914 construction began shortly before the opening of the major shipping route Berlin-Stettin. The port was located "at the Charlottenburg Canal near this diversion of Berlin-Spandau Ship Canal and opposite the southern mouth of the Hohenzollern canal in the connecting channel."[133]

Many cities internationally struggled to reconcile the liberal commitment to the transportation of commodities, consumers, and labour through the urban environment, on the one hand, and suburbanization of industry, on the other hand.[134] The Plan for Chicago moved heavy industry outside of the city, shifted the rail lines from the shore of Lake Michigan to underground tunnels, and constructed new rail hubs at the edge of the commercial centre. This move was an attempt to fix, spatially, threats to capital investment in the city that Burnham and his Commercial Club sponsors saw in the city's air and water pollution, its reputation for corruption, and a history of violent labour conflict.[135] Similarly, Vienna needed to balance urban growth, transportation, and the natural environment. With industrialization, Vienna expanded real estate development to the Danube's floodplain and increased traffic by steamboat on the Danube, as well as on railroad lines that met in the Leopoldstadt district of the city to an island in the middle of the Danube.[136] A built environment that once had facilitated the accumulation of capital in a particular location became an impediment to continued accumulation.

This crisis in the liberal form, function, and perception of urbanism inspired some to reconsider the social implications of the liberal focus on transportation. For Willy Wygodzinski the demand for punctuality in transportation, as well as in production and administration, revealed domination by a new socioeconomic-temporal regime. He argued that the "spatial compression" of "such strong demand and such strong production" into the metropolis made it necessary that the "whole economy must be shaped ever more rationally, ever more accurately, so that it functions smoothly also under these increasingly difficult circumstances."[137] Transportation was fundamental, because "the arrangement or division of time is so sharply stressed that the producer must use for instance a certain metropolitan railway line and can compute its arrival to the working site by the minute." Furthermore, labour time was "exactly chronologically specified," and in the modern economy "the regularity and systematization of all economic procedures become almost living conditions of the metropolis." Wygodzinski claimed that cities, even those in the midst of an agricultural area, would starve without efficiently functioning transportation. He wrote that metropolitans lived under a "reign of terror" that they could become "slave[s] of the methodical organization, which [they] created."[138] William Cronon makes a similar argument about the role of transportation, urban economies, and the generalization of one time-zone system across North America.[139] And Oscar Handlin, among others, describes how capitalism made the efficiency of movement and time the determining factor for urban spatial layout.[140] Not only were cities subjected to time-oriented measures of efficiency, but the concept and practice of time, according to Handlin, were transformed. He argues that, before capitalism, the season was the meaningful unit of time; time was flexible and task-dependent.[141] However, Handlin maintains, the complexity of the modern city demanded a historically more rigorous regime of time.[142] Yet mass transit could improve the quality of life of those caught in inner-city slums, so it was believed, by enabling them to settle less dense suburbs. Transportation and coordinated time fundamentally structured the character of the metropolis.

The combination of old and outmoded transportation corridors, a growing and changing urban geography, and the suburbanization and the expanded scale of raw material consumption and commodity production in Greater Berlin created a complex set of logistical and political problems. Both the municipal and private transit providers wanted to rationalize the system through either cartelization or municipalization. According to the Zweckverband law for Greater Berlin, the new institution would take control of and rationalize the regional mass-transit network. Between 1900 and 1910 ridership on all train lines had grown 80 per cent.[143] In the fall of 1905 the major regional streetcar companies pushed the municipalities to sign one contract with all of them for a ninety-year period of service and to improve the regional traffic infrastructure.[144] Angered by this suggestion, Berlin, Charlottenburg, Schöneberg, Rixdorf, Wilmersdorf, Lichtenberg, Tegel, Tempelhof, and Steglitz, as well as county and provincial authorities gathered in October 1905 to discuss regional transit problems and decided to block a transit monopoly by sharing information and collectively bargaining with the transit companies.[145] In 1907 they created an administrative structure with an assembly, a committee, and a chairman to deal with transit issues and agreed to extend the contracts through 1 January 1920, then to acquire and operate streetcars in Berlin or the suburbs as well as power stations.[146]

The Greater Berlin Zweckverband law hoped to establish the legal means and administrative authority to resolve these conflicts in the regional transit system generated by the crisis of liberal city planning and municipal administration. Gustav Böß, among the more prominent administrators of this process, worked in the Hessian financial service and then the Prussian-Hessian Railway Administration, before being elected to the Berlin-Schöneberg city council; in 1912 he became treasurer of Berlin. (In 1921 he was elected the first mayor of the new municipality of Greater Berlin.)[147] He argued that a capital-starved, haphazard rationalization would retard progress; therefore, the Zweckverband, he contended, would "joyfully celebrate" the willingness by large private capital, like Hochbahngesellschaft, Siemens & Halske A. -G., and AEG, to undertake this rationalization and draw extensively on their large factories.[148] Despite the goals laid out in the Zweckverband law and the importance of the transit system to the prevailing understanding of economic growth, the new institution accomplished relatively little at this stage.

The Role of Urban Green Space

As capitalism developed, it transformed the urban geography of Greater Berlin. This geography included the commodification of formerly royal land into real estate for housing and production. The forest, once a cultural institution tied to corporate privileges and prohibitions, became both a raw material and a site for industry. It also became a locus for modern romantic individual contemplation and for the spectacle of modernized corporate privileges. The forestry and woodworking industries in Germany were an important part of the economy. As such, they were rationalized for the goal of turnover on investment or speculative real-estate development. In response, a movement developed to preserve old-growth forests that fought against the rationalized forestry in favour of what was believed to be a more organic and German form of forestry. This critique attacked forestry as too abstract and celebrated the concrete experience of the forest and its purportedly transformative psychological effects. The Crown, the largest landholder in the vicinity of Greater Berlin, was speculating on its land and wanted to sell it in a laissez-faire manner for the greatest value. However, representatives of the Crown and in government generally worried about the purported effects of lack of access to nature on a radicalizing working class. The Zweckverband took over forest preservation in the midst of this ideological climate.

The reterritorialization of the Greater Berlin region through the Zweckverband law was intended to address deforestation in part, which, like transportation, was a regional problem brought on by the changing urban geography. The politics of German forests, however, has a longer history that creates the context for turn-of-the-twentieth-century forest politics. Before the advent of capitalism, a forest was a historically constituted and organic social form. Like city planning, forestry underwent a significant rationalization and abstraction, and those who pushed for liberal economics in forestry were not necessarily liberal. In addition, a criticism of this mode of forestry arose that attacked the abstraction and purported foreignness of scientific forestry and advocated more ecological and German form. This formal similarity between distinct fields suggests capitalism mediates the formation of these ideologies.

Forests, despite romantic rhetoric, did not stand outside of modern life or capitalism. Indeed, modern capitalism constituted the natural forest. In the late nineteenth and early twentieth centuries, roughly a quarter of Germany's territory was forest and the forest owners managed their forests as profit centres, producing 430 million marks gross and 200 million net in the 1890s, or about 2 per cent of total national income in 1895. Beyond the processing of lumber, wood-related industries employed 600,000 people and produced 500 million marks, or 2 per cent of GNP. Prussian state forests produced 15 per cent of the gross forest income and employed 150,000 workers.[149] The aristocracy or Crown used forest land for royal hunting and recreation and as a source of revenue, including speculatively hoarding their land to corner the market.[150] Beginning in the 1870s, the public trespassed in Grunwald as spectators for grand hunts, driving the royal hunting party further afield from Berlin in 1904. Grunwald became a destination for working-class and bourgeoisie recreation.[151]

The discourse about forests, too, was dualistic, opposing the purportedly concrete and organic dimensions of forests to the abstract and imposed dimensions. In the late eighteenth century, increasing wood consumption from early capitalist production, population growth, and a desire to profit from this consumption led forest owners to manage their properties, using statistics and mathematical models to increase output and create steady profits. They reconstituted the natural, ecological dynamics of a forest into an "abstract natural resource," and, like in other forms of capitalist enclosure and industrial rationalization, forest owners pushed peasants from their traditional access to these forests and simplified the labour of forest workers. However, unlike many capitalist entrepreneurs, the forest owners were aristocrats or royalty.[152]

Beginning in the 1860s, a second discourse attacked the abstract, scientific, and geometrical form of forestry and celebrated the organic development of forests for aesthetic and ecological reasons, mobilizing antinomies similar to those of aesthetic city-planning discourse, disapproving of the "materialism" of the foresters, and alleging that a Jewish conspiracy in the forest administration made foresters think like "homeless nomads."[153] Nationalists hoped to use the metaphor of forests to unite the German Reich. Wilhelm Riehl argued that Germany's "primeval forests" gave the Germans a hardy and resourceful character, while Friedrich Ratzel believed Germans had "the nature of the forest interlaced with their entire being."[154] The movement to preserve forests combatted the social, cultural, and environmental consequences of industrialization, urbanization, and capitalism and fused ecological concerns with pre-modern cultural traditions. Ernst Rudorff, a writer and a composer, coined the term *Heimatschutz* and inveighed against the "prostitution of nature" and celebrated the capacity of the *Heimat* to "morally cleanse" with its "'ennobling' magic."[155] While often less acute than the versions discussed above, most arguments still favoured preservation of organic nature and inveighed against abstraction.

While the dualism in forestry discourse may seem distant from the crisis of the liberal form, function, and perception of urbanism, the two issues are closely related. Forests, on the one hand, were felled to create space and raw materials for new buildings, and, on the other hand, they were seen as a site of existential recreation and rehabilitation for urbanites. This dualistic approach to forests combined with the dualistic discourse of city planning. Paul Schultze-Naumburg, an architect, Greater Berlin Contest judge, and president of the Deutsche Bund Heimatschutz, attacked what he saw as an international pattern of rationality that corrupted German cultural and historical particularity. He warned that all of Germany would soon be converted into "proletarian suburbs whose buildings are in the style of a penitentiary."[156] Inexpensive access to green space, according to nationalists, protected against the metropolitan "Moloch."[157] The Oberbürgermeister of Berlin-Lichtenberg contended that green space could ameliorate urban social problems, but its absence created a somnambulism or narcolepsy and insufficient patriotism in the population.[158] Joseph August Lux, a Catholic modernist who sought to reintroduce the human soul into the modern world, regarded the houseplant as a symptom of "the longing for nature in the bleakness of this [urban] stone desert." He blamed these conditions on the profit motive, which preferred abstract, quantitative growth – which Lux associated with British utilitarianism – to the concrete, qualitative condition of that property and those who lived there.[159] Heinrich Pudor, an anti-Semitic activist, pioneering nudist, and critic of urban life, argued that without more green space the masses would "suffocate in the inextricable grid of houses and rental barracks," and cities would be "the mass graves of mankind."[160] Hermann Kötschke posited that "the octopus-like arms of a new colony of villas" in Grunwald blurred the "distinction of culture and barbarism."[161] This thinking was not limited to Germany, American lawmakers at a variety of levels sought to preserve natural environments and distribute the population in less density and over more territory.[162] The Socialist understandings of the forest were similarly dualistic. They opposed a spiritualized and abstract sense of culture, on the one hand, rather than a functionalist sense of the quotidian, on the other hand. Some Socialists defended Berlin's forests as essential for the recovery and recreation of Greater Berlin's working class and as the "lungs" of the metropolis.[163] Others, like Martin Wagner, were interested in the "use value" of green space for games or sports, roads or park promenades.[164]

A testament to the crisis of liberal ideology caused by early twentieth-century capitalism, liberals used categories such as inalienable rights to argue for a medieval form of forest, while conservative aristocrats defended modern concepts of private property.[165] This shift suggests an important change in the meaning of *liberalism* to the point where it nearly abandoned its central features. The defender of classical liberal ideas of real estate property as a commodity was the Prussian state – a state long associated with anti-liberal politics. The Prussian treasury, with management by the Ministry of Agriculture, owned much of the forest land around Berlin and held it as collateral for Prussian state debts. However, it managed the land as a monopoly on speculative real estate. In the 1890s Berlin administrators had offered twice to purchase Grunwald from the Prussian state, but the state was uninterested. The state rejected efforts by conservatives in the Landtag to preserve Grunwald, in response to the 200 hectares levelled since the 1870s, as a "primeval forest." In 1902 Wilhelm II offered to convert Grunwald to a *Volkspark*, but both conservatives and liberals balked, contending that such a conversion would diminish the forest's aesthetic power.[166] Their suspicion was justified when it surfaced that the Ministry of Agriculture wanted to sell 500 hectares for development. Liberals mobilized to defend Grunwald against this "forest slaughter" by land speculators. They tried to position themselves as defenders of the working-class interest while expressing frustration with the SPD for failing to rally to their side, despite the role that forest preservation played in anti-Socialist politics.[167] By 1907 Wilhelm II backed away from this promise, convinced by the Ministry of Agriculture to allow the land to accrue value and then sell it in small parcels.[168] The liberals were angry at the state for behaving like a real estate entrepreneur in a free market.

The struggle over forest preservation in the midst of this crisis of liberalism revealed the limitations of older liberal ideas of municipal self-administration and territory when confronted with regional problems. Before the passage of the Zweckverband law, the municipalities in Greater Berlin had begun a negotiation with the Crown ministries to preserve forest area around Berlin.[169] Indeed, part of the reason the state created the Zweckverband was to sell forest land.[170] A popular movement between 1904 and 1914 forced the state not to speculate on the forest land and instead to sell that land below market value.[171] On 11 June 1909 the Niederbarnim county board chairperson encouraged Oberbürgermeister Kirschner to create "an economically viable [forest] reservation," but Kirschner thought such a reservation was impossible without a regional administration. A large preserve would have meant forgoing future tax revenues, but he believed that more private development near the forests posed a danger to the environment of Greater Berlin.[172] In December 1909 local mayors issued a memorandum demonstrating that Berlin was nearly as dense as Paris and twice as dense as London.[173] Furthermore, its lack of green space threatened both physical and psychic public health.[174]

While liberal social forms structured ideas about the city, economics, and politics, actual liberals remained relatively weak in comparison to the conservatives in the Prussian state. The law assigned the new Zweckverband the task of creating a forest preserve for Greater Berlin through the purchase of state lands. At meetings to decide the fate of Greater Berlin's forests, interior and public works ministries, ambivalent proxies, represented the Zweckverband. Within the negotiations in the Prussian Ministry of State, the public works and the interior ministries were interested in employing forests to resolve housing problems and to mollify the anger of the working class by giving them access to green spaces. The agriculture and finance ministries did not want to concede anything to the urban left and wanted to retain the capital that was in the form of forest land, which was rapidly and speculatively increasing in value, in case the military needed it. The representative from the Ministry of State tried to stay above the fray and argued that "general interest" should be paramount in determining a price.[175]

In the end, those who sought to mollify the working class by creating access to forest land and expanding the land that could be developed for new working-class housing won the day. This type of concern about working-class radicalism and its mollification played an essential role in transforming classical liberalism into a new political and economic ideology. In 1915, in the midst of the First World War, the approach that focused on opposing working-class politics and hoarding capital in the form of land had faded. This decision represented part of a broader shift from direct confrontation with the Socialists to one that sought to incorporate the working class into national political and social life. The forests, they believed, could contribute to this incorporation.

Building Regulation Reforms

The crisis in the liberal mode of urbanism led those concerned with Greater Berlin's problems to place great significance on the built environment; housing conditions, in particular, preoccupied the discourse of city planning and municipal administration. However, despite its authority, the Zweckverband achieved little. The political conflicts of the day were focused on introducing small working-class homes into villa suburbs and on the jurisdiction of the various levels of building authorities and the enforcement of building codes.

Despite the perception that the form and function of housing was *the* key problem for the Zweckverband as liberals tried to address the changed urban geography of Greater Berlin, building regulation could not overcome the plutocratic character of local politics and the power of real-estate property owners. The prevailing building ordinances focused only on the relationship between buildings and the street, the depth of the buildings, the relative size of courtyards and airshafts, and the height of buildings relative to the street.[176] Local authorities could condemn or destroy buildings or expropriate an entire block if necessary.[177]

The limitations of liberal ideas about property and municipal self-administration constrained discussion to the relatively small issue of whether to change the legal code to allow working-class row houses, which were seen as more hygienic, in sparsely populated, wealthy areas, despite all the concern and meaning invested in housing. These measures were defeated.[178] Similarly, the discussion of building codes centred on small issues of enforcement. For example, in 1903 business owners complained that the same regulations addressed both suburban factories and housing, which resulted in cumbersome paperwork that supposedly held back innovations and safety measures in factories.[179] Similarly, in 1904 housing developers objected to the way that Prussian housing ordinances infringed on self-administration and inappropriately focused on maintaining land price and the Crown's land monopoly.[180] Finally, Socialists, in turn, objected to the developers' "unremitting agitation in the interest of the homeowners" against state-mandated improvements in housing conditions, which amounted to appeals to the "the freedom of the possessing classes to use the property-less masses according to their discretion."[181]

In all of these conflicts lay a broader contest over the territories of the state and the municipality as capitalism transformed the urban geography of Greater Berlin. In 1910 the chief of police for Berlin, Traugott von Jagow, rejected a request from municipal authorities to devolve individual branches of the state-run local police administration to Berlin, because he believed that was not in the national interest and would require new legislation. He thought municipal officials would act out of self-interest and transgress jurisdictions and building regulations.

The intensive industrialization and agglomeration of the region had made administration significantly more complex. He believed this was a problem that needed to be solved at a higher level of administration and enforced by an integrated jurisdiction for Greater Berlin.[182] Jagow expressed the need to create a new form of territory to deal with Greater Berlin, but he also believed that the local administrations could not be relied upon to act in the national interest and to uphold local laws. His appeal to the national interest and his defensive appeal to established law, as well as his concern that municipal officials would follow self-interested policies, in certain respects, reflected a positivist approach to legal questions.

This vision of a reterritorialized Greater Berlin adequate to a society that was pushing against the limits of liberal understandings of politics and economy came to fruition in Zweckverband law, but the Zweckverband passed up the authority to regulate housing. Socialists in the Zweckverband assembly believed that the assembly surrendered its regulative responsibility to property owners.[183] Ultimately, this reterritorialization project did result in some mild building reforms. On 19 February 1914 revisions to the building ordinances came into effect. The police authority remained solidly in the hands of the state, regulating all new, reconstructed, and expanded buildings. Local communities had a limited and circuitous path to contesting these rules.[184] The liberal constraints on municipal authority and defence of property relations meant that these mild reforms did little to alter the problem of housing or to facilitate renovation of housing properties.

Conclusion: Liberalism at its Limits

This chapter focused on two attempts to unify and to reterritorialize the Greater Berlin region to address the changing urban geography of the metropolitan region: the Greater Berlin City Planning Contest and the Greater Berlin Zweckverband. The contest and the related exhibition, billed as a great leap forward in planning, remained within the confines of the liberal city-planning ideology and pointed to new directions beyond liberal city planning. The chapter also focused on the creation of a Zweckverband to handle questions of forest preservation, mass transit, and building regulation, in both practice and ideology. In each area, political actors recognized that the liberal form of municipal organization was inadequate, yet remained within its ideological confines. In so doing, they revealed a path beyond liberalism and the continued power of liberal ideas. In terms of the philosophies connected with forests, mass transit, and housing, one sees a curious disjunction, again, between the abstract and the concrete dimensions of urban life.

As was the case in other contemporary discourses discussed so far – namely municipal administration, liberal jurisprudence, forest preservation, mass transportation, housing, and speculation – a formal similarity existed in the ideas of the city planners between the abstract, general, and calculable on the one hand and the concrete, particular, and ineffable on the other. This formal similarity between such disparate areas suggests that something structural was at work that could not be explained by the rational choices of individuals

Chapter Four

City Planning and Municipal Administration in Total War and Revolution

By sovereign edict, a state of war is declared for Berlin and the Province of Brandenburg. Executive authority is thus passed to me. With regard to this, I am hereby suspending articles 5, 6, 27, 28, 29, 30, and 36 of the Constitution of 31 January 1850 for the areas declared above to be in a state of war until further notice, and decree the following:

a) The civil and local authorities retain their functions but must obey my orders and instructions.

b) House searches and arrests may be undertaken at any time by the authorized agencies and state officials.

c) All aliens who are unable to give a proper account of the purpose of their sojourn must leave the area declared to be in a state of war within twenty-four hours when ordered by the local police.

d) The sale of arms, gunpowder, and explosives to civilians is forbidden. Civilians may carry arms only when specifically permitted to do so by myself or by the local police. Whoever does this without such permission will be immediately disarmed.

Commander in Chief Mark Brandenburg and
Governor of Berlin General von Kessel[1]

Introduction: Capitalism at a Crux

By 1914 the era of liberal city planning and municipal administration had reached a crisis as a result of the dynamics of liberal capitalism. The social conditions that made liberalism appealing and seem to comprehend the world so well in the middle of the nineteenth century were transformed over the next seventy years, undermining this liberal world view. The Greater Berlin Contest made an abstract and speculative attempt to think through the transformations in the built environment wrought by liberalism, and the Verband Groß-Berlin was a tentative and pragmatic effort to deal with these same questions through administrative measures. In both city planning and municipal administration, the conditions of the First World War and the November 1918 Revolution reconfigured the territory of Berlin beyond labels, scale, or jurisdiction. This reterritorialization was part of a broad cultural and ideological change in the perception of social space, which, in turn, was part of an even wider, international shift in the character of capitalism that altered not only processes of production and circulation but also the prevailing modes for understanding the world. The war and revolution were the crux points in a long-building transformation in the form, function, and perception of Greater Berlin. With the war, the liberalism that had structured the form, function, and perception of Greater Berlin gave way and, in its place, arose a corporatist set of social forms that structured Greater Berlin.

The change in capitalism had international consequences and permutations. Like Berlin, in London the desire to understand the modern industrial city, Lucy E. Hewitt argues, inspired a broad array of approaches and investigations. Urban scholars and reformers treated urban space as a foreign, dark, and uncharted territory. These studies focused on the environment of the slum and its impoverished and supposedly degenerate inhabitants. A similar discourse developed with regard to French cities.[2] London followed Berlin's example and developed a regional plan and government. As in Berlin, this London project was guided by two pressures: an expanded geographical imagination of the territory of a metropolis and civil society organizations.[3]

Before the First World War, in both municipal self-administration and city planning, the dominant ideology was liberal. It structured the form, function, and perception of Greater Berlin and celebrated the abstract, general, market-mediated, and constitutionalist. Dissenters criticized this liberalism from a position that emphasized the concrete, particular, collective, intimate, and unmediated human exchange. This chapter posits that under the pressures of war, and the opportunities of revolution, a new form of corporatist and producerist city planning and municipal administration emerged, part of a broader shift in the form of capitalism from one that was liberal to one that was corporatist.

In the long transformation from liberal social forms into corporatist ones that took place between 1871 and 1933, the First World War and the

November 1918 Revolution were crucial moments. To explore this shift, this chapter is divided into several sections, that explain: (1) how the First World War and the associated mobilization of society fundamentally transformed the relationships among the state, civil society, the economy, and the military, and consequently how this change altered how the urban region was understood and functioned; (2) how by replacing the market with administratively distributed commodities, German society, like other belligerent societies, took a significant step towards undermining the basis of liberal capitalism and establishing a post-liberal form of capitalism; (3) how the war and the new administrative distribution measures affected the perception of the city, asserting that a new ideology of city planning developed that sought to integrate the particular into a productive urban totality; (4) how the political-economic attempts to understand the war economy led to the widespread introduction of a command economy that facilitated a critique of liberal economics focused on its abstract features, including money, finance, and speculation; (5) how the revolution and the developing critique of abstraction in liberal economics played a prominent role in a new architectural and city-planning aesthetic that emphasized the concrete and the collective; (6) how a new system of welfare state intervention and regional administrative systems shaped assumptions about the scale and territory of Greater Berlin, decentralization, and the need for a single government; and (7) how the war and revolution made the creation of a single city out of Greater Berlin possible in a way that had never been imaginable.

The Integration of the State and the Economy

According to the self-understanding of liberals, the state and the economy, as well as the state and civil society, should be starkly separated. While this was not achieved in a practical sense, this ideal guided liberal political action. However, the war and the associated mobilization reconfigured the relationships among the state, civil society, and the economy. Increasingly the state orchestrated civil society and the economy, accentuating the ongoing social shift away from liberal social forms into ones that were more corporate. The way that the military functioned in the war was laid down, to a certain degree, in the Kaiserreich. Although the military needed a rationalized administrative structure, the new role of the military only made administration more complex. The wartime military dictatorship reconstituted the municipal structure of Berlin and transformed its economic structure.

With the declaration of war and the mobilization of the Reich, the relationships among the state, civil society, and the economy began to change, constituting an increasingly corporatist society, with the state – in particular, the military – gaining increasing control over civil society and the economy. In May 1914 the Reich minister of the interior, Clemens von Delbrück, worried that the market could not provide the necessary raw materials and food in the event of a war and suggested that ministers, bureaucrats, and business people gather to discuss the possibility that a war might engender significant economic dislocation, necessitating plans to stockpile food and to manage its distribution.[4] In Britain, anticipating a short conflict, the state took a hands-off approach to the economy; however, by March 1915 the government had brokered a deal that restrained profit margins for industrial employers in exchange for weakened unions and wage restraint. The government was responding to the needs of the war and also to politicized public discourse about profiteers and the first step in Britain "toward a total war economy"; by 1918, the state controlled more than two-thirds of the British economy.[5] The war produced the expansion of state controls over realms that in liberal periods had been left to the logic of the market economy: production, distribution, and consumption. The state came to agreements with representatives of the workers' movement and labour unions, and it gained the right to control speech, in negative ways, through the suppression of dissent, and in positive ways through the propaganda that built enthusiasm for the war.[6]

Soon the demands of this new conflict began to transform German society towards a more corporatist governmental structure and undermine the foundations of liberalism. The Reichstag, elected by universal male suffrage, represented the only parliamentary structure within the Reich. But it had limited power over military affairs: every five to seven years it voted to approve the military budget, as it did on 4 August 1914. The Law of Siege was enacted in 1851 as part of the reaction to the Revolution of 1848.[7] With the Law of Siege, which declared martial law domestically and prepared for war internationally, the Bundesrat took legislative power from the Reichstag and focused on mobilizing the economy. The Prussian Ministry of War, while legally equivalent to similar ministries in the other states, functioned as the Reich institution charged with economic mobilization.[8] The declaration of martial law and of the "fortress peace" vastly expanded the associated administrative structures. The Kaiser took the title "supreme warlord," but this position had no basis in the constitutions of 1867 or 1871 or in the treaties with the other German kingdoms. It was a personal oath of allegiance from the officers and soldiers that granted this authority. Under the Kaiser were forty generals and eight admirals, all of whom could approach him directly and go over the heads of their commanders. Just below the Kaiser were the commanding generals of the twenty-five military districts. They could suppress civil unrest, censor mail and newspapers, regulate transportation and communication, and police the courts.[9] This chain of command created a military dictatorship, led by the Kaiser, as the commander-in-chief, and not subject to parliamentary oversight. Under the Law of Siege, the only limit to the military's power to command was the commander's personal judgment. The Law of Siege granted the military commander "direct control over the administration in his geographical area of jurisdiction" and the right to suspend the basic rights of the Prussian constitution.[10] On 31 July 1914 the Kaiser declared martial law, and the next day military governors commandeered the railroads, warehouses, and local government offices for the military.[11] Upon declaration of martial law, local authority passed to the commanders in each military district. The commanders, who were at the front, in turn, devolved authority to the deputy commanders. These deputies had nearly dictatorial power over civilian and military life, including transportation, censorship, and public order, as well as recruitment, training, logistical support, and deployment of the troops.[12]

The Law of Siege reconstituted the former liberal bulwark of liberal form, function, and perception of Greater Berlin: municipal organization. In a peaceful and more liberal time, the Berlin Polizeipräsidium, the largest and most powerful in the Reich, and its Polizeipräsident were directly subordinate to the Prussian Ministry of the Interior and Reich authorities, with the Polizeipräsident acting both as president of the district of Berlin and as the chief of police. With the start of the war, the Kaiser bolstered, enlarged, and militarized the Polizeipräsident's position and made him report directly to the high commander of the Mark. The police acted as soldiers enforcing the "fortress peace" on the domestic front. Gustav von Kessel, the high commander of the Mark and Präsident of the district of Berlin, reported only to the Kaiser and to the Oberpräsident of Brandenburg. He and the chief of police, Traugott von Jagow, shared control of the city with Oberbürgermeister Adolf Wermuth, who was also directly subordinate to the Kaiser and to the Oberpräsident. Belinda Davis argues that while the state focused on mobilizing the society and projecting an aura of order on Berlin, war industries further proletarianized the city. This social change troubled the authorities because of the easy interaction between garrisoned soldiers and radicalized civilians.[13] The state had to balance the conditions of the working class, whose labour and whose role as soldiers were necessary to win the war, with the potential for working-class radicalization.

The funding of the German war effort altered state finances, shifting the relationship between the state and society from a liberal one and into a corporatist one. Unlike the British, the Germans did not have access to international, especially American, capital, and they could not raise taxes on an already burdened population. The Reich budget, even for non-military areas, relied on deficit spending, and tax revenues paid only the interest on German loans. The war bonds were oversubscribed at the beginning of the war, but by the fall of 1916, the fifth war loan was under-subscribed by about 1.4 million subscribers. This inflationary policy redirected capital flows from private investment into military production.[14] Germany mobilized inflationary spending but did not adjust wages, and consequently wages decreased relative to living expenses, and the price controls were ineffective. However, those with private debts could more easily service them. With a decline in real wages and salaries, reduced end-point consumption meant that the state and industrialists could invest more capital in war production.[15]

This war-accelerated transformation from a liberal to a corporatist form, function, and perception of Greater Berlin changed the economy of cities like Berlin. As Maureen Healy argues about Vienna, for Berliners, social conditions shaped their relationship to the Kaiserreich.[16] Before 1914, German war planners were prepared for rapid mobilization, including 800,000 men. Within two weeks of the declaration of war, the military absorbed more than 2 million civilians and put 1.5 million at the front. By January 1915, 4,357,934 men were in the military, of whom 2,618,158 were at the front.[17] This outflow of the population (industrial employment fell by nearly 24 per cent) made unemployment rise from roughly 6 per cent to more than 19 per cent as the owners closed their doors, fired their employees, and enlisted. Conditions were particularly dire in businesses not related to the war effort, like the textile, furniture, and tanning works concentrated in southeastern Greater Berlin. In addition, the military commandeered much of the transit infrastructure, disconnecting workers from their employment and leaving factories without coal and other key raw materials.[18] However, unemployment was short-lived, and by January 1915, men found employment at rates higher than pre-war levels. Female unemployment had peaked in October 1914 but did not recover as rapidly.[19] Skilled labour became scarce, and one key concern of military planners was balancing the military's need for bodies and the competition between employers for workers. Germany put about two-thirds of the 1.6 million prisoners of war it captured to work, especially those from Poland, and women increasingly were drawn into war industries.[20] Cities in the Ottoman Empire saw a similar re-gendering of the workforce that entailed many women working for the first time – often for long hours and at low pay – and significant impoverishment.[21]

War-related shortages in labour and raw materials forced the state to break from liberal norms and to intervene in the economy. By the spring of 1915 the extreme shortages in raw materials, food, and labour that would characterize the rest of the war had set in. Both male and female workers moved into heavy industry, particularly machine, metal, and chemical works, with male employment increasing by 36 per cent and female by 50 per cent in these sectors after June 1914.[22] The military conscripted many labourers and often ignored local economic needs. As Matthias Blum argues, "Neither German society nor Germany's production capacities were prepared for a modern war: the German supply of food and military equipment was insufficient."[23] The economy stabilized in the winter, though with decreased productivity, despite a 20 per cent increase in hours worked.[24] Foodstuffs such as flour and potatoes were also in short supply in the fall of 1914.[25] By late fall 1916 Germany radically increased munitions production in a short period, seeking to harmonize the home front with the needs of the war. On 28 August 1916 the Kaiser promoted Paul von Hindenberg and Erich Ludendorff to the chief of the General Staff and first quartermaster general, respectively. Their "Hindenburg Plan," introduced through the 5 December 1916 Auxiliary Service Law, ordered this increase in munitions production without consideration of available resources, either economic or human.[26]

Further shortages in raw materials pushed the state to expand its intervention in the economy. The war and the North Sea blockade affected German food supplies, preventing the flow of food, fertilizer, labour, and animal feed, and taking away roughly 40 per cent of the male labour force, horses, and cattle in the agricultural industry in Germany. These conditions of shortage further reduced agricultural output because of malnourished and unmotivated workers and, between 1913 and 1919, agricultural production was halved, leading to speculation, corruption, and hoarding. Beginning in 1916 officials attempted to counteract this situation with price ceilings and rationing. In turn, black markets developed for food, through which roughly half of all foodstuffs that were produced exchanged hands. The legal rations supported 50 to 60 per cent of the needs of an adult, and by 1916–17 the ration fell to 1,000 calories a day and led to average adult weight loss of 20 per cent.[27] The blockade entailed a more than 80 per cent reduction in protein foods by October 1918, with famine persisting in urban industrial regions.[28] Before 1914 Germany had been the world's largest importer of agricultural products, comprising about 38 per cent of all German imports.[29] In Paris, French citizens were generally able to secure the food they needed, though prices rose significantly. The government did not immediately place price controls on foods, as it did on rent, but by the end of the war the government strongly regulated most food. As Tyler Stovall notes with respect to Paris, "The study of food thus best illustrates the transition from the liberal to the interventionist state in consumer affairs."[30] Maureen Healy describes a similar introduction of a new role for the state in what had been liberal spheres, like the market.[31]

The drive to rationalize government was coupled with dramatic reductions in the available funds and raw materials for non-military governmental concerns. By early 1915 in Germany, the shortages in materials, labour power, and tax revenues significantly constrained municipal budgets. Berlin's Bürgermeister Georg Reicke was forced to demand spending cuts in all city government departments. In February the Berlin structural engineering department froze all building beyond what was necessary.[32] In July, during the 1916 budget process, Reicke explained to the city departments that they should "observe the largest self-restraint and most scrupulous care," during the war and its immediate aftermath, because of the value of money on the money markets and the significant demands on the economy after the war.[33] In 1916 the municipalities shouldered a growing burden of the cost of war-relief funding and consequently demanded that the state or Reich either support or take over this responsibility, ceding a part of their self-administration. On 11 February 1916, Berlin Oberbürgermeister Adolf Wermuth complained to the Oberpräsident about Berlin's war-related costs, which totalled 60 million M per quarter on the one hand and increased interest rates on the other.[34] The duration of the war was making it difficult for leftist parties to pass budgets that responded to war-related forms of poverty.[35] By April 1916 Wermuth, as representative of the Städtetag, wrote to the Reich chancellor that the length of the war convinced urban districts that the Reich would cover their municipal expenditures in the name of social peace.[36] Wermuth's plea convinced the state to reimburse the cities and their citizens for the expenses associated with quartering soldiers.[37] As Belinda Davis has noted, the Städtetag had once exemplified the strength of German cities, but now it employed that power to call for national coordination of food distribution and to decry the ability of local administrations' ability to address the problems.[38] The Bürgerbund Groß-Berlin, a group that once would have defended the self-administration of the (richer) suburbs, presented to Greater Berlin communal officials the Bürgerbund's vision for the city, which recognized that "a uniformity of the interests of the population of Greater Berlin" had recently overcome "splintered" municipal self-interests.[39] This war-related fiscal state of affairs led formerly self-administering municipalities to seek out state and Reich intervention.

The Rise of Planning

One of the key changes in the shift from liberal social forms to corporatist ones was the transformation in attitudes towards the market and the rise of economic planning. While the right wing had long disliked the market for the ways that it levelled society and erased feudal privileges and responsibilities, now it disapproved because it regarded the market as inefficient for the needs of the war. Almost as soon as the war began, the conservative state and the military intervened to make the market more efficient for their purposes. This was a key step in a long process of constituting a new form of capitalism that would be less dependent on the market and private property and created an integrated, goal-directed society.

The rise of form, functions, and perceptions of urbanism structured by corporatism included a shift away from the market and towards planning. Desires for efficiency shifted the social perception of the market, a central institution in liberalism. The Left had long argued that the market and private property were constraints on the possibilities of human freedom, but during the war, the right wing, too, attacked the market for being inefficient and inhibiting war production. The war-related shortages, increased prices, and inadequate reimbursement made city governments desire better distribution of commodities and inspired a sense that the market was inadequate to deal with the problems the war presented. These economic and administrative conditions pressured the municipality, the state, and the Reich into further integration, and, according to Roger Chickering, to meet the needs of the military emergency, the state needed to alter the market because it was too slow to react to fluctuating conditions. The solution for the military planners was the introduction of collectivistic measures such as administrative compulsion of a "command economy."[40] This pressure to administer state aid efficiently created a need to plan a regional economy of scale in aid distribution through an administrative integration of Greater Berlin.

Wartime state administration of the economy turned the government away from the liberal division between the state and the economy when the war began. In August 1914 the government gathered food, and bills passed on 2 August of that year empowered the local administrations to set upper limits on prices.[41] Wermuth asked Delbrück to institute a national food-distribution system in the fall of 1914, but it was Georg Michaelis in the Prussian finance ministry who initiated the War Grain Society in November 1914, which stockpiled enough grain for urban Prussia to last through the 1915 harvest. In January 1915 the War Grain Society became a national grain monopoly, and in February major cities established grain-rationing systems. In 1914 Wichard von Moellendorff and Walther Rathenau, both of AEG, successfully pressured the state to found the War Raw Materials Division. They envisioned this division as superseding the traditional wartime rationing to establish a centrally planned industrial economy.[42] Like his French counterpart, the Socialist Albert Thomas, Rathenau combined socialistic elements with a capitalism that catered to the needs of large businesses.[43] This new planning strategy challenged liberal dichotomies between public and private and between state and society.[44]

The war and the demands that it placed on capitalist social relations completed a longer-term process of reconstituting capitalism from a social system organized by liberal social forms to one organized by corporatist social forms. Between the outbreak of war and the introduction of the Hindenburg Plan in late 1916, liberal institutions like the market, civil society, and municipal self-administration became tenuous. The cities that had once prized their self-administration and celebrated the market, by October of 1916 demanded the "centralized control" of food provisioning to ensure "fair" and "equitable" access to food.[45] As Joseph Bloch, the long-time editor of the *Sozialistische Monatshefte,* saw it in 1914, the war "brought about the unification of the German people" and "interrupted" the class struggle, replacing it with an interclass solidarity in defence of the national totality.[46] By 1916, as Leopold von Wiese argued, a liberal society in which the welfare of the society at large was determined by the activity of the affiliated individuals was fading, while a society wherein the unified whole took precedence over the individual was taking its place.[47]

The government attempted to reduce inefficiencies in the housing market by introducing more administrative measures and planning, especially in large cities with substantial military contingents, like Berlin. The existing barracks were insufficient, so the military decreed that businesses and households had to quarter soldiers stationed in or passing through Berlin.[48] The responsibility for providing the soldier with food varied according to the particular soldier, but reimbursement to municipalities was a point of contention.[49] The city of Berlin sought bureaucratic means to reclaim funds it spent on quartering soldiers and other social services.[50] In September 1915 Wermuth was thankful for the 310 million M in support from the Ministry of the Interior to Berlin, but he argued that this support was waning as demand continued to increase.[51] The Oberpräsident of Brandenburg assured Wermuth that the state would reimburse Berlin for 45 per cent of its 14,201,223 M expenditure.[52] On 1 May 1916 the Kaiser disbursed an additional 200 million M to municipal governments.[53] In August 1916 the Department for the People's Provisioning in the Berlin Magistrat established "necessary," rational, and economical public kitchens. The municipalities shouldered much of the cost, though the Reich and the state would partially reimburse the municipalities.[54] With the goal of promoting military production, the Reich, the state, and the municipal government interceded into commodity distribution. Maureen Healy presents the failure of the Austrian state to adequately provision Vienna as evidence of poor governance, but this responsibility to provision the population was at most five years old. Healy does not sufficiently acknowledge the extent to which the war changed the state and its responsibilities.[55]

City Planning in Wartime

The shift in the form, function, and perception of Greater Berlin from ones structured by liberalism to ones by corporatism changed the goal of city planning from creating the spatial conditions of possibility for the flourishing of the individual to integration of the particular individual, building, or neighbourhood into the social totality, and the war accelerated and accentuated that change. Planners, in this new corporatist form, function, and perception of Greater Berlin, commonly proposed to address the urban environment by decentralizing the city. Rationalization and the reduction of building costs would enable this decentralization, and a new aesthetic developed that accentuated these rationalized modes of production and criticized ornamentation. Planners connected ornamentation to self-interested and unproductive forms of profit-taking, such as speculation.

In the later years of the war, the scale of the planning and the concern for overcoming shortage through coordinated and productive spatial relations became central interests. Planners believed it was necessary to make cities suitable to the newly found social solidarity.[56] Martin Wagner argued that the municipality needed to bring together structural engineering, underground engineering, building police, housing inspection, and settlement offices into "a single organism," and create a corresponding university curriculum.[57] A similar spirit affected architecture: Bruno Taut argued that Berlin's new opera house revealed that "in all levels of our civilization … the productive, progressive element" was being realized in new architecture so that "the individual was subordinated to a greater community" and the building became a "living organism" of the city.[58] For Felix Linke, an engineer from Charlottenburg, modern architecture combined this subordination of the individual to the social totality, with a faith that charismatic individuals could make society "bow to the power of brilliant invention and the objective awareness of the builder."[59] While this shift to a more integrative vision of the role of the architect, the building itself, and the urban society within which it was located took place over roughly twenty years, nonetheless the conditions of the world war significantly accelerated and deepened this transformation.

The pressure of the war conditions on the state to reterritorialize the jurisdictions of Greater Berlin made it possible for the state to change regional housing laws such that they surmounted local legal particularities and to facilitate suburban housing for the working class. On 1 December 1916 Minister of Public Works Breitenbach introduced a new housing law to the Haus der Abgeordneten, but the representatives did not read it before both houses of the Landtag until 15 January 1918.[60] In the Ministry of Public Works, architects and building bureaucrats met to discuss a single building code for Greater Berlin, including the distribution of industry, merchant, and housing structures, as well as smaller-scale regulations of the building itself.[61] Despite the reduced population and the state involvement, more than 24,000 apartments in Greater Berlin still had no heat, and this fed the disenchantment with the Zweckverband.[62] On 28 March 1918 the new housing law came into force.[63] While the Architects Committee for Greater Berlin praised these reforms, they thought that the Zweckverband for Greater Berlin could not "naturally" form an "organic whole."[64] There was an increasing sense that unification was necessary, but the Zweckverband was insufficient. London was undergoing a similar transformation at the same time, as increasingly planners considered the urban area through a regional lens.[65] On 12 May 1917 local authorities discussed creating a single building code for Greater Berlin.[66] Fritz Beuster regarded this reform as a "pleasing" consequence of the war. Furthermore, the conditions of the war economy and martial law in Greater Berlin meant that the Zweckverband could more effectively enforce building laws.[67] The Polizeipräsident requested guidance from the minister of public works on Beuster's proposal, despite opposition from local authorities that wanted to maintain existing codes to preserve local historical particularity.[68] While in the past this appeal to local particularity could thwart unification efforts, the conditions of the war had changed the state's position, and this appeal to liberal values of municipal self-administration had lost its purchase with the state.

In the corporatist form, function, and perception of city planning, the most common solution offered to these problems of the urban environment created by liberal city planning was to decentralize the city. Right-wing Socialists pressed planners to "separate the smoke and noise-filled large-scale industry quarters from the residential districts" and create "purely industrial" quarters, where building height did not "totally cut off the city from the fresh air." They believed this spatial arrangement would allow people to "convalesce" from the physical and psychic experience of the war.[69] The architect Hans Schliepmann noted that a "purely socialist state" would mean "exodus of industry from the cities" and improved working conditions.[70] Bruno Taut wrote that such a change was an essential requirement for the peaceful unification of all people and elimination of poverty.[71] Conventional wisdom held that the existing housing stock "cooped-up with the healthy, in culturally depraved and immoral disorder," and new housing was necessary to bring back population growth.[72] However, housing in Berlin was not much different from housing in Paris, where, though residents paid less, it was older, smaller, and in poorer condition than housing in comparable cities.[73]

Planners believed that this decentralization project demanded lowering costs by bringing the rationality of the factory to the construction industry. As SPD member Friedrich Wilhelm Sollman wrote, in order to control rents, it was "necessary to pull all indices of the construction costs, reducing them as far as can be made to coincide with the basic composition of work-efficiency work and the protection of lives and health."[74] Peter Behrens and Heinrich de Fries argued that new housing should release "the working masses from the painful inadequacy of the dwellings of the large cities" and provide workers space for gardening, roomy living quarters, and plenty of light. Making such housing fiscally possible, they believed, necessitated a thoroughgoing industrialization of building parts.[75] Furthermore, they supported the notion that experts needed to scientifically analyse the bodily practice of the construction worker, breaking it down into individual movements and reassembling it, to reduce muscle strain with the Taylor system. With this knowledge, they thought, the contractor could "attain a more intense exploitation of the human labour power and a reduction of the labour time." With the Taylor system, "the bricks of the wall builder are not cast to the scaffold, rather they are at the height of the layer so that they can be shifted straight so that he only needs to move it horizontally." This change enabled the worker to "work with both hands symmetrically" so that "the left hand presses the brick into a pre-made mortar bed, while the right hand at the same time and in similar motion spreads the bed for the next stone." The experts believed that "scientific management [of labour] could contribute very substantially to reducing in price the construction of small flats."[76] The war and its technological means created the conditions of possibility to see society as a massive human machine.[77] The state created the Advisory Council for City Planning and an Urban Settlement Policy, which pursued cost and production time reduction through prefabrication and typification of housing products.[78] In 1920 Paul Schmitthenner, an architect and city planner who played a prominent role in architecture during the National Socialist period, claimed, "The economic emergency will be equally coercive for all," which meant "building more cheaply but without degradation in handiwork, hygiene, or technique and with more discipline."[79] He characterized typification as the "universal remedy for cheaper building" and declared that a strict limit on unique parts and the manufacture of a few versatile pieces could lead to unexpected savings.[80]

This emphasis on efficiency in the new corporatist form, function, and perception of cities extended beyond changes to the labour process and density, to include architectural aesthetics. The mass production of housing transformed building aesthetics to emphasize the totality, cohesion, and stripping down of buildings to their productive essence. Martin Wagner argued that this social and aesthetic transformation "undressed" the structure, exposing the mode of building to the layman.[81] Historians of American city planning in this same period emphasized a shift from the "City Beautiful" to the "City Practical" paradigm. However, as Robert Freestone argues, historians exaggerated this dichotomy between the beautiful and the practical. What this literature misses is that internationally, the meaning of "the beautiful" had changed. Functionalism arose as an aesthetic as part of an overt populist or social democratic political critique of the interests that "City Beautiful" served, but also as an imminent response to the development of the modern city.[82]

In this new corporatist form, function, and perception of urbanism, housing production and speculation became key parts of a political critique of urban space. City planning discourse regarded speculation as detrimental to the housing stock and thereby to public health, social politics, financial stability, and population growth. Hans Schliepmann hoped that speculation was "dead once and for all," because it forced the "shameful" question: "How do I use a property until it is bled white, how do I pay interest on my money for me alone in the most advantageous way?"[83] Right-wing Socialists offered a similar discourse, celebrating concrete productivity and criticizing abstract profit making.[84] This aesthetic attacked speculation in urban real estate as an especially destructive, abstract, and unproductive mode of profit taking. The view celebrated concrete technical productive capacity. In this new ideology of productivity, fused with a theory that sought to decentralize the city and increase access to nature, one finds celebrations of both technology and organicism in the same work.

A long transition from liberal to corporatist social forms structured the form, function, and perception of Greater Berlin. City planning was drawn into this transformation, and the war accelerated and accentuated that change. Planning, in this new era, sought to integrate the particular into a socially productive totality. As the war progressed, the territory of planning now included coordinating productive spatial relations.

The Political Economic Explanations of the War Economy

The shift from a liberal to a corporate set of social forms shaped not just ideas about municipal administration, architecture, and city planning, it changed the understanding of political economy. Within the political economic discourse about the war economy, a consensus developed that the era of liberal economics had ended. The shift from market-distributed commodities to administratively distributed commodities also created a new understanding of the territory of Berlin and promoted regional thinking. While the state had removed market and private property from their central positions in the war economy, capitalism remained, which inspired political economists to ask what exactly capitalism was. This new social order revealed that the market was not essential to capitalism, which gave rise to a desire to remove money and other similarly abstract and financial elements of capitalism.

Political economists commonly argued that the war had ended a period of liberal economics. As Edgar Jaffé explained, the First World War meant "a complete shift of virtually all previous conditions of life," one in which the population "gains a new, unified view," becoming a "cohesive unit, ... what it should be."[85] Jaffé was an editor with the *Archiv für Sozialwissenschaft*, an assimilated Jew, and a participant in the Bavarian Revolution of 1918–19.[86] Paul Lensch argued that the war had integrated the interests of German society, and protective tariffs had already "broken the backbone of the old liberalism by the elimination of free competition." Lensch was a proponent of anti-revisionist orthodoxy in the SPD and an opponent of war bonds in 1914, though he came to support them in 1915 for what he saw as Marxist reasons.[87]

Increasingly the political Left, Right, and Centre attacked liberal concepts of the individual. Those individuals who profited from the irrationalities of the market, seemingly at the expense of the totality, were the objects of scrutiny. According to Julius Hirsch, the war and the British blockade had "radically transformed" the structure of that economy: overseas supplies became scarce, and the army sucked up labour power, lowering domestic production and contributing to the rise in prices. Hirsch claimed that food prices escalated further as the result of speculative hoarding, making price no longer a "reliable regulator of economic life" and generating a "false economy" in which a small group "controlled too much of the nation's wealth."[88] For Karl Thieß the profit motive no longer "automatically steered" commodity distribution; rather, monopolized production meant that commands, quotas, and deadlines played a greater role.[89] And for August Skalweit, who in 1933 was driven from his position as rector of Christian Albrechts-Universität in Kiel because he was Jewish and was critical of the new Nazi state, the "private economy" was inefficient and "inevitably" led to high prices.[90] The war had crystallized a new political-economic structure that inverted the classical liberal understanding of the effect of monopoly and the free market: the former led to rational prices and the latter to irrationally high prices.

Breaking with the division in liberal dogma between the state and the economy, the state interceded in the market to manage food distribution. This management of distribution created regional bureaucracies, which concretized the concept of territory in Greater Berlin and made a unified Greater Berlin practical and possible. In October 1917, seeking funds equal to those of Berlin and Charlottenburg, the Berlin-Wilmersdorf Magistrat proposed a more efficient unified form of distribution.[91] Regional municipal authorities determined regionwide rations of barley, semolina, pasta, and other basics distributed to workplaces, with a single bread card to standardize food expenditure in Greater Berlin. On 21 January 1918 the Greater Berlin Provisioning Association, governed by a committee with equal numbers of workers and employers, absorbed the other provisioning organizations and expanded its reach to include all of Teltow and Niederbarnim.[92] To unify services for Greater Berlin, the Berlin Magistrat established the Department of Egg Provisioning on 22 January; the Grocery Necessities Association, on 4 February; and an office of ersatz coffee on 16 February.[93] In March 1918 the chair of the State Distribution Office told his colleagues in the Grocery Necessities Association of Greater Berlin that to counteract the black market in factories and to facilitate the ability to work and a positive work atmosphere, roughly 500,000 armaments workers in Greater Berlin would be granted extra food, as determined by their bosses.[94] Corporations wanting to secure their workers to their jobs needed to include those workers' names on an armament workers protection list, and after 12 March, each week they needed to report the workers' numbers and identities to the state distribution office, which then gave out the necessary grocery provisions. The state created individual auxiliary food-support distribution services (eggs, fat, bread, meat, etc.) and centralized their administration for all of Greater Berlin.[95]

Political economists questioned liberal assumptions about the centrality of the market and private property to a capitalist economy as the war economy phased them out; yet capitalism seemed to endure. For example, Otto Neurath, who was a prominent figure in a few intellectual spheres, including the Vienna Circle of logical positivists, modernist architecture, and social housing, and a reform-minded Socialist, argued that a "state-managed in-kind economy was set up on a large scale," because the pre-war "monetary economy" could not meet the new requirements. Neurath argued that the change in focus of political economy from money and finance to production and distribution made him wonder why political economists accepted what he regarded as the consequences of the "monetary economy," which were "limitations on production, mass unemployment, emigration, as some kind of fate." Factories were closed to increase "monetary income," but, in the war economy, they were closed in order to be repurposed to produce something more important to social needs.[96] Exchanges based on utility, he believed, would overcome the irrationalities of the market economy.[97] He thought that this moneyless system eliminated abstract, quantitative, exchange-value-oriented relations, replacing them with concrete, qualitative, use-value-determined relations.[98]

The ideological change in the attitude towards money played a significant role in the formation of a new corporatist form, function, and perception of urbanism and of Berlin. In city planning discourse, a critique of money as a mediator of economic life and a celebration of a new social cohesion similar to Neurath's critique flourished. Unlike in the "mammonist" and "soulless" form of exchange between the country and the city in other nations, architect Franz Steinbrucker believed that Germans uniquely and organically united the rural and the urban.[99] Architect Hans Schliepmann thought that a German victory would mean "the utter destruction of the arch enemy of all the peaceful development of all civilized nations[:] … England, the stronghold of Mammon." In his view, architects needed to move from self-indulgent, profit-focused, and vacuous activities towards a heroic fusion of the people and the state and a communal feeling of participating in "the great birth pangs of a greater Germany." Schliepmann, however, worried that "an economic frenzy" in which Germans would "dance around the golden calf until an [economic] crash" would follow "the wonderful ethos of this period of struggle." Rather, he suggested, architecture needed to prevent this by overcoming "ruthless speculation" through cooperation between employers and employees.[100] In this ideology of planning, a cohesive, productive, eternal, and concrete community is set against a selfish, abstract, ephemeral, and monetary enemy, and the same rootlessness and concern for ephemeral monetary gain that is ontologically connected here to the British poses the threat of infecting and corrupting "Greater Germany." The Socialist Heinrich Peus regarded the war as essentially capitalist, but also an anomaly in the progress towards socialism. Nonetheless, he believed that "individualistic private capitalism" had collapsed during the war.[101] As Pierre Purseigle notes, an opposition between participant and victim shaped the perception of social roles in the war mobilization.[102] The differentiating feature was whether the individual provided what was considered productive labour. In Austria-Hungary and in Germany, the soldiers' wives who received a stipend were seen as squandering government funds and profiting from their husband's sacrifice and from the war.[103] In Parisian discourse, struggle and war were used to describe the challenge of procuring consumer goods. Access to consumer goods became a site of conflict, with arguments about speculators, "monopolist rich, bourgeois wastefulness, the luxurious habits of workers in war industries, and the venality of both landlords and tenants."[104]

The Revolution in Architecture and City Planning

The November 1918 Revolution in Germany transformed the aesthetics and self-understanding of architects, encouraging them to find the meaning of their work through the collective and through the revolution. This political and social rupture made manifest a new corporatist aesthetic that was latent in the liberal era. This aesthetic could be progressive, but it could also fuse revolutionary rhetoric with reactionary and romantic politics that blamed abstract and unproductive social forms for the current problems with society.

As the radical Left began to publicly press its critique of the war, the state, and the right-wing Social Democrats, many of the most important meetings, discussions, and protests occurred in the streets, bars, homes, and assembly halls of Greater Berlin. The revolution affected the politics of city government, bringing to power a reformist city council and state government and a competing form of government in the Workers' and Soldiers' Council. This dichotomy had consequences for the debates about the creation of a single city out of Greater Berlin. However, the particular details of the revolution are beyond the purview of this book. The revolution represented a potentially world-historical break in the basic forms of social relations. To some this was a hopeful development; to others it was terrifying. A new corporatist society took shape, built on agreements between collectives and on a goal of social cohesion. The revolution, as Franz Neumann observed, made the concerns and politics of the working classes and class conflict impossible to ignore. The Weimar constitution attempted to both acknowledge this conflict and to incorporate it, peacefully, into the structure of the state. Within liberalism, the social form of the contract legalized the ability of individuals or firms to agree to the terms of an exchange. In the corporatist capitalism that was taking shape, the contract as a social form remained, but it recognized two social groups, two institutions, coming to an agreement. For Neumann, the Weimar Republic was founded on five of these new corporate contracts: "The contract between [Friedrich] Ebert [the right-wing Social Democrat serving as chancellor], on the one hand, and [generals] Hindenburg and Groener, on the other hand," provided "for the re-establishment of 'peace and order,' and for the fight against Bolshevism." The "Stinnes-Legien Agreement" addressed the same problems by forcing "employers [to] promise not to tolerate 'yellow' labour unions and to recognize only independent unions, to cooperate with them, and to fix working conditions by means of wage contracts," forcing unions to reject politics that extended beyond wages and working conditions. On 4 March 1919 the Berlin SPD and the Reich incorporated factory councils into the state apparatus, separating them from the revolutionary Workers' and Soldiers' Councils. A 26 January 1920 agreement between the Reich and the federal states preserved the Reich's federal character, and, finally, the Centre, Socialist, and Democratic parties "preserved the bureaucracy and judiciary; rejected the Soviet system; stabilized the political power of the church; sanctioned civil liberties, even though they were somewhat restricted by new social fundamental rights; and introduced parliamentary democracy." Each of these agreements was not a contract between legal individuals but between social groups or institutions, and this new system "attempted rather to transform [class struggle] into a form of inter-class co-operation."[105] The success of overthrowing the Kaiserreich and establishing a reform-oriented democratic republic, and the failure to overthrow capitalism in Germany, with all its global implications, contributed significantly to the particular corporatist form of society in the Weimar Republic. This duality of a hope deferred or denied, and of a new corporatist society, were consequences of long-term developments in German society and of a new form of government.

For many in the architectural and city-planning community, the revolution solidified a progressive version of the new corporate vision of urban life and made a unity of humanity real. Most architects believed that this new unity of humanity would be achieved through the integration of all individuals into a collective project. On 24 December 1918 members of the newly formed Working Council for Art attacked what they saw as a false division of labour in the arts and proclaimed that the arts should be unified "under the wing of a new architecture," which was the "immediate carrier of the mental power, shaper of the feelings of the whole." They used explicitly utopian ideas to expand the German populace's vision of a better future.[106] The members claimed that the architect's freedom was "not expressed in the arbitrary and illusory freedom of the individual" but through the collective.[107] They rejected the creation of minimal apartments, referring to them as "caves and cells, mass quarters and man stables," because in creating them they were "only tools of the profiteers and exploiters."[108] Instead, this vision of a new architecture and city planning placed both aesthetics and pragmatics at the centre of a new, more humane world.

The political stakes of this change in social forms from liberal to corporatist were still relatively fluid. Some contemporary discourses blended left-leaning ideas with ideas that were reactionary. Within one branch of architectural and city-planning discourse, a revolutionary romanticism attacked individuals engaged in businesses that appeared abstract and unproductive, such as speculators, believing that these individuals constrained the creative, productive generality – nation, race, class, and society. Landscape architect Leberecht Migge, for example, who collaborated with many modernist and left-leaning architects, such as Ernst May, Bruno Taut, and Martin Wagner, argued that the central idea of the nineteenth century was the city, but the city was dead. Its industry, technology, position in global trade, wealth, pleasures, misery, and lifelessness were all gone, along with cargo ships, factories, raw materials, finance, and credit. However, he claimed, the central idea of the twentieth century would be the land, and it would save the city through autonomous individual farming plots for new rural settlers and through new configurations of urban space, including sports parks, playgrounds, pools, and youth parks.[109] For Migge, the revolutionaries needed to rejuvenate the land from the consequences of abstract and vampire-like cities through the most intensive agriculture possible, including mechanization.[110] David Haney notes Migge's affinity for Adolf Damaschke's and Henry George's land-reform ideas but is more dismissive of the nationalism in Migge's work than is warranted.[111] Migge was not a completely anti-modern figure; rather, he wanted to join what he saw as the elemental social and environmental conditions of the pre-modern society with the highest levels of technological advancement.[112]

Further fluidity in the political stakes of this change in the immediate post-war environment can be seen in the efforts to create socialist spaces in an otherwise capitalist society. These efforts interpret capitalism as concerned only with the market and the individual; in other words, they conflate capitalism with its liberal form. Non-profit building associations and left-leaning planners regarded the market as unfair and selfish as well as inefficient, distorting communal needs. They sought to build the city as a concrete totality, a productive organism.[113] Martin Wagner founded Bauhütte Berlin, a prominent of the non-profit builder, which advocated a communal economy, which meant production for socially determined and administratively managed needs.[114] Although this institution was not the success that Wagner and his allies envisioned, the private builders' predictions of failure did not come true, either.[115] Wagner believed that builders needed to strip the housing industry of all that was individualistic and thus unproductive.[116] Therefore, for these builders, the mode of construction and the orientation of the building were both social and political.

New State Forms and the Economy

The post-war period witnessed the development of a new form of capitalism that could be described as corporatist and that created the social forms governing the perceptions of cities and their territories. This new corporatist form of capitalism included work-creation programs, state mediation between capital and labour, municipal ownership of key utilities, and a governmental role in the economy.

In the immediate post-war period, a new corporatist form of capitalism took shape in Greater Berlin and in cities more generally, affecting not only the production and circulation of commodities, but also the constitution of social space and of ideas about society. In conditions of mass unemployment following the war and the revolution, the state hired unemployed people for communal purposes, attempting to make joblessness "productive." In February 1919 the state formed the Reich and State Committee for Public Relief Labour of Greater Berlin and paid roughly 130 million M to businesses and municipalities to respond to shortages in materials and to unemployment.[117] Soon after the group was started, committee members expanded the committee's purview to include delayed maintenance as a way to employ workers and because cities were already conducting these repairs under the assumption of state support. Greater Berlin employed 7,574 (4,300 in Berlin itself) workers in public relief labour, and only 500 to 600 (300 to 400 in Berlin) were involved in new projects. Berlin needed 12.4 million M for this work, while other Greater Berlin municipalities would require 2.5 million M, and this program would employ about 10,000 workers by 15 August 1919. If the state and the Reich agreed to that number of workers, then Greater Berlin could expect 20 million M in support. The committee "recognized the special dangers, which unemployment meant in the vicinity of Berlin, would probably justify a deviation from the principles."[118] However, state support of the Productive Unemployment Emergency Public Labour Program did not keep pace with rising wages, driven by workers' political or economic demands and accelerating increases in the price of necessities, and so the German Städtetag pressed for more funding.[119] Minister of Labour Schlicke considered it important that the wages in this program remain consistently below those of the unions to promote a desire for normal employment.[120] The Reich was significantly expanding its role as a provider of welfare: no longer was it providing a minimal safety net; now it was finding productive work for the unemployed.

In addition to creating jobs servicing public-sector utilities and deferred maintenance, this new corporatist form of capitalism had the government placing itself as the mediator between workers and employers as the last resort, such as an acrimonious transit workers' strike that began on 2 July 1919. The Executive Committee of the Greater Berlin Workers' and Soldiers' Council (GBW&SC) tried to resolve the strike, selecting a commission to explain the situation to Minister Schlicke. The state told the transit workers, transit businesses, and the Executive Committee of the GBW&SC to make a new attempt at reconciliation, with Schlicke leading the negotiations.[121] Six days later, the workers concluded their strike and returned to work.[122]

Municipalities took ownership or quasi-ownership of basic utilities and services in this new corporatist form of capitalism. At the conclusion of the strike, the Zweckverband purchased the Ostbahn commuter rail that served the eastern suburbs.[123] The Zweckverband also made an offer on the Groß-Berliner Straßenbahn that would make this private company a publicly owned institution.[124] While the Zweckverband valued the company at 131.5 million M, the director assessed the company's productive value at 152 million Reichsmark (RM).[125] A meeting on 18 July between the Zweckverband and the Groß-Berlin Straßenbahn grew heated, as large shareholding banks and small shareholders faced off, but the banks promised to cover the small holders' losses.[126] The radicalized workers, in part, had pressed the Zweckverband into action, while the large holders, the Zweckverband's goal of public ownership, and the radicalized workers pinched the small holders.[127] The Reich and the Zweckverband now municipalized private companies as well as mediated disputes between capital and labour. This new urban political economy in Greater Berlin and of other cities marked the beginning of the form of capitalism that would characterize the middle of the twentieth century.

The political-economic structure of the Greater Berlin region was not changed from liberal to corporatist only by municipalization of formerly private businesses. With the state mediating conflicts between labour and capital, and the Reich instituting job-creation programs, a number of wartime commodity-distribution-programs continued and even expanded in peacetime. This continuation of wartime systems into peacetime reterritorialized Greater Berlin deepened the political economic relations created by the war.

The Housing Question

The housing industry and the government's efforts to address social questions through housing played a key role in the development of a new corporatist form of capitalism. The revolution and demobilization made a government role in the housing economy justifiable and even expected. In this new system, housing administrators were encouraged to act aggressively to address problems and to support the provision in the Weimar constitution for adequate housing for all citizens. The state granted the new housing authorities significant new influence to confiscate existing housing for housing the homeless, while it attempted to build housing as quickly as possible. In this corporatist form of capitalism in the housing industry, the Reich, the state, and the municipality played a role either in administering the market or in eliminating it altogether. Housing shortage, on the one hand, created significant social angst and access to housing, while on the other hand, purportedly it had the power to address the trauma of the war, to placate or reward – depending on one's point of view – the radicalism of the working class, to increase food sources, and to rebuild the population growth rate.

The revolution and demobilization provided the grounds for a corporatist effort by the Reich to administer the distribution of housing. The Reich named a new housing administrator and, breaking from liberal norms, granted him arbitrary, extra-legal power over the housing market and over the market for commodities related to housing production. In the late fall and early winter of 1918–19, housing authorities at various levels of government and private business associations struggled to find the necessary materials to begin housing construction, including the Reich and the State Commissar for Housing Policy, the Demobilization Committee for Greater Berlin, the Federation of Building Businesses, and the Berlin Structural Engineering Administration.[128] On 15 January 1919 the Reich issued a new housing regulation that obligated state authorities to find small and middle-sized apartments for homeless families during the demobilization and that gave a district housing commissioner the power to expropriate properties. Before expropriation, the owner could sell the property to the municipality or to the martial federation, and the State Secretary of the Reich Labour Office could determine the details and grant exemptions in cases of hereditary property – which protected aristocratic and wealthy bourgeois property holders from expropriation. The secretary could determine the production of building materials; the creating, halting, or closing of brickyards and similar institutions; and the expropriation of forest for timber or real estate.[129] The state gave the regulator the power to make significant interventions in the market.

The new administrator of this corporatist housing economy was encouraged to act in an aggressive manner. The state instructed him to "intervene without fear," even if in the process he made minor mistakes in individual cases. The war economy had reconstituted the economic geography of production and housing, clustering population around militarily useful factories, moving the population from one city to another, and accentuating the suburbanization of industry. To demobilize the economy, new housing was necessary, and the authorities preferred decentralization of population and so declared that the state should only fund low-rise, diffused housing.[130] However, the several conflicting interests battled for influence over housing policy. The Reichs-Arbeitsgemeinschaft für das Baugewerbe, which legally represented construction employers and employees within the Demobilization Office, was frustrated that the Reich Economic Office and the Reich Office for the Economic Demobilization created general principles for the communalization of building and housing without consulting them.[131] As a short-term measure, municipal authorities were allowed to expropriate unused land or buildings suitable for dwelling, including factories, camps, workshops, and service buildings; unused commercial areas in hotels, pensions, and similar spaces, and unused parts of large apartments and homes that were suitable for habitation, with little or no alteration, even if economic separation was impossible. Municipal authorities could determine a lease with the owner and renter, as a last resort, and direct those in search of housing as to where to live and provide necessary renovations to the building.[132] This new approach to housing granted the municipality significant power to address those areas of the housing economy that were ill-served by the housing market.

The gears of this large corporatist housing mission had begun to turn in the immediate post-war period. Berlin city planner Ludwig Hoffmann proposed the two municipal housing projects in Buch and Jungfernheide to the city council on 24 May 1919. The land in Buch, adjacent to city facilities and a mental hospital, was inexpensive. They would be built with fifty-six homes in a simple style and with inexpensive materials, electric lights, gas stoves, in-house bathing apparatuses, a shared modern water boiler, sun-filled windows, and a backyard garden. Nevertheless, this housing would be priced 300 per cent higher than pre-war prices, so state and Reich subsidies compensated the purchaser for 50–60 per cent of the war-related price increase.[133] Home construction and furniture-making firms sought clients in municipalities. H. Reimer and Insterburger Holzindustrie GmbH declared to the Magistrat of Berlin that their business would address the housing shortage, presenting a design for a four-family housing barrack. Exemplifying the rationalization of the housing industry, this firm claimed that their special mode of construction made it possible "to build a barrack with four dwellings in approximately six days" with the assembler they provided and four workers hired by the municipality.[134] Along similar lines, the Berlinische Grundgesellschaft wanted to start construction as rapidly as possible on land it had just purchased near the Tiergarten Bahnhof, with one-, two-, and three-room apartments with kitchens, baths, and central heating as well as "social facilities" like central kitchens, washrooms, and kindergartens, to attract "good taxpayers."[135]

The Weimar constitution rooted this corporatist housing economy in the legal structure of the state. Passed on 11 August 1919, the constitution included article 155, which demanded that every German citizen have a healthy place to live. The state purchased land for public projects, supported low-profit building societies and research institutes, and set minimum standards for housing quality.[136] In Germany, generally, builders used mass models to build 2.5 million homes during the Weimar Republic and to provide housing for between 7 and 9 million people.[137] This effort, like Lloyd George's Homes for Heroes program that created working-class housing in Britain, was intended to respond to the sacrifices of soldiers and workers and to foster population growth for the recovery of national power, or as George called it, "the Imperial race." In both cases, as well, the focus of the housing planning was on the dispersal of the population from dense slums.[138]

The Unification of Greater Berlin

In the early twentieth century the Zweckverband appeared to challenge the liberal principle of municipal self-administration. But in the new corporate society after the First World War and the revolution, the Zweckverband seemed insufficient, and a more thoroughgoing integration of the urban region seemed necessary. Previously only poor cities with significant welfare responsibilities and a small tax base were interested in a broad incorporation of the region into a single city; but that changed, and even wealthy cities and civil society organizations were interested. Although those interested in defending local privileges and particularities among wealthy towns continued to exist, they no longer had the power to stop unification.

Whereas once the Zweckverband seemed to be a radical departure from municipal self-administration, its role now seemed paltry, and the creation of a total municipality, in which the whole subsumed the parts in a corporatist manner, appeared necessary and adequate for this moment in capitalism. While the Zweckverband might have met its prescribed goals in peacetime, the development of the war proved to be more than the institution could handle.[139] SPD members Paul Hirsch and Wolfgang Heine, in a historical jurisprudential grounding of the Greater Berlin unification law, argued that the rapid growth of Berlin's suburbs had led to an "unnatural" relationship between the centre and the periphery.[140] In the war, isolated communities struggled with grocery provisioning, and in response the state formed a number of Zweckverbände to supply the region, which, the authors posited, "forced the amalgamation of Greater Berlin." The list of organizations included the Grocery Necessities Federation of Greater Berlin, which served sixty-nine municipalities and property districts; the Bread Card Community of Greater Berlin; the Fat Office of Greater Berlin, which regulated milk and cooking fat for thirty-one municipalities and property districts; the Flour Distribution Office of Greater Berlin, which served Berlin, Charlottenburg, Berlin-Lichtenberg, Neukölln, Berlin-Schöneberg, and Berlin Wilmersdorf; and the Coal Federation of Greater Berlin, which distributed coal and regulated the gas and electricity consumption to the same six municipalities as well as to Teltow and Niederbarnim. The Price Auditing Office of Greater Berlin, the Cattle Distribution

Office of Greater Berlin, the Horse Meat Provisioning Community of Greater Berlin, and the Economic District of Greater Berlin for Clothing Utilization served this same area. The Housing Federation of Greater Berlin included this same group of municipalities, with the addition of Spandau, and prepared and executed common measures to combat housing shortages. The Fish Provisioning Office of Greater Berlin served that same territory. Finally, Hirsch and Heine acknowledged the work of the Greater Berlin Office for Rescue, which standardized rescue and hospital policy for thirty-six municipalities and property districts, and the demobilization commissioner and the Demobilization Committee of Greater Berlin, which attempted to formulate coherent responses to economic questions related to demobilization, particularly by creating uniform certificates of employment, unemployment relief, and supply and execution of public relief labour.[141] Beyond these organizations, Hirsch and Heine explained, the effects of the war inspired informal contacts among municipal leaders throughout the region, forming an "organic unity."[142] These institutions created the conditions of possibility for the region's unification.[143]

Unlike in the liberal pre-war period, when only the poor cities lobbied the state to unify Greater Berlin and address their tax revenue shortages, in this new period belief was widespread that some sort of administrative unification of the region was necessary. The twenty-seven municipalities of Greater Berlin, the six Gutsbezirke (estate districts), and the state forestlands lobbied to create a single municipality, known as Greater Berlin. In December 1918 Berlin-Reinickendorf asked the minister of the interior to incorporate his city into Berlin as soon as possible. Before that, in 1914, the two cities had declared themselves in agreement on incorporation. They presented the issue to the Oberpräsident in 1914, in 1915, and in 1918, but each of these attempts was rejected. The Reinickendorf Magistrat and the local W&SC agreed on 17 December 1918 to press the issue with the minister of the interior, because they believed he would be sympathetic. The taxes in Reinickendorf represented, the municipal chairperson argued, the highest rates of taxation in Greater Berlin, but, because of the limited tax base, had a very low yield.[144]

Political groups that in the past would have been more liberal in their approach and offered a defence of municipal self-administration put forth ideas about how to create a single regional city. The Bürgerausschuss Groß-Berlin campaigned for a draft law to unify Greater Berlin.[145] In this plan, the Berlin Oberbürgermeister would head the

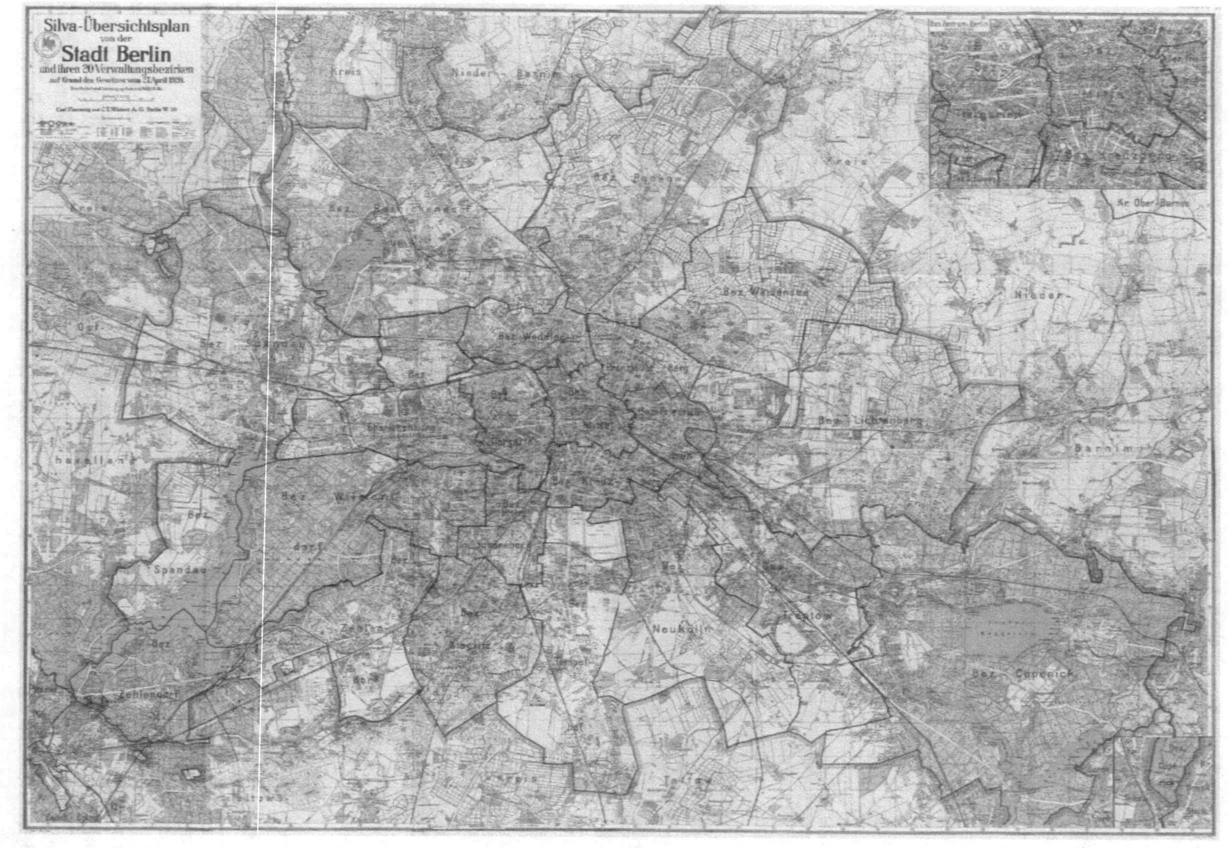

6 Berlin after 27 April 1920. Willy Holz, "Silva-Übersichtsplan von der Stadt Berlin und ihren 20 Verwaltungsbezirken" (Berlin: Flemming, 1925).

new municipality, which included "Berlin, Charlottenburg, Neukölln, Berlin-Schöneberg, Berlin-Lichtenberg, Berlin Wilmersdorf, and Spandau, as well as rural municipalities and property districts of the districts Teltow, Niederbarnim, and Osthavelland." The bill allowed the parts to opt out and to remain the same insofar as they did not conflict with the jurisdiction of the whole. The unified municipality would manage housing policy, provisioning of water, gas, and electricity, sewer systems, traffic, and railway administration.[146] The Bürgerausschuss expanded the Zweckverband, but it did not create an integrated totality, and the ability to opt out of the arrangement would enable the wealthy suburbs to remain independent and create a union of impoverished municipalities.[147] The Bürgerausschuss Groß-Berlin created voter education programs, held between 5 and 10 May 1919, about Greater Berlin questions.[148] They offered classes on the new communal constitution for Greater Berlin: on the future local bodies, their composition, and their tasks on Reich and state administration in Greater Berlin; on Greater Berlin's financial structure and on Greater Berlin as a city-planning problem; on Greater Berlin's business concerns (electricity, gas, water, sewerization, and the possibilities for communalization); and on the communalization of the food economy, mass supply, recycling of waste, and the provisioning of coal.[149] Because of the war, the ideology that governed the popular understanding of Greater Berlin as a region and as a governmental territory had shifted.

As evidence of this shift from a liberal to corporate social forms, a single city comprising the social and economic region of Greater Berlin had become both desirable and possible. In 1919 two bills were working their way through the Prussian parliament: one that addressed municipalities generally and the other that dealt with Greater Berlin. In April 1919 the Greater Berlin law took legislative precedence over the general law.[150] To formulate this Greater Berlin law, the state created a committee on 5 July that would meet to determine the structure of the municipal government, the constitution of Greater Berlin, and the relationship of former local administrations to the now "total" administration. The deputation intended to include a roughly fifteen-kilometre radius of moderately developed land around Berlin. Blankenfelde, Schildung, Machnow, Buch, Hobrechtsfelde, and Greater Ziethen were included, and though Spandau resisted incorporation, the deputation fought to draw it in later. The state divided the new city into eighteen districts, with Berlin itself into six. The deputation members believed that unifying Greater Berlin was the only option; otherwise the region would remain an agglomeration of poor cities surrounding wealthy suburbs.[151] These conditions would significantly limit the ability of the SPD to address the needs of its constituents.

Pockets of liberal resistance to creating a single corporatist regional city government continued, but they now could not derail the process. According to liberal newspapers, the SPD dominated the discussion and pushed for unification for the party's political reasons. Those fighting against the SPD presented themselves as fighting layers of "ponderous" bureaucracy and "a degradation and a descent" of "local work and efficiency," in the name of "the most extensive decentralization" to preserve the "independence" of large suburban municipalities.[152] Other councillors forced the SPD to defend its proletarian politics against charges of particularism.[153] Reinickendorf came to an agreement over the law, while Tegel worried about representation in the unified municipality.[154] The communal Workers' and Soldiers' Councils addressed the topic on 17 July, and the Berlin council included the USPD leadership.[155] In subsequent days Lichtefeld, Tempelhof, Friednau, Steglitz, Lichtenburg, and Neukölln all supported incorporation.[156] Charlottenburg opposed the incorporation, as did its local Deutsche Volkspartei[157] (the German People's Party, a successor of the National Liberal Party, which held right-wing liberal or conservative-liberal positions). In late September, Potsdam requested that the state exclude it from the Grocery Necessities Association, because it wanted the state to also exclude it from incorporation.[158] On 16 and 17 July the local papers reported that Schmargendorf and Spandau rejected the Greater Berlin law.[159] Spandau, in particular, put up a vigorous struggle.[160]

With the sense of cohesion in the corporatist ideology, those forming a single city out of Greater Berlin celebrated unity and condemned particular interests. The Prussian minister of the interior began formulating a law on 4 August 1919, which was to be read in the Landesversammlung (Prussian constituent assembly) on 6 December and be transferred to a committee of predominantly Greater Berlin representatives.[161] On 4 December 1919 the committee for drafting the law was determined,[162] with twenty-seven members set to meet on 5 December for the first time with many members familiar with Greater Berlin though with political differences.[163] The liberal Bürgerausschuss Groß-Berlin praised the efforts to overcome the "splintering of economic interests," which were "retarding the economic totality."[164] Importantly, as Social Democrats Hirsch and Heine claimed, the law differed from the Zweckverband law in that it granted the new municipality competence-competence, i.e., the ability to determine whether it had jurisdiction, enabling the city to eliminate economic and political obstacles to the development of the totality. They conceded that "a unified municipality [represented] a significant intervention into the autonomy of the independent municipalities," and it would have "certain victims among its members," but a totality that could act as a fully integrated corporation would have greater autonomy than the accumulating idiosyncrasies of the individual municipalities.[165] Therefore, the weakness and idiosyncrasies of the Zweckverband and self-administering, individual municipalities actually made them less autonomous, according to this vision, and only an integration of all municipalities into a single totality could autonomy actually exist.

Heine presented the bill to the Prussian Landesversammlung on 2 December 1919. He argued that fear of the proletarian character of the Greater Berlin electorate had blocked the creation of a "more efficient and larger local federation," but the revolution created new possibilities. He asked that the legislators act quickly, because delay would only make the transition more difficult, and a new era had begun. With the examples of the Peace of Tislit in 1807 and the Stein Reforms, Heine's State Undersecretary Friedrich Freund argued that defeats and crises could make possible a redefinition of the state and bring the nation to a new level. He argued that, during the war, the state created an "abundance of federations" to address inadequacies of the Zweckverband that "exerted a pressure toward concentration."[166]

Just as the process was concluding, the unification plan faced renewed calls for municipal self-administration by the wealthy suburbs. As *Vorwärts* stated, "The unconditional annexation of the suburbs to Berlin has been a program point of the Berlin Social Democrats for decades. We want the unified community in Berlin for political and economic reasons." While the republic mandated fair local elections, Greater Berlin's disunity enabled some suburbs, the SPD argued, to block the migration of the working class into their city and the advance of proletarian politics.[167] On 23 January 1920 Wermuth encouraged the Landesversammlung committee to resist "the disastrous consequences" of efforts to block the law.[168] City Councillor Bruns responded on 24 January that the state had scrapped the total community in favour of a unified community, and this transition would "undoubtedly be more difficult."[169] On 17 April 1920 the state unified Greater Berlin into a single city of nearly four million people extending across an area twice the size of old Berlin. The practical integration of the municipality was yet to come.

Conclusion: A Formally Unified City

Through the course of the First World War and the November Revolution, city planning and municipal administration underwent a fundamental transformation, changing the goals, values, and the very terms with which city planners and municipal administrators characterized themselves. Before the war, both realms of activity had a hollowed-out, "late" liberal quality, but they metamorphosed into institutions that attempted to facilitate the "corporate" cohesion of society. This change was part of a larger social transformation away from a liberal form of capitalism into its corporatist incarnation. When the war began, martial law and, increasingly, the demands of the war economy transformed the administrative structures that had once governed Berlin. In the face of this war economy, contemporaries increasingly saw the market as an impediment to the efficient functioning of war production. The ideology of city planning, political economy, and political science in this period all emphasized the new cohesive character of the society; meanwhile, though, a great rupture was brewing in working-class politics, as Socialists battled over the meaning of totality – nation or class – and whether the best path was cooperation with the war effort or revolution.

This revolutionary energy culminated in the winter of 1918–19, beginning with the 9 November Revolution and continuing into the following spring. The revolution inspired a significant shift in city planning to emphasize a planned, unified, productive society, assisted by artistic and technocratic city planners setting the conditions for the possibility of this new peaceful, civilian, and cohesive society. Many of the programs for planning the distribution of commodities, particularly of building materials, continued and even expanded after the war. This was especially the case in housing, with the appointment of a new administrator with dictatorial powers over the market and private property. Finally, the development of the war and the administrative systems created to distribute commodities rendered the unification of Greater Berlin into a single city possible in a new way, and on 27 April 1920 a single city came into being.

Chapter Five

Organic Municipal Government, 1920–1933

The path to an organic structure and with it to the regaining of the masses was opened by the law of 27 April 1920 [which created a single city out of Greater Berlin]. Now the woods and the meadows, the rivers and lakes no longer belong to Köpenick, Spandau, or whatever lucky previous owners were called; they no longer belong to the state or to a bloodless interest group [Zweckverband], but to each and every Berliner embraced by the expansive boundary of the metropolis. Once again, the Berliner has a share of nature. The most general and liberal right to vote gives him a direct right of disposal over his valuable real estate and over the mighty economic enterprises and social institutions of the unified metropolis. Possessing equal rights and responsibilities, every inhabitant becomes a full citizen.

Ernst Kaeber, 1926[1]

Introduction: A Unified Berlin Takes Shape

On 7 October 1918 the Spartakusbund concluded that Germany was in a "revolutionary situation in which the problems that the German bourgeoisie could not solve in the Revolution of 1848 are being posed in a new way."[2] In other words, the fulfilment of the promise of rights and full citizenship for all citizens, to which the Revolution of 1848 had been dedicated, was a point of contention between the old state and the revolutionary social movements. With the 1918 Revolution, the working class won those rights as liberal citizens, but to do so they had needed to act not as an agglomeration of individuals but as a unified class and through collective action.[3] While the 1918 Revolution did not achieve the fuller sense of freedom and liberation from capital that the

Spartakists expressed in this statement, the working class managed to gain formal liberal rights through actions such as abolishing the three-tier voting system. Nonetheless, these liberal rights became collective rights and at the same time were made obsolete by the workers' movement on the one hand, and the "mighty economic enterprises and social institutions of the unified metropolis" on the other.

For many, this new corporatist form, function, and perception of Greater Berlin and of cities more generally created the opportunity for and necessity of a new form of city government and new economic policies towards cities. Ernst Kaeber, the city archivist, argued that the unification of Greater Berlin created a capacity to create an organic home out of the metropolis through a reworked connection to the soil, the forests, and the expanded spaces of the city. This collectivized form of citizenship granted citizens a sort of ownership over the municipally owned natural spaces. For Kaeber this new collective society was able to free itself from the inefficient weight of both the Prussian state and the Zweckverband. He placed the organic, productive, and collective in a positive light, and the imposed or inorganic, speculative, and individualized signified the negative. This dichotomy shaped much of the discussion about municipal administration in the Weimar Republic in Berlin. Elements of a liberal society, ironically, were made real in this period in Berlin, but they took on a new and changed form. If this form was liberal, as Kaeber claimed, then the meaning of liberalism had fundamentally changed when compared to perceptions from earlier eras.

During the Weimar Republic this new corporatist form, function, and perception of municipal government was institutionalized. This chapter argues that this institutionalization is particularly clear in three areas: the way that the complex economic conditions of the Weimar Republic affected the responsibilities and capacities of municipal government; the development of a coercive, tenuous, and interdependent dynamic between the state, banks, industry, municipalities, and the housing industry in the late years of the Weimar Republic; and the way that the Great Depression contributed to the collapse of that dynamic. Furthermore, the institutionalization of this corporatist mode of urbanism engendered a shift in the spatial scale of city planning and a reterritorialization of the powers of the municipality; fused arguments about urban and rural population density with concerns about birth rates and living space through these new corporatist social relations; and integrated the formerly independent municipal administrations into a unified, efficient Greater Berlin government. A self-identified liberal, Oberbürgermeister Gustav Böß drove this effort to create one municipality by integrating and rationalizing old institutional structures and municipal utilities. In so doing, Böß took positions that were distinctly opposed to what had once been bedrock liberal thinking. The way that liberals like Böß framed their activity through a corporatist understanding of the world indicates this shift from liberal to corporatist social forms. Finally, the chapter contends that the crime, violence, and corruption shaped perceptions of Berlin during the late years of the Weimar Republic and reaffirmed commitments to a corporatist vision of the city, a vision of society supported by the rules that guided the relationship between the municipality and the higher levels of government.

The Hyperinflation and the Currency Stabilization

The pre-war liberal form of capitalism was transformed in the early years of the twentieth century, and the First World War and the Revolution of 1918 accentuated certain post-liberal elements and introduced new ones, such as state administration of markets. This section argues that the post-war hyperinflation and stabilization of the currency provided the last steps necessary to create this new form of corporatist capitalism. This new form of capitalism is evident in the way that the inflation affected city budgets and politics and the ideology that celebrated the concrete and productive elements of society and attacked the abstract and speculative elements. The local economy had been oriented towards the armaments industry and changed to a centre of revolutionary and counter-revolutionary politics, making the transition to the post-war and hyperinflation economy challenging. Finally, the stabilization of the currency, which moved significant amounts of capital from the hands of those who kept their assets in paper form and lived off the interest into the hands of those who controlled industry, i.e., in this ideology, from those engaged in abstract profit taking to those engaged in concrete production.

The transformation of capitalism from one organized around liberal principles to one organized around corporatist principles was not limited to Germany; indeed, it was an international phenomenon that took both progressive and reactionary forms. During the interwar period, the positive perception of abstract forms of capitalism, like banking and speculation, diminished as this dimension of capitalism appeared unnecessary to production. It appeared that the lingering power of this abstract dimension of capitalism was constraining progress, whether economic, social, or racial in some circles. The hyperinflation of 1921–3, the stabilization of the currency and subsequent boom, and then the Great Depression all caused the theory and practice of both city planning and municipal administration to emphasize efficiency and productivity, favouring the concrete and collective over the abstract and individual. Inflation, during the war and certainly afterward, moved capital from the hands of creditors to debtors and significantly benefited production over finance.[4] One could view the inflation as moving capital from the "unproductive" rentier to the "productive" large-scale industrialist.[5] The inflation hurt small-business owners and those living on interest, but insofar as wages kept pace with the price of necessities, the inflation spared the working class.[6] As the economist Franz Eulenburg wrote in 1924, "The disintegration of the currency did not occur in isolation but in constant connection with all the other factors of societal existence. It is itself only the consequence of factors underlying it."[7] Gerald Feldman argues that significant inflation took hold during the First World War and accelerated in the fall and winter of 1919–20. Between the springs of 1920 and 1921, the inflation stabilized but then "made a dramatic leap upward to qualitatively new levels, beginning in the late summer of 1921 and continuing through the winter and spring of 1922 before the true hyperinflation began in the summer of 1922."[8] Theo Balderston explains that the inflation meant both a significant demand for credit to take advantage of the debt shrinking with inflation and the increasing difficulty of finding working capital, since creditors were not interested in lending, fearful that their investment would be inflated away.[9] The inflation undermined the authority of the new republic, because the state had difficulty collecting the full value of the taxes due. And although the Reichstag passed a progressive tax on personal and corporate income in March 1920, the inflation made it possible to delay payment and thereby reduce the value of the tax remitted. Indeed, the nominal growth in wages forced five changes to the bottom tax bracket.[10] These new conditions shifted power from bankers to industrialists but also contributed to a sense among industrialists that banks were constraining their growth, making anti-financial ideas more appealing.

The new ideology of the corporatist society included a significant anti-financial bias, which the conditions of hyperinflation emboldened. This ideology celebrated labour, productivity, and concrete social conditions over speculative and abstract forms of business. This thinking could already be seen in the political economic discourse of the First

World War, and the hyperinflation only accentuated it. This ideology often revealed itself in the social forms that it attacked and in the "good" conditions it assumed. For example, the liberal Italian economist Costantino Bresciani-Turroni argued in 1931 that the inflation led to

> falling productivity; a misallocation of resources; 'profound disequilibrium in the economic organism'; 'the vastest expropriation of some classes of society that has ever been effected in time of peace'; and declines in public health and morality. Annihilated thrift … Destroyed … moral and intellectual values … It poisoned the German people by spreading among all classes the spirit of speculation and by diverting them from proper and regular work, and it was the cause of incessant political and moral disturbance. [Moreover,] by reinforcing the economic position of those classes who formed the backbone of the "Right" parties, i.e., the great industrialists and financiers, [it] encouraged the political reaction against democracy.[11]

Bresciani-Turroni was concerned that the new conditions devalued labour and distracted people from what he saw as morally upright and productive.

This opposition in the corporatist ideology between the concrete and productive, on the one hand, and the abstract and speculative or financial, on the other hand, also shaped cultural ideas. Feldman argues that literary works of the time focused on profiteers living off the misery and labour of others and anthropomorphized the abstract process of the hyperinflation through images of master puppeteers. Furthermore, he claims that it was not surprising that the hyperinflation coincided with significant increases in anti-Semitism and right-wing radicalism.[12] Nevertheless, an explanation is needed for why events like the inflation gave rise to anti-Semitism.[13] Hyperinflation made Germans feel as if they were trapped in an abstract and dominating system that was beyond their control or understanding. Anti-Semites conflated this abstract dimension of capitalism with "International Jewry." Drawing on the theory explained in the introduction to this book, this ideology can be explained with reference to a theory of capitalist social forms rooted in the historically specific, dualistic mediations of the commodity form. The commodity form creates a mutually constitutive opposition between value and use value. The two dimensions tended to appear separate and external, such that one dimension of the commodity was viewed as money and the other as things: commodities, machines, nature, etc. Consequently, it appeared that the useful dimension was natural and the value dimension was imposed from outside. Within this mode of thought, money appeared "as abstract," as the "root of all evil," even though it was just as rooted in the commodity as use value, and consequently "capitalist social relations" appeared to "find their expression only in the abstract dimension."[14] This abstract dimension was seen as the power of Jews. Anti-Semites associated Jews with "abstractness, intangibility, universality, mobility," all of which were characteristics of the value dimension of the commodity and of capital. As Moishe Postone argues, "Moreover, this dimension – like the supposed power of the Jews – does not appear as such, rather always in the form of a material carrier, such as the commodity."[15] The apparent power of this abstract dimension of capitalism is not concrete, is not rooted. It seems immense and difficult to resist. It fundamentally shapes phenomena but is not identical to them. Therefore the source of this power seems conspiratorial.[16] This dualistic mode of thought is particularly appealing in a society wracked first by currency inflation and later by deflation.

The social conditions in Berlin made this corporatist ideology more acute in its celebration of production and attacks on finance and speculation. Greater Berlin had been dedicated to the armaments industry, and then the war effort was rapidly demobilized. The city was also a centre of revolutionary and counter-revolutionary activity. These conditions combined with the hyperinflation to create dire conditions in the city, though the social gains of the November Revolution averted the worst effects. The number of unemployed people in Berlin fell from the demobilization period high of 271,000 (in a city of 4 million) in February 1919 to 60,000 in 1920. However, as inflation accelerated, the number of unemployed increased to 126,000 in April 1921. While the numbers of unemployed shrank over time, their politics became radicalized and hyperinflation devalued their welfare support.[17] The state had last adjusted payments to the unemployed for inflation in 1920, and even then the amounts were insufficient for the purchase of food, housing, heating, water, and warm clothing. The Greater Berlin Magistrat issued lump-sum payments, but the local branch of the confederation of unions [Allgemeiner Deutscher Gewerkschaftsbund, or ADGB] and the Communist Party (Kommunistische Partei Deutschlands or KPD) demanded further compensation. The Magistrat wanted to expand services, despite resistance from the republic and the state.[18] Therefore the state had city administrators design and implement "productive unemployment relief" programs that were believed would directly benefit the social whole and that determined worthiness of the participants by their "willingness to work" and "ability to work."[19] In April 1921, under pressure from the USPD and KPD, the city expanded job creation to include construction of housing and museums, and a continuation of the north-south subway line.[20] As Gerald Feldman has noted, Berlin Oberbürgermeister Gustav Böß maintained that it was more cost-effective to pay adequate support to the unemployed through labour on public works than it was to deal with the destruction caused by social unrest. At the time Böß voiced this concern, the unemployment benefit per week for a family of four was 88.5 million M and the subsistence minimum was 683.3 billion M per week.[21] Programs like the "productive unemployment relief" and the conditions of inflation fostered the growth of an ideology that privileged labour and productivity over market relations and finance.

Stabilization of the currency solidified this new corporatist political economy and completed a significant movement of capital and power from the parts of the economy that held capital in abstract, interest-bearing paper forms to those that held capital in machinery and the ability to command labour power. In 1924, in order to bring hyperinflation under control, the mark was stabilized at one-trillionth of its pre-war value, completing a dramatic devaluation of capital held in paper, which benefited industrialists over bankers.[22] In December 1924 the Reichsbank cut off all international loans to the states and municipalities to force them to pursue domestic loans.[23] However, as a result of the upheaval between 1914 and 1924, little remained of the German capital markets, and what capital was available was loaned at real interest rates of nearly 50 per cent. In response, German businesses and municipalities turned to American capital markets. The foreign capital created competition between private firms that advocated expanding national productive capacity and reformist liberals, unions, and Social Democrats interested in extending the welfare state, public utilities, and public works. Between 1925 and 1930 American banks lent nearly $3 billion to Germans – more than twice the amount the Marshall Plan made available following the Second World War.[24] The German municipalities absorbed about 12 per cent of the long-term American loans in that period.[25] The inflation had eliminated municipal debts and made municipal bonds attractive investments.[26] The stabilization enabled right-wing business interests to reverse reforms from the revolutionary period, such as the eight-hour workday, and the balance of power shifted among businesses, the state, and the unions. By 1924 businesses that were once nationalized for more equitable distribution of profits were being catered to by the state in order to facilitate increased production.[27] The stabilization caused a contraction of the Germany economy, which increased unemployment, further undermining the bargaining power of workers.[28] According to Thomas Childers and Larry Eugene Jones, stabilization negatively affected liberal parties and accelerated the crisis of legitimacy in the parliamentary system.[29]

The Building Economy

During the war, the revolution, and the hyperinflation, the construction industry was largely dormant. In this period, among the few construction projects that were completed was Westhafen freight port. On New Year's Day 1923, Berlin acquired the harbour facilities to create the Berlin Hafen und Logistik Aktiengesellschaft (Behala).[30] Westhafen had several varieties of powerful cranes for unloading freight barges. Through somewhat circuitous paths, commodities could go to either the Hamburg-Lehrter freight station or the Charlottenburg-Westend one. Despite the difficult conditions, construction was finished in November 1920.[31]

After stabilization, housing construction became a key piece of governmental policy, and industry planned as if this policy would expand, generating a new dynamic that was simultaneously necessary and unsustainable. This dynamic made it appear, consistent with a corporatist view of the world, that financial interests were constraining the ability of more productive parts of society to address fundamental social questions. Five factors interacted to create a tenuous, even coercive interdependence in the building economy and in the economy more broadly that helped to constitute the new corporatist urban economy: (1) the insufficient supply of housing stock, which was worsened by delayed maintenance and from wartime and post-war population movements; (2) the incorporation of rent controls and housing subsidies into the calculation of labour costs; (3) a short supply of capital and high interest rates in domestic capital markets because of hyperinflation and stabilization; (4) capital flowing into Germany from US banks to municipalities and businesses at high interest rates; and (5) a dynamic wherein significant capital expenditures on escalating labour and material costs still could not meet the needs of the housing market and conditions.

Between the stabilization of the currency and the stock market crash in 1929, housing construction boomed with significant public funding.

Nonetheless, housing conditions were shaped by rents that exceeded residents' budgets, high labour and material costs, high-interest loans, state intervention in the housing market, significant yet insufficient state support, and attempts to reduce the cost of housing through rationalization of production. Ultimately the problems of the financing of housing production became too much and were the first signs of the impending economic depression.

First, while housing stock had been insufficient in the liberal era before the First World War, these conditions were worsened by wartime and post-war population movements and delayed maintenance. Though the war decreased population growth, shifting population increased the use of attics, subdivided rooms, and subdivided apartments. Immediately after the war, the nascent corporate society had only "barely enough housing" for the homeless because of the number of newly married couples in search of their own apartments. Costs of labour, land, and materials further limited the supply of housing, and the Housing Committee assumed that the pressure on the housing market would increase.[32] After January 1921 a new tax law removed the state's power to directly tax citizens, giving it to the national government, which decreased state authority and expanded the municipal responsibilities for welfare, public utilities, and unemployment relief. Municipalities demanded reimbursement from the Reich for their increased fiscal commitments.[33] Two decree-laws – one from 5 November and the other from 28 December 1926 – altered what had been the law since 1884 and expanded municipal capacity to address housing and utilities. The 5 November 1926 law enabled municipalities to intervene in the activity of private businesses directly or to garner a financial stake to provide public services and housing. The 28 December 1926 law made the municipal council the manager of city services.[34] Berlin took advantage of these changes and unified its mass transit system in 1926 when it bought the majority of shares in the Hochbahngesellschaft and established the Berlin Transit Corporation (BVG).[35]

After nearly a decade of little construction, housing was scarce and rents or mortgage payments were high. A Department for Settlement and Housing Policy report declared that at the end of 1923 the city had 25,769 apartments available for rent and 219,981 people searching for them. A 17 December 1923 resolution bound cities to address the needs of Eastern European refugees first, exacerbating the housing shortage. The city of Berlin played a role in the housing market and created 137 refugee camps in city buildings.[36] According to the report, a 1 June 1923 edict further hurt the housing market by requiring municipalities to assign new housing immediately to those made homeless by eviction or foreclosure. The available houses were of poor quality, particularly in the east of the city, and changed hands regularly or were owned by foreigners.[37] Apathetic housing inspectors and shortages made possible habitation in spaces not designed for that purpose, such as attics and cellars.[38]

As the rest of the economy improved following the stabilization of the currency, in 1926, according to the Deutschen Bau- und Bodenbank Aktiengesellschaft, housing production did not fully stabilize, but there were signs of improvement from the capital invested: 200,000 dwellings were built nationwide with funds made available through new mortgage loans and as large banks doubled their mortgage holdings.[39] In 1926, in Berlin, luxury-housing taxes financed approximately 10,000 new apartments.[40] Of the state housing assistance expended in 1926, two-thirds went to home mortgages and one-third to specific projects already under way, with an additional 7.5 million M for building projects.[41] On 1 April 1926 the Labour Ministry dedicated another 100 million M to the construction of small homes with typified materials and specified dimensions.[42]

Second, the new corporatist economy had incorporated and started to assume the existence of rent controls and housing subsidies in the calculation of labour costs. On 28 February 1924 the Reich Labour Ministry established public funding for mortgages on new construction of apartment buildings, particularly those built with standardized parts, that were for "one- and two-family houses with garden land ... in contiguous settlements" for "large families and injured, particularly blinded, veterans" on completed roads or roads that could be completed cheaply.[43] On 3 April 1924 the Reich Labour Ministry added to this measure "housing assistance funds" to encourage government bureaucrats and workers, as well as veterans and widows, to buy small and medium-sized apartments.[44] New housing taxes increased revenues on urban housing, and nominally charitable housing corporations used these new rules to accumulate significant capital reserves, and, in the case of Berlin, create real estate monopolies.[45]

Not only non-profit builders built housing; private corporations, too, expanded their concerns from production of specific products to social reproduction and a corporatist policy that endeavoured to ameliorate the conditions of the workers to lower total production costs. Seeing the possibility of savings on wages, private industrial firms formed their own housing subsidiaries and built housing for their employees.[46] The major banking lobbies agreed that housing production was central to social and hygienic concerns and requested further state involvement.[47] The state enforced rent controls and, as Bruno Schwan of the Reichsverband der Wohnungsfürsorgegesellschaften (Reich Association of Housing Relief Societies) argued, a rapid rise in rent to the pre-war levels would mean a large and rapid increase in homelessness; therefore, housing construction was "an economic necessity."[48]

As part of a corporatist policy of amelioration of workers' conditions to lower total production costs, non-profit building corporations encouraged the state to expand further its role in the housing economy. In 1925, the Arbeitsgemeinschaft gemeindlichen Siedlungsgesellschaften in Berlin and the Bezirksverband Berlin-Brandenburg des Reichsverbandes Deutscher Baugenossenschaften posited that the state needed to use its taxing power to inject more capital into the building economy.[49] Though organizations like the Reichsverband der Wohnungsfürsorge-Gesellschaften and Deutsche Bau- und Bodenbank did not favour the role of the government in the housing industry, they conceded that it was necessary. Once the command economy entered the housing industry, it became difficult to remove, because housing prices affected the cost of living and thus wages.[50] The Reichsverband trusted that the private market could counteract usury but argued that state grants were inefficient and their outlays too small.[51] In November 1924 the Deutsche Städtetag supported the notion and petitioned the Prussian minister of welfare to use revenues from a tax on the increase in value to rental properties brought about by improvements to the property to pay for housing development and to lower the cost of raw materials and building capital.[52] However, a few months later, in February 1925, the Deutsche Städtetag advocated removal of the tax increase, believing that the housing shortage could be addressed only through new building and repair of old homes, and thinking that the command economy led people to retain apartments instead of repairing them.[53] Karl Elkart, the city planning director for Greater Berlin, argued in a lecture to the Berlin-BDA that this command economy was necessary and logical, but that its coercive methods did not solve the housing question.[54] The Berlin-BDA criticized state intervention in the market but wanted the state to promote housing through an "emergency tax decree" to mitigate unemployment.[55] These contradictory desires suggested that even organizations ideologically committed to the free market felt compelled by the social conditions to demand government involvement.

Third, this new dynamic in housing construction became a key piece of governmental policy and was both necessary and unsustainable. The new corporatist social forms made it appear that the financial constraints inhibited the ability of productive parts of society to address fundamental questions about productivity and social equality. Hyperinflation and stabilization damaged the domestic capital markets, making capital in short supply and interest rates high. The state, to rebuild those markets, pressured businesses to take out domestic loans. The Industrie- und Handelskammer zu Berlin claimed that "expensive mortgages" caused housing prices to increase by 166.2 per cent, compared to the prices before the war.[56] According to a Department for Settlement and Housing Policy report, private construction, which had been restrained by hyperinflation, was, after the stabilization, constrained by interest rates. Public construction gained some of the financing it needed through the Tax Emergency Decree [Steuernotverordnung] of 1924, through which 50 and later 40 per cent of the revenues were dedicated to housing construction.[57]

This shortage of capital also had consequences for non-profit builders. In 1925 the Arbeitsgemeinschaft gemeindliches Siedlungsgesellschaften in Berlin reported and the Bezirksverband Berlin-Brandenburg des Reichsverbandes Deutscher Baugenossenschaften observed that in order to finance the production of new apartments and houses, the settler or apartment seeker had been expected to pay 10 per cent of the costs, although most buyers and tenants could not meet this condition, leaving the housing that remained unfinished.[58] A similar project of working-class decentralization to the suburbs was also occurring in Britain as well as in U.S. cities like Chicago. The working-class customers were offered "easy terms" under which they could purchase a home.[59] Conditions in Berlin improved slightly in 1926.[60] Both the Deutschen Bau- und Bodenbank Aktiengesellschaft and the Deutschen Wohnstätten-Hypothekenbank Aktiengesellschaft believed they could supply the necessary capital for affordable housing construction.[61]

Fourth, municipalities and businesses used the significant capital flowing into Germany from United States banks, also with high interest rates, to enable a large-scale corporatist building policy. However, the high interest rates accentuated the sense that abstract, financial interests were constraining the concrete, productive possibilities of this new corporatist society. The infusion of American capital, a practical response to practical problems, wove German municipal finances into the fate of large American banks. Since capital from the U.S. banks came at a steep price, municipalities and housing construction firms rigged together complex systems of funding. The Deutsche Bau- und Bodenbank, founded on 20 July 1923, was established to revive the construction industry.[62] However, the Bau- und Bodenbank reported that, by 1925, domestic capital for construction was insufficient and foreign funds were essential, although the Reichsbank held that foreign loans should be for industrial purposes only.[63] In 1925, throughout the republic, 150,000–180,000 homes were built with capital from the mortgage banks and public-sector loans; foreign capital had become too expensive.[64] At a 9 March 1926 meeting convened by the Prussian Ministry of Welfare, representatives from the Bayerischen Handelsbank, the Württembergischen Hypothekenbank, the Special Committee for Mortgage Bank Policy, the Reich Labour Ministry, and the Prussian Ministry for Welfare discussed the extent to which mortgage banks were willing to implement the 1926 housing program. The Welfare Ministry feared that the difficulty of finding secured credit for affordable housing led banks to prefer to lend to agriculture, industrial building, and villa construction, driving building firms to seek foreign capital for first mortgages.[65]

Fifth, this corporatist society seemed to be constrained by the cost of labour and raw materials, which escalated and hampered builders and bureaucrats interested in rectifying the housing shortage. Building demanded a higher financing threshold, necessitating a higher final price for the apartment. With revenue from the rental property tax, municipalities were able to purchase equipment and large parcels of land, but this raised prices on the means of production and interest rates on building capital.[66] Increased building taxes garnered the Prussian Finance Ministry 374 million M in gross revenues in 1924 and 360 million M in 1925; however, the finance minister noted that in Berlin, brick prices had more than doubled in eight months, and construction workers were paid 150 per cent their prior standard wage.[67] In fact, building in Berlin cost 70 per cent more than before the war. The answer appeared to be "stronger state control of the so-called charitable construction companies" in order to reduce costs.[68]

Changing Conditions

The features of this corporatist building economy that maintained the balance in the dynamic discussed in the previous section lost their capacity to stave off economic disaster: a shortage of domestic capital led to high interest rates; cities in search of capital through the issuing of bonds increasingly found there was no market for their bonds and so they turned to international lenders, principally from the United States; and the housing and related employment strategies appeared to be well designed for conditions of increased poverty, homelessness, and unemployment. Despite these factors, increasingly the government felt pressed to take a more austere approach.

In this corporatist society, the shortage of capital and high interest rates were interpreted as abstract and financial constraint on concrete, productive building. Beginning in 1926 and intensifying in 1927, the structures of housing finance became strained. According to the Reich Labour Ministry's ministerial director, Erwin Ritter, "The 1926 capacity of the banks was over-estimated" with the "need to procure capital from foreign banks" to pay for housing construction.[69] As city councillor, union leader, and Social Democrat Emil Wutztky wrote in the same year, in Greater Berlin contemporary economic conditions had rendered the freestanding single-family home financially and spatially impossible.[70] The Deutschen Bau- und Bodenbank AG noted that the savings banks had "yet to prove whether they are in fact able to keep their large and alluring promises"; the savings cooperatives were "only to a certain extent able to muster the necessary funds."[71] Conditions worsened in 1927. On 21 May 1927 the Preußische Landespfandbriefanstalt requested a larger loan from the Finance Ministry, after an effort to increase funds through institutional bonds had failed, so that it could provide bridge loans to finance construction. Under prevailing conditions, the Landespfandbriefanstalt could offer only 10 million RM per year.[72] On 3 June 1927 the Deutschen Bau- und Bodenbank AG reported that "the capacity of the German bond market has declined continuously since March" and recovery was unlikely. Indeed, many mortgage banks had stopped accepting mortgage applications altogether and had begun creating reserves for loans for small-home construction that they were legally bound to fulfil or open themselves up to foreign capital by selling bonds, though that required their getting permission from the republic.[73]

Cities sought to raise capital for building through the sale of bonds. Struggling to find buyers in Germany, they turned to banks in the United States, deepening their connections to the American financial system. On 30 August 1927 the Prussian State Mortgage Bank wrote to the ministers of finance and welfare about the secured credit market, "which for weeks and months has experienced a deterioration," and "recently ... was experiencing a worsening crisis." They reported that the stock market had gradually fallen, but investors had not turned to mortgage bonds, and so "the pace of capital formation [had] slowed significantly" for the savings banks. Consequently, the institutional bonds had lost value, and attempts to raise funds on the capital markets and through new tax revenues failed too.[74] This meant that the banks could not fulfil their decreed responsibility to provide bridge loans for construction activity undertaken or planned in 1926. Thus builders turned to foreign capital in search of bridge loans and large new loans for 1927 in the hope of improved conditions.[75] The cost of those bridge loans from 1927 made the Reich responsible for 350 million RM in foreign bonds; the payments on the interest and principal of that would be made through the rental tax.[76]

The capital shortage and interest rates had limited the possibilities of building. The shortcomings in financing for 1927 caused the financing and construction plans for 1928 to develop slowly. The Deutsche Wohnstätten-Hypothekenbank reported that "the relatively favourable" conditions of the mortgage market in early 1928 encouraged bankers and builders to believe the stagnation was over, but that was not to be.[77] In early 1928 the Deutsche Bau- und Bodenbank had difficulty procuring the necessary capital as a result of the lingering effects of 1927.[78] Serious building began only at midyear. The bank estimated that the capital held in bonds was about 1.95 billion RM for 1928, and it assumed that this portfolio would garner 350 million RM more than in 1927.[79] But as of 7 March 1929 short-term financing of housing construction through bridge loans had become unpredictable because of fear of the risks of speculative building.[80] And by 1927 the financing of housing construction and of German municipalities had become increasingly tied to the fate of international finance. Much of the demand to attract international capital investment was made necessary by state building measures, and much of the capital was moved through semi-state-owned institutions like the Prussian Mortgage Bank. What one found, then, was simultaneous state intervention in the housing industry and increasing dependence on international capital flows, particularly from the United States.

After the collapse of the German economy, housing policymakers were to continue the funding methods of the boom years in keeping with a corporatist view of the world, but increasingly the various levels of government were forced to take a more austere approach. In February 1929 Minister of Labour Rudolf Wissell, a long-time member of the SPD, presented a draft law that would address the provision of credit to encourage small-housing construction. The bill made possible loans from the state to guarantee loans to the Deutsche Bau- und Boden Bank between April 1929 and March 1932, which, in turn, was obligated to use these funds as bridge loans so that small residential building projects from the previous year could be completed.[81] The Prussian minister of welfare granted funds from the municipal share of the Hauszinssteuer (home interest tax) revenues for continued or expanded construction, with the hope of providing jobs for the unemployed. Municipalities would be allowed to use up to 90 per cent of their portion of the revenues and could push back their repayments by a quarter.[82] In February 1930, despite the Ministry of Labour declaring their request "without proof of special emergency," the Preussische Landespfandbriefanstalt and Deutsche Wohnstätten-Hypothekenbank were allowed to delay their loan repayments to the state by three months. Both financial institutions requested more funding from the ministry: 6.5 million RM for the Landespfandbriefanstalt and 250,000 RM for the Wohnstätten-Hypothekenbank.[83]

The Scope of the Solution

With the corporatist celebration of the organic, concrete, and productive, some concerned with urban issues saw social revolution as the solution to overcrowded cities, post-war industrial geography, inadequate housing, and industrial productivity, while others saw urban decentralization as the solution. This discourse on decentralization invoked theories concerned with issues of birth rates, living space, and at times race, and employed a new and dynamic understanding that invested space with the power to affect social relations.

City planners and municipal administrators tied these corporatist concerns of post-war population movement and affordable housing to regional planning, conceptions of geography, living space, birth rates, and productivity. In 1930, in a critical analysis of the previous forty years of city planning, Alexander Schwab posited that modernist architecture was fundamentally new, because it recognized how embedded building was in a broader urban socio-economic environment and how it tried to mediate between the building and the environment, and therefore formal architectural curricula increasingly began to include study in city planning. Schwab argued that a crisis in architectural thought and practice had developed, and, in response, architects and planners dramatically changed the scale of their work.[84] According to Schwab, this crisis had taken place when, in the 1890s, "the economic and social contradictions rending capitalism" confronted architecture and city planning. But city planners at the time shrank from a general solution to this crisis and pursued "temporary partial solutions" and "innocuous details such as traffic issues, questions of the limits building heights, where lawns begin, and the like." He observed that bureaucrats and civil servants in the liberal era delimited the scope of planning and turned planning concerns into questions of "beauty." He asserted that both the pragmatism and aestheticism in city planning were a retreat from the question of capitalism and from determining whether liberal city planning could create the liberated world those planners envisioned. To the contrary, a true solution was "dependent on a complete transformation of the economic order" to address urban questions from the perspective of the needs of humanity, because the "inner logic of the facts" demanded a social revolution.[85]

The concern for decentralization in the corporatist urban ideology was widespread and existed on both the right and the left. In this discourse one can see the development of connections between urban life, population politics, living space, and race. In the late summer and fall of 1923 the Prussian state began to revise the law that regulated urban building in order to require cities to develop comprehensive city plans that accounted for future development.[86] The Bund Deutscher Architekten (BDA) viewed the law as important, since it drastically changed local self-administration and the work of freelance urban planners.[87] In October 1923 the Freie Deutsche Akademie des Städtebau endorsed an expanded law regulating building height but was concerned that densely settled industrial areas dominated the bill and that the plan would limit national agricultural capacity and wanted provisions to address the access to food for Germans through decentralization of the population from "over-populated" areas.[88] The Gesellschaft zur Förderung der inneren Kolonisation, a more radically right-wing and anti-urban organization, pushing an ideology of decentralization and depopulation of the cities, envisioned a migration from the "full" space of Germany to the "empty" spaces in the Baltic region.[89] They believed this migration would create autarkic agriculture, improve public health, and foster population growth, and eastern borderlands of Germany with ethnic Germans, believing that these changes in population politics would positively affect national power and productivity. Like many others, the group believed that problems of urban housing stock and urban density alienated Germans from a concrete relationship with their soil and nation, and weakened the people through a parasitic, abstract, and superficial form of social life, especially in the context of inflation and occupation of the Ruhr industrial region.[90] A common assumption among planners and architects held that the city limited the (demographically) productive capacity of Germany.

This corporatist discourse on urban density and decentralization employed a dynamic sense of space. As David T. Murphy argues, the German word they used was *Raum*, but the word *space* does not capture the political meaning invested in *Raum*. Space was passive, while *Raum* had "a dynamic force in its own right." As Murphy claims, this discourse on *Raum* was "characterized by anti-urbanism, visions of German eugenic improvement, imperialism and racial anxiety." And this discussion on both the built and the natural environments attributed to *Raum* the power to determine key facets of national and cultural life.[91] Bernhard Dietz notes that after the First World War a qualitative shift occurred in the character of anti-urbanism in Britain and in Germany, becoming more than "conservative agricultural lobbyism or a sentiment limited to a moralistic cultural pessimism," but rather a "comprehensive and complex" critique that sought "political solutions beyond Capitalism and Socialism."[92]

Demographic and Economic Productivity and Space

Working within this corporatist ideology, municipal administrators and planners widely agreed that addressing the relationship between population density and birth rates demanded planning on a regional scale. Those who wrote on urban questions often understood fluctuations in birth rates to be the result of issues of space. Politics shaped whether the decentralization pushed people to the eastern borderlands or simply to the outer limits of cities' rapid transit lines. Planners and administrators agreed that these rural spaces needed to shed the superfluous, stifling, and even parasitic liberal form of urban spatial planning to create concrete, organic, and productive spaces for this new corporate era. However, not everyone agreed.

In addition to economic rationalization, according to most planners in this corporatist era, population politics demanded planning on a vast scale. A shift was occurring in the scale of urban and architectural imagination. In 1920 the Prussian minister of welfare from the Centre Party, Adam Stegerwald, believed that a new regional plan of zoning and regulations of building height that emphasized zoning unused land for development, encouraging municipal intervention in building, and promoting cooperation among experts to address questions about urban aesthetics could best address the consequences of the war.[93] Max Klesse argued that Germans increasingly saw falling birth rates as a concern. He asserted that cities like Berlin, which had significantly reduced stillbirths and infant deaths, nonetheless were only barely producing more children than the rate of deaths and were shrinking in population; this trajectory for several decades, he believed, spelled "catastrophe" for German productivity, economy, and working-class politics.[94] Gustav Langen agreed about population growth in Berlin and expected an exodus from Berlin to the suburbs over the course of the succeeding twenty-five years.[95] Martin Pfannschmidt related housing problems to "the changes in the social, economic and demographic structure," and slowing population meant that "growth of large cities on their own" was "no longer generally available."[96] Jean-François Gravier, an influential French planner, and Armin Meili, an important Swiss planner, also shared this concern for birth rates, urban density, and city planning.[97] Within the corporatist discourse, birth rates were often related to spaces of habitation, and researchers sought to determine the amount of space per person necessary for a productive individual and region, both economically and demographically. Using statistics, Philip Rappaport tried to determine the necessary living space (which included a garden) for each urbanite and the extent to which cities met this mark.[98] Alexander Klein, who was born in Odessa and trained in St Petersburg (and a Jew who fled Germany for Palestine in 1933), became a *Baurat*, or city building officer, in Berlin in 1927. He developed housing standards, which were applied to housing projects in Berlin, and then in Wilmersdorf in 1927 and Zehlendorf in 1928–9.[99] He noted that the discussion of affordable rents often moved to conversation about "suitable floor plans," dimensions, and frontage, avoiding the contentious question of whether "still more primitive dwellings should be constructed that satisfy the minimal demands of living and hygiene, or more sophisticated floor plans are acceptable."[100] On this tension between creating less dense urban space through minimum homes, on the one hand, and supplying people with adequate domestic space, on the other, Roman Heiligenthal complained that the concept of hygiene had become so circumscribed that the population could not take advantage of advances.[101]

Assumed in this corporatist investigation into the relative need for living space was expansion either into exurban regions surrounding the major cities or East Prussia. Social scientist Ernst Runge believed that, if urban expansion continued along contemporary lines, one needed to investigate "the structural exploitability of the adjacent land."[102] In the case of Berlin, Gustav Langen explained, before the First World War, the most intense urbanization occurred in the immediate vicinity of the developed areas; however, during the war and post-war years, diffused development enabled urban and suburban vegetable gardens and depended on "the electrification of the suburban railway and motor transport, creating a fifty-kilometre sphere of influence and planning for Berlin."[103] He was thankful that "the desire for a small piece of land," even among the less wealthy, was "still widespread" and believed that a mechanization of work and reduction of the bodily strain on workers would only increase this search for rural places to recreate.[104] Fritz Elsas, a German-Jewish academic who stayed in Berlin during the National Socialist period and contributed significantly to the anti-NS resistance, was a member of the German Democratic Party and vice president of the Deutschen and Preußischen Städtetages during the Weimar Republic.[105] To address the population decline, he advocated "green spaces within the city and its perimeters, playgrounds and sports courts, swimming pools, roomy settlements and many other facilities" so as to administer to "the human health and welfare of a large urban population."[106] And for Martin Pfannschmidt, sweeping migration from cities to suburban areas and the country could follow the movement of industries to exurban areas that "utilize modern transportation improvements in order to seize the advantages of cheaper land and cheaper business taxes outside the large urban agglomerations." Elsas thought that cities would welcome this migration both politically and socially, because it eased popular protest and municipal fiscal responsibilities.[107] Peter Scott maintains that a similar demographic shift occurred between the world wars in Britain, as the "outer" areas of Britain suffered economic depression, the industrial Midlands and Southeast grew rapidly, in particular, smaller towns at the edge of Greater London and towns and cities near the West Midlands. In Britain, the state facilitated this internal migration by creating labour exchanges to manage the regional and national labour supply.[108] Similarly, Tyler Stovall observes that in the 1920s there culminated "a process which transformed the Paris suburbs into a vast zone of working class habitation" that included a population increase of one million in the Department of the Seine.[109]

These rural spaces, however, required a particular form within the corporatist form, function, and perception of space: they needed to abandon what planners deemed the superficial affect of liberal capitalism and to include only productive and vital spatial layouts. Leberecht Migge argued that old "ornamental squares, promenades and parks" from the nineteenth century were designed for the "dispassionate citizen," the stroller who had the time to spare, but that style was no longer "vital green." The "new green" was connected with sports and "young people," as well as with "the horticulturist and gardeners" using the "green of the millions of parcel gardens."[110] Theodor Nußbaum, a garden architect from Cologne, agreed with Migge's historical sketch and believed that contemporary planning focused on accentuating the use value of parks near "crowded rental barracks as spaces for recreation and reconnecting with nature."[111] Workers who could afford to move to the periphery often did, leaving traditionally working-class inner-city neighbourhoods like Wedding, Kreuzberg, Friedrichshain, Mitte, and Moabit with only the poorest, who were precariously employed, lived a long distance from consistent employment, or were unemployed. These inner-city proletarian districts became strongholds of the Communist Party, areas with perceptions of high rates of crime and with the greatest welfare expenditure.[112] Some, however, viewed the movement of population and the discourse about it with a critical eye. The rise of this new corporatist vision, as has already been noted, did not happen entirely behind the backs of social actors. Alexander Schwab contended that those who worried about population politics were not coming to terms with the real problem: large-scale movements of population characteristic of modern capitalist society, where the labour market and the market in general generated "convulsive spasms" and "crisis-like destruction of manpower and equipment" that periodically shook society.[113] He explained that there was the technical capacity to create an unlimited number of homes, but capitalism had constrained fulfilment of this capacity.[114] At the heart of the migration, for Schwab, was agriculture in Germany, which, like other advanced capitalist countries, did not keep up with the innovative pace set by industry, but "exodus" from the countryside was a consequence not only of rural backwardness but also a result of the industrialization of agriculture, which reduced the necessary labour time for agriculture.[115] By placing urban space and population politics in the context of the recent history of capitalism, Schwab argued, one could illuminate the ideological focus on the family, on population growth, and on fertility in the corporatist city planning discourse. He argued that the prevailing concept of family was historically specific.[116] Schwab mocked those population politicians who were concerned that urbanites, especially the working class and migrants from the east, were not rooted in a particular home, for discovering the "urban nomad" "as the bourgeoisie itself was drawn into the vortex and felt the restlessness of constantly revolutionizing modern capitalism."[117]

The Character of the State

In the building industry, governmental intervention altered the functioning of a central liberal institution – the market. A similar change occurred when the state sought to incorporate the totality of the levels of government into one corporate, integrated, and "organic" entity, by eliminating formerly independent entities of government, like the municipality, with the goal of an efficient and corporate community. This section argues that in this period municipal self-administration eroded as social actors sought to incorporate of all parts of government into one institution; it will also argue that contemporary legal theorists understood this historical shift as one part of a change in the character of capitalism. Instead of treating the levels of administration as distinct, legally determined entities, as had been the case before the war, the developing corporatist ideology viewed the administrative strata as a single, integrated, living institution. This vision of government mirrored the organic conception of the city.

When the corporatist discourse about the nature of society employed classical liberal language, the meaning was inverted to fit the new corporatist society. Migge proclaimed, "Self-administration is dead; long live self-administration!" He argued that Germans could build a new society only on the basis of "responsibility, freedom, independence and self-administration." While these ideas sound liberal, Migge, in fact, argued that formal and abstract responsibility, freedom, independence, and self-administration that had characterized liberalism were insufficient and unproductive; on the contrary, he asserted, communal autarky was necessary and could be made real in form and content through inner colonization, that is the redevelopment of depopulated lands at the eastern edge of Germany with ethnic Germans. He contended that this was the only way to heal the weakened body of Germany.[118] The corporatist vision incorporated this seemingly liberal claim.

As discussed in chapter 1, Hugo Preuß claimed that economic transformation led to an incremental change in legal concepts like self-administration, which could be masked by the fact that these conventions appeared the same on the surface. Preuß's insight into this misrecognition was one side of a duality. The other side was that historically specific problems, such as the relationship between the self-administering city and the state in the corporatist period, could appear to be long-term problems. For example, in 1922 the sociologist Abroteles Eleutheropulos posited that the relationship between state and society had never truly been resolved.[119] Eleutheropulos argued that since the French Revolution, liberals understood state and society as opposites. In Germany, he asserted, society was synonymous with the "material interests associated with the ownership," but "such a view of society and state could not be sustained," because the purpose of a society was "the unity of people with the specific intention to achieve a purpose."[120] Where once there were a series of antagonisms, there was now an integrated whole.

German society and capitalism more generally were commonly understood to be in the midst of a transformation. The political scientist Kurt Wolzendorff suggested that German society lay on the cusp of a new epoch in political life, one that would require "a new calibration of the problem [of man and the state] according to the changed practicalities of social life."[121] Wolzendorff agreed with Preuß's argument about historical specificity, arguing that in the liberal epoch, people believed they could address the relationship of the individual to the state through formal rights, but that the "German spirit" could not tolerate this formalism. Therefore, he argued, the "German spirit" recognizing that "the bond of community is rooted in man" and that community was the reservoir of "human rights and cooperative self-governing social communities" sought to overcome formalism. In other words, human rights were not categories of the individual or citizen but of the social totality, of the organic community.[122] He explained, the liberal conception of the state was defined through an opposition between the state and "the individual sphere of freedom of its citizens"; however, the corporatist conception was defined through an opposition between "the social jurisdiction of the state and of non-governmental organizations."[123] The struggle over jurisdiction was not between the sovereign state and the citizen; it was between institutions of different orders.

The shift from liberal social forms to corporatist social forms was also evident in legal theory, including to contemporaries. Franz Neumann argued that those supporting this new institutionalist theory of law, which was sympathetic to and symptomatic of the corporatist society, considered themselves to be engaged in a "progressive debunking" of liberal theories of law, because they attacked the central liberal concept of the abstract equality of legal persons. In its place, this school offered "the concept of the institution," attesting that it, unlike the legal person, did not "mask [social] differentiations." They viewed the state as "a community, which rests organically upon communities of a lower order." This change affected the conception of property, for example, in that a factory was no longer understood as just a means of production but as "'social work and factory community' in which the worker is not only an instrument of the entrepreneur but also is 'a living member of the working community of entrepreneurs and workers.'"[124] Furthermore, contract relationships in corporate society were no longer "the reciprocal obligations of exchange," as they were in liberal society; they became the "work in the community on a common task and aim."[125]

This turn away from liberal norms and towards corporatist social structure was not limited to German government or jurisprudence. The critical legal theorist Otto Kirchheimer contended that these new corporatist governments depended on executive authority and emergency decrees, even in liberal governments, such as that of the Third Republic in France, because of a sense that liberal political norms, like parliamentary democracy, were weak, indecisive, and abstract. This, in turn, hollowed out liberal principles under the pressure of radical and contentious politics, but also under the pressure of a changed form of capitalism. The executive power of the state, which institutionalist law saw as decisive and concrete, was preferred to the abstract representation and deliberative mode of the legislative branch. The French government had introduced enabling acts in 1916 that granted the executive branch power to act without parliamentary approval, in the same year as the Hindenburg Plan went into effect, then a second similar bill in 1924, and a third in 1934, which was terminated four months after it was enacted. But as Kirchheimer noted, the debate was not about whether it should be allowed at all, but about whether to limit it to a particular government.[126]

The Unification of Greater Berlin

As Greater Berlin became a single municipality with the 1920 law, discussions about the administrative integration and rationalization of older administrative structures reveal a shift – even among liberals – towards a corporate vision of government. This section argues that the liberal Oberbürgermeister of Berlin, Gustav Böß, emphasized the efficiencies of an economy of scale over municipal self-administration, that conservatives inverted and mobilized formerly classical liberal positions, like self-administration, to defend pre-revolutionary governmental structures, and that the Left and liberals inverted former positions to defend the power of the centralized bureaucracy. Böß regarded the liberal principle of self-administration, as will be analysed here, as excessively deliberative, corrupt, and inefficient. Furthermore, he held that the market, the key locus of equality and freedom within liberal understandings of the world, fundamentally distorted the ability of the city to address pressing needs.

This shift in the form, function, and perception of Greater Berlin inspired transformations in long-held political positions and in the meaning and power of key terms with regard to administration of the region. While the 27 April 1920 Greater Berlin Law created a single legal entity and reterritorialized the Greater Berlin region, it did not establish the practical functioning of this new administration. Analysis of efforts to create that administration reveal an ideology of municipal administration that emphasized efficiency and economy of scale. The new municipal government had to integrate and rationalize the formerly independent administrations, while purging the unproductive and purportedly parasitic elements.[127] Administrators justified this new form of city government by claiming that the state did not impose the new single municipality of Greater Berlin from the outside according to abstract norms of liberal law; rather, it was "organic" and "concrete" historical and economic connections within the Greater Berlin region, accentuated during the war, that created the unified city.[128] In 1921 Greater Berlin's Oberbürgermeister, Gustav Böß, believed that an expansion of scope and a centralization of control of housing were necessary.[129] Martin Wagner recalled that the Greater Berlin Law "revolted against the 19th century spirit of isolational individualism."[130] The Berlin city planner Roman Heiligenthal claimed that statistics provided the planner with the means to grasp "the manifestations of the urban 'organism' and a picture of future development" as well as "the basis for understanding the economic processes."[131] And he believed that such a comprehensive form of planning demanded regional and state cooperation.[132] Projects of regional planning were already under way in the industrial Ruhr region of Germany. Siedlungsverband Ruhrkohlenbezirk was the first regional planning authority in Germany, formed in 1913 with the goal of rationalizing the road system and preserving open space. Like the Verband Groß-Berlin and the new city of Berlin, it was not until after the stabilization that planning on a genuinely regional scale began in earnest.[133]

While during the war, conservatives sought to consolidate administrative power in a regional government centred on Greater Berlin, during the Weimar Republic they used formerly liberal arguments to decentralize the administration of the integrated community, as the Left and liberal parties looked to create a unified administration with significant power vested in the central bureaucracy. Martin Wagner recalled that Karl Steiniger, the executive of the Zweckverband, had succeeded through "dexterous exploitations of First World War conditions" and that Steiniger was "an experienced administrator and financier. Although he happened to be a conservative of the first rank, he nevertheless went the whole way with [me] in zoning down square miles of overly zoned suburban building land; he approved many radical building code revisions; he bought from the Prussian State some 25,000 acres of forests to be set aside as permanently secured recreation areas for the people; he laid the foundation for the acquisition of all commuter traffic facilities."[134] The Left succeeded in creating a unified and centralized city government, because in the Landtag it worked as a unified and powerful block, despite its factions.[135] A similar left-wing block dominated city government. A 20 June 1920 election brought a new city council to power that was 38.4 per cent USPD and 17.2 per cent SPD, making a total of 55.6 per cent representing left-wing parties, while the rest of the vote was split among bourgeois factions, with the German People's Party (DVP) and the German National People's Party (DNVP) leading that coalition.[136]

Formerly independent municipalities resisted the integration of Greater Berlin, invoked the liberal category of municipal self-administration, and were reluctant to give up the privileges that the old budgets and borders protected. In the discourse, an ideological opposition developed between deliberative and self-administering administrative bodies, on the one hand, and a centralized bureaucracy, on the other. In this dichotomy, the deliberative bodies represented the corrupt and entrenched traditional interests and inequalities, while the bureaucracy spoke for equality and the needs of the greater society. At a May 1920 meeting to determine the finances of the new Berlin and consolidate the municipal technical apparatus, Böß argued that district self-administration ran counter to the goal of eliminating competition, redundancy, and complexity.[137] Böß contended that the law made "centralization of housing policy" possible when connected to the emergency law, which facilitated an equal if not stronger "implementation of the command economy."[138]

As further evidence in this shift, the liberal idea of municipal self-administration in this new corporatist society had significantly less power to convince than it had before the war. Böß, who was a member of the liberal German Democratic Party, largely dismissed these claims of self-administration because he believed it to be inefficient. The longest-lasting challenge to the new municipal structure came from the right-liberal *Deutsche Volkspartei*, which sought to increase district self-administration. Böß claimed that their request was a "constitutional impossibility" and would "actually dissolve even old Berlin," replacing it with "six new public law entities" that would result in "completely unacceptable" effects on "existing economic and historical conditions."[139] When addressing a similar problem in 1922 of whether to create a federal structure of the districts of Greater Berlin, Böß contended that city government could eliminate district assemblies or empower them "like small-town council meetings," but the latter would generate "serious ongoing disputes between the headquarters and districts." Furthermore, such a change would recreate the old inequalities among rich and poor districts, which those who drafted the law sought to overcome.[140] In 1922 he argued that the deliberations of local district committees were slow and redundant.[141] He wanted to eliminate district assemblies.[142] Larger and wealthier former suburbs fought against Berlin's takeover of municipal water, gas, and electricity.[143] However, centralization was not the answer to every question, and in April 1922 Böß sought to eliminate the six inner districts in old Berlin and to decentralize civil engineering as well as the distribution of general welfare, youth welfare, unemployment welfare, and veterans and wounded welfare.[144] At the height of the inflation in the fall of 1923, Spandau attacked the central administration for "overly emphasized centralism, clumsiness and slowness of business, redundancy in the central administration and the districts, inadequate regard for local interests and characteristics." Böß responded that the diversity of the incorporated communities made the process uneven, but the only way forward was a "well-planned unification of all existing local administrations" with the goal of unity and equality.[145]

Even social institutions as central to liberal understandings of the world as the market were deemed inefficient in this new corporatist society. Böß believed that private ownership of key municipal services distorted the ability of the city to deal with pressing needs. Spandau had claimed that its municipal services could be more efficient if they were independent and operated as private, for-profit entities.[146] Böß challenged this celebration of "the alleged principles of the private sector" and responded with an example of private trash collection in Stieglitz that led to significantly higher profits for the waste disposal contractors than in the rest of Berlin.[147] For Böß, the Greater Berlin law made management simpler and more economical, eliminating jurisdictional conflicts and competition among the gas, electricity, and waterworks.[148] Böß believed that the municipal administrators had nearly harmonized the district interests with that of the Greater Berlin totality, and an amendment to the Greater Berlin law threatened that success.[149] The left-wing parties and unions resisted these efficiency measures because of concerns about working conditions, the city's conduct as an employer, tariffs for municipal utilities, and the closing of redundant and unprofitable plants. Within the left wing, city councillors disagreed about operating public utilities as non-profits or using profits to pay for other city services; however, the Socialists and the Communists agreed that the city government remained capitalist and behaved accordingly.[150]

As was the case in other parts of this corporatist society, a series of oppositions sustained this discussion about the integration of the formerly independent cities and towns into the new Greater Berlin municipality. One can see antimonies between self-administering municipalities and a centralized and efficient central government; between ineffective and unequal deliberative bodies and efficient, egalitarian, and productive bureaucracy; between profit-seeking, inefficient, expensive, and irrational private business and non-profit, productive, cheap, and rational public utilities; and finally between imposed and abstract structures of government and organic, historically constituted, and concrete governmental structures. In each case, the key administrators preferred the more concrete and institutional to the more abstract and market-mediated forces.

Urban Politics

Perceptions of political and criminal violence and corruption shaped the political conditions in Berlin during the late period of the Weimar Republic. Yet this development did not inspire a desire to return to a more liberal form of government; rather, it caused Berliners to want to deepen the roots of the corporatist society.

Table 1. Percentage votes for the Reichstag, Landtag, and communal governmental votes in Berlin, 1928–1933

	KPD	NSDAP
Reichstag vote 20 May 1928	24.64	1.57
Reichstag vote 14 September 1930	27.29	14.62
Reichstag vote 31 July 1932	27.33	28.65
Reichstag vote 6 November 1932	31.02	25.97
Reichstag vote 5 March 1933	19.47	34.62
Landtag vote 20 May 1928	24.69	1.54
Landtag vote 24 April 1932	23.65	27.90
Landtag vote 5 March 1933	24.32	34.21
City Council vote 17 November 1929	24,64	5.76
City Council vote 12 March 1933	19.47	38.26
County Council vote 17 November 1933	24.64	5.71
County Council vote 12 March 1933	19.47	38.22

In the late 1920s and early 1930s Berlin struggled with paramilitary violence, economic crisis, and political scandal. The National Socialists and the Communists battled for control of the streets. While the National Socialists attacked all left-wing parties, the Communists focused on the National Socialists. Despite the Communist rhetoric against the Socialists, they generally refrained from violence in their confrontations.[151] The Sturmabteilung (SA) of the NSDAP defined themselves and their party through street battles with the Communist Red Front in "Red Berlin," especially after Joseph Goebbels became the *Gauleiter* for Berlin in 1926. Goebbels emphasized – accurately or not – the proletarian character of the Berlin SA. The NSDAP saw Berlin as Jewish, Red, decadent, and a symptom of cultural decline, as did many right-wing groups and thinkers throughout Europe.[152] The Communists, for their part, returned the fight but also tried to sabotage and subvert the SA through the deployment of spies and the publication of fake SA newsletters.[153]

The city of Berlin was increasingly politically polarized. The rise of the National Socialists in Berlin elections was rapid, while the Communists maintained their position.[154]

Scandals racked the Berlin city government during this period, with the Kutisker-Barmat Scandal setting the tone. Julius Barmat, originally from the Ukraine but living in Berlin, and Ivan Kutisker, originally from Lithuania but also living in Berlin, were Jewish businessmen who created conglomerates during the inflation that then went bankrupt with the stabilization. Kutisker fraudulently submitted collateral in order to obtain increasingly large loans from the Reichspost and Prussian State Bank. He then consolidated the credit in a period of capital shortage; Barmat did much the same thing. Kutisker ended up with 11 million M and Barmat with 14 million RM from the state at a time when the hourly wage for the unskilled worker was 0.67 RM. The key feature, though, was not the amount of capital but their close connection to the Berlin SPD. This opened the SPD to (further) accusations of class betrayal from the Left and of subservience to Jews, and the state itself as being "Jewish" from the Right. This scandal connected the state and the SPD to corruption and to the influx of Jews from Eastern Europe that so worried the Right.[155]

The ignominious Sklarek Scandal involved Leo, Max, and Willy Sklarek, who were also Jews, though natives of Berlin. They were millionaire textile manufacturers and, like Kutisker and Barmat, they were associated with socialist and liberal politicians. Wealthy conservatives saw them as parvenus. In 1925 the brothers bought a second-hand clothing business.[156] In 1926 they purchased low-quality clothing stocks that the city had bought to support the poor during the inflation. The next year the brothers forced the city to pay a significant amount by claiming that the quality of the clothing, which the city had advertised as poor, was worse than expected. Simultaneously, the brothers won a monopoly on supplying the city with clothing, by bribing the head of city purchasing and offering other city officials merchandise at very cheap prices and then delaying or never sending bills. The Sklareks provided Böß with a deeply discounted fur coat for his wife and thereby ended his career.[157] The Sklarek brothers defrauded the city of at least 10 million M and were put on trial in October 1931 and were convicted on June 1932.[158] Also violent organized crime syndicates engaged in street fights, prostitution, protection rackets, and the drug trade in Berlin, creating a culture of fear in poorer neighbourhoods.[159]

Municipal Independence

This new corporatist understanding of society and the city altered the theories of the relationship between the city government and the state and Reich governments. First, the expansion of the welfare state responsibilities of municipalities made municipalities into arms of state and Reich policies. Second, while the austerity measures of the Brüning government constrained these responsibilities, they did not lead to a return of liberal municipal self-administration. Finally, the fascist legal theorist Carl Schmitt appropriated and transformed the left-liberal Hugo Preuß's approach to questions of government and politics.

The expansion of the welfare state and the growth of the corporate society during the Weimar Republic challenged the liberal tradition of municipal self-administration in fundamental ways. But this expansion met a significant challenge with the arrival of the Great Depression and the austerity policy of the Brüning government. Fritz Elsas argued that various levels of government, prior to the austerity measures, had restructured municipalities, like Greater Berlin, to better serve the interest of the public good and affect economic development.[160] Herman Kranold lamented that within the Prussian legal code, municipal government remained bound to pre-war liberal structures, and he believed that the state needed to overcome what he regarded as this empty formalism of municipal democracy.[161] Ernst Runge argued that the incorporation of Greater Berlin effectively concentrated technical and city-planning capacity at a regional level, which could "only be seen as a precursor to a stronger form of government."[162]

The conditions of the Great Depression seemed to create a barrier for corporatist expansion of municipal responsibilities, which had significant economic consequences for local economic conditions. Theodor von Pistorius propounded the view that poor Reich, state, and municipal financial conditions were driving the economy into bankruptcy.[163] Kranold blamed local financial difficulty and corruption on "insufficient financial compensation by Reich and state, the removal of revenue, dependence of local authorities [upon tax] revenue from sources (capital gains tax, property transfer tax, entertainment tax, business tax and other items)" that were especially affected by most cyclical changes as well as "new responsibilities without adequate funds."[164] In fiscal years 1928–30 municipalities received 33.7 per cent of total income and corporate taxes in Germany, or 1205.9 million RM, but the revenue dedicated to the cities was decreased by roughly half or more (depending on the year) between 1930 and 1933. In addition, the Reich restricted the ability of municipalities to raise taxes, and the December 1930 emergency decree included cuts in municipal taxes of 10 and 20 per cent, as well as measures prohibiting the increase of real estate taxes.[165] Nonetheless, Kranold claimed, the local press focused on sensational local scandals and "a pogrom atmosphere had been created against the self-administration," blocking autonomy from the state that was more genuine.[166] Reich, state, and provincial officials also fanned the flames of controversy to distract from the relationship between tax revenues and municipal welfare responsibilities.[167]

A Catholic theorist of the fascist state, Carl Schmitt, crystallized this transformation of municipal self-administration between 1900 and 1930 in a 1930 lecture on Hugo Preuß. Preuß defended municipal autonomy and saw it as a necessary but unfulfilled task of liberal revolution. However, unlike many of his predecessors, Schmitt contended, Preuß did not make claims for municipal self-administration based on positivist jurisprudence. Schmitt, an arch-critic of the liberalism and abstraction of the Weimar constitution, celebrated the constitution's primary author, Preuß, as a pioneer in the corporate theory of the state. Schmitt maintained that categories such as "sovereignty, freedom, democracy, and rule of law preserved their precise meaning only through a concrete antithesis." He built his theory of politics and law on an antithesis between the abstract and superficial, on the one hand, and the concrete, organic, and essential, on the other. For Schmitt, all categories of law and state theory were political and polemical and were aimed at a political enemy. Schmitt contended that the works of Preuß, who spent his life in the opposition until he had the opportunity to contribute to the writing of the Weimar constitution, must have appeared polemical to his contemporaries; therefore, it was easy to attack him for politicizing what should have been pure jurisprudence. However, Schmitt argued, Preuß was revealing the concrete and essential political oppositions behind the jurisprudence.[168] Schmitt asserted that the apolitical character of pure jurisprudence was a "political trick." Presenting a certain political approach in the name of "the technical interests of a quickly and smoothly functioning bureaucracy" was only superficially apolitical. Embedded in bureaucracy were "foreign and domestic political conditions and in a concrete political situation."[169] Schmitt's supposed revelation of the political essence of Preuß's insights exemplified the pseudo-progressive debunking that Franz Neumann describes.[170] Schmitt claimed that despite Preuß's intellectual debts to the abstract and positivist jurisprudence of Gneist and Laband, Preuß retained Gierke's concrete, Germanist, and institutionalist idea of an "organic state" and used this category "to refute the existing monarchical authoritarian state."[171] Schmitt defined Preuß's organic state in a positive light, as one that was "built up from below" by democracy and not a mechanical fusion state with the bureaucracy. For Schmitt, the organic state was "the whole, the unity of the whole in the concrete political situation" and not classically liberal "atomistic," "individualistic," or "particularistic."[172]

Conclusion: The Corporate City

In important formal ways, the Weimar Republic made it possible for the working class to become full-fledged citizens and to experience certain liberal rights. This occurred, however, as the social basis for such liberalism was being undermined. And the working-class movement itself played no small role in weakening the grounds for liberalism. Because of the successful and effective assertion of working-class power and a broader social transformation towards a corporatist society, a different, more collective form of society developed. Much of the discourse of the time connected this new corporatist society, the new city of Berlin, and the interventionist state to a newly defined capacity to connect with the natural world and organic social structures. This new ideology celebrated the organic, productive, and collective while attacking the inorganic, speculative, and individualized. This dichotomy shaped much of the discussion about municipal administration in the Weimar Republic in Berlin.

Chapter Six

The Organic Machine: City Planning in the Weimar Republic

The physical image of the modern city is not naturally grown, but somewhat artificially imposed. An enormous blood pressure jams into a few abnormal veins, which threaten to explode at any moment, a ruthless accumulation of forces, regardless of whether they are healthy or sick, and accordingly a haphazard alignment across the functional design. The entire literature of the last forty years on cities proves the correctness of these statements for both the physiognomy and the physiology of the city.

Martin Mächler[1]

Introduction: Transformation in City Planning

In the 1922 epigraph above, Martin Mächler, with Greater Berlin in mind, characterized the major themes of city planning and municipal administration in the Weimar Republic. Though it is difficult to determine Mächler's political party affiliations, he was comfortable with the continued existence of a "pyramidical structure of society," which he believed had endured since ancient times.[2]

Planners and architects of the time asserted that a fundamental break from the building industry of the past was necessary. During this corporatist period, they commonly saw modern capitalist society as a massive organism connected with population growth, urban space, and economic productivity. Their discourse connected this vision of capitalism to an existential angst about national decline and to a veneration of the supposedly redemptive powers of the soil of Germany. This corporatist attention to the soil and the concrete became more intense with the onset of the Great Depression. However, as Molly Loberg has explained, while a transnational history of capitalist cityscapes in boom periods exists, a history of the same spaces in crises of capitalism does not.[3]

This sense of a breach with the liberal past was not limited to Berlin or even to Germany. Paul Ashton describes a very similar transformation from liberal to corporatist social forms in Australian urban discourse, away from laissez-faire city planning and towards a "new social order" that emphasized national efficiency and productivity, eugenics, and environmental determinism.[4] New corporatist policies in the 1930s in Brazilian cities led to increasing administrative centralization, a rejection of liberalism, a greater role for the state in urban affairs, and an interventionist and industrially focused economic policy. Brazilian planners turned to German and American examples, but not simply because these foreign models represented modernity, but because these models seemed uniquely suitable to their own urban conditions.[5] In both Brazil and Mexico, modernist architecture was adopted by revolutionary governments and by reformist architects interested in expressing a progressive and modernizing structure in their relatively non-industrialized societies. In Argentina, where industrialization was more firmly established, architects and patrons more haphazardly adopted modernism.[6] (This suggests that the relationship between industrialization and architectural form is an international issue, and not only a question of isolated nation states and their economies.) In Germany, as in Britain, political economists hoped that a period of post-war prosperity could be created by "physically and morally revitaliz[ing] the labor force, improv[ing] industrial relations, and an enhanced technical and administrative structure."[7]

This chapter examines institutionalization of a corporatist model of city planning and architecture in the Weimar Republic through seven sections. The first section argues that this corporatist form, function, and perception of cities shaped the development of housing construction and its ideology during the Weimar Republic. The second section argues that this ideology emphasized access to nature and small-scale agriculture within city planning and housing design. The third part of the chapter contends that a new corporatist aesthetic ideology shaped housing construction that celebrated production, efficiency, and functionality, and its proponents attacked what they regarded as superfluous or contrary to these values. In the fourth section, the chapter maintains that a belief that space causes and can solve social problems led to new approaches to the perceived social consequences of the built environment and new attempts to build the city as a productive totality. The fifth section argues that the corporatist form, function, and perception of cities led to a vastly expanded scale and perceived territory of planning, while the sixth contends that the city planners and architects wished to rationalize the built environment by eliminating those elements of the city that were inefficient, including domestic spaces, and thereby bring the logic of the factory to the built environment. In the seventh and final part, this chapter maintains that the development of city planning, architecture, and housing production called into question long-held assumptions about capitalism, as many of the features of capitalism that were regarded as essential were significantly ameliorated or eliminated, while capitalism itself survived.

Housing and Productivity

The combination of the First World War and the 1918 Revolution institutionalized the corporatist discourse that prior to these events had been a critical discourse. This discursive change was part of a broader change in capitalism and in the form, function, and perception of cities like Greater Berlin and shifted the approach to the long-term problem of housing shortages in Berlin. This attempt to deal with the housing issue involved a critique of the free market and its role in creating the poor conditions, as well as a new corporatist celebration of the possibility of coordinating the society to increase productivity. Concerns about psychic, physiological, economic, and political consequences of inadequate housing contributed to this effort to expand housing. To pay for the housing policy, the national government reorganized the tax structure, and to enact the policy, government at all levels created new programs and institutions that it was hoped would address concerns about both housing and employment. In the brief period between the stabilization of the currency following the hyperinflation and the Great Depression, the government and non- or low-profit housing construction firms made headway in addressing the housing shortage. However, in the late 1920s the housing market began to feel the first tremors of the Great Depression, following which the austerity policy of the Brüning government removed the state from the concern about housing.

In this new corporatist social order, housing shortage remained a problem for city planning, in Germany and internationally. Planners used the corporatist ideology of the state to address that long-term insufficiency. Manfredo Tafuri argues that housing construction was a "cornerstone of Weimar *Sozialpolitik*."[8] Gerald Feldman posits that housing construction presented a "vicious circle" of social and economic policy.[9] David Abraham claims that political and economic changes could pressure the state to increase its role in the economy. However, as the state became increasingly involved in the economy, it also became increasingly dependent on private capital, because, while the state regulated capital, it did not control the development and movement of capital. Those whose business depended on the housing economy assumed that the state was involved, and it became increasingly difficult for the state to retreat to a more liberal position.[10]

Though the government was involved in the housing economy in Berlin in a limited in scope in the liberal era, a qualitative and quantitative change occurred in 1914 with new laws to protect tenants, publicly manage housing, limit rent increases, and provide financial support for housing.[11] During the Kaiserreich, liberal philanthropy and right-wing populism dominated housing reform discourse, but after the war, the Left entered this discussion.[12] The First World War had brought rent-control measures to Germany, as it did to Britain and Belgium. In all three nations, rent control became part of the assumed conditions of the national economy. In Britain during and after the war, property rented from private landlords declined rapidly, and new construction of publicly supported council housing became an important source of new homes. By 1938 one-third of the existing housing stock had been built after 1914 and one-third of that was government-sponsored housing. Likewise, rent control in Belgium survived into the mid-1920s and was slowly dismantled in the 1930s.[13] In Vienna after the war, the power of the tenant was increased relative to the landlord in evictions and rent increases; however, employers used these rent controls as a reason not to increase wages.[14]

In the corporatist ideology, critics of the existing housing conditions blamed them on the free market. This criticism combined with economic goals and imperatives to expand the role of the government. The Socialist city planner Martin Wagner argued that the free market was "hostile" to "social and cultural housing production" and created "plan-less settlements."[15] Wisso Weiß blamed the housing problem on a "liberal-capitalist economy," wherein housing was considered a commodity whose price was determined by supply and demand.[16] He was unsure how far social movements could push socialization after the 1918 Revolution.[17] Robert Sachs, among others, believed that municipalities should acquire large tracts of land and construct "housing estates, roads, playgrounds and green spaces, play areas," to avoid real estate speculation.[18] Weiß thought that Wagner's Bauhütte movement took steps towards "the realization of socialism" in housing, but its vision of socialism was romantic.[19] He argued that the diffusion of capital in the construction industry limited the possibilities for establishing Socialism and, in the place of workers' control, the state revolutionized the mode of construction.[20] Lotte Abrahamsohn argued that the appeal to the government to resolve housing shortage was as old as the shortage, but housing reform movements could not force change on private capital. For Abrahamsohn, "The liberal conception of the autonomy of the private sector was too deeply rooted even in public places, [for] drastic measures by the state or local [government to] be realized." However, the First World War, she noted, provided cause for drastic measures, and after the war the government funding supported new residential construction. She contended that housing construction was unprofitable for private firms because construction costs and rebuilding and restarting dormant industries soaked up capital. Responsibility fell to the government, which intended its housing policy to re-establish the private market, Abrahamsohn argued, but Socialists used the opportunity to attempt to solve the housing shortage with public funds.[21]

The government expanded its role in the housing economy, because it believed, following this corporatist ideology, that poor-quality housing had social and economic consequences, which affect the political and economic health of the new republic. The state used new taxes to encourage and focus housing production on low-income habitations. In April 1920 the Wohnungsverband Groß Berlin wrote to the Reich Ministerpräsidenten Otto Braun that, in Greater Berlin, the Prussian state had created about 12,000 emergency apartments and nearly completed 4,000 new permanent dwellings. These structures were built or prepared with the assumption of 150 million M in subsidies, and the Wohnungsverband warned that a failure to pass the tax bill to cover these costs would lead to a paralysis of construction.[22] In October 1920 city council president Hermann Weyl and his colleagues in the Wohnungsverband Groß-Berlin, as well as Oberbürgermeister Adolf Wermuth, pressed the city government to fund and facilitate the purchase of land and the construction of housing that included small-scale agriculture.[23] In a letter to the National Assembly, the Housing Committee argued that construction of new homes, especially small apartments, was necessary immediately, because rationing of the existing housing was reaching the limits of its effectiveness.[24] The Reich, the state, the province, and the municipality were all willing to fund housing construction in Berlin because of the "dangerous repercussions" of the shortage on the "overall economy and the mood of the population."[25] The liberal city planner Joseph Stübben argued that the housing shortage was becoming more acute: each year, before the war, private enterprise had built about 200,000 new housing units of all types. After five years of war and revolution and little building, new housing construction was short 1 million apartments. For Stübben, both public financial support and private enterprise were necessary.[26]

The conditions in Berlin were often compared to those in Vienna. In the Austrian capital in 1912, the liberal era, housing consumed roughly a quarter of the average worker's pay, and according to some estimates, more than 550,000 people (or one-quarter of the city's population) had been in emergency housing for the homeless that year. The First World War only made these conditions worse, as many soldiers chose not to return to the countryside and instead sought housing in the capital. As in Berlin, while new family formation stagnated during the war, it surged afterward. Vienna had 254 vacant apartments in early 1918, and by September 1919 there were only 105 inhabitable apartments available.[27]

With these new funds, the corporatist government created novel ways of addressing the long-term housing shortage and regulation. In May the municipality passed the Greater Berlin Housing Crisis Law, which enabled the development of regional housing policy and instituted new rent laws and policies. The act created housing offices in twelve districts in old Berlin and fourteen in the formerly independent cities and towns; a housing and settlement committee in the Magistrat oversaw regulatory uniformity.[28] But in November 1923 the problem of housing was still pressing, and the Brandenburg District of the Association of German Architects (BDA) demanded that the Prussian Finance Ministry act immediately to solve the housing shortage and restart construction. The BDA proposed a 50 per cent tax on the increase in the value of an upgraded rental property in order to finance new buildings and protect old ones.[29]

The hyperinflation significantly limited the capacity of the new corporatist state to actually address these problems; after the stabilization of the currency, however, housing construction firms finally were able to begin to manage the shortage. In September 1923 Martin Wagner's construction firm, Bauhütte Berlin, agreed with the German

Confederation of Unions, Allgemeiner Deutscher Gewerkschaftsbund (ADGB), to create a social service network based on the provision of public housing.[30] The Bauhütte group was non-profit but competed in the market. They were able to underbid for-profit builders, because they paid their workers the going wage but required the highest level of work discipline, used the most advanced forms of rationalized labour, and expected the unions to refrain from striking.[31] In 1924 they developed a workers' bank (Bank der Arbeiter, Angestellten und Beamten), housing insurance companies (Deutsche Wohnungsfürsorge A. G. für Beamte, Angestellte und Arbeiter, or DEWOG), and with a subsidiary of Volksfürsorge, provided social insurance. The most prominent branch was the Berlin Gemeinnützige Heimstätten- Spar- und Bau- Aktien-Gesellschaft (GEHAG), which performed many tasks and built many settlements, including Britz in Schöneberg, begun in 1924 and designed by Bruno Taut and Wagner.[32] In 1926 Wagner became city planner for all of Berlin.[33] There he tried to create a capital of a democracy, improve working-class conditions, and establish a productive and efficient city.[34]

In Germany, and in Berlin, as part of the corporatist vision and practice of government and the economy, all levels of government were committed to integrating themselves and to expanding the housing stock. The Deutsche Bau- und Bodenbank reported that construction firms built about 300,000 homes in 1928; they had constructed roughly the same number the year before. In the fiscal year 1928–9 another 150,000 homes were under construction, which, the bank officers believed, was proof of the favourable condition of the German economy and the construction industry. But between 1927 and 1929 some 4 to 6 per cent of construction workers were unemployed. The bank noted that the 600,000 required minimum of new apartments developed by the Reich Housing Census covered "only the most urgent needs," because the census found that 950,000 to 1,000,000 independent households were in search of housing. The bank assumed that housing demand would continue to be strong because of the housing shortage, of the need to replace unusable housing, and of migration in response to changes in industrial geography. The "general decline" in the economy in 1929, according to the Bau- und Bodenbank, did not stop construction, which continued at the same pace as it had the previous year.[35] But the bank also noted that the number of housing starts had lagged because of the unfinished buildings from 1928.[36] Approved building permits far exceeded housing starts in 1929, and fewer dwellings were completed than in 1928.[37] The bank claimed that employers increased construction workers' wages twice in 1928 and again in April 1929, and the prices for building materials increased as well, making the average costs in 1929 higher than they had been in 1928 or in 1927.[38] Thus in 1929, because of increased costs and a shortage of domestic and foreign capital, the bank argued, the number of unemployed construction workers began to rise, especially beginning in August.[39] In response to a drive by the Brüning government to remove the state from the housing economy, Kurt Bloch argued that the private market could not supply a million homes.[40] He contended that the housing industry set a record with 250,000 apartments built in 1927, but at that rate, a real decrease in demand would not occur until 1935.[41]

By the late 1920s these corporatist governmental housing policies began to reach their economic limits. At this time the government was funding 60 per cent of house construction in the Weimar Republic. Just as the housing industry was finally beginning to address the shortage in a substantive manner, the economic and policy conditions that made it possible to do so had deteriorated. The housing industry collapsed in the financial crises of 1929 and 1931, and as a result of the policies of the Brüning government.[42] On 17 December 1928 architect Ludwig Hilberseimer reported that the Berlin City Council had approved a four-year construction program to occur between 1929 and 1932, with the goal of building 32,000 apartments. He believed that after many futile efforts, the city government had taken the first step to funding Martin Wagner's efforts for the long term.[43] Hilberseimer endorsed the program because he believed it placed collective needs above those of the individual, and it contributed to the effectiveness of "the most important means of production, human labour."[44] In Vienna, in the first year of enactment of the 1923 tax measure, 2,200 apartments were built and quickly surpassed the goal of 5,000 in 1924. By the third year of the program, in 1926, the city was creating 12,000 new apartments a year. While this building program was significant, proportional to the population it was not as large as the effort in Frankfurt, accomplished in less time, or the effort in the United States.[45] Despite the Austrian Social Democrats' initiatives, as of 1928 they believed they had failed to overcome the housing shortage.[46]

In 1931, in response to the financial constraints brought on by the Great Depression and the 1931 run on banks, the austerity programs of the Brüning government withdrew public control of the housing market. This change strengthened the idea in this corporatist society that abstract, financial parts of social life were constraining the development of concrete, productive endeavours. For Ferdinand Falk, this set back the housing industry years, adversely affecting housing conditions, the health of the working class, economic productivity, and social reproduction.[47] Abrahamsohn added that the October 1932 reorganization of the state, which included eliminating the Prussian welfare ministry, also wiped out the gains from centralization; in the new austerity effort, the government shifted responsibility for housing policy to three other ministries, including, most detrimentally, the Ministry of Finance.[48] Abrahamsohn argued that social policy during the Weimar Republic reduced the power of capital in favour of the workers, but the imperatives of the capitalism still governed social policy.[49] Expressing a common sentiment, she endorsed urban decentralization to eastern Germany to improve the economy, where agricultural "living space [was] in abundance."[50]

Decentralization, Agriculture, and Access to Nature

Nature and agriculture played an important role in the development of corporatist housing policy in Berlin and in Germany at this time. In this corporatist form, function, and perception of cities, urban decentralization became a goal, in part because of changes in economic geography that had been underway since before the First World War. But the consequences of the war and the 1918 Revolution inflected this spatial change with new ideological meaning: it was believed that access to nature and cultivation of gardens could ameliorate social and economic problems.

Decentralization became a goal of the corporatist housing policy because of changing economic geography, on the one hand, and new ideologies about the relationship between nature and national health and productivity, on the other. Ministerial president Otto Braun and Minister of Welfare Hirtsiefer justified the city planning bill to the Staatsrat on 11 June 1926, on the basis of the rapid and random urban agglomeration in Prussia in the nineteenth century. They argued that cities grew in concentric circles, eliminated natural and agricultural landscapes, and created an "expectant wasteland" in which speculators bought out farmers or drove them off the land by making it unworkable. This nineteenth-century development resulted from "the economic ideas of the time" that were "based on the free play of market forces," rather than from policymakers, who "lacked an understanding of the dangers that result from urban expansion." Dense cities "killed the feeling of beauty," formed "apathy and despair," and were characterized by "spreading disease, sunless courtyards, [and no] playgrounds."[51] This corporatist attitude towards urban space and population density was dominant in Britain, too. The Homes for Heroes program brought attention to overcrowding and "unhealthy areas" with its introduction in 1919. As in Berlin, British planners saw better housing as a key means to combat the radicalization of the working class.[52]

In this corporatist era, city planners and architects believed that decentralizing the Greater Berlin population would increase agricultural production. Deutscher Bund Heimatschutz praised the new city-planning law for assuming building and nature conservation were "in indissoluble connection."[53] The Bund endorsed the law's effort to create satellite towns separated by green belts, dedicated to "permanent agriculture, gardens, livestock, etc.," and to avoid urban sprawl.[54] This type of reconfiguration of space demanded a significant role for planning, but the Bund stated that the plan had to be organic and moderate and guided by the "influence of economic interests," promoting industrial and working-class decentralization.[55] Siedlungswissenschaftliche Arbeitsgemeinschaft agreed and praised the law for intensifying and consolidating agriculture "in the thinly populated regions ... especially in the east."[56] Vegetable gardens played an important role in the new mode of planning, providing the necessary nutrition to workers in times of scarcity, such as those of the First World War, and enabling workers to work productively. Moreover, these gardens, as a garden advocate, Otto Albrecht, asserted, gave the urban population its "last opportunity for direct contact with this primordial power source of physical, mental, and moral health." While before the war landscape architects designed parks for bourgeois walkers, after the war the advent of the small garden transformed parkland towards egalitarian and productive ends.[57] Most new housing developments included space for gardening, as found, for example, in the "Lichtenberger Gartenheim."[58] The Deutscher Bund Heimatschutz's Heinrich Keller thought that large-scale plans were necessary to preserve the areas outside of administrative jurisdictions from being developed with mines, dumps, and industrial or housing projects, which destroyed "the last natural and recreational opportunities in these areas."[59] The Siedlungswissenschaftliche Arbeitsgemeinschaft believed the law would mitigate the mass "estrangement" from nature and counteract land speculation.[60] As Konstanze Sylva Domhardt shows, architects expected green space to mediate conflict and constitute civic culture even beyond the Second World War through the Congrès Internationaux d'Architecture Moderne.[61]

Architectural Form

The First World War and the 1918 Revolution had helped to create a new aesthetic ideology that then was crystallized in the tumultuous environment of the Weimar Republic. This new corporatist aesthetic ideology criticized pre-war liberal urban social relations and held that the urban built environment had profound consequences for those who inhabited it. It celebrated concrete social relations, cohesiveness, efficiency, and productivity, emphasizing its proletarian character as part of a broader corporatist reorganization of society. This corporatist aesthetic sought to coordinate the functionality of the interior with the simplicity of the exterior. It brought the logic of the factory to the home and eliminated distinctions between work and home life, as part of an effort to create a productive, coordinated society. In keeping with this factory logic and as part of a critique of excess, on the one hand, and of a political project to build as much housing as possible, on the other hand, the government and civil-society research organizations attempted to determine the minimal space necessary for apartments and the least expensive way to create them. While this theory emphasized the concrete and productive side of social life, architects and planners, nonetheless, organized their work according to abstract principles. However, these principles were different from the abstract precepts that had characterized planning and architecture before the First World War.

During the Weimar Republic a corporatist architectural ideology developed that blamed liberal social relations for the poor conditions of the built environment. Art historian, critic, and proponent of modernism Paul Ferdinand Schmidt argued that the City Committee in the Reichstag had become "increasingly architecturally conscious to the fact Berlin is a world city"; however, liberal city planning since the 1850s was filled with "irretrievably lost opportunities" due to "the horrors of Wilhelmine architecture facades" and speculation. The citizens of Berlin felt "at home nowhere" and fled en masse to the areas whose natural beauty was "unblemished" by the "trampling and raping of speculation." He did not want to free Berlin from responsibility by comparing it to "the horror of New York or Chicago," and so he compared it to Paris.[62] Within this world view, liberalism caused a type of abstract urban development – speculation – that eliminated immediate and intuitive, and arguably concrete, urban experiences. This led to an alienation from concrete nature and a need to seek out concrete nature wherever Berliners could find it.

The aesthetic and practical form of building purportedly had social, cultural, and economic consequences. For many planners and architects in this corporatist society, the dichotomy between the historicist decoration used to enhance the sale of the rental barrack, on the outside, and the decrepit and inadequate conditions, on the inside, expressed the problems of the Wilhelmian society.[63] Heinrich de Fries contended that rental barracks contained "excessive constriction, bad air, [and] bodily illness" as well as, in terms of "*Daseins-Formen*, great hate, great despair ... concentrated behind ridiculous facades."[64] For de Fries the superficial decoration on rental barracks masked poor use value. De Fries saw a similar difference between surface and depth in pre-war industrial architecture: the exterior was just a superficial skin on a dynamic interior; instead he wanted industrial buildings to "merge body and the outside wall into an inseparable unit" or "organic" link.[65] Le Corbusier expressed this sentiment when he referred to his apartment buildings as "a machine for living," as did Bauhaus artist Oskar Schlemmer when he advocated that dwelling machines should replace cathedrals.[66] De Fries saw modern architecture as a project of de-reification: it removed that which he regarded as the superficial and oriented towards quantification, like decoration intended to raise the market value. Modern architecture revealed the essential, working materials that the market had masked. This view held that pre–First World War society valued form over function, superficiality over depth, and market value over use value. By declaring "form follows function," the high modernist architects in the Weimar Republic criticized the Wilhelmine conditions and proposed that use value and not market value should determine the character of a building.

The 1918 Revolution and the First World War influenced architectural aesthetics in the Weimar Republic and fostered a corporatist aesthetic of cohesiveness and integration. In the early 1920s the sense of possibility that characterized the architecture of the revolutionary period endured. Standardization of building parts represented a way of reducing labour time and freeing the worker for leisure; however, by 1924 standardization of parts simply allowed builders to build more housing at a lower cost without reducing labour time. These prefabricated, standardized parts brought the efficiency and the aesthetics of factory production into architecture. Economist Ernst Schuster defined *typification* as a design of industrial products that emphasized standardization, specialization, and normalization, with the goal of the rationalization of industry. Schuster warned that this development also was "a process of de-individualization," an "economic fact of mass production," and a result of quantification.[67] Karl von Mangoldt proclaimed that typification enabled a "degree of freedom" while simultaneously facilitating "aesthetic subordination to the individual building and typification of its parts to the whole."[68]

This corporatist sense of the city as a machine comes through in the first act of Walter Ruttmann's classic silent film *Die Sinfonie der Großstadt*, where, once the city comes alive and wakes up, the film offers an extensive montage of industrial machines. This industrial order becomes still clearer when one considers the orderliness and the uniformity of the people in the first act of the film, exiting trains and entering factories. Compare this with the discussion of chaos and hyperbolic particularity in Georg Simmel's pre–First World War essay "The Metropolis and Mental Life."[69] Architects and city planners connected individualism with the inequalities and irrationalities of the Kaiserreich. Robert Atkinson posited that "mass production, new forms of trade and social reconstruction" eliminated or simplified the individualistic forms of buildings, and this development "compelled attention" to "the fundamental questions of architecture" and spatial planning.[70] In this corporatist society, the prevailing discourse expected the aesthetic of this new era to be productive and proletarian and to transform the population to increase efficiency. As Mary Nolan offers, literature and artistic works of all types proposed rationalizing spatial relations as a means of overcoming class conflict.[71] In 1924 Otto Neurath explained that the grand architectonic scale and unity came as consequences of proletarian labour and labour movement: "Big, clear, *inherently truthful* building ideas will once again be realized because the proletariat is a class in the ascendant ... that has *no need for empty appearances*."[72] The architecture emphasized parsimony, directness, honesty, and productivity.[73]

This corporatist desire to unify the outside and inside of the built environment transformed housing interiors, making the space of apartments more efficient and rational and rationalizing housework and, as Mary Nolan has noted, working-class women's behaviour. The prototype of this rationalized domestic workspace was the "Frankfurt kitchen," designed by Margarete Lihotzky.[74] Nolan argues that proponents of Neues Bauen, especially Martin Wagner and Bruno Taut, pushed rationalization and increased the productivity of the apartment to transform working-class life. They believed that a new organization of space could create a "'new person,' who would be 'modern, clean, rational, disciplined, as well as family oriented.'" This goal for the efficient household was two-sided: it could expand women's leisure time, according to some, and it could enable women to get more done in less time but expand her responsibilities, not her free time, according to others.[75] Historians influenced by postmodern theorists, like Michel Foucault, focus on the invasive and dominating micromanagement of what had once been the private domestic sphere of women. These historians diminish the goal of freeing women from the domestic sphere and affording them free time to use as they pleased.[76] For example, Leif Jerram affirms the "backbreaking nature of women's and girls' domestic work" and "complicated spatial and visual arrangements" because the historical subjects valued it. He criticizes the efforts of self-proclaimed experts, some of whom were trying to free women from labour.[77] This argument challenges the ideology of the experts, but it also takes for granted a self-understanding of the historical subjects and surrenders the historian's critical insight.[78] In addition, this postmodern critique of design tends inadvertently to assume that the privacy of the feminized domestic sphere is worth preserving and not, itself, a historically specific and gendered form of domination.

The new corporatist aesthetics brought the logic of the factory to habitations through the apartment rationalization and an attempt to eliminate a separate domestic sphere. In the words of Irene Witte, a proponent of rationalizing home economics, "If we view the housewife in her totality, or in other words, if we consider housework not as an individual activity but as a social function ... we see that an hour of previously wasted energy saved in every household amounts to many days and years. The meaning of waste in the household becomes clear."[79] Witte echoes the same dichotomy between the possibility for the time free from work and for more work in the same amount of time. Women working in old kitchens were encouraged to rearrange furniture to maximize hygiene and eliminate superfluous movement.[80] The liberal era had separated the public and private spheres. The new corporatist era melded the area of work and of the home into a single unit.[81] However, these housing developments were not all the same. The mass housing in Berlin included individualized functional spaces, like kitchens, while the mass housing in Vienna emphasized spaces for collective recreational activities and childcare.[82]

The government in this corporatist era took interest in scientifically defining the minimum space necessary for a dwelling and determining the cheapest way to construct the most efficient home. For example, the Reich Society for Research in Efficient Construction and

Housing divided the society's mission into two groups: one for scientific research and one for testing and evaluation of research results in actual buildings. By calculating the space necessary for furniture, storage space, and home appliances, the group precisely determined apartment dimensions that would provide a basis for researching what the population needed and would contribute to eliminating the housing shortage.[83] For Walter Curt Behrendt, the industrialization of building components and the attendant change in architectural styles was part of a large-scale transformation of society brought on by capitalism and its architecture.[84]

Modernist architecture, an aesthetic form that emphasized this corporatist ideology of productivity, became the dominant form. In 1928 German and French architects founded the Congrès Internationaux d'Architecture Moderne, which included, from the architects discussed here, Le Corbusier, Mies van der Rohe, Walter Gropius, and Hugo Häring, among others, to press for these ideas internationally.[85] In an issue of *Moderne Bauformen* focused on "The Ring" architects, Häring argued that modern architecture no longer needed to defend its right to exist: "It correspond[ed] to deeper causes" and was "on its way to becoming official."[86] Roger Ginsburger agreed and argued that "New Building" was "a new, more serious view of the architectural profession" that no longer needed to ape past artistic styles. He expanded the vision of the beautiful to include "a plane or a steel bridge" and wanted to "subvert [the] usual dualistic world view" that opposed the beautiful to the useful.[87] Others were less convinced. In July 1929 Peter Meyer remarked that the proponents of New Building were celebrating too soon and they offered catchphrases, not arguments.[88] Werner Hegemann asserted, in January 1929, that New Building stole "degenerated old themes from the Baroque or Classical."[89]

In the corporatist era, the literature on housing and architecture in the Weimar Republic and internationally emphasized the concrete, practical character of modernist buildings, yet architects rationalized and organized these buildings according to abstract principles. This contradiction compelled Taut to argue against mathematically determined spaces, because "mathematics is pure logic and therefore a totally abstract discipline. Architecture is the complete opposite, concrete in every way and not in the least abstract."[90] Taut and many historians of this period misunderstood the form of the abstraction in modernist architecture. The architecture and city planning of both the liberal period and the Weimar Republic were guided by abstract principles, which can lead one to overemphasize the continuity between the periods. However, the abstract rationality of the liberal period differed from the rationalism of Neue Sachlichkeit. In the liberal period, the abstract laws of circulation and of the citizen provided the intellectual framework for the liberal form of rationalism, while the abstraction of Neue Sachlichkeit was focused on the abstraction created through increased efficiency in the sphere of production, which often took the aesthetic form of a factory floor, facilitating productivity – from kitchens to a regional plan.

Architectural Form and Its Relationship to Urban Problems

In this corporatist era, architects and planners believed that the proper arrangement of urban space could address social problems. The particular goals of building in Berlin and in other cities during the Weimar Republic become clearer when one compares them to building in Vienna in the 1920s and early 1930s. Addressing urban space meant transforming the built environment remaining from the liberal era, but it also meant choosing from new modes of architecture, including the skyscrapers proliferating in the United States. With the question of the skyscraper, though, the debate moved beyond aesthetics and functionality to consider the character of American capitalism. The administrative centre of the new republic in Berlin still bore the aesthetics of the Kaiserreich, and architects and planners hoped to redesign the space to better fit the needs of the new society.

Architects in the Weimar Republic commonly believed that they could address social problems through the proper arrangement of urban space. Walter Gropius sought to determine the best architecture for public housing and proposed a 20,000-person project in southern Berlin. He argued that the needs of the citizens for basic economic consumption – electricity, heat, food, clothing – should determine the spatial layout of the "organism of the city." Gropius wanted to integrate housing and transportation efficiently with production and recreation. He believed that housing should be free from noise and have plenty of light and air, limited population density, access to convenient transit routes, and comfortable floor plans.[91] Gropius's goal was not facilitating market relations; indeed, he regarded production and consumption as separable from the market. Beyond noise and pollution, he observed, "unscrupulous exploitation of the soil," i.e., land speculation and rental barrack construction, did the worst damage to cities.[92] This new housing,

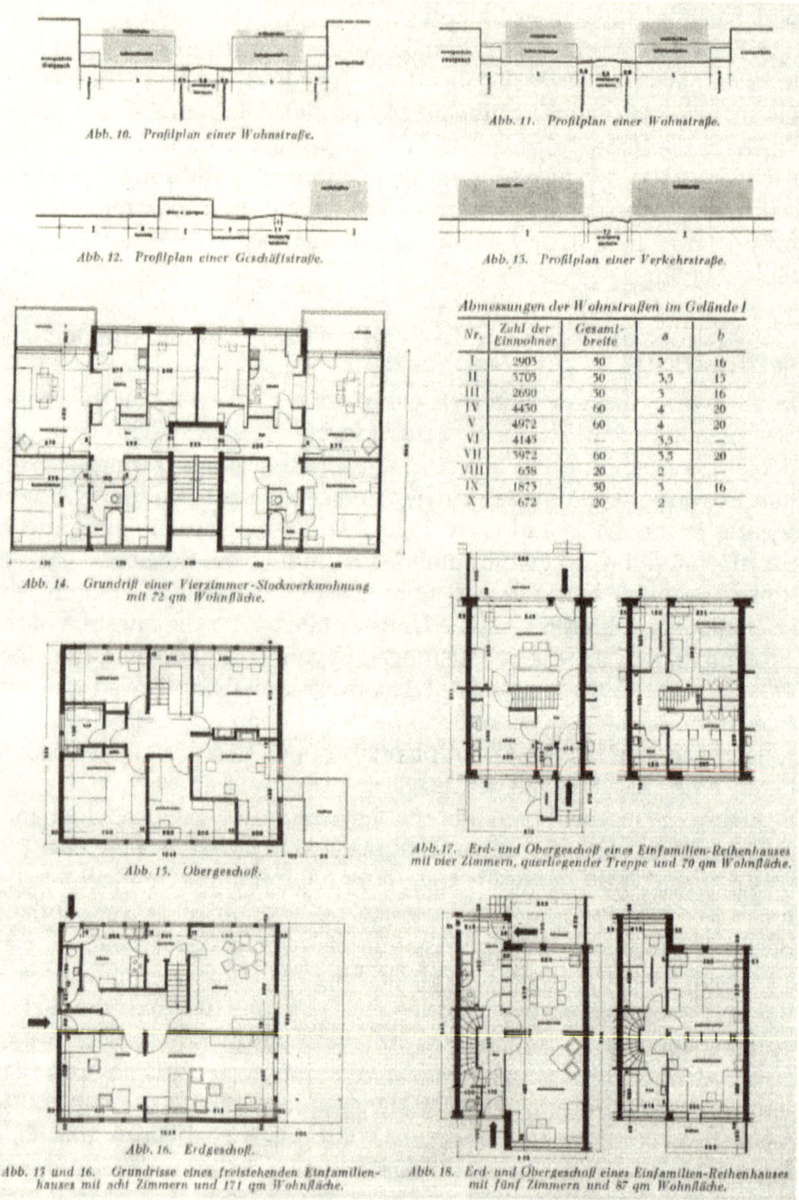

Abb. 10. Profilplan einer Wohnstraße.

Abb. 11. Profilplan einer Wohnstraße.

Abb. 12. Profilplan einer Geschäftsstraße.

Abb. 13. Profilplan einer Verkehrstraße.

Abmessungen der Wohnstraßen im Gelände I

Nr.	Zahl der Einwohner	Gesamtbreite	a	b
I	2903	30	3	16
II	3703	30	3,5	13
III	2690	30	3	16
IV	4430	60	4	20
V	4972	60	4	20
VI	4143	—	3,5	—
VII	3972	60	3,5	20
VIII	658	20	2	—
IX	1873	30	3	16
X	672	20	2	—

Abb. 14. Grundriß einer Vierzimmer-Stockwerkwohnung mit 72 qm Wohnfläche.

Abb. 15. Obergeschoß.

Abb. 17. Erd- und Obergeschoß eines Einfamilien-Reihenhauses mit vier Zimmern, querliegender Treppe und 70 qm Wohnfläche.

Abb. 16. Erdgeschoß.

Abb. 15 und 16. Grundrisse eines freistehenden Einfamilienhauses mit acht Zimmern und 171 qm Wohnfläche.

Abb. 18. Erd- und Obergeschoß eines Einfamilien-Reihenhauses mit fünf Zimmern und 87 qm Wohnfläche.

7 Interior Plans from Walter Gropius. Walter Gropius, "Groß-Siedlungen." *Zentralblatt der Bauverwaltung* 50, no. 12 (26 March 1930): 238. © 2015 Artists Rights Society (ARS), New York / VG Bild-Kunst, Bonn

he argued, should progressively socialize "formerly family functions" of an authoritative, educational, and home-economic nature. Rejecting the idea that the rational should be limited to economic efficiency, he used this as a sociology of the "inner structure of the modern industrial working class family" to determine the optimal building height, "because the economy is, for all its importance, not an end in itself, but only means to an end."[93] While Gropius endorsed Weimar Republic housing policy, he questioned whether housing alone was "responsible for physically and mentally mature people."[94] Gropius envisioned new social relations, wherein space played an important role, along with a broader socialization of private property and of the domestic sphere, in constituting the new freer and more humane society.

The development of housing settlements in Berlin, unlike Vienna, focused on building in the exurban areas, with their large-scale layout, austere design, and incorporation of nature into the housing. Wagner undertook many developments in the Berlin area together with Taut, but the Hufeisensiedlung in Britz in Neukölln to the south-southeast of the city centre was one of the more famous structures, erected between 1924 and 1928. A large building with single-family dwellings surrounding a park area, it featured rows of houses radiating out. The builders used repetition and mass-produced parts to emphasize their vision of the future of architecture. When entering the development from the main road, one saw first a red wall, and then once past that a bright white, three-story horseshoe building surrounding a park area, a pond, a small café, and a few stores. Outside the horseshoe, the roads stretched like rays, though they turned to become roughly parallel at about their midpoint. This area had two types of two-story homes: one five metres wide and the other six metres wide. While the ideology of the garden city did play a role in the development of this structure, this development was decidedly modernist and not nostalgic.[95] The Onkel Toms Hütte development, in Zehlendorf, was constructed between 1928 and 1932. Here Taut and Häring incorporated the buildings into the pine forest of Grunwald surrounding them. The main buildings made a long, 400-metre curve and were surrounded by perpendicular structures. These apartments, as well, were either of two or three stories with five- or six-metre-wide fronts. Prominent, periodic staircases among calm and unadorned fronts marked the facades of Taut's buildings. In response to the development's broad colour palette, it was popularly referred to as the parrot settlement.[96]

These Berlin housing developments were different from contemporaneous developments in Vienna. Vienna developments were less avant-garde, less focused on rationalized production, and tiny in comparison to the developments in Berlin.[97] In Vienna, builders created apartments of two sizes: thirty-eight or forty-eight square metres, each with a kitchen that doubled as a living room. In 1926 architects added a third size of fifty-seven square metres for the very largest families, but included a smaller kitchen in order to rationalize the work there. The apartments did not have private baths, but they did have a faucet and a cooking stove or plate.[98] The exteriors of the Viennese structures were modelled on the "official imperial style of the Ringstrasse buildings" and "on Vienna art nouveau architecture," and were massive structures surrounding a courtyard garden or park, though not modernist in style.[99] German architects regarded the Viennese plans with disdain. In 1926 Hegemann wrote that these buildings were a "missed opportunity," because instead of devising a "large-scale artistic unity," they created chaos. Wagner argued that the buildings failed to "find the proper artistic character [of Socialism] ... which is unity and equality."[100] Eve Blau notes that Adolf Loos, Josef Frank, Franz Schuster, and Margarete Lihotzky criticized Viennese building for the absence of a "comprehensive plan, technologically advanced building methods, and innovative spatial arrangements."[101]

Skyscrapers would come to play a central role in modernist architecture, but in the late 1920s German architects were ambivalent. Nonetheless, their praise and criticism of skyscrapers were framed by corporatist dualisms. Attitudes towards skyscrapers served as a proxy for attitudes towards the United States, its purportedly superficial and abstract form of capitalism, its purportedly cultureless cities, and its wages and mass consumption. In December 1925 the Deutscher Bund Heimatschutz criticized the proposed city-planning law for promoting what they regarded as an *Allerweltstype* of urban development. The Bund believed that "progressive standardization of style and construction methods" would lead "in a few decades to the complete Americanization" of the built environment and destruction of the best of the old buildings.[102] Though the Bund did not oppose skyscrapers on principle, it objected to "the haphazard erection of towers" in Berlin to feed the landlord's desire to exploit his real estate.[103] Others argued that these structures provided no "architectural enrichment" to the city image and expressed the overpowering, cultureless, and materialistic character of American capitalism.[104] Martin Mächler saw skyscrapers as "not an expression of a planned, rational housing policy evolved in the interests of a collective mass of people"; rather, as "the ruthlessness of the pure capitalist entrepreneur, solely concerned with extracting huge profit from material goods." However, he believed that "German genius" could discover and express the essence of the skyscraper.[105]

From another perspective, Robert Atkinson cited the example of one skyscraper as constructed in "the pattern of a factory, as it should be."[106] For Behrendt, skyscrapers could provide interest to the cityscape and particular types of space, but not solve housing problems; they "only increased utilization of the inner city real estate." He held that skyscrapers revealed the "critical illness of these extra-large organisms," i.e., metropolises, and expressed "a one-sided metropolitan and world-economically discontinued intellectual course" as well as the "last flare-up of a dying imperialism."[107] Heinrich Mendelssohn promoted building skyscrapers anywhere appropriate, because they reflect the dynamism of the metropolis, and while social and cultural relations shape the built environment, Berlin was stuck in the nineteenth century. He blamed this state of affairs on mortgage policy and the cost of credit, i.e., on the abstract dimensions of capitalism, which made it profitable to allow buildings to stand that in America would have been demolished.[108] Mendelssohn celebrated the churn of building in New York as "progressive renewal."[109]

While the shortage of space used to explain skyscrapers in Manhattan did not exist in Berlin, Martin Wagner argued that a socially and culturally rooted shortage did. Space in Berlin was subdivided into many small plots, and the property owners were typically either unwilling to sell or demanded such steep prices that projects tended to fail.[110] Hegemann and Charles du Vinage believed that skyscrapers were impractical in Berlin because of the prevailing laws and cultural assumptions about the proportion between building height, street width, and sunlight.[111] Hegemann explained that skyscrapers would need to be set back significantly if they exceeded ten stories, giving them a smaller footprint and making a taller building necessary to have the same space available for rent; thus, a ten-story building became a fifteen-story building. And, they argued, skyscrapers did not address density: "A skyscraper is like a suction pump" for life and traffic, and despite the decentralization effects of telephones and fast cars, builders still focused on small spaces as part of a "mass psychosis."[112] Hegemann and du Vinage condemned German architects who were "intoxicated" by "the 'gorgeous cathedral-like beauty' of American cities" and failed to realize that "American high wages, short hours, amazing transport" were a way to compensate for a "day's work in poorly lit and poorly ventilated offices." Hegemann and du Vinage believed that Berliners, already confined to rental barracks, could not tolerate working in high-rises.[113]

8 Contribution "Wabe" (Honeycomb) to the Ideas Competition for a Skyscraper at Friedrichstrasse Station, Berlin. Photograph, reworked in various media, Inv. Nr. 8238 Bauhaus-Archiv, Berlin © 2015 Artists Rights Society (ARS), New York / VG Bild-Kunst, Bonn

The business and administrative centre of Berlin bore the heavy imprint of the Kaiserreich built environment. Despite the uneven way that the Kaiserreich adopted liberalism, architects and city planners associated that regime with a liberal world view. After the revolution they attempted to reconsider how this space should look and function in order to make it commensurate with the democratic culture of the Weimar Republic. However, because of the shifts in capitalism and in the form, function, and perception of Greater Berlin, the focus of this new democratic culture was collectivist and corporatist. Most architects regarded the Reichstag building as ugly and inadequate for meeting the needs of lawmakers.[114] Cornelius Gurlitt wrote sarcastically that, for many, the Reichstag building sinned against functionalism.[115] Taut wanted to redesign the Reichstag as part of a large-scale transformation of central Berlin.[116] The Reichstag needed office space to accommodate the activities of the new government, providing an opportunity for planners and architects. Hegemann explained that the Reichstag needed 400 private offices and a connection between the old building and the extension. The lot proposed for this extension was a 3,100-square-metre triangle that had "ample room for a skyscraper."[117]

Greater Berlin held a design contest for this office building to be connected to the Reichstag that would fit this new democratic collectivism and the shifts in the form, function, and perception of Greater Berlin. However, the contest resulted in no design selection, as many had predicted.[118] Prize committee member Ludwig Hoffmann's antipathy towards modernist architecture sank the contest.[119] Greater Berlin tried again, but that one failed, too.[120] As a result of this experience, critics such as Hugo Häring questioned determining new architectural plans through contests, which they associated with the market and liberalism. They instead desired a more centralized method of creating cohesive associations.[121] Häring suggested that just as every building has both an architect and a builder, every building has a material and an intellectual underpinning, and competition interrupts the interaction between these two and leads to banal architecture.[122] According to Fritz Hoger, the most radical designers wanted to destroy the Reichstag, not just provide a new facade.[123] Max Berg worried that redesigning the Reichstag area would cause "ever-increasing traffic on the roads through the Tiergarten" that would "entirely destroy this green area in the foreseeable future as a recreational area," and it thus would be "eliminated as a lung and nerve-strengthening green area."[124]

With the termination of the contest, architects nevertheless sought to transform the architecture of Berlin into one appropriate for a republic and to this new corporatist era by redesigning the Reichstag and creating a Platz der Republik. The 1927 Greater Berlin Art Exhibition, which introduced a city-planning section for the first time, presented Mächler's 1917 idea for a Platz der Reich in front of the Reichstag.[125] Similarly, Wagner organized a contest to redesign this governmental district in 1929 inspired by Mächler's schema and by his own desire to make capital city spaces that fit the new government.[126] The contest jury, which included Hans Grässel of Munich, Ludwig Hoffmann of Berlin, Fritz Schumacher of Hamburg, Theodor Veil of Aachen, and Wagner himself, sorted through 278 proposals but did not award the first prize.[127] According to Gustav Lampmann, the same triangular lot between the Reichstag, the Spree, and the Hindersinstraße continued to challenge planners.[128]

As Wolfgang Sonne observes, the unification of Greater Berlin did not alter the layout of the administrative district of Greater Berlin. While the political and economic challenges were too great, planners still envisioned a new, corporatist city centre. Mächler's plan for Greater Berlin, developed in 1917, included a new north-south axis for the city and a new governmental centre in Spreebogen. Similarly, architect Otto Kohtz tried in 1920 to propose grouping Reich ministries on Königsplatz, which would become the Platz der Republic. Kohtz wanted to replace the conventional city centre with a massive government pyramid high-rise, as part of an expressionist city crown. Sonne argues that the most practical plan was that of the avant-garde "Ring" group of architects, including Häring, presented at the Greater Berlin Art Exhibition in 1927, which was similar to the high-rise administrative district that Le Corbusier designed for his Ville contemporaine of 1922.[129] Architect and planner Max Berg wrote that the 1927 exhibition popularized Mächler's vision of scientific "universal planners" and productive city planning, who took into consideration "the issues of industry, commerce, management of transport, housing and recreation, hygiene, intellectual culture," and especially the "labour problem of the masses."[130] When the world economy went into the Great Depression, beginning in 1929, the funding for building and the political will to build a new governmental district collapsed.[131]

The City Planning Law

A new city planning law changed the practice of planning during the Weimar Republic and expanded the scope of the city planning in keeping with corporatist ideology. As the Deutscher Wirtschaftsbund für das

Baugewerbe maintained in April 1924, the 1923 draft of the law introduced the legal concept of a settlement plan, while previous laws had included only zoning and flight-line planning.[132] Preußischer Landesverband der Haus- und Grundbesitzerverein, which regarded similar, earlier efforts in the Housing Act of 28 March 1918 as "successful in only a hateful patchwork," praised the effort to rationalize city planning laws and to make the welfare ministry in charge of enforcement.[133] This association held onto older liberal ideas, believing that the rules about expropriation in the law established "an entirely new concept of real property" that challenged "our entire legal and economic system." The association members argued that the new law did not ground "the differences between the legal sphere of the private man and the general public" in the new legislation, nor the "institution" of "expropriation" in private law. They thought that the "inseparability of the concepts of land ownership and the right of development ... should not be summarily denied," because the "command economy ... taught ... that the housing problem [could] not be solved by magisterial action, but only through ... private initiative."[134] This association worried that the law would inhibit a return to pre-war economic conditions.[135] Ironically, given this group's liberal leanings, they worried that communities enacting the provisions of this law would act in their self-interest and not in the common good.[136] The Landesausschuß der preußischen Industrie und Handelskammern held the law in the same regard.[137] They argued that these features would scare the mortgage loan business and weaken foreign confidence in the German economy.[138]

As evidence of the changed relationship between the state, society, and the economy in the corporatist form, function, and perception of cities, other commentators on the law assumed the expropriation of property for social and economic purposes would exist and worried only about compensation to the owners. In November 1925 the housing reformer Karl von Mangoldt of the Siedlungswissenschaftliche Arbeitsgemeinschaft presupposed the new powers of expropriation and was concerned only with the compensation for the expropriated.[139] He questioned whether the market value of the land should determine the compensation of the former owners, as the law from 1874 determined, because the interest of society in healthy dwellings was at least equal to that of the former owner. Therefore he believed the state should determine financial compensation by the use value of the land to development companies, because the social and national interests in green space were pre-eminent.[140] Through this vision of compensation,

Mangoldt, a conservative, criticized exchange value in the name of the use value and praised administrative determinations of value not those of the market. In both cases he valued the apparently concrete dimension (use value and administration) over the abstract dimension (exchange value and the market).

Within this corporatist world view, the groups opposing the expropriation measure represented those who believed the law went too far, but also those who believed it did not go far enough. Mangoldt, in the same letter, praised that the expropriation measures and a new division of powers between communities and the state enabled regional planning, but wished to expand the law "as far as possible" to coordinate the planning efforts of the state, counties, and municipalities; demarcate green space; and counteract exurban real-estate speculation.[141] In late May 1925 Bruno Möhring and Paul Fischer complained to Minister of Welfare Heinrich Hirtsiefer on behalf of the Freie Deutsche Akademie des Städtebaues that the new law only combined existing structural engineering regulations, urban planning regulations, and building police ordinances.[142] They favoured a fundamental revision that expanded planning powers. In November 1925 the Deutscher Bund Heimatschutz similarly praised the way the law empowered the state to plan.[143] Heinrich Keller, in that Bund letter, endorsed the bill as "a major advance" and suggested that planners focus the scale of their work on economic regions, not administrative ones.[144] Carl Johannes Fuchs, also a Bund representative, viewed the bill as "an extremely significant step forward," on which depended "the future of our entire [German] culture" and the "rebuilding [of] our economy and the resurgence of our country."[145] He stated that while it did oppose the forces that had made the city a site of "mass tenements," impinging upon "public health and the economy," he thought that "an arbitrary limit of the growth of cities" would significantly hurt the economy.[146] In January 1926 the Preußischen Städtetag praised the bill for its "modern views and clear insights" and claimed that it "killed [private property] in the name of the public interest."[147] Later in June they welcomed the "contemporary and comprehensive revision of all legal relations of city planning," proclaiming zoning "the indispensable instrument of the urban planner."[148] By 1929, though, the instability in the mortgage market caused some to worry about the effects of the law on investor confidence. Hermann Ehlgötz denied that expropriation was a problem, and members of the community committee did not want to alter the "organic" development of the existing laws; however, they worried about "interference with private property" as a threat to mortgage loans and demanded cautious enforcement of expropriation and full compensation.[149]

In keeping with the corporatist ideology, both the law and the commentators on the law focused on urban population density. Many believed that, at its current levels, density was detrimental to public health, and that the law's intended redistribution of the urban German population would benefit both public health and birth rates.[150] Fuchs of the Bund welcomed the provisions in the law that adhered to ideas presented at the International Federation for Housing and Planning meeting in Amsterdam in 1924: in particular, that "unlimited growth of big cities" was undesirable and cities should be "decentraliz[ed] by means of 'satellite towns' and isolated ... by greenbelts."[151] Mangoldt was similarly pleased by the decentralizing aims of the law and its provisions for planning of industrial location and nature preservation.[152]

Those concerned with city planning regarded their era as fundamentally different from the pre-First World War liberal era. On 8 March 1929 when the Prussian Staatsrat considered a new draft of a city planning bill, the authors argued that the circumstances had changed significantly since nineteenth-century liberal city plans, and so, in this corporatist era, a new law that accounted for the increased role of the "public hand" was necessary. Principally, the expansion of cities, the development of housing settlements, and the agglomeration of cities made it no longer possible to address a city as an isolated entity rather than as a regional economy.[153] Wagner, speaking for a collection of city planners, declared that the bill lacked clarity and detail, but that a "zoning plan" had become an "indispensable prerequisite."[154]

While the law did have critics, criticisms remained within the corporatist form, function, and perception of the city. A June 1929 meeting of the Staatsrat, the Deutsche Vaterlandspartei, the SPD, and the Centre Party welcomed the intent of the draft of the City Planning Law to synthesize leading theories of city planning law. However, they thought that zoning could inspire speculation and would alter the "organic" development of the existing laws.[155] For the BDA the draft was "too narrow" as a city planning law and should have been a unified building law that with not only with urban, but with rural settings as well, to facilitate "planning for the whole country ... including the major transport routes by sea and by land, state highways, airports, gas pipelines and electric lines, distribution of various economic areas, resettlement possibilities, and necessities considered."[156] The City Committee welcomed the legal pretext for planning in the law but felt it was "insufficient for the urban development of a world city." They believed that the draft law should be less "for the regulation and implementation of an organic development of the cities" according to "modern city planning principles" and more of an attempt to "awaken the labour process of the Volksgemeinschaft." They wanted the law to eliminate the necessity for large cities and to follow the principles of the 1924 International Federation for Housing and Planning.[157] The City Committee wished to solve the cultural and economic "problems of Berlin" through collaboration between business and administration and affirmation of the suburbanization of industry.[158] Ehlgötz observed that zoning had no legal consequences for municipal self-administration, though the bill limited community autonomy.[159] Martin Wagner believed a state project might trample the particularity of individual cities but thought that it was necessary nonetheless.[160] However, the community committee and the Preußischen Städtetag believed that the law violated municipal self-administration.[161] For some, the violation of municipal self-administration was a question of creating greater uniformity, improving hygienic conditions, and maximizing efficiency in city planning.

Scale, Rationalization, and City Planning

The corporatist discourse about rationalization posited that it could bring about profound changes in the economy, and architects and planners conceived of their territory on an expanding scale. They sought the rationalization of industrial production and celebrated what they regarded as the social and cultural possibilities created by rationalization. They understood the city as an integrated organic machine, accentuating, on the one hand, the organic and environmental character of the city or, on the other hand, a vision of the city as a machine within a larger global organic apparatus. The more planners considered the problems of the city, the more they saw them as part of a broader system.

Corporatist city planners sought to plan larger territory, so they could, as one put it, "create in Berlin, the real spiritual and architectural centre, the proper capital [Germany] deserve[d]."[162] The planner Ernst Runge noted the "extension of a world city such as Greater Berlin require[d] considerations" that went "far beyond the purely technical and artistic challenges." He believed "the consideration of public health and public hygiene require[d] a new kind of city" and that city planning was dependent upon state financing.[163] The architect Hellmut Delius agreed that economic development made city planning, even regional planning, insufficient and asserted that planners needed to do so on a national scale.[164] Planner Gustav Langen believed that these plans should only be limited by the "natural" boundaries.[165] Delius maintained that planning was "the use of scientific, rational analysis to promote the economy of a particular place [and] the improved performance and efficiency of each individual," which would include "increased ordering of communal life [and] the raising of public health and welfare."[166] At this time regional or national planning was an international phenomenon, and proponents of planning on this scale saw it as part of larger initiatives of economic rationalization that influenced business and administration, including public land management, in response to what they saw as a fundamental irrationality in economics.[167]

Rationalization, in corporatist political economic discourse, referred to the well-planned organization of the economy and large-scale mechanization, precision time-management, and ergonometric configuration of the production process. The discourse of rationalization assumed that the economy was a unified structure and that rationalization could solve social problems.[168] Bernhard Harms, the founder of the Institut für Weltwirtschaft at the University of Kiel who was later forced from his directorship by the National Socialists in 1933 for his defence of his Jewish colleagues, explored structural changes in the economy. With the word *structure* he meant socially general features that appeared everywhere as "elements, [which] together ... constitute a unity," and took form "as a result of historical development" and according to "the way the parts are assembled into a whole." He thought that structural changes differed from business cycles, which were of "declining significance."[169] The discourse on rationalization coupled economic efficiency with a diminished role for the individual. Roderick von Ungern-Sternberg argued that industry is inherently social and that the state should manage "the totality of all of the productivity of industry."[170] Criticisms of rationalization argued for still more effective rationalization: Friedrich Olk wrote that during the Great Depression the German rationalization followed a one-sided American model that focused on mechanization, which created a large and unprecedented cheap labour force and made the same tasks possible with 20–50 per cent fewer workers.[171] Olk, a trade unionist, believed that mechanization was an "inevitable" "reorganization of our labour market" that would temporarily "increase our industrial reserve army" as well as "the capacity for overproduction."[172] According to Olk, this form of rationalization increased the intensity of labour and production at the cost of the workers, which provoked concern among employers for working-class "mental-psychological" conditions. In response, employers focused on "the idea of community [and] a sense of belonging" they believed were found in older forms of production such as those of guilds.[173]

This corporatist ideology and society was structured by a dualism that is especially well grasped by Walter Gropius. This dichotomy revealed a social and cultural transformation at the end of the hyperinflation and the establishment of a more stable social order. In 1923 Gropius attempted to come to terms with this moment, claiming that social life had entered a new epoch, in which nineteenth-century (liberal) oppositions had been overcome in favour of an integrated society.

> The dominant spirit of the epoch is already recognizable although its form is not yet clearly defined. The old dualistic world-concept, which envisioned the ego in opposition to the universe, is rapidly losing ground. In its place is the idea of a universal unity in which all opposing forces exist in a state of absolute balance. This dawning recognition of the essential oneness of all things that their appearance endows creative effort with a fundamental inner meaning. No longer can anything exist in isolation. We perceive every form as the embodiment of an idea, every piece of work as a manifestation of our inner selves. Only work, which is the product of inner compulsion, can have spiritual meaning. Mechanized work is lifeless, proper only to the lifeless machine. So long, however, as machine-economy remains an end in itself rather than a means of freeing the intellect from the burden of mechanical labor, the individual will remain enslaved and society will remain disordered. The solution depends on a change in the individual's attitude towards his work, not on the betterment of his outward circumstances, and the acceptance of this new principle is of decisive importance for new creative work.[174]

Alan Colquhoun notes that for Gropius, while industrial division of labour eliminated personality, it afforded individuals access to something greater: the collective, human machine as a social totality. As Colquhoun explains, at this point Gropius perceived of industrial production not as creating distance between the individual and community but as creating community.[175] Gropius argued that labour with machines was lifeless and should be left to the machines. In so doing, he hoped, people could experience liberation *from* labour. However, he contended that what he called the machine economy was an ever-renewing end in itself. For Gropius the impediment to the realization of an economy beyond labour was subjective, the era of the bourgeois subject was over, liberation from labour was possible and desirable, and no objective limitations existed to the realization of this better world. By 1924, however, Gropius's sense of revolutionary possibilities of making technology serve human ends was gone. In its place was a "striving to create buildings with a simple, organic body, naked and radiating from an inner law, without falsehood or playfulness, which responds affirmatively to our world of machines, wires and fast vehicles, which expresses its purpose and function through the tension of its masses, casting off all that is not essential, that would veil the absolute form of the building."[176] A new order had overcome the dichotomies that had characterized urban life in the liberal period, but the society remained capitalist.

City planners and municipal administrators in this corporatist era sought an integrated, productive, and efficient metropolitan region, and this logic extended to areas that had previously been outside debates about efficiency, such as housing. In 1920, an article in *Wasmuths Monatshefte für Baukunst* asked how a new residential development fit into the economic body of Greater Berlin. Were these homes "productive or consumptive in our economy"? How would they affect a weakened Germany? Were these new homes "value-creating" or just "ruin to the German economic body" and "pointless spending of money"? The article concluded that developments in the industrial areas in the north and east of Berlin were not "value dissipating," because a permanent job opportunity lay nearby.[177] This discourse perceived the German economy not only as a unity but also as a single biological entity, whose various parts needed to contribute to the creation of value. Planning was also framed in terms of its productivity: Joseph Brix, as president of the Freie Deutsche Akademie des Städtebaues, emphasized that regional zoning was an economically, socially, and culturally significant labour.[178] Mächler asserted that planners needed to liberate the productive biological totality of the city from the domination of technical, inorganic, and arbitrary design of liberal city planning. For Mächler, the city was "one cell, though the main cell, in the large communal concept of the state." The ideas from Mächler quoted at the beginning of this chapter fused biological, city-planning, and economic ideas as a way of rejecting liberal city planning.[179] Mächler believed that population density was the central problem of urban development, especially for the working class, which was not "integrate[d] appropriately into the whole organism" because of lingering housing problems. Mächler claimed that the 1862 liberal Hobrecht plan for Berlin was class interest in city-plan form and had debilitating mass-psychological consequences. For him, settlements, on the contrary, would integrate cities as "a cell in the total state, as an organic part in a greater organism."[180] Mächler believed that the cooperative settlement, at whose heart was "eminently peaceful, unifying and community-building" productive labour, could answer the "deep longing of renewal" that pervaded society. This productive labour, he argued, was as old as human history, and only later did "ideas of envy and competition" arrive.[181] This was a view of the city that celebrated labour and treated it as essentially a constant throughout human history. It attacked liberal social forms like liberal planning and competition, and even envy. For Mächler, these liberal social forms had been imposed on humans and their labour, and they dominated the city's physical plan and psychology.

While many planners in this corporatist era regarded the city or the nation as a socially productive organism, others saw the totality of the world economy as an organism as well. Hilberseimer shared Mächler's assumptions about the relationship of society to space, but Hilberseimer understood urbanization globally: "Design of the environment is the main task of mankind. Essential components of such design are the mutually dependent state building and the urban planning. The city ... cannot be considered as independent, to be considered in isolation of the existing organism. It is fused and connected to the omnipresence of her people and by the overall economy of the whole civilization; the organized world ... This world is a whole organism."[182]

Hilberseimer argued that the metropolis is an unprecedented "creation of the modern age," which results "naturally and necessarily" from "the industrialization of the world." He believed it was the most appropriate form of settlement for "the economic system of capitalist imperialism." He continued, "Extreme concentration and comprehensive organization" characterized modern imperialist capitalist cities. A form of production whose needs were necessarily international and generative of hostile international relations constituted these cities.[183] Therefore, he posited, the metropolis appeared "as a creation of the almighty big business, as an expression of its anonymity, as a type of city that foster[ed] a peculiar set of socio-economic and collective psychological foundations," bringing together "the greatest insulation and closest union of its inhabitants." Hilberseimer argued that capitalism created a private-interest-driven and historically specific and international form of urbanization and alienation and it "displace[d] local particularity at a rapid pace."[184] Pier Vittorio Aureli argues that Hilberseimer's city plans were especially abstract, because he understood that abstract social relations such as value and capital fundamentally structured capitalist cities. For Aureli, Hilberseimer understood that a liberated society could be found by pushing the reifying tendencies and contradictions of capitalism to their extremes and then beyond. Unlike many of his colleagues, he did not retain a romantic hope of a space outside of capitalism.[185] Hilberseimer offered that, while both the street layout and the building code were currently overly schematic, urban development could be rationally planned and decentralized to facilitate better conditions for the population.[186]

Hilberseimer's corporatist vision of urban development was abstract, but not in the same way that Hobrecht's liberal vision had been abstract. Hobrecht used abstract, liberal principles (figure 2) to create the conditions of possibility for individual success and entrepreneurial activity, and emphasized efficient, circulation-of-capital-oriented traffic movement to structure the influence on the built environment. Hilberseimer, however, was interested in the abstraction of the factory to architecture and the home (figure 9). The functionalist uniformity of his structures and the infinitely extending straight streets spoke to his desire to make housing productive. The layout of a factory is abstract in the sense that principles of time and capital-accumulation-determined efficiency influence its layout; in its concrete dimension, a factory is interested in the creation of a particular commodity. For Hilberseimer, the city-factory produced workers. The difference between Hobrecht's and Hilberseimer's abstractions lay in the different time pressures that they were invoking. New technologies, from paper money to internet commerce, can accelerate the time of circulation, but as Henryk Grossmann explains, "The exchange relations among 'economic magnitudes' on markets are in fact not real processes of change over time but transfers, representing an atemporal 'movement' – a circular motion."[187] The time of production, however, can become more "dense" as the same quantity of labour can produce more commodities in the same amount of time, especially with the introduction of science and technology into the production process. This increased efficiency spreads the same amount of value more thinly across more commodities. Increased efficiency can make it possible for the worker to spend less of the day producing the

9 Hilberseimer "Hochhausstadt, East-West Street" from Hochhausstadt, East-West Street, Drawing, 1924. Ludwig Karl Hilberseimer. Ludwig Karl Hilberseimer Papers, Ryerson and Burnham Archives, Art Institute of Chicago, Digital File #070383.HochhOst.

value that would pay his or her wage and more time creating value for the capitalist, because efficiency, for a host of reasons, drives down the value of the wage. Thus, time in the sphere of production has a historical dynamic; it can become increasingly dense, is generative of a historically transformative technological and scientific drive towards greater productivity and efficiency, and is shaped by the abstract demands of value creation.[188]

The Politics of City Planning and Architecture

The amelioration of the role of the market in corporatist social life and the development of an architectural and city planning form that celebrated production and the social totality raised questions about the relationship between capitalism, architecture, and city planning. Alexander Schwab, Adolf Behne, and Siegfried Kracauer separately developed an analysis of modernist city planning and architecture that was critical in the sense that they saw it as both a consequence of present domination and representative of a potential liberated society. The Deutsche Bauausstellung of 1931 in Berlin inspired considerations of social and economic geography and a desire to declare the victory of modernist building and the dulling of its radical edge.

The form of architecture and city planning in the corporatist era offered a political critique of the liberal period before the First World War. Schwab argued that within capitalist societies, the outer form of buildings was more important than the interior and was "mostly stolen from older styles and mingled together." Modernist architecture was seen as "the great enemy" of bourgeois society, because eclectic ornamentation was an expression of the "rising capitalist bourgeoisie" and their failed revolution in 1848.[189] Housing, Schwab noted, was produced for exchange value and not use value, using "ornaments, flourishes, little roofs, pillars, stucco and other unnecessary things" to increase the price.[190] He argued that the social consequences of war, revolution, and hyperinflation forced a reconsideration of construction processes and an attempt to drastically reduce manual labour and decoration.[191] Also addressing ornamentation and drawing on Adolf Loos, Behne argued that decoration "increase[d] the work of the people by 100%."[192] In the past, Behne suggested, "our ancestors did not utilize their houses, furniture and appliances enough"; they "exploited their people" in inverse proportion to their exploitation of their house, furniture, and appliances.[193] For Schwab, Behne, and others, there was a class content to the austerity of modernist architecture.

Schwab's analysis brought together the symbolic use of space, new forms of capitalism, and modernist architecture and could begin to account for the shift between liberal and corporatist society. Schwab argued that the expansion of Unter den Linden in Berlin, the parade street of the recently deposed monarch, expressed "the existing political power relations in the structural design of the capital." These "symbolic representations appear[ed] natural" because they expressed a psychological and intellectual world view of the present society.[194] He posited that urban development was "an expression of capitalism" with the increasing concentration of capital, on the one hand, and the prefiguration of socialism, on the other.[195] For Schwab, capitalism generated functionalist architecture, which developed a structure from the inside to the outside, but this aesthetic form nonetheless pointed beyond capitalism.[196] Modernist aesthetics celebrated simplicity and honesty and believed in a unity of form and meaning: that a building, as Schwab put it, "expresse[d] in its outer form what it is: a simple house with apartments for working people."[197]

Critics like Schwab and Behne attempted to develop theories about the relationship between spatial politics, architecture, and capitalism that dealt critically with the shift from the liberal to the corporatist form, function, and perception of cities. Schwab argued that reformist city planners' concerns with urban nomadism coincided with the "new, rapidly emerging custom to provide new homes with built-in furniture, especially cabinets," for people without homes. He contended that this feature responded to the dissolution of the bourgeois family and to the relative liberation of women from the domestic sphere.[198] He claimed that marriage changed as capitalism changed, even as the dominant ideologies of capitalism proclaimed marriage the "official basis of the regulation of sexual life" and "one of the most important foundations of society." For Schwab, this development clarified marriage as an agreement between two people in love and demonstrated that marriage was historically formed and not immutable.[199] Schwab argued that "the war of all against all" in capitalism generated "a tremendous inner loneliness" because it monetized all relationships and in turn inspired a desire for a refuge and thus for the private sphere and the private home.[200] Schwab contended that the concept of the private sphere was central to the idea of "private property" and shaped architecture. As capitalism undermined private property, it did the same to the private sphere.[201] Behne, like Schwab, believed that "every building [was] a battlefield of that class struggle" and located this struggle in terms of a battle between "form and function." For Behne, "Form [represented] the interest of the ruler. Form employ[ed] the ruled" and brought him "into the hand of the ruler." The class interests of the workers, he claimed, were in the function of a building or piece of furniture.[202]

The development of city planning from liberal to corporatist suggested that in certain respects key components of a capitalist society had been replaced by more Socialist means, but in other respects capitalist social relations remained in place. The critical theorist Siegfried Kracauer, who reported on the Deutsche Bauausstellung of 1931 in Berlin for the *Frankfurter Zeitung*, argued that the chaos of the juxtaposed exhibits corresponded well "to the anarchical conditions that prevail[ed] in the [capitalist] economy."[203] However, "at the first glance at least it [was] already obvious that the more advanced urban planning policies [were] permeated by a spirit" in which "private economic and political principles [were not] tolerated any more." This spirit, he argued, was that of "modern state planning" and gave rise to "complaints about arbitrary political boundaries" and was striving "for a systematic organization of urban and rural areas; if you will, it ha[d] the character of the planned economy." Kracauer considered it possible that "these exhibited urban designs signal[led] essential social transformation, beneath the surface."[204] In response to the 1931 exhibition, architect Franz Lowitsch posited, "Now there is little doubt that what we have experienced in recent decades represents a revolution in the economic, social, cultural, artistic, and especially architectural area of unprecedented magnitude," which in turn demanded a new form of city planning within which the whole city was expected to express its function through its form.[205]

Finally, by the early 1930s the modernist architectural revolution and its corporatist vision of the built environment began to claim victory, but its achievements were milder than early claims suggested they might be, and the radical architects backed away from their more extreme positions. The 1931 Berlin exhibition, after the coming-out party of modernist building in Stuttgart in 1927, established modernism's hegemony and orthodoxy. For the first time one can see critiques of modernism from the standpoint of the avant-garde. On Mies van der Rohe's "House of Our Time" exhibit, critic Behne wrote that building aesthetics had been so inverted that where once "the renunciation of 'painting and sculpture in building' [was] originally meant as a blow to the decorative," now it was "decorative not to have picture on the wall." He argued, "The attack on the image in its original, once revolutionary, form is now 'reactionary,' because of the way it became a brand." Behne drew two possible conclusions from the exhibits: either architects had not solved the problems presented in Stuttgart in 1927 and Breslau in 1929, or the Berlin exhibits evidenced "the solidification of style."[206] Joseph Gantner thought that after Stuttgart in 1927 "the aesthetic revolution" climaxed there and [had] now subsided.[207] Behne was concerned that the rationalism of modernist architecture had passed from a rationality developed out of concrete practice into a rationality that was schematic and imposed from the outside.[208] Left-leaning city planners and architects began to develop a critique of modernism that pointed to the immanent tendencies towards both liberation and further domination in modernism.

Conclusion: Corporatist City Planning

During this period, planners and architects commonly saw modern capitalist society as a massive organism connected to population growth, urban space, and economic productivity. The discourse connected this vision of capitalism to an existential angst about national decline and to a veneration of the supposedly redemptive powers of the soil of Germany. This attention to the soil and the concrete became more intense, not less, with the arrival of the Great Depression. During the Weimar Republic, housing construction and rent controls helped to regulate wage rates, address serious social grievances, and respond to a host of environmental concerns. The design of the new housing and its location enabled a revised engagement with nature and agriculture that was assumed to have significant social and cultural benefits. An ideology that celebrated production and efficiency came to dominate the concerns of both city planners and architects. This desire to incorporate nature into the city and to make the city as efficient as possible led to a vastly larger scale of planning. Finally, increasingly a critique developed that attempted to come to terms with the politics that gave rise to architectural and city-planning modernism. Left-wing critics of modernism developed an analysis that worked through a dialectical tension between those elements of modernism that were potentially liberating and those that continued the dominating aspects of capitalism.

Conclusion

The Corporate City and a New Regime of Accumulation

All programs of an anti-technological character, all propaganda for an anti-industrial revolution, serve only those who regard human needs as a by-product of the utilization of technics. The enemies of technics readily join forces with a terroristic technocracy. The philosophy of the simple life, the struggle against big cities and their culture frequently serves to teach men distrust of the potential instruments that could liberate them.

Herbert Marcuse, 1941[1]

Between 1871 and 1933 a metamorphosis in the form, function, and perception of the city of Greater Berlin took place in discourses on city planning and municipal administration. During this period a sense of crisis regarding the status of Greater Berlin pervaded the thinking and activities of city planners, municipal administrators, and concerned citizens relating to the city's rapid urbanization, population growth, inadequate housing, working-class radicalism, and regional incoherence. Over time, however, the form and the content of this sense of crisis and the attempts to respond to it changed. The transformation was affected by a variety of historical events and processes, including the failure of liberalism, the rise of Socialism, the First World War, the November 1918 Revolution, the hyperinflation of 1921–3, the Great Depression, and the rise of fascism. But these events and processes can mask or distract from a more fundamental change that occurred at this time, as the form, function, and perception of Greater Berlin shifted from a city constituted through liberal social forms to one organized along "corporatist" social forms.

Across the nineteenth century, municipal administration in Germany became increasingly autonomous and liberal in its political structure, despite the enduring power of the conservative Prussian bureaucracy. Over time, however, industrialization began to undermine the foundation of this autonomy. Cities became sites of social conflict, welfare services, and expanding geographic-economic influence and integration, all of which attracted the attention of the higher levels of government. In this same period a form of city planning developed that was structured around basic ideas of liberal political economy and politics, incorporating the abstract equality of citizens as buyers and sellers; the sanctity of private property; the value of regular, legal, calculable exchange; the importance of the bourgeois pedestrian and the public landscape; and the ease of free circulation of commodities and people. The planners developing these ideas were not necessarily liberal in an overtly political sense, but they believed that liberalism was the natural and rational response to the demands of the city.

Industrialization and urbanization in Greater Berlin, however, challenged this liberal city planning framework. The concrete consequences of liberal city planning, politics, and economics rendered many of the ideas about abstract equality deficient. The freedom of the market and of the private property holder had not created the conditions of possibility in the built environment for the society that liberals had envisioned. The poor-quality housing, monopoly of real-estate property ownership, inefficient (from the point of view of capitalism) layout of the city, poor hygienic conditions, and absence of green space all seemed to demand that liberals modify their previous ideals and intervene in the functioning of the market and private property to address the spatial consequences of capitalism.

While these conditions undermined liberal city planning and municipal self-administration, the First World War and the November 1918 Revolution fundamentally transformed these liberal social forms. The war and revolution underscored certain tendencies in the Kaiserreich but in the process utterly changed them. For capitalists in the face of the war economy, the market and liberalism more generally appeared to be impediments to efficiency, while city planning and municipal administration needed to focus on the new cohesive character of society and on expanding the role of the planning process. The revolution inspired a further shift to emphasize a planned, unified, productive society, especially with regard to housing. Finally, institutions established by the war economy rendered the unification of Greater Berlin into a single city possible in a way that it never was before. This new form of planning and administration no longer fostered liberal values of individual autonomy, abstract law, private property, and rational self-interest; instead, it emphasized the integration of the individual into the collective, rule by decree, expropriation of private property, and planning for the social totality.

By the 1920s city planners and municipal administrators had begun establishing new theories and practices in their respective fields that celebrated social cohesion and demanded greater state involvement in both urban administration and economic life. During the Weimar Republic, a shortage of capital, an expanded territory for planning, the politics of birth rates and living space, and a new aesthetic that emphasized form that followed function and productivity shaped Berlin's city planning and municipal administration. These discourses related Germany's well-being and power to the productivity of the nation and the productive dimensions of capitalism, believing that new spatial arrangements could remove whatever fetters on production existed.

Across this period one can see an inversion of the form, function, and perception of cities. The abstraction and generality of the liberal era and the sense that social progress was inhibited by concrete problems and particular interests were replaced by a celebration of the concrete and the particular function of a city, as well as a critique of abstraction associated with money and liberalism that inhibited the health of the nation. This shift is associated with a change in the form of capitalism, in what David Harvey calls a "regime of accumulation."[2] A historian, however, should mediate between the deep, structural level of this transformation and its form of appearance, such as in the rise of a particular style of architecture. Historians should not reduce such an aesthetic transformation simply to meeting the needs of capitalists, the will of great individuals, or the will-to-power of a technocracy. Capitalism, as well as its attendant urban agglomeration, was often envisioned in the Weimar Republic (and arguably until the 1970s) through a "corporatist," even biological lens. This book argues that one can account for this turn with reference to the commodity form as a totalizing social form that constitutes social relations.

This celebration of the productive and concrete dimensions of capitalism remains the governing logic of city planning in Berlin and Germany until the 1970s. But it is an international phenomenon: this logic also governs the development of cities and economic regions in France, Britain, and the United States. Moreover, it governs the logic of city planning in ostensibly communist nations. This book suggests that, as was the case in Germany during the First World War, societies can significantly diminish or eliminate the power of the market and private property while remaining capitalist, implying that the market and private property are integral to a specific form of capitalism – liberal capitalism – but are not essential to capitalism itself.

It is possible to conceive of the communist nations as not completely separate from capitalism but as a particularly acute version of a more general form of capitalism that significantly regulated the market and private property, that emphasized Fordist production, and that assumed significant state intervention.[3] Certainly, more work needs to be done on this front. Andrew Sloin and Oscar Sanchez-Sibony have argued that if one used the conception of capitalism developed by Moishe Postone and William Sewell Jr, one could begin to understand how capitalism might have structured Soviet society.[4] Sanchez-Sibony's work has placed Soviet international trade in the context of global capitalism.[5] Jake Werner makes a similar suggestion about understanding Maoist China.[6]

Corporatist Planning in the Trajectory of the Twentieth Century

During the National Socialist period some city planners and architects embraced the new regime; others tried to accommodate themselves without buying into its ideology; and still others fled the country. City planners in the NS period created the industrial cities of Wolfsburg and Salzgitter. They redesigned areas of Berlin, Munich, Hamburg, Nuremberg, and Linz as "Führerstädte," incorporating "major axes, construction of monumental government and party buildings and the relocation of [displaced] residents and institutions." These Führerstädte were set pieces designed to honour and encourage a "cult of the state." The planners created new housing for NS supporters that would "'renew' urban residential districts containing rundown buildings and occupied by members of the working class." In the newly conquered areas in Poland, for example, city planners sought to coordinate the region and to decentralize Warsaw into a network of smaller cities. Finally, planners re-envisioned the German cities that had been levelled by bombing in the Second World War. The architectural style was eclectic, combining "bombastic neoclassicism ... with modernist architecture" and spaces intended to "intimidate" with "more intimate 'organic' settlements."[7]

While architects did develop an aesthetic vocabulary to express the racial theories of the party and the Third Reich, the plans to reorganize Berlin also had a more concrete goal: a desire to eliminate Jewish spaces. Paul Jaskot argues that architect Albert Speer used the areas created through the destruction of Jewish spaces in Berlin to create his new Third Reich capital, and he sought to build new housing for the German working class while being open to modernist designs.[8] Speer tried to relocate residents displaced by his triumphal projects by depriving Jews of their rights as tenants and as property holders.[9] While Speer's vision of Berlin, like NS ideology, combined both anachronistic and archaic ideas with celebrations of modern technology and (pseudo-) science, he was planning the city for a coordinated and integrated purpose: the glorification of Hitler and the Nazi Party. And though Speer, and Baron Georges-Eugène Haussmann in Paris, as well as a number of the contestants in the Greater Berlin Contest of 1910, planned the totality of the city and had triumphal visions of their respective designs, the concerns that constituted that totality were quite different. Unlike the previously discussed goals of Speer's comprehensive plan, Haussmann's plan for Paris was liberal. It levelled uncoordinated local development plans and neighbourhood parochialism in municipal government that constrained the creation of a higher, abstract unity of the municipality. Haussmann's form of abstraction was specific to the liberal period of capitalism, in that he focused on moving commodities, making business predictable and facilitating freedom of the market and of civil society. He valued symmetry among buildings, which hearkened to the abstract equality of citizens. For Haussmann the city should be abstractly integrated, like a nation of particularities forming a single, politically mediated totality. Movement and free exchange structured the aesthetic of Haussmann's Paris, which was designed to be equalizing, rational, and symmetrical. With this context, Haussmann was historically specific to his liberal capitalist moment, while Speer was bound to his corporatist point in time.

In the 1930s anti-Semitic city planning was not limited to Germany. In French colonial Algeria, for example, municipal politicians relied on anti-Semitic views to appeal to voters. (Algerian Jews and non-French European settlers in the colony could vote. And although Algerian Muslims did not have the vote, right-wing groups sought their support for anti-Semitic platforms.[10]) This type of politics grew in popularity after 1933.[11] In Tunis and in Paris, Jews lived in "an overcrowded and insalubrious ... quarter." The French Protectorate offered to "cleanse" this quarter of Tunis with the cooperation of French Jews. Between May 1933 and 1939 the Tunis Municipal Council expropriated and demolished nearly all of the Jewish Quarter. The council had offered "1,400 'luxury' and 1,100 'semi-luxury' apartments," but by 1939 had built only 400 apartments. Contemporaneously, the Paris municipal government attempted to "cleanse" the Saint-Gervais ghetto in Paris because municipal officials in Paris valued maintaining the socioeconomic status quo of landowners and their wealthy allies more than new housing the project failed.[12] Rosemary Wakeman characterizes Parisian attitudes towards their city's built environment in this period as nostalgic modernism, because no high modernist plans, outside Le Corbusier's Plan Voisin, sought to express a new metropolitan spirit.[13]

In Britain, like in Germany, the Labour government of the early 1930s sought to expand measures from the 1920s to address the problems of housing quantity and quality. However, in response to the crises of 1931, voters replaced the Labour government with a more conservative administration that instituted austerity measures. But by the end of the 1930s politicians viewed city planning as "essential to the health of the nation." Among the goals was addressing overcrowding and reconfiguring interiors to free women from housework through new technologies and efficient layouts, so that these women could engage in fuller lives as citizens.[14] Women in Britain were integrated into civil society and political life outside of the house, while in France and Germany similar measures to intensify and "professionalize" household work enabled housewives to either do more in the same amount of labour time or experience greater leisure time.[15]

Functionalist and producerist architecture and city planning gained its international institutional power in 1933 when the Congrès Internationaux d'Architecture Moderne (CIAM) created the Athens Charter. The CIAM members who developed this charter retained the ideological critique of nineteenth-century architecture that had characterized discourses during the Weimar Republic. They rejected "nineteenth-century cities as overly dense, unsanitary, and given over to traffic and industrial uses," but they also rejected "detached-house suburban sprawl and center-city abandonment." Instead, they created four concrete "functional categories" to describe parts of urban industrial agglomerations – "dwelling, working, recreation, and circulation" – and provided solutions for each. Le Corbusier's version of the CIAM charter "called for the abolition of private property and the re-planning of cities on the basis of the hierarchy of 'four functions.'" However, Le

Corbusier advocated an "architectural rather than a political solution to the problem," driven by a technocratic and "powerful elite of architect planners."[16]

The CIAM architects who made their way to the United States found a receptive audience in the Roosevelt administration, which built garden city suburbs, created the regional plans for the Tennessee Valley Authority, and developed the Regional Planning Association of America. The CIAM argued for "an 'urban biology' with cities viewed as living organisms." Similarly, the urban sociology of Robert E. Park and the University of Chicago pioneered urban theory and research that drew on biological metaphors to understand the city.[17]

In the early 1930s Le Corbusier introduced the CIAM's ideas about cities into the Soviet Union and might have found a welcoming audience because of the emphasis on a professional avant-garde in both Leninism and the discourse of the CIAM. For a brief period the ideology of the CIAM and the architectural aesthetics of the Soviet state coincided, giving credence to the idea that CIAM's ideas were communist. But by the mid-1930s Stalin preferred a triumphal style that eliminated the audience for the ideas promulgated by the CIAM.[18]

The Fordist City from 1945 to 1972

After the Second World War, in West Germany the Marshall Plan made significant investments to address the housing needs of ten to twelve million refugees and coal miners in the Ruhr region. The nation had roughly six million dwellings fewer than the necessary number as the result of low housing production during the NS regime and even earlier.[19] The new housing drew on "pre-war proposals for garden cities, the modernist visions of CIAM, and National Socialist plans" of "functional zoning, green belts and new parks, high-rise housing blocks, roadways for growing motor vehicle traffic, revitalized neighborhoods of 5,000–10,000 inhabitants, and monumental axes and buildings to shape or represent the identity of a city."[20]

In the aftermath of the Second World War, during the period of Soviet occupation, much of the reconstruction in Berlin focused on triumphal and heavily ornamented Stalinist buildings that employed traditional building methods.[21] But this pattern changed quickly after Stalin's death in 1953. The Politbüro of the German Democratic Republic focused its efforts on large Plattenbausiedlungen at the margins of large cities like Berlin instead of rebuilding the old city centres. These new high-rise dwellings adhered to Fordist construction methods, were made of mass-produced parts, and embraced a holistic understanding of the city and economy.[22] This included a reintroduction of CIAM architects into Soviet-controlled areas.[23]

In France in the late 1940s the bulk of public works responsibilities were dedicated to addressing the destroyed cities littered with munitions and homeless residents. With the help of funds from the Marshall Plan, in 1947 the French government launched a national program to address housing, because housing shortage was seen as a limit to national economic growth; birth rates rose and people migrated from the countryside to cities in large numbers in search of jobs.[24] Progressives argued that housing production should follow the example of the automobile industry by incorporating mass production and lowering costs through increased efficiency at old sites for military production.[25] Builders used Taylorist methods to create the new publicly funded high-rises that resolved the "problem of family life." These buildings were based on the idea of a dwelling or "cellule ... whose efficient, rationalized floor plan offered a reconfiguration of domestic space as a streamlined site that actively minimized labor and maximized comfort in the form of central heating and indoor plumbing." This one-size-fits-all style of apartment forced both rich and poor to adapt their lives to a standardized layout. For modernist architects, these dwellings made Le Corbusier's vision of housing as a "machine for living" real, as a result of their emphasis on "scientific management and efficiency instead of status-oriented designs derived from a bourgeois desire for display." These designs frustrated many women who had previously helped to determine the character of the domestic space; however, because of the "gendered understanding of the home as a feminine sphere, ... women's preferences and practices ultimately triumphed."[26] The social relations in the housing designed for poorer people coloured perceptions of both residents and outsiders to this space. Increasingly these buildings were criticized for the "quality of their design and the alienating environment they provided." What was once seen as a means to achieve solidarity and equality were now attacked as inhuman.[27]

The Soviet Union, once Nikita Khrushchev secured power in 1957, undertook a state-funded housing construction project that created thirty-four million dwellings between 1956 and 1970, and ended up housing 126 million people – more than half of the nation's population.[28] Echoing Walter Gropius's desire in 1924 to construct buildings adequate to modern technology, Soviet architects in the 1950s sought to create buildings and cities that were equal to the needs of the mid-twentieth century, with its atomic energy, space flight, automation, and electronics. These new buildings were understood to be constructed "on conveyor belts"; used concrete panels for walls; and included prefabricated stairs, landings, and roofs. The state and the architects believed that these new structures expressed "clarity" and "veracity" through the elimination of ornamentation and the use of geometric simplicity to accentuate functionality. The new housing structures rejected the triumphal architecture of Stalinism and in its place offered "simplicity, plainness, horizontality, asymmetry, and equalization of forms and functions of modernist architecture." Some architecture historians have associated this functionalism with continued totalitarianism, those "totalitarian" features were common to most large-scale housing construction outside of the Soviet sphere of influence.[29] This aesthetic and its critique of ornamentation bear similarity to architectural discourses during the Weimar Republic. Furthermore, though the state eliminated the market and private interests from the Soviet economy, competition thrived in the battles between relatively autonomous interests at various levels of government and with various political, economic, and social responsibilities. This competition affected city planning in Stalinist Russia and after, when planners sought to balance the competing interests, assert their own influence, and mind the political imperatives of the state and party. This competition favoured heavy industry and made conditions challenging for planners.[30]

This similarity in architecture and city planning internationally across the mid-twentieth century could be explained either by disposing of the idea that it is particular to totalitarianism or by claiming that this uniformity expresses the inherent totalitarianism of all mid-twentieth-century urban planning. This book, however, argues for a different interpretation: this vision of the city is connected to a mid-twentieth-century form of capitalism wherein the market and private property were significantly constrained or even eliminated, while capitalist imperatives, particularly those of production, remained as the basic structural forms of society. In other words, as was the case during the command economy of Germany during the First World War, a society can discard the liberal social forms of the market and private property without eliminating capitalism. In the middle of the twentieth century, states whose ideology presented them as communist and post-capitalist were in fact still dominated by the imperatives of capitalist production.

Archival Sources and Abbreviations

This book synthesizes published and archival primary sources concerned with ecology, sociology, local and national politics, political economy, architecture, city planning, and the law of the municipality and of the state. From the Landesarchiv Berlin, it draws on the internal documents of the municipality of Berlin and of surrounding municipalities to address questions of administrative structure and jurisdiction, of public works and city planning, and of municipal finances. The research for this book drew on files in this archive from Stadtverordnetenversammlung der Stadt Berlin; from the Generalbüro, Militärbüro, Deputation für die städtischen Park-, Garten- und Baumanlagen, Deputation für das Siedlungs- und Wohnungswesen, Amt für Siedlungs- und Wohnungswesen, Städtische Hochbaudeputation, Städtische Tiefbaudeputation, Deputation für das Verkehrswesen, Verkehrsamt of the Magistrat der Stadt Berlin; from the Zweckverband von Groß-Berlin and Liegenschaftsstelle der Städtischen Güter und Forsten; from the Lebensmittelverband Groß-Berlin; from the Magistrat der Stadt Köpenick; from the Gemeindeverwaltung Friedrichsfelde. Also in this archive, it drew on files from the Eisenbahndirektion Berlin, A. Borsig Zentralverwaltung GmbH, Siemens-Werke, Gemeinnützige Heimstätten Spar- und Bau AG (GEHAG), Berliner Terrain-Centrale GmbH (BTC), Bauverein Eigenhaus, Boden-Aktiengesellschaft Berlin-Nord, Berliner Verkehrs-Gesellschaft (BVG), as well as the papers of Ernst Reuter, Gustav Böß, Paul Baumgarten, Ludwig Hoffmann, Paul Wittig, and the Grobe family.

The Prussian state had unique influence over the municipality of Berlin and the surrounding region, and therefore it dealt with many of the same municipal and regional questions as found in the documentary evidence held in the Geheimes Staatsarchiv, Preußischer Kulturbesitz. From this archive, this book draws on research in the papers relating to Greater Berlin and city planning from the following ministries: Handel und Gewerbe, Finanz, Volkswohlfahrt, Innern, and öffentlichen Arbeiten. Finally, materials at the Archiv der Akademie der Künste, Baukunstarchiv enable me to address changes in building and city-planning aesthetics. At the Archiv der Akademie der Künste, Baukunstarchiv, the research for this book focused on the files of Die "Gläserne Kette," Arbeitsrat für Kunst, Adolph Behne, Bruno Taut, Erwin Gutkind, August Endell, Hugo Häring, Herman Muthesius, Hans Poelzig, Harry Rosenthal, Josef Scherer, Luckhardt und Anker, Martin Mächler, Max Taut, Franz Mutzenbecher, Martin Wagner, Adolf Otto, Paul Baumgarten, Paul Baumgarten, Adolf Rading, Richard Ermisch, Der Ring, Hans Sharoun, and Thilo Schroder. In addition, this book draws on the public interest in municipal administration and city-planning issues that supported many publications during this period: technical and professional journals, academic journals, political party journals, and monographs, as well as newspapers and popular magazines that periodically addressed these questions. Taking this broad and synthetic approach reveals problems that would not arise in more specialized studies.

Archival Abbreviations

Akademie der Künste-Sammlung Baukunst: AdK-SB

118	Die "Gläserne Kette"
AfK	Arbeitsrat für Kunst
BEH	Adolph Behne Archiv
BT-Slg	Bruno Taut Sammlung
EGA	Erwin Gutkind Archiv
END	August Endell Archiv
HHA	Hugo Häring Archiv
HMA	Herman Muthesius Archiv
HPS	Hans Poelzig Sammlung
HRA	Harry Rosenthal Archiv
JSA	Josef Scherer Archiv
LAA	Luckhardt und Anker Archiv
MMA	Martin Mächler Archiv
MTF	Max Taut Fotosammlung
MUT	Franz Mutzenbecher Archiv

MWA	Martin Wagner Archiv
MWA-SMW	Martin Wagner Archiv-Sammlung Martin Wagner
Ott	Adolf Otto Archiv
PBA	Paul Baumgarten Archiv
PBA	Paul Baumgarten Archiv
RAD	Adolf Rading Archiv
REA	Richard Ermisch Archiv
RIN	Der Ring
SCH	Hans Sharoun Archiv
TSA	Thilo Schroder Archiv

Geheimes Staatsarchiv Preußischer Kulturbesitz: GStA PK

I. HA Rep. 120 A XV	Ministerium für Handel und Gewerbe
I. HA Rep. 151 IC	Finanzministerium
I. HA Rep. 191	Ministerium für Volkswohlfahrt
I. HA Rep. 77 Tit. 803	Ministerium des Innern
I. HA Rep. 93 B	Ministerium der öffentlichen Arbeiten

Landesarchiv Berlin: LAB

A Rep. 000-02-01	Stadtverordnetenversammlung der Stadt Berlin
A Rep. 001-02	Magistrat der Stadt Berlin, Generalbüro
A Rep. 001-04	Magistrat der Stadt Berlin, Militärbüro
A Rep. 007	Magistrat der Stadt Berlin, Deputation für die städtischen Park-, Garten-, und Baumanlagen
A Rep. 009	Magistrat der Stadt Berlin, Deputation für das Siedlungs- und Wohnungswesen/Amt für Siedlungs- und Wohnungswesen
A Rep. 010-01-01	Magistrat der Stadt Berlin, Städtische Hochbaudeputation
A Rep. 010-01-02	Magistrat der Stadt Berlin, Städtische Tiefbaudeputation
A Rep. 012-03	Zweckverband von Groß-Berlin/Liegenschaftsstelle der Städtischen Güter und Forsten
A Rep. 013-03	Lebensmittelverband Groß-Berlin
A Rep. 014	Magistrat der Stadt Berlin, Deputation für das Verkehrswesen/Verkehrsamt
A Rep. 046-03	Magistrat der Stadt Köpenick (ab 1809)
A Rep. 047-05-03	Gemeindeverwaltung Friedrichsfelde

A Rep. 082-01	Eisenbahndirektion Berlin
A Rep. 226	A. Borsig Zentralverwaltung GmbH
A Rep. 230-02	Siemens-Werke
A Rep. 251-05	Gemeinnützige Heimstätten Spar- und Bau AG (GEHAG)
A Rep. 251-09	Berliner Terrain-Centrale GmbH (BTC)
A Rep. 251-10	Bauverein Eigenhaus
A Rep. 251-11	Boden-Aktiengesellschaft Berlin-Nord
A Rep. 260	Berliner Verkehrs-Gesellschaft (BVG)
E Rep. 200-21	Nachlass Ernst Reuter
E Rep. 200-24	Nachlass Gustav Böß
E Rep. 200-38	Nachlass Paul Baumgarten
E Rep. 200-50	Nachlass Ludwig Hoffmann
E Rep. 200-83	Nachlass Paul Wittig
E Rep. 300-43	Nachlass Grobe

Notes

Introduction: Towards a Critical Historical Study of Greater Berlin

1 Le Corbusier, *Toward an Architecture [1924]* (Los Angeles: Getty Research Institute, 2007), 290.
2 Rudolf von Gneist, *Berliner Zustände* (Berlin: Bessersche Buchhandlung, 1849), 3–4.
3 Ibid., 6.
4 Andreas Heusler, *Der Ursprung der deutschen Stadtverfassung* (Weimar: Hermann Böhlau, 1872), 249–50.
5 Gustav von Roessler, "Zur Bauart deutscher Städte (I–II)," Deutsche Bauzeitung 8, no. 39 (1874): 153. (The complete article by Roessler is serialized in three issues no. 39 [p. 153–4], 41 [p. 162–5], and 101 [p. 402–5].)
6 Ibid., 164.
7 Walter Ruttmann, *Berlin* (Berlin: Deutsche Vereins-Film, 1927); Fritz Lang, *Metropolis* (Berlin: Erich Pommer, 1927).
8 Georg Simmel, "The Metropolis and Mental Life," in *Metropolis*, ed. Philip Kasinitz (New York: New York University Press, 1995), 32–3.
9 James J. Sheehan, "Liberalism and the City in Nineteenth-Century Germany," *Past and Present* 51, no. 1 (1971): 116–20.
10 Ibid., 117–20, quoted text from 120.
11 Ibid., 122–3.
12 Ibid., 134.
13 Jan Palmowski, "The Politics of the 'Unpolitical German,'" *Historical Journal* 42, no. 3 (1999): 667–8, 680, 688.
14 Hans Ulrich Wehler, "Der Aufstieg des Organisierten Kapitalismus und Interventionsstaates in Deutschland," in *Organisierter Kapitalismus*, ed.

Heinrich August Winkler (Göttingen: Vandenhoeck & Ruprecht, 1974), 36–7.

15 Ibid., 38–9. Jürgen Kocka, "Class Formation, Interest Articulation, and Public Policy," in *Organizing Interests in Western Europe*, ed. Suzanne Berger (Cambridge: Cambridge University Press, 1981), 76.

16 Heinrich August Winkler, "Einleitende Bemerkungen zu Hilferdings Theorie des Organisierten Kapitalismus," in *Organisierter Kapitalismus*, ed. Helmut Berding et al., (Göttingen: Vandenhoeck & Ruprecht, 1974), 9.

17 This new state was distinct from the early Prussian state interventions that sought to foster entrepreneurialism in the first half of the nineteenth century. Wehler, "Der Aufstieg des Organisierten Kapitalismus und Interventionsstaates in Deutschland," 45–7.

18 David Blackbourn, "The Discreet Charm of the Bourgeoisie," in *The Peculiarities of German History*, David Blackbourn and Geoff Eley (Oxford: Oxford University Press, 1984), 175; Geoff Eley, "The British Model and the German Road," ibid., 86–87.

19 Eley, "British Model and the German Road," 84–5, quoted text from 84; see also 90.

20 Charles S. Maier, "Strukturen kapitalistischer Stabilität in den zwanziger Jahren," in *Organisierter Kapitalismus*, ed. Heinrich August Winkler (Göttingen: Vandenhoeck & Ruprecht, 1974), 196–7.

21 Charles S. Maier, *Recasting Bourgeois Europe*, 2nd ed. (Princeton, NJ: Princeton University Press, 1988), 593.

22 Ibid., 593–4.

23 Dennis Sweeney, *Work, Race, and the Emergence of Radical Right Corporatism in Imperial Germany* (Ann Arbor: University of Michigan Press, 2009), 1–2.

24 Ibid., 2–3.

25 Ibid., 3.

26 Ibid., 4.

27 Lynn K. Nyhart, *Modern Nature* (Chicago: University of Chicago Press, 2009), 1–2.

28 Wolfgang von Oettingen, *Berlin* (Leipzig: Klinkhardt & Biermann, 1907); Oskar Schwebel, *Geschichte der Stadt Berlin*, 2 vols (Berlin: Brachvogel & Ranft, 1888).

29 Ludwig Geiger, *Geschichte der Juden in Berlin* (Berlin: J. Guttentag, 1871); Dora Meyer, "Das öffentliche Leben in Berlin im Jahr vor der Märzrevolution," *Schriften des Vereins für die Geschichte Berlins* 46 (1912): 1–116.

30 Lothar Baar, "Probleme der industriellen Revolution in großstädtischen Industriezentren," in *Wirtschafts- und sozialgeschichtliche Probleme der frühen Industrialisierung*, ed. Wolfram Fischer, 529–42 (Berlin: Colloquium

Verlag, 1968); Ingrid Thienel, "Industrialisierung und Städtewachstum," in *Untersuchungen zur Geschichte der frühen Industrialisierung vornehmlich im Wirtschaftsraum Berlin/Brandenburg*, ed. Otto Büsch, 105–50 (Berlin: Colloquium Verlag, 1971); Thienel, *Städtewachstum im Industrialisierungsprozess des 19. Jahrhunderts: Das Berliner Beispiel* (Berlin: Walter de Gruyter, 1973). See also Otto Büsch, *Geschichte der Berliner Kommunalwirtschaft in der Weimarer Epoche*, vol. 1 (Berlin: De Gruyter, 1960); Hans Herzfeld, *Demokratie und Selbstverwaltung in der Weimarer Epoche* (Stuttgart: Kohlhammer, 1957); Hertzfeld, *Geschichte von Brandenburg und Berlin*, vol. 3 (Berlin: Walter de Gruyter, 1968).

31 Joan Wallach Scott, "A Statistical Representation of Work," in *Gender and the Politics of History*, 113–38 (New York: Columbia University Press, 1999).

32 Andrew Lees, *Cities Perceived* (Manchester: Manchester University Press, 1985), 3, 5–6.

33 Andrew Lees, "Berlin and Modern Urbanity in German Discourse, 1845–1945," *Journal of Urban History* 17, no. 2 (1991): 155.

34 Ibid., 153.

35 Peter Fritzsche, *Reading Berlin 1900* (Cambridge, MA: Harvard University Press, 1996), 1–4.

36 Ibid.

37 Michel Foucault, "Governmentality," in *The Foucault Effect*, ed. Graham Burchell, Colin Gordon, and Peter Miller, 87–104 (Chicago: University of Chicago Press, 1991).

38 Leif Jerram, *Streetlife* (Oxford: Oxford University Press, 2011), 3. By conceptualizing this process by way of individual choices, this interpretation reifies these choices, making urbanization appear natural. Because he relies on textual analysis alone and rejects abstract arguments, he cannot account for this shift.

39 Ibid., 11–12. Jerram reveals a significant discursive shift, but the logic of "governmentality" struggles to explain that shift. Some social actors, suddenly, must be able to step outside of the reigning discourse and create a new one. In other words, "experts" gained power, then addressed their "obsessions." As is the case with his critique of abstraction in historiography, Jerram criticizes "expert" technical knowledge as inherently dominating. While he may find it surprising, one could describe this type of argument as one that sees social rationalization as an assertion of *Gesellschaft* into *Gemeinschaft*, to use Ferdinand Tönnies's terms.

40 Ibid., 11–12. Chris Otter offers a similar critique of technology and a supposed will-to-domination of the state. Like Jerram, he focuses on the concrete technologies and strategies of the state to order social life.

Otter treats liberalism as immediately concerned with the body and as concretely dominating. He argues that new infrastructural technologies – plumbing, street lighting, sewers, etc. – created liberal governmentality. Chris Otter, "Making Liberalism Durable," *Social History* 27, no. 1 (2002): 1, 4. Taking an apparently critical stance, Maiken Umbach emphasizes agency into what she regards as an overly deterministic – and abstract – mode of history writing. Maiken Umbach, "A Tale of Second Cities," *American Historical Review* 110, no. 3 (2005): 659.

41 James C. Scott, *Seeing like a State* (New Haven, CT: Yale University Press, 1998), 53.

42 Ibid., 54.

43 Ibid., 88–9.

44 Scott's account bears important similarities to Tönnies' antinomy of *Gemeinschaft* and *Gesellschaft*. Scott attributes this desire to a state will-to-power and a technologically driven teleology of increasing intervention into privacy. Scott posits that human interaction is naturally chaotic, *Gemeinschaft*, and resists this abstract and rationalizing tendency of the Enlightenment ideas, *Gesellschaft*. Scott contrasts the cultural space of *Gemeinschaft*, which is characterized by immediate, local understanding of the built environment, with the social space of *Gesellschaft*.

45 Jan van Ballegooijen and Roberto Rocco, "The Ideologies of Informality," *Third World Quarterly* 34, no. 10 (2013): 1794–5.

46 Ibid., 1795–6.

47 Moishe Postone, "Theorizing the Contemporary World," in *History and Heteronomy*, ed. Viren Murthy and Yasuo Kobayashi, 85–109 (Tokyo: University of Tokyo Center for Philosophy, 2009), 106.

48 The quotation in Brenner's text cited as Neil Smith, "Homeless/Global," in *Mapping the Futures*, ed. Jon Bird et al., 87–119 (London: Routledge, 1993); Neil Brenner, "Globalisation as Reterritorialisation," *Urban Studies* 36, no. 3 (1999): 432.

49 Henri Lefebvre, *The Production of Space* (Oxford: Blackwell, 1991), 25.

50 David Harvey, *The Condition of Postmodernity: An Enquiry into the Origins of Cultural Change* (Oxford: Basil Blackwell, 1989), 266–70.

51 Cited as Elmar Altvater, "Fordist and Post-Fordist International Division of Labor and Monetary Regimes," in *Pathways to Industrialization and Regional Development*, ed. Michael Storper and Allen J. Scott, 21–45 (London: Routledge, 1992); Michael Charles Storper and Allen John Scott, "The Wealth of Regions," *Futures* 27, no. 5 (1995): 505–26; Saskia Sassen, *The Global City* (Princeton, NJ: Princeton University Press, 1991); Brenner, "Globalisation as Reterritorialisation," 432.

52 J. Taylor Vurpillat, "Empire, Industry, and Globalization," *History Compass* 12, no. 6 (2014): 531–40; Paolo Mauro, Nathan Sussman, and Yishay Yafeh, *Emerging Markets and Financial Globalization* (Oxford: Oxford University Press, 2006); Manuel Llorca-Jaña, "Shaping Globalization," *Business History Review* 88, no. 3 (2014): 469–95; Weimin Zhong, "The Roles of Tea and Opium in Early Economic Globalization," *Frontiers of History in China* 5, no. 1 (2010): 86–105; Isabella Löhr and Roland Wenzlhuemer, eds, *The Nation State and Beyond* (New York: Springer Verlag, 2013); Ian Phimister, "Late Nineteenth-Century Globalization: London and Lomagundi Perspectives on Mining Speculation in Southern Africa, 1894–1904," *Journal of Global History* 10, no. 1 (2015): 27–52; Robert M. Schwartz, "Rail Transport, Agrarian Crisis, and the Restructuring of Agriculture: France and Great Britain Confront Globalization, 1860–1900," *Social Science History* 34, no. 2 (2010): 229–55.

53 Harvey, *Condition of Postmodernity*, 121.

54 As Moishe Postone argues, the regimes of accumulation "indicate that capitalism cannot be identified completely with any of its configurations"; but capitalism retains an essential core. This book, like Postone's, does not assume a teleological dynamic of history or that history is an accumulation of contingent events. Rather, it builds on Postone's argument that "the form of social domination intrinsic to modern, capitalist society is generative of a historical dynamic" and that the conditions of that dynamic are "historically specific social forms at the heart of capitalism – such as commodity and capital." Postone, "Theorizing the Contemporary World," 105–6.

55 Max Horkheimer, "The End of Reason [1941]," in *The Essential Frankfurt School*, ed. Andrew Arato and Eike Gebhardt (New York: Continuum, 1982), 131–2.

56 This sense is echoed by both Walter Benjamin and Theodor Adorno in that as Adorno explains, Benjamin's *Arcades Project* and *A Berlin Childhood around 1900* together were intended to grasp the dawn and sunset of a particular urban liberal subjectivity. Theodor W. Adorno, "Nachwort zur 'Berliner Kindheit um neunzehnhundert,'" in *Über Walter Benjamin*, ed. Rolf Tiedemann (Frankfurt am Main: Suhrkamp Verlag, 1990), 74–6.

57 As I will explain later, this contradiction between abstract, universal values and concrete, particular functionality is rooted in the commodity form. Herbert Marcuse, "The Affirmative Character of Culture," trans. Jeremy J. Shapiro, in *Negations: Essays in Critical Theory* (London: Mayfly Books, 2009), 67.

58 Ibid., 70.

59 Ibid., 71–2.
60 Ibid., 73–4.
61 Ibid., 92–3.
62 Ibid., 95.
63 Georg Lukács, "Reification and the Consciousness of the Proletariat: Studies in Marxist Dialectics," in *History and Class Consciousness,* (Cambridge, MA: MIT Press, 1971), 93. Georg Simmel developed the idea of social forms as trans-historical, recurring patterns that have the same form, despite different contents. For example, he argued that an antinomy between the individual and society is ontological. (Georg Simmel, "Individual and Society in Eighteenth and Nineteenth Century Views of Life [1917]," trans. Kurt H. Wolff, in *The Sociology of Georg Simmel,* ed. Kurt H. Wolff [Glencoe, IL: Free Press, 1950], 60.) Lukacs, Simmel's friend and student, criticized Simmel for isolating social forms from their specific moment in social history and making them ontological. Lukacs regarded Simmel's ontologization of one phenomenon in a broader social history as symptomatic of a social process called reification that, as a part of capitalism, like capitalism, was historically specific.
64 Lukács, "Reification and the Consciousness of the Proletariat," 83.
65 Moishe Postone, "The Holocaust and the Trajectory of the Twentieth Century," in *Catastrophe and Meaning: the Holocaust and the Twentieth Century,* ed. Moishe Postone and Eric L. Santner (Chicago: University of Chicago Press, 2003), 90–1. Postone's shorter texts introduce key categories like the commodity or capitalism succinctly, but full understanding can be gained only by reading his book. *Time, Labor, and Social Domination* (Cambridge: Cambridge University Press, 1993).
66 Moishe Postone, "Anti-Semitism and National Socialism," in "Germans and Jews," special issue, *New German Critique* 19 (Winter 1980): 110.
67 Postone, "The Holocaust and the Trajectory," 92–4; Postone, *Time, Labor, and Social Domination,* 174n15; Postone, "Anti-Semitism and National Socialism."

1. The Rise of Industrial Berlin

1 Karl Scheffler, *Berlin,* 3rd ed. (Berlin-Westend: Erich Reiss Verlag, 1910), 182–3.
2 By the term *form,* I mean the appearance of the built environment and of plans for the built environment, as well as the organization of municipal and regional government. By *content,* I am referring to the functioning of the built environment and of regional government.

3 Carl E. Schorske, *Fin-de-siècle Vienna*, 1st Vintage Book ed. (New York: Vintage Books, 1981), 4.
4 Harvey, *Condition of Postmodernity*, 121.
5 Brenner, "Globalisation as Reterritorialisation."
6 Blackbourn, "Discreet Charm of the Bourgeoisie," 175; Geoff Eley, "The British Model and the German Road," ibid., 86–87.
7 Cited as Gareth Stedman Jones, "Society and Politics at the Beginning of the World Economy," *Cambridge Journal of Economics* 1, no. 1 (1977): 84; in Eley, "The British Model and the German Road," 76.
8 Blackbourn, "Discreet Charm of the Bourgeoisie," 190.
9 Eley, "The British Model and the German Road," 84–5.
10 Blackbourn, "The Discreet Charm of the Bourgeoisie," 190–1.
11 Ibid., 192.
12 Ibid., 193.
13 Michael John, "The Peculiarities of the German State," *Past and Present*, no. 119 (1988): 105–31.
14 William H. Sewell Jr, "Refiguring the 'Social' in Social Science," in *Logics of History*, 318–73 (Chicago: University of Chicago Press, 2005); Theodor W. Adorno, "Society [1963]," in *Critical Theory and Society*, ed. Stephen Eric Bronner and Douglas Kellner, 267–76 (New York: Routledge, 1989).
15 Elaine Hadley, *Living Liberalism* (Chicago: University of Chicago Press, 2010), 64–5.
16 Blackbourn, "Discreet Charm of the Bourgeoisie," 203–4.
17 Marion W. Gray, "Government by Property Owners," *Journal of Modern History* 48, no. 1 (1976): 74.
18 Ibid., 75–9; Marion W. Gray, "Prussia in Transition," *Transactions of the American Philosophical Society* 76, no. 1 (1986): 86.
19 Gray, "Prussia in Transition," 106–8.
20 Jeffrey K. Wilson, *The German Forest, 1871–1914* (Toronto: University of Toronto Press, 2012), 53–4.
21 Alfred Baron a. Wernigerode, "Der Haus- und Grundbesitzer in Preussens Städten einst und jetzt (unter Berücksichtung von Steins Städteordnung)" (Vereinigten Friedrichs-Universität Halle-Wittenberg, 1911), 16–17.
22 *Städte-Ordnung für die sechs östlichen Provinzen der Preußischen Monarchie: Vom 30. Mai 1853* (Berlin: Carl Salewski, 1853), § 16; Håkan Forsell, *Property, Tenancy and Urban Growth in Stockholm and Berlin, 1860–1920*, (Aldershot, Hampshire, UK: Ashgate, 2006), 26; Günter Richter, "Zwischen Revolution und Reichsgründung (1848–1871)," in *Geschichte Berlins*, ed. Wolfgang Ribbe, (München: C.H. Beck, 1987), 644.

23 *Städte-Ordnung für die sechs östlichen Provinzen der Preußischen Monarchie,* § 5; Forsell, *Property, Tenancy and Urban Growth*, 29; Richter, "Zwischen Revolution und Reichsgründung," 646.
24 Forsell, *Property, Tenancy and Urban Growth*, 28–30.
25 Wolfgang Hardtwig, "Großstadt und Bürgerlichkeit in der politischen Ordnung des Kaiserreichs," *Historische Zeitschrift: Beihefte* 12 (1990): 26–7.
26 Forsell, *Property, Tenancy and Urban Growth*, 31.
27 Brian Ladd, *Urban Planning and Civic Order in Germany, 1860–1914* (Cambridge, MA: Harvard University Press, 1990), 91.
28 Ibid., 93.
29 Büsch, *Geschichte der Berliner Kommunalwirtschaft*, 1; Herzfeld, *Demokratie und Selbstverwaltung*.
30 Adolf Streckfuss, *500 Jahre Berliner Geschichte*, 4th ed., vol. 2 (Berlin: Albert Goldschmidt, 1886); Schwebel, *Geschichte der Stadt Berlin*, vol. 1; Maxime Du Camp, *Paris: ses organes, ses fonctions et sa vie dans la seconde moitié du XIX e siècle*, 6 vols (Paris: Hachette, 1869–1875); Bessie Louise Pierce, *A History of Chicago*, 3 vols (New York: A.A. Knopf, 1937–57); Carl Bridenbaugh, *Cities in the Wilderness*, 2nd ed. (New York: Alfred A. Knopf, 1955); William George Hoskins, *Industry, Trade and People in Exeter, 1688–1800* (Manchester: Manchester University Press, 1935).
31 Richter, "Zwischen Revolution und Reichsgründung," 646, 677.
32 Michael Erbe, "Berlin im Kaiserreich (1871–1918)," in *Geschichte Berlins*, ed. Wolfgang Ribbe (Munich: C.H. Beck, 1987), 770–5.
33 Ladd, *Urban Planning and Civic Order*, 31; Shulamit Volkov, *The Rise of Popular Antimodernism in Germany* (Princeton, NJ: Princeton University Press, 1978).
34 Ladd, *Urban Planning and Civic Order*, 26; Erbe, "Berlin im Kaiserreich," 767–70.
35 John W. Boyer, *Political Radicalism in Late Imperial Vienna* (Chicago: University of Chicago Press, 1981); Boyer, *Culture and Political Crisis in Vienna*, (Chicago: University of Chicago Press, 1995).
36 Gerd Heinrich, "Hauptstadtraum und Miltärstaat," in *Stadt und militärische Anlagen*, ed. Akademie für Raumforschung und Landesplanung (Hannover: Hermann Schroedel Verlag, 1977), 238; Martin Zippel, "Untersuchungen zur Militärgeschichte der Reichshauptstadt Berlin von 1871 bis 1945" (Geschichte, Westfälischen Wilhelms-Universität, 1981), 158.
37 Ladd, *Urban Planning and Civic Order in Germany*, 93.
38 Heinrich Dove, "Berlin," in *Verfassung und Verwaltungsorganisation der Städte*, ed. Vereins für Sozialpolitik (Leipzig: Duncker & Humblot, 1906), 96.

39 Heinrich, "Hauptstadtraum und Miltärstaat," 238; Zippel, "Untersuchungen zur Militärgeschichte der Reichshauptstadt Berlin," 158.
40 Richter, "Zwischen Revolution und Reichsgründung," 647–50.
41 Erbe, "Berlin im Kaiserreich," 759–63.
42 Ernst Schraepler, "Berlin als Zentrale der deutschen sozialistischen Arbeiterbewegung," in *Berlin im Europa der Neuzeit*, ed. Wolfgang Ribbe and Jürgen Schmädeke, 155–64 (Berlin: Walter de Gruyter, 1990). An early example of this work is Eduard Bernstein, *Die Geschichte der Berliner Arbeiter-Bewegung*, 3 vols. (Berlin: Buchhandlung Vorwärts [Hans Weber], 1910).
43 Erbe, "Berlin im Kaiserreich," 763–7.
44 Ladd, *Urban Planning and Civic Order in Germany*, 31.
45 Eduard Bernstein, ed. *Fünfzehn Jahre Berliner Arbeiterbewegung unter dem gemeinen Recht* (Berlin: Buchhandlung Vorwärts [Hans Weber], 1910), 3:264–8.
46 Carl Hugo Lindemann, "Zur Kritik der socialdemokratischen Communalprogramme," *Socialistische Monatshefte* 6, no. 4 (1902): 277–88. He wrote a follow-up article detailing the communal successes of the SPD. Lindemann, "Unsere Forderungen an die Communen," *Socialistische Monatshefte* 6, no. 6 (1902): 437–47.
47 Hsi-Huey Liang, "The Berlin Police and the Weimar Republic," *Journal of Contemporary History* 4, no. 4 (1969): 160; Gernot Wittling, "Zivil-militärische Beziehungen im Spannungsfeld von Residenz und entstehendem großstädtischen Industriezentrum," in *Stadt und Militär 1815–1914*, ed. Bernhard Sicken (Paderborn: Ferdinand Schöningh, 1998), 216.
48 Heinrich, "Hauptstadtraum und Miltärstaat," 238; Zippel, "Untersuchungen zur Militärgeschichte der Reichshauptstadt Berlin," 158.
49 F[riedrich] Freiherr von Dincklage[-Campe], "Das militärische Berlin," in *Groß-Berlin: Bilder von der Ausstellungsstadt*, ed. Albert Kühnemann and Richard Schott (Berlin: W. Pauli's Nachfolge, 1896), 158.
50 Anja Johansen, *Soldiers as Police* (Aldershot, UK: Ashgate, 2005), 60–6; Nicholas Stargardt, *The German Idea of Militarism* (Cambridge: Cambridge University Press, 1994), 19–90.
51 Stargardt, *German Idea of Militarism*, 91–108.
52 Karl Liebknecht, *Militarism and Anti-Militarism* (New York: Howard Fertig, 1969), 56.
53 Wittling, "Zivil-militärische Beziehungen," 240–2.
54 Albert Sigrist, *Das Buch vom Bauen* (Berlin: Der Bucherkreis GmbH, 1930), 207–8. Sigrist was a pseudonym for Alexander Schwab. Diethart Kerbs, "Alexander Schwab (1887–1943)," *Internationale wissenschaftliche*

Korrespondenz zur Geschichte der deutschen Arbeiterbewegung 41, no. 4 (2005): 487–95.

55 Arthur M. Schlesinger Sr., *The Rise of the City, 1878–1898* (New York: Macmillan, 1933); Schlesinger Sr., "The City in American History," *The Mississippi Valley Historical Review* 27, no. 1 (1940): 43–66; Oscar Handlin, "The Modern City as a Field of Historical Study," in *The Historian and the City*, ed. Oscar Handlin and John Burchard, 1–26 (Cambridge, MA: MIT Press and Harvard University Press, 1963); Blake McKelvey, "American Urban History Today," *American Historical Review* 57, no. 4 (1952): 919–29.

56 McKelvey, "American Urban History Today," 927–8. Curiously, McKelvey suggests that the modern city organized around a number of antitheses: "diffusion versus centralization, heterogeneity versus standardization, expressionism versus planning, to mention only a few," but does not pursue this further. This tendency toward dualism, in the perception of cities, is of particular interest to this dissertation, as will be discussed later.

57 Wolfgang Köllmann, "The Process of Urbanization in Germany at the Height of the Industrialization Period," *Journal of Contemporary History* 4, no. 3 (1969): 76.

58 Eric E. Lampard, "The History of Cities in Economically Advanced Areas," *Economic Development and Cultural Change* 3, no. 2 (1955): 89–91; Lampard, "The Urbanizing World," in *The Victorian City*, ed. Harold James Dyos and Michael Wolff, (London: Routledge & Kegan Paul, 1973), 40; Handlin, "Modern City as a Field of Historical Study," 5.

59 Eric E. Lampard, "American Historians and the Study of Urbanization," *American Historical Review* 67, no. 1 (1961): 54.

60 Wolfgang Hofmann, "Wachsen Berlins im Industriezeitalter," in *Probleme des Städtewesens im industriellen Zeitalter*, ed. Helmut Jäger (Cologne: Böhlau Verlag, 1978), 160–3.

61 Simone Gingrich, Gertrud Haidvogl, and Fridolin Krausmann, "The Danube and Vienna," *Regional Environmental Change* 12, no. 2 (2012): 284, 286.

62 Jim Clifford, "The River Lea in West Ham," in *Urban Rivers*, ed. Stéphane Castonguay and Matthew Evenden (Pittsburgh: University of Pittsburgh Press, 2012), 37, 44.

63 Handlin, "Modern City as a Field of Historical Study," 8.

64 Baar, "Probleme der industriellen Revolution," 539–42.

65 Karl Flesch, "Referaten: Verhandlungen des Vereins für Sozialpolitik über die Verfassung und Verwaltungsorganisation der Städte," in *Schriften des Vereins für Socialpolitik: Verhandlungen der Generalsammulung in Magdeburg,*

30. September, 1. und 2. Oktober 1907, ed. Verein für Socialpolitik (Leipzig: Duncker & Humblot, 1908), 225–6, 230.

66 Heinrich Herkner, *Die sociale Reform als Gebot des wirtschaftlichen Fortschrittes* (Leipzig: Duncker & Humblot, 1891), 1, 3–4. A sympathetic social reformer argued that modern industry created "unfavourable consequences" on "the life and the health of the working population," who are forced to live in densely populated housing with "with all its bad economic, health and moral accompaniments." Lujo Brentano, *Die Schrecken des überwiegenden Industriestaats* (Berlin: L. Simion, 1901), 30.

67 Franz Adickes, "Vortrage von Oberbürgermeister D. Adickes in Frankfurt a.M.," in *Die sozialen Aufgaben der deutschen Städte*, ed. Franz Adickes and Gustav Otto Beutler (Leipzig: Druncker und Humbolt, 1903), 11; Hugo Preuß, *Entwicklungsgeschichte der Deutschen Städteverfassung* (Leipzig: B.G. Teubner, 1906), 1:377–9.

68 Ernst Scholz, "Die moderne Stadtverwaltung [1]," *Zeitschrift für Kommunalwirtschaft und Kommunalpolitik*, no. 1 (11 January 1913): 2–3. Scholz was trained as a jurist and worked in a variety of court-related bureaucratic roles in German cities, as well as serving as the first secretary of the General Federation German Trade and Industrial Cooperatives and as Oberbürgermeister of Kassel [1912–13] and of Charlottenburg [1913–20]. During the Weimar Republic, he played a leading role in developing the platform of the German National People's Party and served as minister of economics from 1920 to 1921. Barbara Hillen, *Scholz, Ernst August Gustav*, vol. 23 (Berlin: Duncker & Humblot, 2007).

69 Robert Millward, "Urban Government, Finance and Public Health in Victorian Britain," in *Urban Governance: Britain and Beyond since 1750*, ed. Richard H. Trainor and Robert Morris, (Burlington, VT: Ashgate, 2000), 48–9.

70 James R. Moore, "Liberalism and the Politics of Suburbia," *Urban History* 30, no. 2 (2003): 247.

71 Ernst Scholz, "Die moderne Stadtverwaltung [15]," *Zeitschrift für Kommunalwirtschaft und Kommunalpolitik*, no. 22 (25 November 1913): 674–5.

72 Christoph Bernhardt, "At the Limits of the European Sanitary City: Water-Related Environmental Inequalities in Berlin-Brandenburg, 1900–1939," in *Environmental and Social Justice in the City: Historical Perspectives*, ed. Geneviève Massard-Guilbaud and Richard Rodger (Cambridge: White Horse, 2011), 155–6.

73 Ibid., 156.

74 Adam Smith, *An Inquiry into the Nature and Causes of the Wealth of Nations [1776]* (Chicago: University of Chicago Press, 1976), bk V, chap. 1, pp. 302–9, 340.

75 Otter, "Making Liberalism Durable," 1.

76 Gustav Adolf Kuhfahl, "Verfassung und Verwaltung der deutschen Städte," in *Die deutschen Städte*, ed. Robert Wuttke (Leipzig: Friedrich Brandstetter, 1903), 8–9; Preuß, *Entwicklungsgeschichte der Deutschen Städteverfassung*, 1:1, 377–9.

77 Paul Mombert, *Die deutschen Stadtgemeinden und ihre Arbeiter* (Stuttgart: J.G. Cotta'sche Buchhandlung Nachfolger, 1902), 214–16.

78 Preuß, *Entwicklungsgeschichte der Deutschen Städteverfassung*, 1, 375, 377–8. As Dieter Langewiesche notes, liberal discomfort with this choice can be seen in the way municipal issues were excluded or buried in their party literature, despite their municipal power. Dieter Langewiesche, *Liberalism in Germany*, ed. trans. Christiane Banerji (Princeton, NJ: Princeton University Press, 2000), 220–1.

79 Carl Hugo Lindemann, "Probleme des Munizipalsozialismus," *Sozialistische Monatshefte* 14, no. 8 (1910): 508–13.

80 Sam Bass Warner, "If All the World Were Philadelphia," *American Historical Review* 74, no. 1 (1968). 35, 39, 42.

81 Hofmann, "Wachsen Berlins im Industriezeitalter," 160–3.

82 Robert Lewis and Richard Walker, "Beyond the Crabgrass Frontier," *Journal of Historical Geography* 27, no. 1 (2001): 3–4, 7–8; Richard Harris and Robert Lewis, "The Geography of North American Cities and Suburbs, 1900–1950," *Journal of Urban History* 27, no. 3 (2001): 262–92; Richard Walker, "Industry Builds the City," *Journal of Historical Geography* 27, no. 1 (2001): 36–57.

83 Tyler Stovall, "French Communism and Suburban Development," *Journal of Contemporary History* 24, no. 3 (July 1989): 438–41. Though the suburbanization of industry, in part due to inner city rents, was a global phenomenon, French historians attribute the centrifugal pressure to Baron von Haussmann destroying affordable inner city housing in the 1860s.

84 For a very early English example of this type of population movement, see Robert L. Fishman, "American Suburbs/English Suburbs," *Journal of Urban History* 13, no. 3 (1987): 237–51.

85 David Ward, "Environs and Neighbours in the 'Two Nations' Residential Differentiation in Mid-Nineteenth-Century Leeds," *Journal of Historical Geography* 6, no. 2 (1980): 139–40.

86 Stovall, "French Communism and Suburban Development," 438–41.

87 Horst Matzerath, "Städtwachstum und Eingemeindungen im 19. Jahrhundert," in *Die deutsche Stadt im Industriezeitalter*, ed. Jürgen Reulecke, (Wuppertal: Peter Hammer, 1978), 68–9.

88 Hans Guradze, "Der Einfluß der Eingemeindung auf die Bevölkerungsbewegung der Großstädte," *Jahrbücher für Nationalökonomie und Statistik* 90, no. 5 (1908): 626–32.
89 Dove, "Berlin," 102–6.
90 Fritz Besgen, "Die Wirkung der Eingemeindung auf Polizeiverordnungen nach preußischem Rechte" (Leipzig: Universität Leipzig, 1909), 1.
91 Scholz, "Die moderne Stadtverwaltung [1]," 2–3.
92 Carl Hugo Lindemann, *Die deutsche Städteverwaltung*, 2, improved and expanded ed. (Stuttgart: J.H.W. Dietz nachf., 1906), 429–31.
93 Ernst Hirschberg, "Die Wohnungsfrage und die Eingemeindung der Berliner Vororte," *Volkswirtschaftliche Zeitfragen, Vorträge und Abhandlungen* 27, no. 4 (1905): 15–17.
94 Ibid., 12–16, 18, quotation from 18.
95 Georg Haberland, *Der Einfluss des Privatkapitals auf die bauliche Entwicklung Gross-Berlins* (Berlin: Carl Heymanns Verlag, 1913), 10–11.
96 Ernst W. Burgess, "The Growth of the City," in *The City*, ed. Robert Park, Ernst W. Burgess, and Roderick McKenzie, 47–62 (Chicago: University of Chicago Press, 1967).
97 Henri Lefebvre, *The Urban Revolution [1970]*, ed. trans. Robert Bononno, (Minneapolis; London: University of Minnesota Press, 2003), 15.
98 Neil Brenner, "Urban Theory without an Outside," in *Implosions/ Explosions*, ed. Neil Brenner (Berlin: Jovis, 2013), 17.
99 Wolfgang Hofmann, "Die Entwicklung der kommunalen Selbstverwaltung von 1848 bis 1918," in *Grundlagen und Kommunalverfassung*, ed. Thomas Mann and Günter Püttner (Berlin: Springer-Verlag, 2007), 83; Erbe, "Berlin im Kaiserreich," 748.
100 Haberland, *Der Einfluss des Privatkapitals auf die bauliche Entwicklung Gross-Berlin*, 5.
101 Albert Frank, "Die Eingemeindung von Vororten in Städte" (Jurist-Doktor, Juristenfakultät der Universität Rostock, 1908), 1–5, 10, 37–8.
102 Martin Queis, *Begriff und Wirkung der Eingemeindung nach preußischem Verwaltungsrecht* (Greifswald: J. Abel, 1913), 11.
103 Hermann Dittmar, "Das Recht der Eingemeindung in Preußen" (Universität zu Rostock, 1908), 1–3, 12–13, 31–3.
104 Besgen, "Die Wirkung der Eingemeindung auf Polizeiverordnungen nach preußischem Rechte," 1.
105 This follows Franz Neumann's idea that abstract norms of law and the executive power of administration are in a dialectical tension. Franz L. Neumann, "The Change in the Function of Law in Modern Society," translated by Klaus Knorr, in *The Democratic and the Authoritarian State,*

ed. Herbert Marcuse (Glencoe, IL: Free Press, 1957), 22–3. He also cautions his reader from taking too seriously the liberal claims about the near non-existence of the state and to mistake its negative legal structure for the totality of the state. The executive power of the state was perfectly capable of crushing rebellion or waging war when the time came.

106 Gneist, *Berliner Zustände*, 3–4, 6, 29–30, 39–42, quotations from 3–4, 6.

107 Ernst von Möller, *Preussisches Stadtrecht* (Breslau: W. Clar, 1864), 4, 43–5. Otto Friedrich von Gierke makes a very similar point about the character of medieval municipal autonomy. Otto Gierke, *Das deutsche Genossenschaftsrecht*, vol. 1 (Berlin: Weidmannsche Buchhandlung, 1868).

108 Rudolph Gneist, *Verwaltung, Justiz, Rechtsweg* (Berlin: J. Springer, 1869), 56.

109 Berthold Grzywatz, *Stadt, Bürgertum und Staat im 19. Jahrhundert* (Berlin: Duncker & Humblot, 2003), 648–84.

110 John, "Peculiarities of the German State," 121–2.

111 Sheehan, "Liberalism and the City," 135; Palmowski, "Politics of the 'Unpolitical German,'" 698.

112 Blackbourn, "Discreet Charm of the Bourgeoisie," 223.

113 Sheehan, "Liberalism and the City," 130–4; Jan Palmowski, "Liberalism and Local Government in Late Nineteenth-Century Germany and England," *Historical Journal* 45, no. 2 (2002): 382–3.

114 Rudolph Gneist, *Der Rechtsstaat* (Berlin: J. Springer, 1872), 105.

115 Ibid., 3, 19.

116 Ibid., 36.

117 Michael Stolleis, *Public Law in Germany, 1800–1914*, ed. trans. Pamela Beil (New York: Berghahn, 2001), 324–35.

118 Neumann, "Change in the Function of Law in Modern Society," 37.

119 Otto Kirchheimer, "The Socialist and Bolshevik Theory of the State [1928]," in *Politics, Law, and Social Change*, ed. Frederic Burin and Kurt L. Shell (New York: Columbia University Press, 1969), 7–8.

120 Neumann, "Change in the Function of Law in Modern Society," 39; Stolleis, *Public Law in Germany*, 292.

121 Sheehan, "Liberalism and the City in Nineteenth-Century Germany," 133–4; Langewiesche, *Liberalism in Germany*, 133; Dieter Langewiesche attributed the declining position of the liberals to the fact that they had achieved their main goal, unification, already and had no further political and ideological goals. This does not fully take into account the changing society.

122 Wilhelm von Blume, "Autonomie Körperschaften," in *Handbuch der Politik*, ed. Paul Laband et al. (Berlin: Dr Walther Rothschild, 1912),

219–22; Franz Neumann, "Types of Natural Law," *Studies in Philosophy and Social Science [Zeitschrift für Sozialforschung]* 8, no. 3 (1939/40): 338–61. For example, Laband dismissed municipal independence as merely a transference of state responsibilities; for him, the municipality was only the direct executor of state business. Paul Laband, *Das Staatsrecht des deutschen Reiches* (Tübingen: J.C.B. Mohr [Paul Seibeck], 1901), 2:187; ibid.

123 Heusler, *Der Ursprung der deutschen Stadtverfassung*, 249–51.

124 Gierke, "Rechtsgeschichte der deutschen Genossenschaft," 312–14.

125 Karl Siegfried Bader, "Gierke, Otto Friedrich von," in *Neue Deutsche Biographie*, ed. Der Historischen Kommission bei der Bayerischen Akademie der Wissenschaft, 374–5 (Berlin: Duncker & Humblot, 1964).

126 Stolleis, *Public Law in Germany*, 345.

127 Otto Gierke, *Die Genossenschaftstheorie und die deutsche Rechtsprechung* (Berlin: Weidmannsche Buchhandlung, 1887), 663–6.

128 Stolleis, *Public Law in Germany*, 326–7.

129 Ibid., 339.

130 Ibid., 337–40.

131 Hugo Preuß, *Gemeinde, Staat, Reich als Gebietskörperschaften* (Berlin: J. Springer, 1889), 204–8, 211, 219.

132 Hugo Preuß, *Das Völkerrecht im Dienste des Wirthschaftslebens* (Berlin: Leonhard Simion, 1891), 12–13.

133 Eugen Leidig, *Preußisches Stadtrecht* (Berlin: Siemenroth & Worms, 1891), 9–10.

134 Preuß, *Das Völkerrecht im Dienste des Wirthschaftslebens*, 12–13; Preuß, *Das städtische Amtsrecht in Preußen* (Berlin: Georg Reimer, 1902), 117; ibid.

135 Preuß, *Das städtische Amtsrecht in Preußen*, 120.

136 Ibid., 123–5.

137 Lukács, "Reification and the Consciousness of the Proletariat," 99–100.

2. The Decline of Liberal City Planning

1 Walther Rathenau, *Zur Mechanik des Geistes*, 3rd ed. (Berlin: Fischer Verlag, 1913), 43–4.

2 Rathenau, *Zur Kritik der Zeit*, 3rd ed. (Berlin: S. Fischer Verlag, 1912), 15–17.

3 Brenner, "Globalisation as Reterritorialisation"; Harvey, *Condition of Postmodernity*.

4 Claus Bernet, "The 'Hobrecht Plan' (1862) and Berlin's Urban Structure," *Urban History* 31, no. 3 (2004): 400–2.

5 Ibid., 400.

6 Bernhardt, "At the Limits of the European Sanitary City," 156.

7 John Robert Mullin, "Ideology, Planning Theory and the German City in the Inter-War Years: Part I," *Town Planning Review* 53, no. 2 (1982): 115–16.
8 Anthony Sutcliffe, "Introduction," in *The Rise of Modern Urban Planning, 1800–1914*, ed. Anthony Sutcliffe (New York: St Martin's, 1980), 2.
9 Wolfgang Sonne, "Specific Intentions, General Realities," *Planning Perspectives* 19, no. 3 (2004): 284–5.
10 Wolfgang Sonne, "'The Entire City Shall Be Planned as a Work of Art,'" *Zeitschrift für Kunstgeschichte* 66, no. 2 (2003): 207–36.
11 Sonne, "Specific Intentions, General Realities," 283–4.
12 Carl S. Smith, *The Plan of Chicago* (Chicago: University of Chicago Press, 2006); Rebecca C. Retzlaff, "The Illinois Forest Preserve District Act of 1913 and the Emergence of Metropolitan Park System Planning in the USA," *Planning Perspectives* 25, no. 4 (2010): 433–55; Christiane Crasemann Collins, *Werner Hegemann and the Search for Universal Urbanism* (New York: W.W. Norton, 2005), 19–31; Steven T. Moga, "Marginal Lands and Suburban Nature," *Journal of Planning History* 8, no. 4 (2009): 308–29; Paolo Capuzzo, "The Defeat of Planning," *Planning Perspectives* 13, no. 1 (2010): 24; Richard Dennis, "The Geography of Victorian Values," *Journal of Historical Geography* 15, no. 1 (1989): 40–54; Colin G. Pooley, "Housing for the Poorest Poor," *Journal of Historical Geography* 11, no. 1 (1985): 70–88; J.A. Yelling, "The Selection of Sites for Slum Clearance in London, 1875–1888," *Journal of Historical Geography* 7, no. 2 (1981): 155–65.
13 Mullin, "Ideology, Planning Theory and the German City," 119–20.
14 Ladd, *Urban Planning and Civic Order in Germany*, 1–6.
15 Ibid., 236–8.
16 Ibid.
17 Adorno, "Society [1963]"; Karl Marx, "Theses on Feuerbach [1845]," in *The Marx-Engels Reader*, ed. Robert C. Tucker (New York: W.W. Norton, 1978), theses III and IV.
18 David Harvey, *Paris* (New York: Routledge, 2003), 96–9.
19 Gerd Albers, *Zur Entwicklung der Stadtplanung in Europa* (Braunschweig: Vieweg, 1997), 47.
20 Herbert J. Gans, *The Urban Villagers: Group and Class in the Life of Italian-Americans* (New York: Free Press of Glencoe, 1962); Edward G. Goetz, "The Audacity of Hope VI," *Cities* 35 (2013): 342–8; Leslie Page Moch and Rachel G. Fuchs, "Getting Along," *French Historical Studies* 18, no. 1 (1993): 34–49; Eliza Ferguson, "The Cosmos of the Paris Apartment," *Journal of Urban History* 37, no. 1 (2011): 59–67.
21 Alain Faure, "Local Life in Working-Class Paris at the End of the Nineteenth Century," *Journal of Urban History* 32, no. 5 (2006): 761–2.

22 Harvey, *Paris*, 111–14.
23 Louis Girard, *La politique des travaux publics du Second Empire* (Paris: A. Colin, 1952), Cinquieme Partie (277–358).
24 Albers, *Zur Entwicklung der Stadtplanung in Europa*, 117, 84–5; Schorske, *Fin-de-siècle Vienna*, 24–116.
25 Walter Benjamin, "Paris: Capital of the Nineteenth Century," *New Left Review* 1, no. 48 (1968): 77–88; William H. Sewell Jr., "Connecting Capitalism to the French Revolution," *Critical Historical Studies* 1, no. 1 (2014): 5–46.
26 Smith, *Wealth of Nations*, bk V, chap. 1, p. 340.
27 Neumann, "Change in the Function of Law in Modern Society," 22.
28 Kristin Poling, "Shantytowns and Pioneers beyond the City Wall," *Central European History* 47, no. 2 (2014): 245.
29 Ladd, *Urban Planning and Civic Order*, 67, 69.
30 Frederick D. Marquardt, "A Working Class in Berlin in the 1840s?," in *Sozialgeschichte Heute: Festschrift für Hans Rosenberg zum 70. Geburtstag*, ed. Hans Ulrich Wehler (Göttigen: Vandenhoeck & Ruprecht, 1974), 197.
31 Poling, "Shantytowns and Pioneers beyond the City Wall," 252–4.
32 Ibid., 253–7.
33 Richter, "Zwischen Revolution und Reichsgründung," 662–3.
34 He drew on Peter Joseph Lenné – the landscape architect of the above parks – and on King Frederick William IV, who had worked with Karl Friedrich Schinkel in the 1830s. Cited as Obertribunalentscheidung of 1869, in T. Striethorst, Archiv für Rechtsfälle, 3rd ser., 1 (Berlin, 1870), 217–18; in Bernet, "'Hobrecht Plan,'" 402; Albers, *Zur Entwicklung der Stadtplanung in Europa*, 117, 35.
35 Richter, "Zwischen Revolution und Reichsgründung," 662–9.
36 Bernhardt, "At the Limits of the European Sanitary City," 156–7.
37 Ladd, *Urban Planning and Civic Order in Germany*, 80–1.
38 Marianne Rodenstein, *Mehr Licht, mehr Luft: Gesundheitskonzepte im Städtebau seit 1750* (Frankfurt/Main: Campus, 1988), 68.
39 Juan Rodriguez Lores, "Stadtentwicklung und sozialer Wohnungsbau: die Anfänge in Europa," *Die Alte Stadt* 23, no. 2 (1996): 181–2.
40 Capuzzo, "Defeat of Planning," 24.
41 Ward, "Environs and Neighbours in the 'Two Nations,'" 155–6.
42 Eli Rubin, "From the Grünen Wiesen to Urban Space: Berlin, Expansion, and the Longue Durée," *Central European History* 47, no. 2 (2014): 223–6.
43 Klaus Bergmann, *Agrarromantik und Großstadtfeindschaft* (Meisenheim a. Glan: Verlag Anton Hain, 1970), 4–5, 41–42; Mary Beth Stein, "Wilhelm Heinrich Riehl and the Scientific-Literary Formation of 'Volkskunde,'" *German Studies Review* 24, no. 3 (2001): 487–8.

44 Wilhelm Heinrich Riehl, *Land und Leute*, 3rd ed. (Stuttgart: J.G. Cotta'scher Verlag, 1856), 91–5.

45 Tobias Metzler, "Secularization and Pluralism: Urban Jewish Cultures in Early Twentieth-Century Berlin," *Journal of Urban History* 37, no. 6 (2011): 871–4.

46 Poling, "Shantytowns and Pioneers beyond the City Wall," 270–2.

47 Reinhard Baumeister, *Stadt-Erweiterungen in technischer, baupolizeilicher, und wirthschaftlicher Beziehung* (Berlin: Ernst & Korn, 1876), 3–6.

48 Ibid., 2–3.

49 Josef Stübben, *Der Städtebau [1890]*, 2nd ed. (Stuttgart: Alfred Kröner Verlag, 1907), 42–3; Brian Ladd, "Urban Aesthetics and the Discovery of the Urban Fabric in Turn-of-the-Century Germany," *Planning Perspectives* 2, no. 3 (1987): 271.

50 Baumeister, *Stadt-Erweiterungen*, 6–7.

51 Stübben, *Der Städtebau [1890]*, 54–5.

52 Baumeister, *Stadt-Erweiterungen*, 80.

53 Ibid., 82–3.

54 Ernst Bruch, "Berlin's bauliche Zukunft und der Bebauungsplan," *Deutsche Bauzeitung* 4, no. 9, 10, 12, 13, 15, 16, 19, 20, 21, 23, 24, and 25 (1870): 79.

55 Forsell, *Property, Tenancy and Urban Growth*, 117; Ladd, *Urban Planning and Civic Order*, 84, 132.

56 Baumeister, *Stadt-Erweiterungen*, 80.

57 Bruch, "Berlin's bauliche Zukunft und der Bebauungsplan," 93–4, 159. See also Gustav Assmann, "Die Wohnungsnoth in Berlin Einvertrag gehalten im Architekten-Verein zu Berlin," *Zeitschrift für Bauwesen* 23, no. 3/5 (1873): 120–1.

58 Roessler, "Zur Bauart deutscher Städte (I–II)," *Deutsche Bauzeitung* 8, no. 39 (1874): 153.

59 Ibid., 164.

60 Stübben, *Der Städtebau [1890]*, 9, 616.

61 Peter Marcuse, "The Grid as City Plan: New York City and *Laissez-Faire* Planning in the Nineteenth Century," *Planning Perspectives* 2, no. 3 (1987): 289.

62 For a theoretical elaboration of the reconstitution of money, time, and labour by capitalism, see Postone, *Time, Labor, and Social Domination*, 123–225; Lukács, "Reification and the Consciousness of the Proletariat," 83–6.

63 Roessler, "Zur Bauart deutscher Städte (I–II)," *Deutsche Bauzeitung* 8, no. 39 (1874): 153.

64 Ibid., 164.

65 Ibid., 165.

66 Baumeister, *Stadt-Erweiterungen*, 76–7.
67 Bruch, "Berlin's bauliche Zukunft und der Bebauungsplan," 79.
68 Ibid., 151.
69 Ibid., 78, 95.
70 Ibid., 161.
71 Baumeister, *Stadt-Erweiterungen*, 6–7.
72 Ibid., 49–53.
73 Ibid., 52–3.
74 Ibid., 26–8.
75 Ibid., 19–20.
76 Ibid.
77 Stübben, *Der Städtebau [1890]*, 20.
78 Baumeister, *Stadt-Erweiterungen*, 26–8.
79 Roessler, "Zur Bauart deutscher Städte (I–II)," *Deutsche Bauzeitung* 8, no. 41 (1874): 165.
80 Assmann, "Die Wohungsnoth in Berlin," 113–14.
81 Baumeister, *Stadt-Erweiterungen*, 51–2.
82 Ladd, *Urban Planning and Civic Order*, 89–90; Elaine Lewinnek, "Better than a Bank for a Poor Man? Home Financing Strategies in Early Chicago," *Journal of Urban History* 32, no. 2 (2006): 280.
83 Ladd, *Urban Planning and Civic Order*, 95.
84 Baumeister, *Stadt-Erweiterungen*, 49–53.
85 Ibid., 26–8.
86 Assmann, "Die Wohungsnoth in Berlin," 130.
87 Robert Home, "Peri-Urban Informal Housing Development in Victorian England," *Planning Perspectives* 25, no. 3 (2010): 366.
88 Stübben, *Der Städtebau [1890]*, 9, 9.
89 Assmann, "Die Wohungsnoth in Berlin," 114–15. There was a conservative counterpoint to this liberal city planning on the question of housing prices. Arminius [Gräfin Adelheid zu Dohna-Poninska], *Die Großstädte in ihrer Wohnungsnoth und die Grundlagen einer durchgreifenden Abhilfe* (Leipzig: Duncker & Humblot, 1874).
90 Peter Hall, "Metropolis 1890–1940," in *Metropolis, 1890–1940*, ed. Anthony Sutcliffe (Chicago: University of Chicago Press, 1984), 21–2; Erbe, "Berlin im Kaiserreich," 693–9, 704–10.
91 Erbe,"Berlin im Kaiserreich," 727–30, 732–42; Jürgen Kocka, "Family and Bureaucracy in German Industrial Management, 1850–1914," *Business History Review* 45, no. 2 (1971): 148.
92 Wilhelm Loesche, "Berlin North [1890]," in *Metropolis Berlin*, ed. David Frisby and Iain Boyd Whyte, 16–17 (Berkeley: University of California Press, 2012).

93 Forsell, *Property, Tenancy and Urban Growth*, 162–4; Wolfgang Sonne, "Dwelling in the Metropolis," *Progress in Planning* 72, no. 2 (2009): 58.
94 Erbe, "Berlin im Kaiserreich," 701–2; Richter, "Zwischen Revolution und Reichsgründung, 664–7.
95 Rodenstein, *Mehr Licht, mehr Luft*, 110–22.
96 Erbe, "Berlin im Kaiserreich," 701–2.
97 Carl Hugo Lindemann, "Wohnungsstatistik," in *Verhandlungen des Vereins für Socialpolitik über die Wohnungsfrage und die Handelspolitik: Deutschland und Österreich*, ed. Carl Johannes Fuchs and Vereins für Socialpolitik (Leipzig: Duncker & Humblot, 1901), 266–7, 272–3, 278–9, 282–3, respectively.
98 Ladd, *Urban Planning and Civic Order*, 152.
99 Capuzzo, "Defeat of Planning," 23–4.
100 Paul Schultze-Naumburg, *Kulturarbeiten* (Munich: Callwey, 1909), 4:6; Christian Welzbacher, "Schultze-Naumburg, Paul Eduard," in *Neue Deutsche Biographie*, vol. 23 (Berlin: Duncker & Humblot, 2007).
101 Scheffler, *Berlin*, 140.
102 Karl Scheffler, *Die Architektur der Großstadt* (Berlin: Gebr. Mann, 1998), 9.
103 Scheffler, *Berlin*, 140–1.
104 Ibid., 182–3.
105 Mark Twain, "The German Chicago [1892]," in *Metropolis Berlin, 1880–1940*, ed. Iain Boyd Whyte and David Frisby (Berkeley: University of California Press, 2012), 17.
106 Egon Friedell, *Ecce Poeta [1912]* (Zurich: Diogenes, 1992), 260; Gordon Patterson, "Race and Anti-Semitism in the Life and Work of Egon Friedell," *Jahrbuch des Instituts für deutsche Geschichte* 10 (1981): 319.
107 August Endell, *Die Schönheit der großen Stadt* (Stuttgart: Strecker & Schröder, 1908), 21–2; Otto zu Stolberg-Wernigerode, "Endell, Ernst Moritz August," in *Neue Deutsche Biographie*, vol. 4 (Berlin: Duncker & Humblot, 1959).
108 Endell, *Die Schönheit der großen Stadt*, 24–5.
109 Hans Ostwald, *Berliner Kaffeehäuser*, 3rd ed. (Berlin: Hermann Seemann Nachfolger, GmbH, 1905), 7:19; Peter Fritzsche, "Vagabond in the Fugitive City," *Journal of Contemporary History* 29, no. 3 (July 1994): 388.
110 Richard Dietrich, *Lebeweltnächte der Friedrichstadt*, 2nd ed. (Berlin: Hermann Seemann Nachfolger, GmbH, 1907), 30:13–14.
111 Edmund Edel, *Neu-Berlin*, 3rd ed. (Berlin: Hermann Seemann Nachfolger, GmbH, 1908), 86.
112 Chad Heap, *Slumming* (Chicago: University of Chicago Press, 2009), 2.
113 Wilhelm Schwenke, "Brix, Joseph," in *Neue Deutsche Biographie*, vol. 2 (Berlin: Duncker & Humblot, 1955).

114 Joseph Brix, *Aus der Geschichte des Städtebaues in den letzten 100 Jahren* (Berlin: Wilhelm Ernst & Sohn, 1912), 11.
115 Conrad Bornhak, *Verwaltungsrechtliches im Städtebau* (Berlin: Wilhelm Ernst & Sohn, 1908), 6; Mark Hewitson, "The *Kaiserreich* in Question: Constitutional Crisis in Germany before the First World War," *Journal of Modern History* 73, no. 4 (2001): 729, 738.
116 Joseph Brix, *Aufgaben und Ziele des Städtebau* (Berlin: Wilhelm Ernst & Sohn, 1908), 9–10.
117 Theodor Goecke, "Von den Beziehungen der Zonenbauordnung zum Bebauungsplane," *Der Städtebau* 2, no. 1 (1905): 2.
118 Walter Lehweß, "Felix Genzmer," *Zentralblatt der Bauverwaltung* 49, no. 33 (14 August 1929): 536.
119 Felix Genzmer, *Die Gestaltung des Straßen- und Platzraumes* (Berlin: Wilhelm Ernst & Sohn, 1909), 8.
120 Felix Genzmer, *Die Ausstattung von Straßen und Plätzen* (Berlin: Wilhelm Ernst & Sohn, 1910), 7.
121 Max Georg Zimmermann, *Künstlerische Lehren aus der Geschichte des Städtebaus* (Berlin: Wilhelm Ernst & Sohn, 1909), 25–6.
122 Sonne, "'Entire City Shall Be Planned as a Work of Art'"; Wofgang Sonne, "'Stadtbaukunst' als Konzept: ein internationales Phänomen um 1910," *Informationen zur modernen Stadtgeschichte* 6, no. 1 (2010): 14–27.
123 Genzmer, *Die Ausstattung von Straßen und Plätzen*, 24.
124 Zimmermann, *Künstlerische Lehren aus der Geschichte des Städtebaus*, 25.
125 [Hans] Mackowsky, "Die geschichtliche Entwicklung des Stadtplanes," *Der Städtebau* 5, no. 3, 4, 5 (1908): 29–30, 45–6, 73–7.
126 Otto Geissler, "Fabrik- und Industrieviertel," *Der Städtebau* 3, no. 4/5 (1906): 51.
127 Bernet, "'Hobrecht Plan,'" 402.
128 Marcuse, "Grid as City Plan," 291.
129 Rudolf Eberstadt, *Handbuch des Wohnungswesens und der Wohnungsfrage* (Jena: Fischer, 1909), 62, as cited in Bernet, "'Hobrecht Plan,'" 410.
130 Camillo Sitte, *Der Städtebau nach seinen künstlerischen Grundsätzen* (Vienna: Graeser, 1909).
131 Frederick Law Olmsted and J. James R. Croes, "Document No. 72 of the Board of the Department of Public Parks … [1876]," in *Landscape into Cityscape*, ed. Albert Fein (Ithaca, NY: Cornell University Press, 1968), 352–4, in Marcuse, "Grid as City Plan," 287.
132 Amy Woodson-Boulton, *Transformative Beauty* (Stanford, CA: Stanford University Press, 2012), 1–2.
133 Ákos Moravánszky, "The Optical Construction of Urban Space," *Journal of Architecture* 17, no. 5 (2012): 655.

134 Karl Henrici, "Gedanken über das moderne Städte-Bausystem," *Deutsche Bauzeitung* 25, no. 14, 15 (18, 21 February 1891): 87–90.
135 Wolfgang Sonne, *Representing the State,* (Munich: Prestel, 2003); Gerhard Fehl, "Camillo Sitte als 'Volkserzieher,'" in *Städtebau um die Jahrhundertwende,* ed. Gordon Emanuel Cherry and Gerhard Fehl, 172–221 (Cologne: Dt. Gemeindeverlag, 1980).
136 Henrici, "Gedanken über das moderne Städte-Bausystem," 81–2.
137 Ibid., 83, 86.
138 Joseph Stübben, "Ueber einige Fragen der Städtebaukunst," *Deutsche Bauzeitung* 25, no. 21, 25 (14 and 28 March 1891): 122–3.
139 Hermann Pfeifer, "Kontrast und Rhythmus im Städtebau," *Der Städtebau* 1, no. 7 (1904): 97–8.
140 Sonne, "'Entire City Shall Be Planned as a Work of Art,'" 208–10.
141 Mark Jarzombek, "The 'Kunstgewerbe,' the 'Werkbund,' and the Aesthetics of Culture in the Wilhelmine Period," *Journal of the Society of Architectural Historians* 53, no. 1 (1994): 9, 11.
142 Walter Curt Behrendt, *Die einheitliche Blockfront als Bauelement im Stadtbau* (Berlin: Bruno Cassirer Verlag, 1912), 12.
143 Ibid., 12–13.
144 Ibid., 14.
145 Ibid., 84.
146 Ibid., 83.
147 John Maciuika, "Wilhelmine Precedents for the Bauhaus," in *Bauhaus Culture,* ed. Kathleen James-Chakraborty (Minneapolis: University of Minnesota Press, 2006), 3.
148 Ibid., 2.
149 Ibid., 3.
150 Alan Colquhoun, "Criticism and Self-Criticism in German Modernism," *AA Files,* no. 28 (1994): 26–7; Maciuika, "Wilhelmine Precedents for the Bauhaus," 2.
151 Colquhoun, "Criticism and Self-Criticism in German Modernism," 26–7; Maciuika, "Wilhelmine Precedents for the Bauhaus," 2.
152 Colquhoun, "Criticism and Self-Criticism in German Modernism," 26–7; Maciuika, "Wilhelmine Precedents for the Bauhaus," 2.
153 Colquhoun, "Criticism and Self-Criticism in German Modernism," 26.
154 Ibid., 26–7; Maciuika, "Wilhelmine Precedents for the Bauhaus," 2.
155 Colquhoun, "Criticism and Self-Criticism in German Modernism," 26.
156 Adolf Loos, "Ornament and Crime [1908]," trans. Michael Mitchell, in *Ornament and Crime,* ed. Adolf Opel (Riverside, CA: Ariadne, 1998), 167; Christopher Long, "The Origins and Context of Adolf Loos's 'Ornament and Crime,'" *Journal of the Society of Architectural Historians* 68, no. 2 (2009): 207.

157 Loos, "Ornament and Crime," 169–70.
158 Theodor W. Adorno, "Functionalism Today," *Oppositions*, no. 17 (1979): 38.
159 Ibid., 33.
160 Adorno, "Veblen's Attack on Culture," in *Prisms*, 75, 77.
161 Frederic J. Schwartz, "Commodity Signs," *Journal of Design History* 9, no. 3 (1996): 156.
162 Ibid., 157.
163 Werner Sombart, "Vienna [1907]," in *Metropolis Berlin: 1880–1940*, ed. David Frisby and Iain Boyd Whyte (Berkeley: University of California Press, 2012), 31–2.
164 Margaret Garb, "Race, Housing, and Burnham's Plan," *Journal of Planning History* 10, no. 2 (2011): 104; Michael B. Kahan, "The Risk of Cholera and the Reform of Urban Space," *Geographical Review* 103, no. 4 (2013): 517–36.
165 John Locke, "Second Treatise," in *Two Treatises of Government and a Letter Concerning Toleration*, ed. Ian Shapiro (New Haven, CT: Yale University Press, 2003), 111 (§ 27); Smith, *Wealth of Nations*, bk I, chap. V, p. 34.
166 Hirschberg, "Die Wohnungsfrage und die Eingemeindung der Berliner Vororte," 6–17.
167 Konrad Sass, *Die Bauklassen der Bauordnung für die Berliner Vororte* (Berlin: A. Seydel, 1906), 12.
168 Paul Alexander-Katz, *Über Preußisches Fluchtlinienrecht* (Berlin: Wilhelm Ernst & Sohn, 1908), 5, 7.
169 Karl Keller and Philipp Nitze, *Gross-Berlins bauliche Zukunft* (Berlin: Renaissance-Verlag Ribert Federn, 1910), 97, 131.
170 Erbe, "Berlin im Kaiserreich," 721–7; Schraepler, "Berlin als Zentrale der deutschen sozialistischen Arbeiterbewegung," 156–7.
171 Richard Harris, "The Rise of Filtering Down," *Social Science History* 37, no. 4 (2013): 535; Andrew Heath, "'Every Man His Own Landlord'," *Journal of Urban History* 38, no. 6 (2012): 1003–20.
172 Lewinnek, "Better Than a Bank for a Poor Man?" 280.
173 Alexia Yates, "Selling Paris," *Enterprise and Society* 13, no. 4 (2012): 774.
174 Richard van der Borght and Paul Lippert, *Grundzüge der Sozialpolitik* (Leipzig: C.L. Hirschfeld, 1904), 386, 394–7, 412–14; Forsell, *Property, Tenancy and Urban Growth*, 167–70.
175 Forsell, *Property, Tenancy and Urban Growth*, 142–50; Richter, "Zwischen Revolution und Reichsgründung," 664–7.
176 Lujo Brentano, *Die Arbeiterwohnungsfrage in den Städten mit besonderer Berücksichtigung Münchens* (Munich: M. Riegersche Universitäts-Buchhandlung, 1909), 1:4–5.

177 Richard Petersen, *Die Verkehrsaufgaben des Verbandes Groß-Berlin* (Berlin: C. Heymann, 1911), 3–4.
178 Otto Blum, "Zur Verkehrspolitik der Großstädte, mit besonderer Berücksichtigung der Berliner Verhältnisse," *Zeitschrift der Vereines Deutscher Ingenieure* 52, no. 27 (4 July 1908): 1083–5.
179 Adolf Damaschke, *Die Bodenreform* (Berlin: Buchverlag der "Hilfe," 1907), 37–8, 40, 51–3.
180 Ibid., 67–69.
181 Adolf Damaschke, *Geschichte der Nationalökonomie*, 7th ed. (Jena: Gustav Fischer, 1913), 554–6.
182 Karl von Mangoldt, "Zur Einführung," in *Gross-Berlins bauliche Zukunft*, ed. Karl Keller and Philipp Nitze (Berlin: Renaissance-Verlag Ribert Federn, 1910), 5–8.
183 Carl Johannes Fuchs, *Zur Wohnungsfrage* (Leipzig: Duncker & Humbolt, 1904), 102–3.
184 Rudolf Eberstadt, *Die Spekulation im neuzeitlichen Städtebau* (Jena: Gustav Fischer, 1907), 17–31, esp. 27.
185 Andreas Voigt and Paul Geldner, *Kleinhaus und Mietkaserne* (Berlin: J. Springer, 1905), 173–6; Haberland, *Der Einfluss des Privatkapitals auf die bauliche Entwicklung Gross-Berlins*, 10–11.
186 Adolf Weber, *Boden und Wohnung* (Leipzig: Verlag von Duncker & Humbolt, 1908), 48.
187 Ludwig Pohle, "Der Kampf um die Wohnungsfrage II," *Zeitschrift für Socialwissenschaft* 8, no. 12 (1905): 759–64.
188 Weber, *Boden und Wohnung*, 44–5.
189 Ibid., 21.
190 Ludwig Pohle, "Der Kampf um die Wohnungsfrage I," *Zeitschrift für Socialwissenschaft* 8, no. 11 (1905): 685–7, 695–8.
191 See Voigt and Geldner, *Kleinhaus und Mietkaserne*.
192 Adolf Weber, *Die Großstadt und ihre sozialen Probleme* (Leipzig: Verlag von Quelle & Meyer, 1908), 10.
193 Frederick Engels, *The Housing Question* (Moscow: Progress Publishers, 1970), 39–40.
194 Ibid.
195 Ibid., 41–2.
196 Ibid., 43.
197 Ibid., 17–21; Karl Marx, "Letter to Friedrich Adolph Sorge: June 21, 1881," trans. Dona Torr, in *Karl Marx and Friedrich Engels: Correspondence, 1846–1895: A Selection with Commentary Notes* (New York: International Publishers, 1942), 394; Marx, *The Poverty of Philosophy: Andwer to the "Philosophy of Poverty" by M. Proudhon* (Peking: Foreign Languages, 1978), 151.

198 Marx, "Letter to Friedrich Adolph Sorge," 395–6.
199 Karl Marx, *Capital: A Critique of Political Economy*, ed. and trans. David Fernbach (London: Penguin Books in association with New Left Review, 1991), 3:759–60.
200 Ibid., 959.
201 Marx, *Poverty of Philosophy*, 154–5.
202 Carl Hugo Lindemann, "Die städtische Grundrente und ihre Bekämpfung," *Socialistische Monatshefte* 9, no. 3 (1905): 248–9.
203 Marx, *Capital* (1991), 1:280.

3. Creating Greater Berlin

1 Alfred Weber, *Ueber den Standort der Industrien [1909]*, 2nd ed. (Tübingen: J.C.B. Mohr, 1922), 2–3; This translation comes from Weber, *Theory of the Location of Industries [1909]*, ed. and trans. Carl Joachim Friedrich (Chicago: University of Chicago Press, 1929), 2–3.
2 Weber, *Ueber den Standort der Industrien*, 1–14.
3 Brenner, "Globalisation as Reterritorialisation," 432, 434.
4 Johann Anton Wilhelm von Carstenn-Lichterfelde, *Die zukünftige Entwicklung Berlins* (Berlin, 1892); von Carstenn-Lichterfelde, *Die Schenkung des Terrains zu Gross-Lichterfelde an den Preussischen Militaer-Fiskus zum Bau der Central Kadetten-Anstalt* (Berlin: E. Staude, 1890); Wilson, *German Forest*, 97–101.
5 John B. Lyon, *Out of Place* (New York: Bloomsbury Academic, 2013), 43; Wilson, *German Forest*, 97–101.
6 Lefebvre, *Production of Space*, 25.
7 Contemporary Berlin integrated some of the ideas set forth in the prize-winning plans, like the location of the central train station, into the reunited city after 1990.
8 Daniel Hudson Burnham, Edward H. Bennett, and Charles Moore, *Plan of Chicago* (Chicago: Commercial Club, 1909); "Boston: 1915, Exhibition," *Art and Progress* 1, no. 1 (1909): 22; Sonja Duempelmann, "Creating Order with Nature," *Planning Perspectives* 24, no. 2 (2009): 143–73; Moga, "Marginal Lands and Suburban Nature"; Sonne, ""Entire City Shall Be Planned as a Work of Art.'"
9 Theodor Köhn, *Wie ist die Schaffung von Groß-Berlin durchführbar?* (Berlin: Carl Heymanns Verlag, 1907), 20–32.
10 Vereinigung Berliner Architekten, and Architekten-Verein zu Berlin, *Anregungen zur Erlangung eines Grundplanes für die städtebauliche Entwicklung von Groß-Berlin* (Berlin: E. Wasmuth A.-G., 1907), i.
11 Ibid., 1–3.

12 Ibid., 3.

13 "Meeting notes: Ver[…] der Denkschrift Gross-Berlin" (LAB A Rep. 001-02 Nr. 72), 5; Otto March, "Erläuterung zu dem in der Denkschrift Gross-Berlin angeregten Wettbewerb zur Erlangung eines Grundplanes. 8. September 1907" (LAB A Rep. 001-02 Nr. 72 Bd. 1), 17VS–22RS.

14 Otto March, Joseph Stübben, and Kayser, "Brief zu den Oberbürgermeister Kirschner. 3 October 1907" (LAB A Rep. 001-02 Nr. 72), 31; Martin Kirschner and Ludwig Hamburger, "Sitzung an November 7, 1907" (LAB A Rep. 001-02 Nr. 72), 39VS–40RS; Otto March, "Brief zu Oberbürgermeister Kirschner. 24. Januar 1908" (LAB A Rep. 001-02 Nr. 72), 58–60; Josef Stübben, "Otto March," *Zentralblatt der Bauverwaltung* 33, no. 29 (12 April 1913): 199–200.

15 Gerhard Kutzsch, "Kirschner, Martin," in *Neue Deutsche Biographie*, vol. 11 (Berlin: Duncker & Humblot, 1977).

16 Collins, *Werner Hegemann and the Search for Universal Urbanism*, 19–31; Thomas C. Palmer Jr., "City Makes Filene's Site a Landmark," *Boston Globe*, 10 May 2006.

17 Samuel Kling, "Wide Boulevards, Narrow Visions," *Journal of Planning History* 12, no. 3 (2013): 245.

18 Garb, "Race, Housing, and Burnham's Plan," 101.

19 Michael P. McCarthy, "Chicago Businessmen and the Burnham Plan," *Journal of the Illinois State Historical Society* 63, no. 3 (1970): 231.

20 Kirschner, "Vorlagen Nr. 24: 427. Vorlage (J-Nr. 50/08 O.B.) – zur Beschlußfassung –, betreffend Bewilligung eines Kostenbeitrages von 82,000 M für das zur Erlangung eines Bebauungsplanes für Groß-Berlin zu veranstaltende Preisausschreiben. Berlin, den 19 März 1908" (LAB A Rep. 001-02 Nr. 72), 106; Vorsteher Michelet, "Vorlage – zur Beschlußfassung –, Betreffend die Bewilligung eines Kostenbeitrages von 82000 M für das Erlangung eines Bebauungsplanes für Groß-Berlin zu veranstaldende Preisauschrieben. – Vorlage 427," in *Auszug aus dem amtlichen Stenographischen Bericht über die Sitzung der Stadtverordneten-Versammlung am 26. März 1908* (LAB A Rep. 000-02-01 Nr. 1566), 180.

21 Otto March, "Brief zu Oberbürgermeister Kirschner. 1. Februar 1910" (LAB A Rep. 001-02 Nr. 73 S. 322–3); Martin Kirschner, "Brief zu Hochbau-Deputation. 16. März 1910" (LAB A Rep. 010-01-01 Nr. 105); Werner Hegeman, "Breif zu Hochbau-Deputation on 22. März 1910" (LAB A Rep. 010-01-01 Nr. 105); von Moltke, "Denkschrift über Votum. 22. Januar 1910" (GStA-PK I. HA Rep. 191 Nr. 133).

22 Sonne, *Representing the State*, 111.

23 The Tägliche Rundschau is quoted at length in the *Berliner Architekturwelt* article. The *Berliner Architekturwelt* was edited by the historicist architect Heinrich Jassoy; by the architect and author of books on the uses of ornamentation, Adolf Hartung; by the architect of villas, business headquarters, and grave markers, Ernst Spindler; and by Bruno Möhring. "Chronik: Wettbewerb Groß-Berlin," *Berliner Architekturwelt* 11, no. 8 (1909): 318; Joachim Pöhls, "Tägliche Rundschau (1881–1933)," in *Deutsche Zeitungen des 17. bis 20. Jahrhunderts*, ed. Heinz-Dietrich Fischer (Pullach bei München: Verlag Dokumentation, 1972), 351–4.

24 "Chronik: Wettbewerb Groß-Berlin," 318.

25 Marcuse, "Affirmative Character of Culture."

26 Fritz Eiselen, "Die Lösung der Verkehrsfragen im Wettbewerb Groß-Berlin," *Deutsche Bauzeitung: Beilage für Wettbewerbe* 44, no. 50, 52, 55, 58, 59 (1910): 385; Albert Hofmann, "Groß-Berlin, sein Verhältnis zur modernen Großstadtbewegung und der Wettbewerb zur Erlangung eines Grundplanes für die städtebauliche Entwicklung Berlins und seiner Vororte im zwanzigsten Jahrhundert [1]," *Deutsche Bauzeitung: Beilage für Wettbewerbe* 44, no. 25 (1910): 169; Walter Lehweß, "Vom Wettbewerb Gross-Berlin," *Tägliche Rundschau, Berlin*, 4 March 1910 (LAB A Rep. 001-02 Nr. 74 S. 20VS–20RS).

27 Eiselen, "Die Lösung der Verkehrsfragen im Wettbewerb Groß-Berlin," 385.

28 Albert Hofmann, "Groß-Berlin, sein Verhältnis zur modernen Großstadtbewegung und der Wettbewerb zur Erlangung eines Grundplanes für die städtebauliche Entwicklung Berlins und seiner Vororte im zwanzigsten Jahrhundert," *Deutschen Bauzeitung: Beilage für Wettbewerbe* 44, no. 42 (25 May 1910): 325–8; Walter Lehweß, "Vom Wettbewerb Gross-Berlin," *Tägliche Rundschau, Berlin*, 4. März 1910 (LAB A Rep. 001-02 Nr. 74 S. 20–20R).

29 Joseph Brix, Felix Genzmer, and Hochbahngesellschaft in Berlin., "Preisgekrönt mit der Hälfte des Zusammengelegten I. und II. Preises: Kennwort: 'Denk an Künftig,'" in *Wettbewerb Groß-Berlin, 1910: Die preisgekrönten Entwürfe mit Erläuterungsberichten* (Berlin: Ernst Wasmuth A.-G., 1911), 3, 32–5.

30 Wolfgang Hofmann, "Der Verkehr beim Wettbewerb Groß-Berlin 1908/10: Am Beispiel von Hermann Jansens Beitrag," in *Stadt und Verkehr im Industriezeitalter*, ed. Horst Matzerath (Cologne: Böhlau Verlag, 1996), 210.

31 Brix, Genzmer, and Berlin, "Denk an Künftig," 5.

32 Ibid., 7–17.

33 Ibid., 25–6; Sonne, *Representing the State*, 114.

34 Brix, Genzmer, and Berlin, "Denk an Künftig," 5.
35 Theodor Goecke and Friedrich Gerlach, "Beurteilung der zum Wettbewerb 'Groß-Berlin' einreichten Entwürfe. April 1910" (LAB A Rep. 001-02 Nr. 74 Bd. 3), 112a: 13.
36 Hofmann, "Der Verkehr beim Wettbewerb Groß-Berlin 1908/10," 209.
37 Hermann Jansen, "Preisgekrönt mit der Hälfte des Zusammengelegten I. und II. Preises: Kennwort: 'In den Grenzen der Möglichkeit,'" in *Wettbewerb Groß-Berlin, 1910; die preisgekrönten entwürfe mit erläuterungsberichten* (Berlin: Ernst Wasmuth A.-G., 1911), 3; Felix Escher, *Berlin und sein Umland: Zur Genese der Berliner Stadtlandschaft bis zum Beginn des 20. Jahrhunderts* (Berlin: Colloquium Verlag, 1985), 317.
38 Goecke and Gerlach, "Beurteilung der zum Wettbewerb "Groß-Berlin" einreichten Entwürfe," 112a: 126.
39 Jansen, "In den Grenzen der Möglichkeit," 3, 19; Escher, *Berlin und sein Umland*, 317.
40 Jansen, "In den Grenzen der Möglichkeit," 20, 16, 18.
41 Ibid., 18; Hofmann, "Der Verkehr beim Wettbewerb Groß-Berlin 1908/10," 217–19.
42 Walter Lehweß, "Die Ergebnisse des Wettbewerbs um einen Bebauungsplan für Groß-Berlin und die Allgemeine Städtebauausstellung in Berlin," *Zentralblatt der Bauverwaltung* 30, no. 41 (21 May 1910): 273–6; Albert Hofmann, "Groß-Berlin, sein Verhältnis zur modernen Großstadtbewegung und der Wettbewerb zur Erlangung eines Grundplanes für städtebauliche Entwicklung Berlins und seiner Vororte im zwanzigsten Jahrhundert," *Deutsche Bauzeitung: Beilage für Wettbewerbe* 44, no. 37 (7 May 1910): 281–7; Goecke and Gerlach, "Beurteilung der zum Wettbewerb 'Groß-Berlin' einreichten Entwürfe," 112a: 23–4.
43 Jansen, "In den Grenzen der Möglichkeit," 20.
44 Sonne, *Representing the State*, 112–13; Hofmann, "Der Verkehr beim Wettbewerb Groß-Berlin 1908/10," 216.
45 Goecke and Gerlach, "Beurteilung der zum Wettbewerb 'Groß-Berlin' einreichten Entwürfe," 112a:34–5; Walter Lehweß, "Bruno Möhring," *Zentralblatt der Bauverwaltung* 49, no. 16 (17 April 1929): 260–1; Ines Wagemann, "Möhring, Bruno," in *Neue Deutsche Biographie*, ed. Der Historischen Kommission bei der Bayerischen Akademie der Wissenschaft, 621–2 (Berlin: Duncker & Humblot, 1994); Wolfgang Sonne, "Berlin," in *Planning Twentieth-Century Capital Cities*, ed. David L.A. Gordon (London: Routledge, 2006), 197.
46 Rudolf Eberstadt, Bruno Möhring, and Richard Petersen, "Preisgekrönt mit dem III. Preise: Kennwort: 'Et in Terra Pax,'" in *Wettbewerb Groß-Berlin,*

1910: Die preisgekrönten Entwürfe mit Erläuterungsberichten (Berlin: Ernst Wasmuth A.-G., 1911), 3.

47 Goecke and Gerlach, "Beurteilung der zum Wettbewerb 'Groß-Berlin' einreichten Entwürfe," 112a: 39–40; Lehweß, "Die Ergebnisse des Wettbewerbs," 274–5.

48 Eberstadt, Möhring, and Petersen, "Et in Terra Pax," 22–8.

49 Ibid., 4–5.

50 Ibid., 8–16; Lehweß, "Die Ergebnisse des Wettbewerbs," 273–4.

51 Eberstadt, Möhring, and Petersen, "Et in Terra Pax," 22–8; Sonne, *Representing the State*, 114, 116.

52 Garb, "Race, Housing, and Burnham's Plan," 99–101.

53 Goecke and Gerlach, "Beurteilung der zum Wettbewerb 'Groß-Berlin' einreichten Entwürfe," 112a: 47–8.

54 Eberstadt, Möhring, and Petersen, "Et in Terra Pax," 3.

55 Möhring, the architect in this group, gained his reputation through the design of civil engineering works, especially bridges. Aesthetically, he was influenced by historicism, especially in his bridges, but around 1900 he adopted Jugendstil and was a central practitioner of that style in Berlin. By 1905 he had moved on to neoclassical styles. Wagemann, "Möhring, Bruno," 621–2.

56 Sonne, *Representing the State*, 115–16.

57 Lehweß, "Die Ergebnisse des Wettbewerbs," 275–6.

58 Havestadt & Contag, Otto Blum, and Bruno Schmitz, "Preisgekrönt mit dem IV. Preise: Kennwort: 'Wo ein Wille, da ein Weg,'" in *Wettbewerb Groß-Berlin, 1910: die preisgekrönten Entwürfe mit Erläuterungsberichten* (Berlin: Ernst Wasmuth A.-G., 1911), 4.

59 Ibid., 41–3; Goecke and Gerlach, "Beurteilung der zum Wettbewerb "Groß-Berlin" einreichten Entwürfe."

60 Garb, "Race, Housing, and Burnham's Plan," 100–1.

61 Havestadt & Contag, Blum, and Schmitz, "Preisgekrönt mit dem IV. Preise: Kennwort: 'Wo ein Wille, da ein Weg,'" 48–56.

62 Goecke and Gerlach, "Beurteilung der zum Wettbewerb 'Groß-Berlin' einreichten Entwürfe," 112a: 65; Lehweß, "Die Ergebnisse des Wettbewerbs," 275. As Sonne notes, for Lehweß urban greatness was synonymous with imperial greatness. Sonne, *Representing the State*, 119. Some historians have connected the monumentality of this plan to the later National Socialist plans. However, Sonne emphasizes that the planners intended their city to be a cultural and not an imperial capital. Ibid., 117.

63 Havestadt & Contag, Blum, and Schmitz, "Preisgekrönt mit dem IV. Preise: Kennwort: 'Wo ein Wille, da ein Weg,'" 43–6; Escher, *Berlin und sein Umland*, 318.

64 Havestadt & Contag, Blum, and Schmitz, "'Wo ein Wille, da ein Weg,'" 39.

65 Ibid., 38. They argued that the military should also move to the outskirts of the city and envisioned the creation of new military training sites there. This would open large tracts of land for civil uses within the urban core. Goecke and Gerlach, "Beurteilung der zum Wettbewerb 'Groß-Berlin' einreichten Entwürfe," 112a: 65.

66 Lehweß, "Die Ergebnisse des Wettbewerbs," 273–4; Havestadt & Contag, Blum, and Schmitz, "Preisgekrönt mit dem IV. Preise: Kennwort: 'Wo ein Wille, da ein Weg,'" 38; Goecke and Gerlach, "Beurteilung der zum Wettbewerb 'Groß-Berlin' einreichten Entwürfe," 112a: 65.

67 The exhibition would be organized by Otto March, the director of the Berlin Parks Department Albert Brodersen, Rudolf Eberstadt, Theodor Goecke, Emanuel Heimann, Hermann Jansen, Hermann Muthesius, and Joseph Stübben. "Allgemeine Städtebau-Ausstellung Berlin 1910," *Deutsche Bauzeitung* 44, no. 1/2 (5 January 1910): 3.

68 Hofmann, "Groß-Berlin, sein Verhältnis zur modernen Großstadtbewegung und der Wettbewerb zur Erlangung eines Grundplanes für die städtebauliche Entwicklung Berlins und seiner Vororte im zwanzigsten Jahrhundert [1]," *Deutsche Bauzeitung: Beilage für Wettbewerbe* 44, no. 25 (26 March 1910): 169.

69 Otto March and Martin Kirschner, "Brief zu Minister des Innern von Moltke, u. A. 14. January 1910" (GStA-PK I. HA Rep. 191 Nr. 133), 6.

70 Rud[olf] Eberstadt, "Die Ziele der ersten Städtebauausstellung in Berlin" (GStA-PK I. HA Rep. 191 Nr. 133), 7.

71 Ibid., 7/1.

72 Ibid., 7/2.

73 Garb, "Race, Housing, and Burnham's Plan," 102.

74 "Allgemeine Städtebau-Ausstellung in Berlin, vom 1. Mai bis 15. Juni 1910."

75 Lehweß, "Die Ergebnisse des Wettbewerbs," 273; Theodor Goecke, "Allgemeine Städtebau-Ausstellung Berlin 1910," *Der Städtebau* 7, no. 7/8 (1910): 74.

76 Garb, "Race, Housing, and Burnham's Plan," 109.

77 Ibid., 99.

78 Lehweß, "Die Ergebnisse des Wettbewerbs," 276.

79 Collins, *Werner Hegemann and the Search for Universal Urbanism*, 15–31.

80 Werner Hegemann, "Einleitung. Rückblick.," in *Der Städtebau nach den Ergebnissen der Allgemeinen Städtbau-Ausstellung in Berlin, nebst einem*

Anhang: Die internationale Städtebau-Ausstellung in Düsseldorf, ed. Werner Hegemann (Berlin: Ernst Wasmuth A.-G., 1911), 7.

81 Ibid.

82 Ibid., 80–1.

83 Ibid., 9–10.

84 Ibid., 8.

85 Ibid., 78.

86 Elek Takáts, "Der Verband Groß-Berlin vom 19. Juli 1911 bis 1. Okt. 1920 seine wirtschaftlichen Aufgaben und Leistungen insbesondere im Verkehrs- und Siedungswesen" (Universität Koln, 1933), 87, 1–2.

87 Hofmann, "Wachsen Berlins im Industriezeitalter," 160–3, 166–72.

88 Ludwig Brühl, Kurt Gordan, and Walter Lebermann, *Zweckverbandsgesetz für Groß-Berlin vom 19. Juli 1911* (Berlin: J. Guttentag Verlagbuchhandlung, 1912), xiv–xvii; Takáts, "Der Verband Groß-Berlin," 2–3; Erbe, "Berlin im Kaiserreich," 747–8.

89 Ian Richard Gordon and Tony Travers, "London," *City, Culture and Society* 1, no. 2 (2010): 50.

90 Richardson Dilworth, "Urban Infrastructure Politics and Metropolitan Growth," *Public Works Management & Policy* 6, no. 3 (2002): 210–11.

91 Ludwig Hamburger, *Denkschrift über die Beziehungen zwischen Berlin und seinen Nachbarorten* (Berlin: W. & S. Loewenthal, 1903), 3–5.

92 "Antrag der Stadtverordneten Dr. Preuß und Genossen," in *Amtliche Stenographische Bericht die Sitzung der Stadtverordneten-Versammlung dem 24. September 1903. Nr.* 22 (LAB A Rep. 001-02 Nr. 638), 3VS–3RS.

93 Ibid., 4VS–4RS.

94 Ludwig Feuth, "Das Problem der Entwickelung Groß Berlins," *Sozialistische Monatshefte* 15, no. 11 (1909): 722–6; Carl Hugo Lindemann, "Selbstverwaltung und Gemeinde in Preussen," *Sozialistische Monatshefte* 11, no. 11 (1907): 918–24; Lindemann," Selbstverwaltung und staatliche Bureaukratie," *Sozialistische Monatshefte* 12, no. 18/19 (1908): 1181–5.

95 "Antrag der Stadtverordneten Dr. Preuß und Genossen," 4VS–4RS. Takáts makes a similar claim about the role of capital flight from Berlin to the suburbs. Takáts, "Der Verband Groß-Berlin," 6.

96 Langenhans, "Stadtverordneten-Versammlung Beschluß: Protokolle No. 10. 26. April 1904" (LAB A Rep. 001-02 Nr. 638 S. 13).

97 Martin Kirschner, "Bericht des Oberbürgermeisters Kirschner an den Minister des Innern vom 3. September 1906" (LAB A Rep. 001-02 Nr. 631 S. 72), 1–2; Takáts, "Der Verband Groß-Berlin," 6; Magistrat der Stadt Berlin, ed. *Bericht über die Gemeinde-Verwaltung der Stadt Berlin in den Verwaltungs-*

Jahren 1906 bis 1910 mit Abildung, Plan und Graphischen Darstellungen, 3 vols, vol. 1 (Berlin: R. Boll, 1912).

98 Kirschner, "Bericht des Oberbürgermeisters Kirschner an den Minister des Innern," 9; Langenhans, "Stadtverordneten-Versammlung Beschluß: Protokolle No. 10. 26. April 1904"; Takáts, "Der Verband Groß-Berlin," 6–7; Ernst Hirschberg, *Bilder aus der Berliner Statistik* (Berlin: Leonhard Simion Nf., 1904), 17; Magistrat der Stadt Berlin, ed. *Bericht über die Gemeinde-Verwaltung der Stadt Berlin in den Verwaltungs* (Berlin: R. Boll, 1912), 1:35–6.

99 Kirschner, "Bericht des Oberbürgermeisters Kirschner an den Minister des Innern," 1–6.

100 von Moltke, "Brief zu den Herrn Oberbürgermeister der Stadt Berlin. 10. Februar 1909" (LAB A Rep. 001-02 Nr. 631 S. 153–4), 153VS–154VS.

101 Elek Takáts, *Der Verband Gross-Berlin vom 19. Juli 1911 bis 1. Okt. 1920, seine wirtschaftlichen Aufgaben und Leistungen insbesondere im Verkehrs- und Siedlungswesen* (Cologne: Kölner studentenburse, 1933), 74–5, 16.

102 Der Magistrat Deutsch-Wilmersdorf, "Brief zu den Magistrat. 4. August 1910" (LAB A Rep. 001-02 Nr. 640 S. 5); Martin Kirschner, "Brief zu den Minister des Innern. 30. Juli 1910" (LAB A Rep. 001-02 Nr. 640 S. 4).

103 Großberliner Magistrat, "Bericht: Auf die Verfügung vom 2. November 1910. An den Herrn Oberpräsidenten der Provinz Brandenburg zu Potsdam" (LAB A Rep. 001-02 Nr. 640 S. 13–17), 14VS–14RS.

104 Edgar Wirckau, "Das preußische Zweckverbandsgesetz vom 19. Juli 1911" (Königlichen Universität Marburg, 1913), 16–18.

105 Brühl, Gordan, and Lebermann, *Zweckverbandsgesetz für Groß-Berlin*, 48, 48, 10.

106 Wilhelm Schröder, "Das Projekt des Zwangszweckverbands für Gross-Berlin," *Sozialistische Monatshefte* 15/17, no. 3 (1911).

107 "Haushaltsplan für 1912," in *Verband Groß Berlin. Stenographischer Bericht über die Sitzung der Verbandsversammlung am Dienstag, den 2. April 1912* (LAB A Rep. 046-03 Nr. 9), 2.

108 Quoted text from Brühl, Gordan, and Lebermann, *Zweckverbandsgesetz für Groß-Berlin vom 19. Juli 1911*, 48, xiv–xvii; see also Erbe, "Berlin im Kaiserreich," 747–8.

109 Takáts, "Der Verband Groß-Berlin," 9; Wilson, *German Forest*, 97–124.

110 Scholz, "Die moderne Stadtverwaltung [15]," 674–5.

111 Ernst Scholz, "Die moderne Stadtverwaltung [2]," *Zeitschrift für Kommunalwirtschaft und Kommunalpolitik*, no. 2 (25 January 1913): 30; Scholz, "Die moderne Stadtverwaltung [15]," 673.

112 Brühl, Gordan, and Lebermann, *Zweckverbandsgesetz für Groß-Berlin*, 48, xviii.

113 Scholz, "Die moderne Stadtverwaltung [15]," 674–5.

114 Takáts, "Der Verband Groß-Berlin," 41.
115 Vakhan Fomich Totomjanz, *Über die wirtschaftlichen Aufgaben der städtischen Verwaltung* (Leipzig: Felix Dietrich, 1906), 11–12.
116 Petersen, *Die Verkehrsaufgaben des Verbandes Groß-Berlin*, 20, 33.
117 Blum, "Zur Verkehrspolitik der Großstädte," 1083–5.
118 Hugo Preuß, "Sozialpolitik im Berliner Verkehr," in *Fragen der kommunalen Sozialpolitik in Groß-Berlin*, ed. Gesellschaft für soziale Reform Ortsgruppe Berlin (Jena: Gustav Fischer, 1911), 1, 25–6.
119 Christopher Wells, "Rebuilding the City, Leaving It Behind," *Journal of Transport History* 35, no. 2 (2014): 190–1.
120 Felix Linke, "Das Berliner Verkehrsproblem," *Sozialistische Monatshefte* 14/16, no. 25 (1910): 1619–26.
121 W[illy] Wygodzinski, *Wandlungen der deutschen Volkswirtschaft im neunzehnten Jahrhundert* (Cologne: M. Du Mont-Schauberg'schen Buchhandlung, 1907), 134–5.
122 Bruch, "Berlin's bauliche Zukunft und der Bebauungsplan," 161.
123 Blum, "Zur Verkehrspolitik der Großstädte," 1084; William Cronon, *Nature's Metropolis* (New York: W.W. Norton, 1991).
124 Bruch, "Berlin's bauliche Zukunft und der Bebauungsplan," 161; Colleen A. Dunlavy, *Politics and Industrialization: Early Railroads in the United States and Prussia* (Princeton, NJ: Princeton University Press, 1994), 4.
125 David Harvey, "The Spatial Fix: Hegel, von Thunen, and Marx," *Antipode* 13, no. 3 (1981): 7–9.
126 Karl Steiniger, "Brief zu die Herren Mitglieder des Verbandsausschusses und Ihre Herren Ersatzmänner. 2. September 1913" (LAB A Rep. 046-03 Nr. 14).
127 Lewis and Walker, "Beyond the Crabgrass Frontier."
128 Architekten-Ausschuß Groß-Berlin et al., "Ist es mit den Interessen von Groß-Berlin vereinbar, die Güterbahnhöfe aus der Innenstadt in die Augenbezirke zu verlegen? 10. Juni 1913" (LAB A Rep. 046-03 Nr. 14), [1]–[2].
129 Ibid., [5]–[7].
130 J. Greve, "Die Verkehr auf dem Wasserstraßen Berlins im Jahre 1906," *Zentralblatt der Bauverwaltung* 27, no. 37 (1907): 251–2; Friedrich Krause, "Der Westhafen von Berlin," *Zentralblatt der Bauverwaltung* 43, no. 69/70–71/72 (1923): 409.
131 "Der Westhafen von Berlin," 409.
132 Ernst Kaeber, *Berlin im Weltkriege* (Berlin: Crowissch, 1921), 399–404; Krause, "Der Westhafen von Berlin," 410.
133 Krause, "Der Westhafen von Berlin," 410–11.

134 Hans Werner Hegemann, "Die neue Bebauungsplan für Chicago," *Deutsche Bauzeitung* 44, no. 40 (1910): 303–7; F.A. Delano, "The Chicago Plan, with Particular Reference to the Railway Terminal Problem," *Journal of Political Economy* 21, no. 9 (1913): 819–31; City Club of Chicago, *The Railway Terminal Problem of Chicago* (Chicago: City Club of Chicago, 1913).

135 Garb, "Race, Housing, and Burnham's Plan," 107.

136 Getrud Haidvogl, "The Channelization of the Danube and Urban Spatial Development in Vienna in the Nineteenth and Early Twentieth Centuries," in *Urban Rivers*, ed. Stéphane Castonguay and Matthew Evenden (Pittsburgh: University of Pittsburgh Press, 2012), 120–1.

137 Wygodzinski, *Wandlungen der deutschen Volkswirtschaft im neunzehnten Jahrhundert*, 134–5.

138 Ibid.

139 Cronon, *Nature's Metropolis*, 74–80.

140 Handlin, "Modern City as a Field of Historical Study," 10–11; Donald J. Olsen, *The Growth of Victorian London* (New York: Holmes & Meier, 1976), 18–19.

141 Handlin, "Modern City as a Field of Historical Study," 13.

142 Ibid., 14–15.

143 von Schorlemer-Lieser, "Brief zu den Minister der öffentlichen Arbeit. 7. November 1912" (GStA-PK I. HA Rep. 191 Nr. 185 S. 248–54), 248VS/1–254VS/13.

144 Heinrich Johannes Schwippe, "Öffentlicher Personen-Nahverkehr, Stadtentwicklung und Dezentralisierung: Berlin 1860–1910," in *Stadt und Verkehr im Industriezeitalter*, ed. Horst Matzerath (Cologne: Böhlau Verlag, 1996), 171.

145 Große Berliner Straßenbahn et al., "Brief zu den Königlichen Polizei-Präsidenten, Herrn Dr. von Borries. 27. September 1905" (LAB A Rep. 047-03 Nr. 20 S. 2–5), 2–5.

146 Martin Kirschner and Werten, "Abschrift. Verhandelt Berlin, den 28. Oktober 1905" (LAB A Rep. 047-03 Nr. 20 S. 37–39), 37VS/1–38VS/3; "Einladung zu einer Sitzung der Vertreter von Gemeinden Groß-Berlins zur Beratung über die in Verkehrsangelegenheiten zu gründende Gemeinschaft am Mittwoch, dem 3. Juli d. J. [1907]" (LAB A Rep. 047-03 Nr. 20 S. 219–25).

147 Ernst Kaeber, "Böß, Gustav August Johann Heinrich," in *Neue Deutsche Biographie*, ed. Der Historischen Kommission bei der Bayerischen Akademie der Wissenschaft, 408–9 (Berlin: Duncker & Humblot, 1955).

148 "§1. Zweck des Verbandes ist … (10. August 1906)" (LAB A Rep. 001-02 Nr. 632 S. 106–10), 106.

149 Wilson, *German Forest*, 54–6.
150 Ibid., 61–2.
151 Ibid., 90–7.
152 Ibid., 54–6.
153 Michael Imort, "A Sylvan People," in *Germany's Nature*, ed. Thomas M. Lekan and Thomas Zeller (New Brunswick, NJ: Rutgers University Press, 2005), 62–4, 66–9.
154 Ibid., 59–61.
155 John Alexander Williams, "'The Chords of the German Soul Are Tuned to Nature,'" *Central European History* 29, no. 3 (1996): 345–7.
156 Ibid., 347–9.
157 Johannes Bartschat, "Das Problem des Grunewaldes [1]," *Der Städtebau* 5, no. 9 (1908): 122–4; Schultze-Naumburg, *Städtebau*, 4, 4, 6.
158 Oskar Ziethen, "Wald- und Wiesengürtel für Groß-Berlin," in *Fragen der kommunalen Sozialpolitik in Groß-Berlin*, ed. Gesellschaft für soziale Reform Ortsgruppe Berlin (Jena: Gustav Fischer, 1912), 38–9, 43.
159 Joseph August Lux, *Die moderne Wohnung und ihre Ausstattung* (Vienna: Wiener Verlag, 1905), 158; Mark Jarzombek, "Joseph August Lux," *Journal of the Society of Architectural Historians* 63, no. 2 (2004): 202–19.
160 Heinrich Pudor, "Der Volkspark von Groß-Berlin," *Der Städtebau* 7, no. 2 (1910): 21–2; Thomas Adam, "Heinrich Pudor: Lebensreformer, Antisemit und Verleger," in *Das bewegte Buch*, ed. Mark Lehmstedt and Andreas Herzog, 183–96 (Wiesbaden: Harrassowitz in Kommission, 1999).
161 Hermann Kötschke, *Die Berliner Waldverwüstung* (Berlin: Ansiedlungsverein, 1910), 7–8.
162 Wells, "Rebuilding the City," 190; Retzlaff, "The Illinois Forest Preserve District Act of 1913 and the Emergence of Metropolitan Park System Planning in the USA," 434; Moga, "Marginal Lands and Suburban Nature," 320–4; James C. O'Connell, "How Metropolitan Parks Shaped Greater Boston, 1893–1945," in *Remaking Boston*, ed. Anthony N. Penna and Conrad Edick Wright (Pittsburgh: University of Pittsburgh Press, 2009), 171.
163 Ludwig Feuth, "Eine neue Etappe der Waldverwüstung," *Sozialistische Monatshefte* 13/15, no. 8 (1909): 508–13.
164 Martin Wagner, *Städtische Freiflachenpolitik*, vol. 11 der neuen Folge der Schriften der Zentralstelle für Arbeiter-Wohlfahrtseinrichtungen (Berlin: Carl Heymanns Verlag, 1915), xi–xii.
165 Wilson, *German Forest*, 53–4.
166 Ibid., 102–4.
167 Ibid., 104–9.

168 Ibid., 119.

169 "On 6 May 1907 the mayors and communal chairpersons of Greater Berlin submitted a petition to preserve the Grunewald to the Ministry of the Interior." Niederschrift der im Landwirtschaftsministerium am 12. Oktober 1912" (GStA-PK I. HA Rep. 191 Nr. 185 S. 231–8), 231VS/1–231RS/2.

170 Brühl, Gordan, and Lebermann, *Zweckverbandsgesetz für Groß-Berlin*, 48, 48, xiv–xvii.

171 Wilson, *German Forest*, 88.

172 Der Vorsitzende des Kreis-Ausschusses des Kreises Niederbarnim, "Brief zu den Herrn Oberbürgermeister der Stadt Berlin Kirschner. 11. Juni 1909" (LAB A Rep. 001-02 Nr. 639 S. 1–2).

173 "Denkschrift betreffend die Erhaltung des Waldbestandes zu Berlin. 3. Dezember 1909" (LAB A Rep. 001-02 Nr. 639), 12–15, 24–5.

174 "Denkschrift betreffend die Erhaltung des Waldbestandes zu Berlin. 17. Februar 1910" (LAB A Rep. 001-02 Nr. 639 S. 26), 26/1–5.

175 Jeffrey K. Wilson, "Environmental Activism in the Kaiserreich," in *The German Forest, 1871–1914* (Toronto: University of Toronto Press, 2012).

176 Karl Steiniger, "6. Vorlage (J.Nr. 529. 12). 5. Oktober 1912," in *Verband Groß Berlin. Drucksachen für die Verbandsversammlung* (GStA-PK I. HA Rep. 191 Nr. 185 S. 245), 245VS; "Brief zu den Minister der öffentlichen Arbeiten. 21. Juli 1912" (GStA-PK I. HA Rep. 191 Nr. 185 S. 203–4), 203VS/1–04RS/4.

177 "Sonderbeilage zum 34sten Stück des Amtsblatts der Königlichen Regierung zu Potsdam und der Stadt Berlin den 26. August 1898: Baupolizeiordnung" (GStA PK HA Rep. 93 B Nr. 1107 Bd. 1 S. 7VS–7RS).

178 Borght and Lippert, *Grundzüge der Sozialpolitik*, 15, 386, 394–7, 412–14.

179 von Ressel, "Erster Petitions-Bericht der Gemeindekommission. 18. März 1904," in *Nr. 167 Haus der Abgeordneten, 20. Legislaturperiode, I Session 1904* (GStA PK I. HA Rep. 77 Tit. 805 Nr. 4 ADH S. 51–3), 51VS/1–51RS/2; Hinekeldeyn, "Brief zu Minister der öffentlichen Arbeiten von Breitenbach. 27. September 1905" (GStA PK I. HA Rep. 93 B Nr. 1093 Bd. 11); "Sitzung der Ministerium der öffentlichen Arbeiten. 2. Februar 1906" (GStA PK I. HA Rep. 93 B Nr. 1094 Bd. 12), 1–3, 17, 22–3, 35–6.

180 Kaempf, "Vorlage – zur Beschlußfassung – betreffend Abschluß eines Vertrages zwischen der Stadtgemeinde Berlin und der Aktien-Gesellschaft Verein zur Verbesserung der kleinen Wohnungen in Berlin," in *Auszug aus dem amtlichen stenographischen Bericht über die Sitzung der Stadtverordneten-Versammlung am 1. Mai 1902* (LAB A Rep. 000-02-01Nr.

2376 S. 31–5), 31/1; "Betrefft der Baupolizeiverordnung für die Vororte von Berlin vom 21. April 1903" (GStA PK I. HA Rep. 77 Tit. 805 Nr. 4 ADH S. 210–12), 210/1–211/3.

181 "Auftrag der Stadtverordneten Haberland und Genossen," in *Auszug aus dem amtlichen stenographischen Bericht über die Sitzung der Stadtverordneten-Versammlung am 29. September 1904* (LAB A Rep. 000-02-01 Nr. 2374 S. 24–41), 24–5.

182 Ibid., 26RS–28VS.

183 "Sitzung der Ministerium der öffentlichen Arbeiten. 2. Februar 1906," 4–6; Fischer, "Brief zu die Herrn Ministern des Innern von Moltke, u. A. 11. September 1907" (GStA-PK I. HA Rep. 93 B Nr. 1077), 1–2, 6; "Etat der Bauverwaltung, Bauordnung," in *Haus der Abgeordneten 129. Sitzung am 10. Februar 1913* (GStA PK I. HA Rep. 93 B Nr. 1100 Bd. 18), 11043–4.

184 "Haushaltsplan für 1912," 2.

4. City Planning and Municipal Administration

1 Gustav von Kessel, "Berlin in a State of War," in *Metropolis Berlin, 1880–1940*, ed. Iain Boyd Whyte and David Frisby (Berkeley: University of California Press, 2012), 279.

2 Lucy E. Hewitt, "The Civic Survey of Greater London," *Journal of Historical Geography* 38, no. 3 (2012): 248–52.

3 Lucy E. Hewitt, "Towards a Greater Urban Geography," *Planning Perspectives* 26, no. 4 (2011): 552.

4 George L. Yaney, *The World of the Manager* (New York: P. Lang, 1994), 35–7; Adam Tooze and Ted Fertik, "The World Economy and the Great War," *Geschichte und Gesellschaft* 40, no. 2 (2014): 217–20.

5 Anthony J. Arnold, "'A Paradise for Profiteers'?" *Accounting History Review* 24, no. 2/3 (2014): 61–2.

6 Pierre Purseigle, "The First World War and the Transformations of the State," *International Affairs* 90, no. 2 (2014): 249–64.

7 Peter C. Caldwell, *Popular Sovereignty and the Crisis of German Constitutional Law* (Durham, NC: Duke University Press, 1997), 55–6.

8 Roger Chickering, *Imperial Germany and the Great War, 1914–1918* (Cambridge: Cambridge University Press, 1998), 32–5.

9 Holger H. Herwig, "Through the Looking Glass," *Historian* 77, no. 2 (2015): 293.

10 Caldwell, *Popular Sovereignty and the Crisis of German Constitutional Law*, 55–6.

11 Yaney, *World of the Manager*, 11, 35–7.

12 Chickering, *Imperial Germany and the Great War*, 13, 32–5.

13 Belinda Davis, *Home Fires Burning* (Chapel Hill: University of North Carolina Press, 2000), 12–14, 18, 20; Yiğit Akın, "War, Women, and the State," *Journal of Women's History* 26, no. 3 (2014): 13.
14 Richard Bessel, "Mobilizing German Society for War," in *Great War, Total War*, ed. Roger Chickering and Stig Förster (Cambridge: Cambridge University Press, 2000), 448–50; Carl-Ludwig Holtfrerich, *The German Inflation, 1914–1923* (Berlin: De Gruyter, 1986), 116–18.
15 Holtfrerich, *German Inflation, 1914–1923*, 107–8.
16 Maureen Healy, *Vienna and the Fall of the Habsburg Empire* (Cambridge: Cambridge University Press, 2004), 8.
17 Bessel, "Mobilizing German Society for War," 438.
18 Ibid., 440.
19 Jon Lawrence, Martin Dean, and Jean-Louis Robert, "The Outbreak of War and the Urban Economy," *Economic History Review* 65, no. 3 (August 1992): 565–90.
20 Bessel, "Mobilizing German Society for War," 441–4.
21 Akın, "War, Women, and the State," 16.
22 Lawrence, Dean, and Robert, "Outbreak of War and the Urban Economy," 565–90.
23 Matthias Blum, "War, Food Rationing, and Socioeconomic Inequality in Germany during the First World War," *Economic History Review* 66, no. 4 (2013): 1063–4.
24 Albrecht Ritschl, "The Pity of Peace," in *The Economics of World War I*, ed. S.N. Broadberry and Mark Harrison (Cambridge: Cambridge University Press, 2005), 41, 43, 47.
25 Davis, *Home Fires Burning*, 25, 29.
26 Holtfrerich, *German Inflation*, 103; Bessel, "Mobilizing German Society for War," 445–7.
27 Matthias Blum, "Government Decisions before and during the First World War and the Living Standards in Germany during a Drastic Natural Experiment," *Explorations in Economic History* 48, no. 4 (2011): 557–8; Blum, "War, Food Rationing, and Socioeconomic Inequality," 1068–70.
28 N.P. Howard, "The Social and Political Consequences of the Allied Food Blockade of Germany, 1918–19," *German History* 11, no. 2 (1993): 162–4.
29 Blum, "War, Food Rationing, and Socioeconomic Inequality," 1066.
30 Tyler Stovall, "The Consumers' War: Paris, 1914–1918," *French Historical Studies* 31, no. 2 (2008): 316.
31 Healy, *Vienna and the Fall of the Habsburg Empire*, 9–10.
32 Reicke, "Brief zu den sämtliche städtischen Verwaltungs-Deputationen, Kuratorien. 18. Januar 1915" (LAB A Rep. 010-01-01 Nr. 323), 20VS; Städtisches

Hochbauamt II, "Unter Bezugnahme auf die Verfügung des Magistrats vom 18. I. d. Jrs … Februar 1915" (LAB A Rep. 010-01-01 Nr. 323), 21VS.

33 Kriegsministerium, "Brief zu den Herrn Bürgermeister Dr. Reicke. 4. Oktober 1909" (LAB A Rep. 007 Nr. 243 S. 119), 270VS/1–271VS/3.

34 Adolf Wermuth and Magistrat der Königlichen Haupt- und Residenzstadt, "Brief zu den Herrn Oberpräsident von Berlin, zu Potsdam. 11. Februar 1916" (LAB A Rep. 001-04 Nr. 3847 Bd. 1), 241VS–242VS.

35 Kaeber, *Berlin im Weltkriege*, 19.

36 Adolf Wermuth and Deutscher Städtetag Zentralstelle, "Brief zu den Herrn Stellvertreter des Reichskanzlers" (LAB A Rep. 001-04 Nr. 3847 Bd. 2), 75VS/1–76VS/3.

37 Hans Luther and Deutsche Städtetag Zentralstelle, "Betr. Erstattung von besonderen Aufwendungen für Standtruppen in Massenquartieren. 10. Juli 1916," (LAB A Rep. 001-04 Nr. 3985 Bd. 3), 54VS/1.

38 Davis, *Home Fires Burning*, 17.

39 Der Vorsitzende des Bürgerbund Groß-Berlin, "Brief zu den Oberbürgermeister" (LAB A Rep. 047-03 Nr. 28), 30VS/1–30RS/2.

40 Chickering, *Imperial Germany and the Great War*, 13, 13, 35–6.

41 Yaney, *World of the Manager*, 11, 35–7.

42 Gerald D. Feldman, *Army, Industry, and Labor in Germany, 1914–1918*, (Princeton, NJ: Princeton University Press, 1966), 45–46.

43 Purseigle, "First World War and the Transformations of the State," 259.

44 Chickering, *Imperial Germany and the Great War*, 13, 13, 37.

45 Davis, *Home Fires Burning*, 114.

46 Joseph Bloch, "Der Krieg und die Sozialdemokratie," *Sozialistische Monatshefte* 20, no. 16 (1914): 1023–5.

47 Leopold von Wiese, "Liberalismus und Demokratismus in ihren Zusammenhängen und Gegensätzen," *Zeitschrift für Politik* 9 (1916): 408–9.

48 Alkoholkranke und Krebskranke in Berlin (E.V.) Zentral-Komitee der Auskunfts- und Fürsorgestellen für Lungenkranke, "Aufschnitt auf den Gemeinde-Blatt Nr. 32 den 9. August 1914. 46–7. 8. August 1914" (LAB A Rep. 001-04 Nr. 3985.1 Bd. 1), 48VS/1–48RS/2.

49 Magistrat der Königlichen Haupt- und Residenzstadt, "Brief zu das Königliche Preußische Kriegsministerium. 18. Februar 1915" (LAB A Rep. 001-04 Nr. 3985 Bd. 2), 18–20. Luther and Deutscher Städtetag Zentralstelle, "Rundschreiben an die Mitgliedsstädte des Deutschen Städtetages. 10. April 1915" (LAB A Rep. 001-04 Nr. 3985 Bd. 2), 32VS–33RS.

50 Friedrich Wilhelm von Loebell and August Lentze, "Brief zu den Magistrat in Berlin. 2. Februar 1915" (LAB A Rep. 001-04 Nr. 3847 Bd. 1), 40VS/1–40RS/4.

51 Adolf Wermuth and Der Vorstand der preußischer Städtetag, "Brief zu den preußischen Minister des Innern. 2. September 1915" (LAB A Rep. 001-04 Nr. 3847 Bd. 1).
52 Rudolf von der Schülenberg, "Brief zu den Magistrat in Berlin. 27. November 1915" (LAB A Rep. 001-04 Nr. 3847 Bd. 1), 222VS/1–223VS/3.
53 "Abschrift. Preußischen Gesetzsammlung. Jahrgang 1916 Nr. 12" (LAB A Rep. 001-04 Nr. 3847 Bd. 2), 57VS/1–57RS/2.
54 Magistrat. Abteilung für Volksspeisung, "Brief an den Kämmerer. 24. August 1916" (LAB A Rep. 001-04 Nr. 3847 Bd. 2), 170VS/1–171RS/3. That fall, the Finance and Interior Ministries secured more funding for the Oberpräsident and Regierungspräsidenten's and their communities but demanded that it be spent on food. "Brief zu die Herrn Regierungspräsidenten und den Herrn Oberpräsidenten in Potsdam" (LAB A Rep. 001-04 Nr. 3847 Bd. 2), 196VS/1–196RS/2.
55 Healy, *Vienna and the Fall of the Habsburg Empire*, 10.
56 B. Hammer, "Moderne Städtgründung," *Der Städtebau* 12, no. 1 (1915): 9; Adelheid von Saldern, "Social Rationalization of Living and Housework in Germany and the United States in the 1920s," *The History of the Family* 2, no. 1 (1997): 73–97.
57 Martin Wagner, "Mehr Organisation im städtischen Siedlungswesen," *Preußisches Verwaltungs-Blatt* 36, no. 50 (1915): 809–10.
58 Bruno Taut, "Das Problem des Opernbaus," *Sozialistische Monatshefte* 20, no. 6 (1914): 356–7.
59 Felix Linke, "Die neue Architektur," *Sozialistische Monatshefte* 20, no. 17 (1914): 1134–5.
60 Paul von Breitenbach et al., "Nr. 299: Entwurf eines Wohnungsgesetzes," in *Haus der Abgeordneten. 22. Legislaturperiode, III Session 1916/17* (GStA PK I. HA Rep. 191 Nr. 56 Bd. 1).
61 "Niederschrift. 23. Februar 1918" (GStA PK I. HA Rep. 93 B Nr. 1115). For example, Berlin-Lichtenberg complained to the minister of public works that only Berlin's representatives were included in the discussion, ignoring Lichtenberg's 160,000 residents. Der Magistrat Berlin-Lichtenberg, "Brief zu den Herrn Minister der öffentlichen Arbeiten. 5. März 1918" (GStA PK I. HA Rep. 93 B Nr. 1115).
62 von Breitenbach et al., "Nr. 299: Entwurf eines Wohnungsgesetzes"; Takáts, "Der Verband Groß-Berlin," 78.
63 Wohnungsgesetz. Vom 28. März 1918," *Preußisches Gesetzsammlung*, no. 9 (1918) (GStA PK I. HA Rep. 191 MfVw Nr. 56); Polizeipräsident von Oppen and Oberbürgermeister der Königl. Haupt- und Residenzstadt Berlin Adolf Wermuth, "Gemeindeblatt Nr. vom 31. 3. 1918. Magistrat.

Bekanntmachung. 20. März 1918" (LAB A Rep. 000-02-01Nr. 2226 Die Städtische Baupolizeiverwaltung [henceforth referred to by Akte Nummer]), 22VS/1.

64 Joseph Stübben and Architekten-Ausschuß Groß-Berlin, "Brief zu den Minister der öffentlichen Arbeiten. 8. April 1918 (GStA PK I. HA Rep. 93 B Nr. 1115).

65 Hewitt, "Towards a Greater Urban Geography," 561–2.

66 Karl Steiniger, "Kommission des Verbandsausschusses zur Vorberatung des VIII. Nachtrages zur Baupolizeiverordnung für die Vororte. Verhandlungsniederschrift über die Sitzung am 12. Mai 1917" (GStA PK I. HA Rep. 93 B Nr. 1115), 1–4.

67 Fritz Beuster, "Einheitliches Baurecht und einheitliche Baupolizei für Groß-Berlin," *Preußisches Verwaltungs-Blatt* 38, no. 38 (1917): 541–2 (GStA PK I. HA Rep. 93 B MdöA Nr. 1115); an argument he developed more fully here: F. Beuster, *Groß-Berlin nach dem Kriege* (Berlin: Carl Henmanns Verlag, 1918).

68 Der Polizeipräsident, "Brief zu den Herrn Minister der öffentlichen Arbeiten. 15. August 1917" (GStA PK I. HA Rep. 93 B Nr. 1115); von Massenbach, "Brief zu den Herrn Ober-Präsident. 15. Juli 1917" (GStA PK I. HA Rep. 93 B Nr. 1115), 2.

69 Victor Roack, "Groß-Berlin Siedlungs- und Wohnungsfrage," *Kommunale Praxis*, 21 September 1918, 596.

70 Hans Schliepmann, "Verbesserung Großstädtischer Bauordnung," *Berliner Architekturwelt* 20, no. 11/12 (1918): 253–5.

71 Bruno Taut, *Die Auflösung der Städte* (Hagen in West Erschienen im Folkwang, 1920).

72 Victor Roack, "Mieterlend in Groß-Berlin," *Kommunale Praxis*, 30 March 1918, 194; see also Paul Gaumitz, "Die künftigen Aufgaben unserer Wohnungsämter," in *Probleme der Neuen Stadt Berlin*, ed. Hans Bennert and Erwin Stein (Berlin-Friednau: Deutscher Kommunal-Verlag GmbH, 1926), 284; Julius Zerfaß, "Die Gartenstadtfrage und das Großstädische Wohnungsproblem," *Kommunale Praxis* 18, no. 29 (20 July 1918): 499.

73 Stovall, "Consumers' War," 304–5.

74 W. Sollman, "Kleinhaus oder Mehrfamilienhaus," *Kommunale Praxis*, 8 June 1918, 355.

75 Peter Behrens and Heinrich de Fries, *Vom Sparsamen Bauen* (Berlin: Verlag der Bauwelt, 1918), 65, 59. For the impact of this mode of labour more generally, see Adelheid von Saldern, "Gesellschaft und Lebensgestaltung Sozialkuturelle Streiflicher," in *Geschichte des Wohnens*, ed. Gert Kähler (Stuttgart: Deutsche Verlags-Anstalt, 1996), 84–8.

76 Behrens and Fries, *Vom Sparsamen Bauen*, 60–1.

77 Rüdiger Hachtmann and Adelheid von Saldern, "'Gesellschaft am Fließband,'" *Zeithistorische Forschungen* 6, no. 2 (2009): 186–7.

78 Beirat für Städtebau und städtisches Siedlungswesen. Ausschuß II, "Niederschrift. Berlin, den 8. Januar 1918" (GStA PK I. HA Rep. 93 B Nr. 5145); "Niederschrift. Berlin, den 24. April 1918" (GStA PK I. HA Rep. 93 B Nr. 5145).

79 Paul Schmitthenner, "Die Siedlung Plaue bei Brandenburg a. H.," *Wasmuths Monatshefte für Baukunst* 4, no. 5/6 (1920): 161; Wolfgang Voigt, "Schmitthenner, Paul," *Neue Deutsche Biographie* 23 (2007): 246–8.

80 Schmitthenner, "Die Siedlung Plaue bei Brandenburg a. H.," 162.

81 Martin Wagner, "Baukostenverbilligung im Kleinwohnungsbau," in *Ein Programm für die Ubergangswirtschaft in Wohnungswesen*, ed. Deutscher Verein für Wohnungsreform (Berlin: F. Siemenroth, 1918), 77.

82 Robert Freestone, "Reconciling Beauty and Utility in Early City Planning," *Journal of Urban History* 37, no. 2 (2011): 256–7.

83 Schliepmann, "Verbesserung Großstädtischer Bauordnung," 253–5.

84 Schultz, "Zur Wohnungsfrage," *Kommunale Praxis*, 5 Oktober 1918, 631.

85 Edgar Jaffé, *Volkswirtschaft und Krieg* (Tübingen: J.C.B. Mohr [P. Siebeck], 1915), 3–4.

86 Guenther Roth, "Edgar Jaffé and Else von Richthofen in the Mirror of Newly Found Letters," *Max Weber Studies* 10, no. 2 (2010): 151–2.

87 Paul Lensch, "Die Neugestaltung der Wirtschaftsordnung," in *Die Arbeiterschaft im neuen Deutschland*, ed. Friedrich Wilhelm Karl Thimme and Carl Legien (Leipzig: S. Hirzel, 1915), 139–40; Abraham Ascher, "'Radical' Imperialists within German Social Democracy, 1912–1918," *Political Science Quarterly* 76, no. 4 (1961): 555–75.

88 Julius Hirsch, "Der Kettenhandel in wirtschaftlicher Darstellung," in *Der Kettenhandel als Kriegserscheinung*, ed. Volkswirtschaftlichen Abteilung des Kriegsernährungsamts (Berlin: Verlag der Beiträge zur Kriegswirtschaft [Reimar Hobbing], 1916), 2–3; Belinda Davis, "Food Scarcity and the Empowerment of the Female Consumer in World War I Berlin," in *The Sex of Things*, ed. Victoria De Grazia and Ellen Furlough (Berkeley: University of California Press, 1996), 288.

89 Karl Thieß, "Höchstpreispolitik," in *Die Preisbildung im Kriege*, ed. Volkwirtschaftlichen Abteilung des Kriegsernährungsamts, 5–33 (Berlin: Verlag der Beiträge zur Kriegswirtschaft [Reimar Hobbing], 1916).

90 August Skalweit, *Die Viehhandelsverbände in der deutschen Kriegswirtschaft* (Berlin: Verlag der Beiträge zur Kriegswirtschaft [Reimar Hobbing], 1917),

40–1; Dirk Henning Hofer, *Karl Konrad Werner Wedemeyer (1870–1934)* (Frankfurt am Main: Peter Lang, 2009), 197.

91 Magistrat der Stadtgemeinde Berlin-Wilmersdorf, "Brief zu den Magistrat Berlin. 12. Oktober 1917" (LAB A Rep. 001-04 Nr. 3847 Bd. 3), 257VS/1–258VS/3.

92 "Ausschnitt aus dem Berliner Tageblatt 17. Oktober 1917: 'Einheitliche Lebensmittelkarten in Groß-Berlin'" (LAB A Rep. 013-03 Nr. 14636), 10VS/1; Simonsohn and Magistrats Abteilung für Brotversorgung, "Urschriftlich dem Nachrichtenamt ..." (LAB A Rep. 013-03 Nr. 14636 Bd. 2), 17VS/1.

93 Magistrat der Königlichen Haupt- und Residenzstadt and Abteilung für Eierversorgung, "Sehr geehrter Herr Stadtrat ... 22. Januar 1918" (LAB A Rep. 013-03 Nr. 14636 Bd. 2), 35VS/1–35RS/2; Simonsohn et al., "Abschrift. Der Ausschuss des Lebensmittelverbandes Groß Berlin. 4. Februar 1918" (LAB A Rep. 013-03 Nr. 14636 Bd. 2), 40aVS/1–40aRS/2; Loehning, Oppler, and Magistrat Berlin Abteilung für Kaffeeersatz, "Protokoll über die Sitzung des Beirats für die Regelung des Verkehrs mit Kaffee-Ersatzmitteln in Groß-Berlin vom 16. Februar 1918" (LAB A Rep. 013-03 Nr. 14636 Bd. 2), 116VS/1–17RS/3.

94 Der Vorsitzende der Staatlichen Verteilungsstelle für Groß Berlin, "Brief zu den Lebensmittelverband Groß Berlin. 4. März 1918" (LAB A Rep. 013-03 Nr. 14636 Bd. 2), 75VS/1–75RS/2; Lehmann and Simm, "Verhandelungsbericht über die Sitzung der Kommission zur Feststellung der Grundsätze für die Zuweisungen an Werkspeisungen, Rüstungsarbeiter und Massenspeisungen am 12. März 1918" (LAB A Rep. 013-03 Nr. 14636 Bd. 2), 72VS/1. On 22 March the same group increased the amount of fat by fifty grams for armament workers because new anti–black market ordinances blocked certain sales.

95 Simonsohn et al., "Niederschrift über eine Besprechung am 17. 4. 18. des Ausschuss zur Beratung der für die Ausgestaltung einer Geschäftsabteilung erforderlichen Maßnahmen, am 17. April 1918" (LAB A Rep. 013-03 Nr. 14636 Bd. 2), 134VS/1–134RS/2.

96 Otto Neurath, "Economics in Kind, Calculation in Kind and Their Relation to War Economics," trans. Christoph Schmidt-Petri and Thomas E. Uebel, in *Otto Neurath Economic Writings Selections 1904–1945*, ed. Thomas E. Uebel and Robert Cohen (New York: Springer, 2005), 304–5; Neurath, "Die Naturalwirtschaftslehre und der Naturalkalkül in ihren Beziehungen zur Kriegswirtschaftslehre [1916]," in *Durch die Kriegswirtschaft zur Naturalwirtschaft*, 174–82 (Callwey: Munich, 1919); Erwin Dekker, "The Intellectual Networks of Otto Neurath," *European Studies* 32, no. 1 (2014): 104.

97 Otto Neurath, "The Conceptual Structure of Economic Theory and Its Foundations [1917]," in *Otto Neurath Economic Writings*, ed. Thomas E. Uebel and Robert Cohen (New York: Springer, 2005), 321–2.

98 "Otto Neurath, "The Economic Order of the Future and the Economic Sciences," in *Otto Neurath Economic Writings Selections 1904–1945*, ed. Thomas E. Uebel and Robert Cohen (New York: Springer, 2005), 251.

99 Franz Steinbrucker, "Wohnungsmangel und Wohungselend," *Der Städtebau* 12, no. 12 (1915): 114–15.

100 Hans Schliepmann, "Der Krieg und die Baukunst," *Berliner Architekturwelt* 17, no. 9 (1915): 319–21.

101 Heinrich Peus, "Der Sozialismus und der sogenannte Kriegssozialismus," *Sozialistische Monatshefte* 23, no. 4 (1917): 190–4.

102 Purseigle, "First World War and the Transformations of the State," 257.

103 Stovall, "Consumers' War," 294–5.

104 Ibid., 298.

105 Neumann, "Change in the Function of Law in Modern Society," 47–9.

106 Bruno Taut, "I. Ein Architektur-Programm," in *Flugschriften des Arbeitsrate für Kunst* (Berlin1918) (AdK-SB AfK Nr. 01–8), 29; Colquhoun, "Criticism and Self-Criticism in German Modernism."

107 Arbeitsrat für Kunst, "Ruf zum Bauen" (AdK-SB AfK Nr. 01–6), 43; Adelheid von Saldern, "'Instead of Cathedrals, Dwelling Machines,'" trans. Bruce Little, in *The Challenge of Modernity* (Ann Arbor: University of Michigan Press, 2002), 97.

108 Arbeitsrat für Kunst, "Ruf zum Bauen," 3–4.

109 David H. Haney, "Leberecht Migge's 'Green Manifesto,'" *Landscape Journal* 26, no. 2 (2007): 201; Spartakus in Grün an dem der rote sterben soll, "Das grüne Manifest," *Die Tat* 10, no. 12 (1919): 912–19; Leberecht Migge, "Das grüne Manifest [1918]," in *Der soziale Garten* (Berlin: Gebr. Mann, 1999), 7–9.

110 David Haney comes to the same conclusion about anti-urbanism and modernity in Migge's work. Haney, "Leberecht Migge's 'Green Manifesto,'" 202–4.

111 Ibid., 202.

112 Migge, "Das grüne Manifest [1918]," 10–15.

113 Hirschberg, "Wege der Wohnungsfürsorge," *Kommunale Praxis*, 3 May 1919, 272.

114 Martin Wagner, *Gemeinwirtschaft im Wohnungswesen* (Kiel: Vollbehr & Riepen, 1920), 5.

115 Klaus Homann and Ludovica Scarpa, "Martin Wagner, the Trades Union Movement and Housing Construction in Berlin in the First Half of the Nineteen Twenties," *Architectural Design* 53, no. 11/12 (1983): 59.
116 Martin Wagner, "Die Sanierung der Mietskasernen," in *Die Wohnungs- und Siedlungsfrage nach dem Kriege*, ed. Carl Johannes Fuchs (Stuttgart: W. Meyer-Ilschen, 1918), 402; Wagner, "Wohnungswirtschaft-Finanzwirtschaft," *Kommunale Praxis*, 20 March 1920, 266.
117 The Demobilization Committee for Greater Berlin had arranged relief labour for the region according to three lists: first, authorized by the Oberpräsident, without the participation of the Demobilization Committee, and totalling 10.63 million M; second, enterprises whose charges would exceed 150,000 M and need consent from the Demobilization Committee – a program expected to cost 118.95 million M; third, those that the Demobilization Committee ruled out from list 1 and 2 – a program expected to cost an extra 1.32 million RM.
118 Lenzmann, "Besprechung über Reichs- und Staatsausschüsse zu öffentlichen Notstandsarbeiten von Groß-Berlin, am 4. II. 1919 im Demobilmachungsamt" (LAB A Rep. 010-01-01 Nr. 61), 137VS/1–142VS/6, quoted text from 140VS/4; Berger, "Dückerung des Schöneberger Regenauslasses unter der Untergrundbahn am Nollendorfplatz in Berlin," *Zentralblatt der Bauverwaltung* 37, no. 71/72 (1, 5 September 1917): 449–52, 453–6.
119 Mitzlaff and Deutscher Städtetag, "Brief zu den Herrn Reichsarbeitsministers. 3 Februar 1920" (LAB A Rep. 010-01-01 Nr. 180 Bd. 1), 2VS.
120 Alexander Schlicke, "Brief zu den Deutschen Städtetag, Berlin. 25. Februar 1920" (LAB A Rep. 010-01-01 Nr. 180).
121 "Neue Einigungsversuche im Straßenbahnerstreik," *Berliner Lokal-Anzeiger*, 10 July 1919 (LAB A Rep. 001-02 Nr. 642), 15RS.
122 "Nach dem Verkehrsstreik," *Berliner Tageblatt*, 16 July 1919 (LAB A Rep. 001-02 Nr. 642), 19RS.
123 "Der geplante Ankauf des Ostbahn," *Die Post*, 15 July 1919 (LAB A Rep. 001-02 Nr. 642), 18VS; "Ankauf der Ostbahn durch den Verband Groß-Berlin," *Berliner Morgenpost*, 15 July 1919 (LAB A Rep. 001-02 Nr. 642); "Zum Ankauf der Ostbahn," *Deutsche Zeitung*, 15 July 1919 (LAB A Rep. 001-02 Nr. 642).
124 "Der Verkauf der Großen Berliner Straßenbahn," *Die Post*, 17 July 1919 (LAB A Rep. 001-02 Nr. 642), 20VS.
125 "Der Verkauf der Straßenbahn," *Vossische Zeitung*, 17 July 1919 (LAB A Rep. 001-02 Nr. 642), 21RS.

126 "Zustimmung der Generalversammlung zum Straßenbahnverkauf," *Tägliche Rundschau*, 18 July 1919 (LAB A Rep. 001-02 Nr. 642), 22RS. Similar articles were run in a number of newspapers: "Die Straßenbahn an den Zweckverband verkauft," *Berliner Tageblatt*, 18 July 1919 (LAB A Rep. 001-02 Nr. 642), 23VS.

127 "Die Verstadtlichung der Großen Berliner," *Deutsche Allgemeine Zeitung*, 18 July 1919 (LAB A Rep. 001-02 Nr. 642); "Zur Kommunalisierung der Straßenbahn," *Die Freiheit*, 9 July 1919 (LAB A Rep. 001-02 Nr. 642); "Zur Aktionärversammlung der Großen Berliner," *Vörwarts*, 18 July 1919 (LAB A Rep. 001-02 Nr. 642); "Die Verstädtlichung der Großen Berliner Straßenbahn genehmigt," *Berliner Morgenpost*, 18 July 1919 (LAB A Rep. 001-02 Nr. 642); "Der Verkauf der Großen Berliner Straßenbahn"; "Zur Aktionärversammlung der Großen Berliner"; "Zur Kommunalisierung der Straßenbahn."

128 Der Reichs- und Staatskommissar für das Wohnungswesen, "Brief zu das Kriegsministerium in Berlin. 23. November 1918" (LAB A Rep. 010-01-01 Nr. 60 Bd. 2), 54; Demobilmachungsausschuß Groß-Berlin, "V. 2. Dezember 1918" (LAB A Rep. 010-01-01 Nr. 60), 53RS; Verband der Baugeschäfte von Groß-Berlin, #356; Verband der Baugeschäfte von Groß-Berlin, "Brief zu die Hochbau-Verwaltung der Stadt Berlin z. Hd. des Herrn Geheimen Baurat Dr. Ing. Ludwig Hoffmann. 6. Dezember 1918" (LAB A Rep. 010-01-01 Nr. 61); ibid. On 14 February the Housing Federation of Greater Berlin and the director of the Zweckverband for Greater Berlin explained to the district administrators and magistrates how each form of commandeered-apartment would be compensated. (Fritz Beuster, Wohnungsverband Groß Berlin, and Verbandsdirektor des Verbandes Groß Berlin, "Brief zu die Magistrate und Herren Landräte im Wohnungsverband Groß Berlin. 14. Februar 1919" (LAB A Rep. 010-01-01 Nr. 61), 165VS/1–168VS/4; ibid.)

129 Reichsarbeitsministerium and Glaß, "Verordnung. 9. Dezember 1919," *Reichs-Gesetzblatt*, no. 237 (1919) (GStA PK I. HA Rep. 151 IC Nr. 12203 Bd. 1).

130 [Adolf] Scheidt, "Brief zu den sämtliche Herren Regierungspräsidenten (außer Sigmaringen) und den Herrn Oberpräsidenten in Charlottenburg. 24. Januar 1919" (GStA PK I. HA Rep. 191 Nr. 56), 150VS/1–150RS/2.

131 Reichs-Arbeitsgemeinschaft für das Baugewerbe, "Brief zu die Sozialisierungskommission. 30. Januar 1919" (LAB A Rep. 010-01-01 Nr. 61), 87VS–87RS); Adolf Wermuth and Magistrat Berlin, "Maßnahmen gegen Wohnungsmangel" (LAB A Rep. 226 Nr. A 277), 2. The Borsig corporation complained that they were forced to lease a property of

theirs at a significant loss. A. Borsig A. G., "Betr. Rücksprache auf der Wohnungsinspektion V: Brunnenstraße 59 betr. das Haus Schlegelstr. 2. 22. September 1919" (LAB A Rep. 226 Borsig Nr. A 277), 8VS. He demanded restitution for the value he would have earned on the property.

132 "Brief zu den Magistrat, Wohnungsamt. 27. September 1919" (LAB A Rep. 226 Borsig Nr. A 277), 11VS–13VS.

133 Ludwig Hoffmann, "Zu 624. 24. Mai 1919" (LAB A Rep. 000-02-01 Nr. 1866), 3.

134 Moritz Lehmann, "Brief zu den Magistrat der Stadt Berlin. 21. Dezember 1918" (LAB A Rep. 010-01-01 Nr. 61), 16VS/1.

135 Berlinische Grundgesellschaft mit beschränkter Haftung, "Bebauung für Grundstücke an der Wullenweberstrasse und Spree, Judenwiesen, nahe Tiergarten. 30. November 1918" (LAB A Rep. 010-01-01 Nr. 59 Bd. 1), 240VS–242VS, quoted text from 241VS.

136 Kiki Kafkoula, "On Garden-City Lines," *Planning Perspectives* 28, no. 2 (2013): 180.

137 von Saldern, "Social Rationalization of Living and Housework," 79.

138 Simon Pepper and Peter Richmond, "Homes Unfit for Heroes," *Town Planning Review* 90, no. 2 (2009): 143–4.

139 Takáts, *Der Verband Gross-Berlin*, 85.

140 Paul Hirsch and Wolfgang Heine, "Nr. 1286 Entwurf eines Gesetzes über die Bildung eines Stadtkrieses Groß-Berlin. 18. November 1919," in *Verfassunggebende Preußische Landesversammlung 1919* (LAB A Rep. 001-02 Nr.659), 21–2.

141 Ibid.

142 Ibid., 24–5.

143 Ibid.

144 Reichhelm and Berlin-Reinickndorf, "Brief zu den Herrn Minister des Innern. 18. Dezember 1918," (LAB A Rep. 001-02 Nr. 644), 25VS–26RS, the quoted text from 25RS.

145 Bürgerausschuss Groß-Berlin and Dominicus, "Einladung. Berlin, den 16. April 1919" (LAB A Rep. 001-02 Nr. 641), 6. Vorstand der "Berliner Vorortgemeinschaft im Kreise Teltow," ed. *Entwurf eines Gesetzes über die Gemeindeverfassung von Berlin* (LAB A Rep. 047-03 Nr. 30), 48VS–52VS.

146 The Citizens Committee was not the only one thinking about this issue. The municipal electrical works and water works in Greater Berlin began to rationalize their service through an economy of scale. Städtische Elektrizitätswerke Berlin, "Brief zu den Herrn Oberbürgermeister.

21. März 1919" (LAB A Rep. 001-02 Nr. 644), 49VS–52VS; Deputation der städtischen Wasserwerke, "Brief zu den Herrn Oberbürgermeister. 28. März 1919" (LAB A Rep. 001-02 Nr. 644), 39VS–41RS.

147 Hans Lohmeyer, "Groß-Berlin: Grundlage zu einem Gesetz betreffend Bildung einer Gesamtgemeinde," *Kommunale Praxis*, 25 January 1919, 33–4.

148 Bürgerausschuss Groß-Berlin and Dominicus, "Einladung. Berlin, den 16. April 1919," 6.

149 Bürgerausschuss Groß-Berlin, "Groß-Berliner Woche: Lehrkursus des Bürgerausschusses Groß-Berlin. 5.–10. Mai 1919" (LAB A Rep. 001-02 Nr.641), 7.

150 Adolf Wermuth, "Brief zu den Herrn Unterstaatssekretär Dr. Freund. Ministerium des Innern. 3. April 1919" (LAB A Rep. 001-02 Nr. 644).

151 Reicke, "Protokoll über die Sitzung der Großen Deputation von 5.7.1919" (LAB A Rep. 001-02 Nr. 644), 15VS/1–16RS/4.

152 "Das Schicksal der Selbstverwaltung in Groß-Berlin," *Deutsche Tageszeitung*, 9 July 1919 (LAB A Rep. 001-02 Nr. 642, 15VS; #336; "Besprechung des Gesetzentwurfes über die Bildung eines Stadtkreises Großberlin," in *Amtlicher stenographischer Bericht über die außerordentliche Sitzung der Berliner Stadtverordnetenversammlung am 10. Juli 1919*, ed. Magistrat Berlin (LAB A Rep. 001-02 Nr. 644).

153 "Besprechung des Gesetzentwurfes über die Bildung eines Stadtkreises Großberlin," 22VS/468–22RS/469. Vorwärts confirmed that SPD majority municipalities strongly supported incorporation. "Die Gemeinden und der Gesetzentwurf Groß-Berlin," *Vorwärts*, 10 July 1919 (LAB A Rep. 001-02 Nr. 642), 15RS.

154 "Groß-Berliner Eingemeindung," *Berliner Lokal-Anzeiger*, 16 July 1919 (LAB A Rep. 001-02 Nr. 642), 18RS; "Für und gegen die Einheitsgemeinde," *Die Post*, 16 July 1919 (LAB A Rep. 001-02 Nr. 642), 19RS; "Für und gegen die Einheitsgemeinde," *Vörwarts*, 16 July 1919 (LAB A Rep. 001-02 Nr. 642), 19RS; "Bedenken Tegels zum Gesetzentwurf Groß-Berlin," *Berliner Börsen Courier*, 17 July 1919 (LAB A Rep. 001-02 Nr. 642), 20RS.

155 "Kommunale Arbeiterräte!," *Die Freiheit*, 13 July 1919 (LAB A Rep. 001-02 Nr. 642), 17RS; "Konferenz der Groß-Berliner Gemeindevertreter der U.S.P.D.," *Die Freiheit*, 13 July 1919 (LAB A Rep. 001-02 Nr. 642), 17RS.

156 "Für und gegen 'Groß-Berlin,'" *Deutsche Tageszeitung*, 18 July 1919 (LAB A Rep. 001-02 Nr. 642), 24VS; "Tempelhof für die Einheitsgemeinde," *Die Post*, 25 July 1919 (LAB A Rep. 001-02 Nr. 642), 31RS; "Tempelhof für die Einheitsgemeinde," *Deutsche Tageszeitung*, 25 July 1919 (LAB A Rep. 001-02 Nr. 642), 32VS; "Auch Tempelhof für die Einheitsgemeinde," *Berliner*

Morgenpost, 26 July 1919 (LAB A Rep. 001-02 Nr. 642), 32VS; "Lichtenberg für die Einheitsgemeinde," *Germania*, 25 July 1919 (LAB A Rep. 001-02 Nr. 642), 32VS.

157 "Charlottenburg gegen Groß-Berlin," *Deutsche Tageszeitung*, 19 July 1919 (LAB A Rep. 001-02 Nr. 642); "Gegen die Eingemeindungszwang," *Tägliche Rundschau*, 24 December 1919 (LAB A Rep. 001-02 Nr. 642).

158 Jacobs et al., "Niederschrift über die Sitzung das Lebensmittelausschuss Groß-Berlin am 23. September 1919" (LAB A Rep. 013-03 Nr. 14636 Bd. 3), 5.

159 "Spandau verlangt vor Eingemeindung eine Volksabstimmung," *Berliner Lokal-Anzeiger*, 18 July 1919 (LAB A Rep. 001-02 Nr. 642), 26VS. See also "Die Verstädtlichung der Großen Berliner Straßenbahn genehmigt," 28RS.

160 "Spandau verlangt vor Eingemeindung eine Volksabstimmung," 26VS. See also "Die Verstädtlichung der Großen Berliner Straßenbahn genehmigt," 28RS; "Spandau gegen die Eingemeindung," *Deutsche Tageszeitung*, 11 July 1919 (LAB A Rep. 001-02 Nr. 642), 16VS; "Spandau verlangt vor Eingemeindung eine Volksabstimmung," 26VS; "Die Verstädtlichung der Großen Berliner Straßenbahn genehmigt," 28RS; "Die Groß-Berliner Eingemeindungsfrage: Spandau verlangt Abstimmung der Einwohnerschaft," *Berliner Tageblatt*, 23 July 1919 (LAB A Rep. 001-02 Nr. 642), 31VS; Peters and Preußischer Staatskommissar für Volksernährung, "Abschrift. 24. September 1919" (LAB A Rep. 013-03 Nr. 14636 Bd. 3), 7VS. This region included Spandau, Staaken, Pichelsdorf with Pichelswerder, Tiefwerder, Dallgow, Döberitz, Rohrbeck, Seegefeld with Gutsbezirk, Falkenhagen, Hennigsdorf, Niederneuendorf with Gutsbezirk, Velten, Marwitz, and the city of Nauen.

161 "Umgestaltung des Gesetzentwurfs Groß-Berlin," *Vossische Zeitung*, 4 August 1919 (LAB A Rep. 001-02 Nr. 642), 32RS; "Der Entwurf über Schaffung einer Groß-Berliner Einheitsgemeinde," *Tägliche Rundschau*, 4 August 1919 (LAB A Rep. 001-02 Nr. 642), 32RS; "Zu dem Gesetzentwurf Groß-Berlin," *Deutsche Zeitung*, 6 August 1919 (LAB A Rep. 001-02 Nr. 642), 32RS; ibid.; "Der Gesetzentwurf 'Groß-Berlin,'" *Neuköllner Tageblatt*, 6 August 1919 (LAB A Rep. 001-02 Nr. 642), 32RS; ibid., 34RS.

162 "Der preußische Ausschuß für das Groß-Berliner Gesetz," *Berliner Lokal-Anzeiger*, 4 December 1919 (LAB A Rep. 001-02 Nr. 642), 35VS; "Der Groß-Berliner Ausschuß der Landesversammlung," *Tägliche Rundschau*, 5 December 1919 (LAB A Rep. 001-02 Nr. 642).

163 "Der preußische Ausschuß für das Groß-Berliner Gesetz," 35VS; "Der Groß-Berliner Ausschuß der Landesversammlung." From the Democrats

Geheime Justizrat Cassel of Berlin, Oberbürgermeister Dominicus of Schöneberg, Dr Frentzel of Charlottenburg und Dr Preuß of Berlin from the SPD Bruns and Frank of Berlin, Heimann of Charlottenburg, Lüdemann of Wilmersdorf, Vieth of Niederschönhauen und Wutzky of Neukölln from the USPD Leid of Berlin from the German People's Party Leidig of Wilmersdorf, from the German Nationalists Lüdicke of Spandau and from the Center Party Dr Fassbender of Südende. "Groß-Berlin im Ausschuß: Die Notwendigkeit einer starkeren Dezentralisation," *Berliner Tageblatt*, 5 December 1919 (LAB A Rep. 001-02 Nr. 642), 36VS.

164 Hamburger, "Urschriftlich. Über den 'Gesetzentwurf über die Bildung einer Stadt Groß-Berlin' … 18. Dezember 1919" (LAB A Rep. 001-02 Nr. 645 Bd. 2), 8VS/1–8RS/2.

165 Hirsch and Heine, "Nr. 1286 Entwurf eines Gesetzes über die Bildung eines Stadtkrieses Groß-Berlin. 18. November 1919," 33–4, 36–7.

166 "Erste Beratung des Gesetzentwurfs über die Bildung einer Stadt Groß-Berlin," in *Verfassunggebende Preußische Landesversammlung 88. Sitzung am 2. Dezember 1919* (LAB A Rep. 001-02 Nr. 654), 87RS/6990.

167 "Groß-Berlin in der Landesversammlung," *Vorwärts*, 14 January 1919 (LAB A Rep. 001-02 Nr. 642), 37RS; "Die Einheit Groß-Berlins," *Vorwärts*, 14 January 1919 (LAB A Rep. 001-02 Nr. 642), 37VS.

168 Adolf Wermuth and Magistrat Berlin, "Brief zu die Mitglieder des Ausschusses der Preuß. Landesversammlung für Vorberatung des Gesetzentwurfs über die Bildung der Stadt Groß-Berlin. 23. Januar 1920" (LAB A Rep. 001-02 Nr. 645), 42cVS/1, 43VS/2.

169 "No. 5," in *Amtlicher stenographischer Bericht über die außerordentliche Sitzung der Berliner Stadtverordnetenversammung am 24. Januar 1920* (LAB A Rep. 001-02 Nr. 655), 99–101.

5. Organic Municipal Government, 1920–1933

1 Ernst Kaeber, "The Metropolis as Home," in *Metropolis Berlin*, ed. David Frisby and Iain Boyd Whyte (Berkeley: University of California Press, 2012), 338.

2 Cited as Institut für Marxismus-Leninismus beim ZK der SED, *Dokumente und Materialen zur Geschichte der deutschen Arbeiterbewegung*, vol. 2/2 (East Berlin: Dietz, 1958), 228–43; in Pierre Broué, *The German Revolution, 1917–1923*, ed. and trans. John Archer (Leiden: Brill, 2005), 131.

3 Postone, *Time, Labor, and Social Domination*, 275.

4 Michael L. Hughes, *Paying for the German Inflation* (Chapel Hill: University of North Carolina Press, 1988), 9; Holtfrerich, *German Inflation*, 119–21;

Niall Ferguson, "Constraints and Room for Manoeuvre in the German Inflation of the Early 1920s," *Economic History Review* 49, no. 4 (1996): 639.

5 Gerald D. Feldman, *The Great Disorder* (New York: Oxford University Press, 1993), 6.

6 Ibid.; Ferguson, "Constraints and Room for Manoeuvre in the German Inflation of the Early 1920s," 639.

7 Cited as Franz Eulenburg, "Die sozialen Wirkungen der Währungsverhältnisse," *Jahrbücher für Nationalökonomie und Statistik* 67, no. 6 (1924): 748–94; in Feldman, *Great Disorder*, 6.

8 Feldman, *Great Disorder*, 5.

9 Theo Balderston, "German Banking between the Wars," *Business History Review* 65, no. 3 (1991): 561.

10 Steven Benjamin Webb, "Government Revenue and Spending in Germany, 1919 to 1923," in *The Adaptation to Inflation*, ed. Gerald D. Feldman et al. (Berlin: W. de Gruyter, 1986), 51.

11 Cited as Costantino Bresciani-Turroni, *The Economics of Inflation*, ed. and trans. Millicent E. Sayers (London: G. Allen & Unwin, 1937), 183, 215, 261, 275, 286, 314, 330, 404; in Ferguson, "Constraints and Room for Manoeuvre in the German Inflation of the Early 1920s," 637; Mikael De Gasperi, "Liberalism in the Economic Thought of Costantino Bresciani-Turroni," in *Issues in Economic Thought*, ed. Miguel-Ángel Galindo Martín and Cristina Nardi Spiller, 57–69 (New York: Nova Science Publishers, 2010).

12 Feldman, *Great Disorder*, 224.

13 Postone, "Anti-Semitism and National Socialism," 112.

14 Ibid., 109.

15 Ibid., 108.

16 Ibid., 106.

17 Robert Scholz, "Die Auswirkunen der Inflation auf das Sozial- und Wohlfahrtswesen der neuen Stadtgemeinde Berlin," in *Konsequenzen der Inflation*, ed. Gerald D. Feldman et al. (Berlin: Colloquium Verlag, 1989), 54–7.

18 Sabine Rudischhauser, "Die parlamentarischen Debatten über die Sozialpolitik der neuen Stadtgemeinde Berlin in der ersten Stadtverordnetenversammlung 1920/21," in *Beiträge zur Geschichte der Berliner Demokratie, 1919–1933/1945–1985*, ed. Otto Büsch and Felix Escher (Berlin: Colloquium Verlag, 1988), 48–59.

19 Scholz, "Die Auswirkunen der Inflation auf das Sozial- und Wohlfahrtswesen der neuen Stadtgemeinde Berlin," 72–4.

20 Rudischhauser, "Die parlamentarischen Debatten über die Sozialpolitik der neuen Stadtgemeinde Berlin in der ersten Stadtverordnetenversammlung 1920/21," 48–59.

21 Feldman, *Great Disorder*, 766–7.

22 Hughes, *Paying for the German Inflation*, 9.

23 Harold James, *The Reichsbank and Public Finance in Germany, 1924–1933* (Frankfurt am Main: F. Knapp, 1985), 45–6.

24 William C. McNeil, *American Money and the Weimar Republic* (New York: Columbia University Press, 1986), 1–2.

25 Harold James, *The German Slump* (Oxford: Clarendon, 1986), 95.

26 McNeil, *American Money and the Weimar Republic*, 85; James, *German Slump*, 95; Michael Ruck, "Der Wohnungsbau Schnittpunkt von Sozial- und Wirtschaftspolitik," in *Die Weimarer Republik als Wohlfahrtsstaat*, ed. Werner Abelshauser (Stuttgart: F. Steiner, 1987), 101.

27 McNeil, *American Money and the Weimar Republic*, 5.

28 Feldman, *Great Disorder*, 766–7.

29 Larry Eugene Jones, "In the Shadow of Stabilization," in *Die Nachwirkungen der Inflation auf die deutsche Geschichte, 1924–1933*, ed. Gerald D. Feldman and Elisabeth Müller-Luckner, 21–41 (Munich: R. Oldenbourg, 1985); Thomas Childers, "Interest and Ideology," In *Die Nachwirkungen der Inflation auf die deutsche Geschichte, 1924–1933*, ed. Gerald D. Feldman and Elisabeth Müller-Luckner (Munich: R. Oldenbourg, 1985), 28.

30 Krause, "Der Westhafen von Berlin," 411.

31 Ibid., 427–9.

32 v. Stein, Zisseler, and Deutschen Wohnungsausschusses, "Brief zu den Verfassunggebende Deutsche Nationalversammlung. Eingabe des Deutschen Wohnungsausschusses. 27. April 1920" (GStA PK I. HA Rep. 151 IC Nr. 12418.1), 2VS–4VS.

33 McNeil, *American Money and the Weimar Republic*, 85.

34 "Die wirtschaftliche Tätigkeit der Gemeinden," *Zeitschrift für Kommunalwirtschaft* 20, no. 2 (25 January 1930): 104, 106.

35 McNeil, *American Money and the Weimar Republic*, 85.

36 Wutzky, "Bericht über den Stand des Wohnungs- und Siedlungswesens in der Stadt Berlin im Jahre 1924: Zu dem Erlass des Herrn Oberpräsident der Provinz Brandenburg und von Berlin vom 17. Dezember 1921" (LAB A Rep. 001-02 Nr. 82 Bd. 2), 17RS/1.

37 Ibid., 18VS/2.

38 Ibid., 18RS/3–19VS/4.

39 Georg Weigle et al., "Geschäftsbericht der Deutschen Bau- und Bodenbank Aktiengesellschaft (früher: Deutsche Wohnstätten-Bank A.G.) und der

Deutschen Wohnstätten-Hypothekenbank Aktiengesellschaft über das Geschäftsjahr 1926," (Berlin 1927) (GStA PK I. HA Rep. 120 A XV Nr. 339).

40 Roman Heiligenthal, "Probleme des Generalsiedlungsplans," in *Probleme der Neuen Stadt Berlin*, ed. Hans Bennert and Erwin Stein (Berlin-Friednau: Deutscher Kommunal-Verlag GmbH, 1926), 256.

41 Finanzminister, "Brief zu den Herrn Minister für Volkswohlfahrt. 23. Dezember 1925" (GStA PK I. HA Rep. 151 IC Nr. 12256).

42 Ritter, Karl Lothholz, and Schäffer, "Verordnung über die Verwendung des Kredits zur Förderung des Kleinwohnungsbaues. 9. April 1926," *Reichsministerialblatt* 54, no. 14 (1926) (GStA PK I. HA Rep. 120 A XV Nr. 180 Bd. 1): 109–10. On 18 March 1926 the Centralverband des Deutschen Bank- und Bankiergewerbes (EV) declared themselves "unanimously willing to finance the proposed construction program in energetic ways." Centralverband des Deutschen Bank- und Bankiergewerbes (E.V.), "Betrifft: Förderung des Kleinwohnungsbaues durch die Hypothekenbanken" (GStA PK I. HA Rep. 120 A XV MHG Nr. 180), 23/1–23/2.

43 "Richtlinien für die Verwendung des für die Neubautätigkeit bestimmten Anteils am Hauszinssteueraufkommen" (GStA PK I. HA Rep. 151 IC Nr. 12256).

44 Glaß and Heinrich Brauns, "Bedingungen für die Gewährung von Tilgungshypotheken und Baugeld (Zwischenkredit) aus dem Wohnungsfürsorgefonds des Reichsarbeitsministeriums" (GStA PK I. HA Rep. 151 IC Nr. 12255), 1.

45 Herrmann, "An die Finanzabteilung. 17. Februar 1925" (GStA PK I. HA Rep. 151 IC Nr. 12255), 1–2, 5.

46 Wutzky, "Bericht über den Stand des Wohnungs- und Siedlungswesens in der Stadt Berlin im Jahre 1924," 27RS/21.

47 Weigle et al., "Geschäftsbericht der Deutschen Bau- und Bodenbank Aktiengesellschaft (früher: Deutsche Wohnstätten-Bank A. G.) und der Deutschen Wohnstätten-Hypothekenbank Aktiengesellschaft über das Geschäftsjahr 1926."

48 Reichsverband der Wohnungsfürsorgegesellschaften and Bruno Schwan, "Leitsätze für die zukünftige Gestaltung des Wohnungsbaues" (GStA PK I. HA Rep. 151 IC Nr. 12254), 31VS/1.

49 Arbeitsgemeinschaft gemein. Siedlungsgesellschaften, "Brief zu den Herrn Preußischen Minister für Volkswohlfahrt. 17. Februar 1925" (GStA PK I. HA Rep. 151 IC Nr. 12255), 1; "Aus Nr. 3 der Zeitschrift für Wohnungswesen: Bezirksverband Berlin-Brandenburg des

Reichsverbandes Deutscher Baugenossenschaften" (GStA PK I. HA Rep. 151 IC Nr. 12255).

50 Gustav Böß, Paul Mitzlaff, and Vorstand der Deutscher Städtetag, "An den Herrn Reichsarbeitsminister, u. A. 24. November 1924" (GStA PK I. HA Rep. 151 IC Nr. 12255), 1, 3; Reichsverband der Wohnungsfürsorgegesellschaften and Schwan, "Leitsätze für die zukünftige Gestaltung des Wohnungsbaues," 31VS/1; Deutsche Bau- und Bodenbank A.-G., "Geschäftsbericht über das Geschäftsjahr 1928" (Berlin 1929) (GStA PK I. HA Rep. 120 A XV MHG Nr. 337 Bd. 2), 8.

51 Reichsverband der Wohnungsfürsorgegesellschaften and Schwan, "Leitsätze für die zukünftige Gestaltung des Wohnungsbaues," 31VS/1, 33VS/3–34VS/4; Bruno Schwan and Reichsverband der Wohnungsfürsorgegesellschaften, "Niederschrift über die Mitgliederversammlung des Reichsverbandes am 8. 1. [1924] vorm. 11 Uhr" (GStA PK I. HA Rep. 151 IC Nr. 12254), 31VS/1–40VS/6.

52 Böß, Mitzlaff, and Städtetag, "An den Herrn Reichsarbeitsminister, u. A. 24. November 1924," 1, 3. Paul Mitzlaff and Vorstand der Preußischer Städtetag, "Brief zu den Preußischen Minister für Volkswohlfahrt, den Preußischen Herrn Finanzminister. 22. November 1924" (GStA PK I. HA Rep. 151 IC Nr. 12255). Two days later, the head of the Preußische Landkreistag concurred. Constantin and Der Preußische Landkreistag, "Brief zu den Herrn Minister für Volkswohlfahrt in Berlin. 24. November 1924" (GStA PK I. HA Rep. 151 IC Nr. 12255), 1.

53 Deutscher Städtetag, "Tagung des Hauptausschusses des Deutschen Städtetages am 6. und 7. Februar 1925 in Berlin" (GStA PK I. HA Rep. 151 IC Nr. 12255).

54 Elkart, "Vorschlage zur Umgestaltung der Wohnungswirtschaft: Vortrag im B.D.A. gehalten," *Zeitschrift für Bauwesen* 74, no. 1/3 (Hochbauabteilung) (1924): 18. Wagner argued that the command housing economy had not resolved conflicts between the renter and the landlord. Martin Wagner, *Neue Wege zum Kleinwohnungsbau: ein Programm der Selbsthilfe* (Berlin: Vorwärts-Buchdruckerei, 1924), 7.

55 Ahrends et al., "Richtlinien für die von Preußen zur Förderung des Wohnungsbaus nach der dritten Steuernotverordnung zu erlassenden Ausführungsbestimmungen" (GStA PK I. HA Rep. 151 IC Nr. 12254 Bd. 1), 20VS/1; Hermann Althoff, "Begründung der Richtlinien für die von Preußen zur Förderung des Wohnungsbaus nach der dritten Steuernot Verordnung zu erlassenden Ausführungsbestimmungen" (GStA PK I. HA Rep. 151 IC Nr. 12254), 20VS/1–20RS/2; Schwartz and Centralverband des Deutschen Bank- und Bankiergewerbes: Sonderausschuss für

Hypothekenbankwesen, "An den Reichskanzler Herrn Dr. Luther. 9. März 1926" (GStA PK I. HA Rep. 120 A XV MHG Nr. 180), 24/1.

56 Franz von Mendelssohn and Die Industrie- und Handelskammer zu Berlin, "Brief zu den Herrn Preußischen Minister für Handel und Gewerbe Berlin. 10 Dezember 1925" (GStA PK I. HA Rep. 151 IC Nr. 12257), 1–2, 5.

57 Wutzky, "Bericht über den Stand des Wohnungs- und Siedlungswesens in der Stadt Berlin im Jahre 1924: Zu dem Erlass des Herrn Oberpräsident der Provinz Brandenburg und von Berlin vom 17. Dezember 1921," 21RS/9–22VS/10, 27VS/20.

58 Arbeitsgemeinschaft gemein. Siedlungsgesellschaften, "Brief zu den Herrn Preußischen Minister für Volkswohlfahrt. 17. Februar 1925," 1; "Aus Nr. 3 der Zeitschrift für Wohnungswesen: Bezirksverband Berlin-Brandenburg des Reichsverbandes Deutscher Baugenossenschaften."

59 Peter Scott, "Marketing Mass Home Ownership and the Creation of the Modern Working-Class Consumer in Inter-War Britain," *Business History* 50, no. 1 (2008): 5; Lewinnek, "Better than a Bank for a Poor Man?" 278.

60 Weigle et al., "Geschäftsbericht der Deutschen Bau- und Bodenbank Aktiengesellschaft (früher: Deutsche Wohnstätten-Bank A. G.) und der Deutschen Wohnstätten-Hypothekenbank Aktiengesellschaft über das Geschäftsjahr 1926."

61 Ibid., 9; Der Preußische Miniser für Volkswohlfahrt, "Brief zu den sämtliche Herren Oberpräsidenten und Regierungspräsidenten, den Herrn Verbandspräsidenten in Essen und den Herrn Polizeipräsidenten ... 7. Mai 1926" (GStA PK I. HA Rep. 120 A XV MHG Nr. 181), 73VS/1.

62 Deutsche Bau- und Bodenbank A.-G., "1923–1929" (Berlin1929) (GStA PK I. HA Rep. 120 A XV MHG Nr. 337), vi.

63 Ibid., xvii.

64 "Konferenzbericht: Auf Einladung des Preußischen Ministeriums für Volkswohlfahrt hatten sich zur Besprechung der Frage, ob und inwieweit die Hyopthekenaktienbanken bie der Durchführung des Wohnbauprogramms für 1926 zur Mitarbeit bereit sind eingefunden. 9. März 1926" (GStA PK I. HA Rep. 120 A XV MHG Nr. 180), 12/1–2.

65 Ibid.

66 Herrmann, "An die Finanzabteilung. 17. Februar 1925," 1–2, 5.

67 "Konferenzbericht: Auf Einladung des Preußischen Ministeriums für Volkswohlfahrt hatten sich zur Besprechung der Frage.

68 "An die Finanzabteilung. 17. Februar 1925," 1–2, 5; von Mendelssohn and Die Industrie- und Handelskammer zu Berlin, "Brief zu den Herrn Preußischen Minister für Handel und Gewerbe Berlin. 10 Dezember 1925," 1–2, 5.

69 Ritter, Fischer, and Curtius, "Nr. 38. Entwurf eines Gesetzes der die Bereitstellung von Kredit zur Förderung des Kleinwohnunbsbaues," in *Reichsrat. Tagung 1926. 15 März 1926* (GStA PK I. HA Rep. 120 A XV MHG Nr. 180).

70 Emil Wutztky, "Städtebau, Siedlung, Wohnung," in *Probleme der Neuen Stadt Berlin*, ed. Hans Bennert and Erwin Stein (Berlin-Friednau: Deutscher Kommunal-Verlag GmbH, 1926), 241.

71 Weigle et al., "Geschäftsbericht der Deutschen Bau- und Bodenbank Aktiengesellschaft (früher: Deutsche Wohnstätten-Bank A. G.) und der Deutschen Wohnstätten-Hypothekenbank Aktiengesellschaft über das Geschäftsjahr 1926," 9.

72 Preußische Landespfandbriefanstalt – Körperschaft des öffentlichen Rechts, "Breif den Herrn Preußischen Minister für Volkswohlfahrt. 21. Mai 1927" (GStA PK I. HA Rep. 120 A XV MHG Nr. 279), 3VS–RS.

73 Zohl, Ohlmer, and Deutschen Bau- und Bodenbank Aktiengesellschaft, "Brief zu den Herrn Reichsarbietsminister. 3. Juni 1927" (GStA PK I. HA Rep. 120 A XV MHG Nr. 278), 1VS–2RS; "Brief zu die Beratungsstelle für Auslandskredite. 10. Juni 1927" (GStA PK I. HA Rep. 120 A XV MHG Nr. 278), 1VS–2RS.

74 Dr Meyer, Vormbaum, and Preußische Landespfandbriefanstalt, "Brief zu den Herrn Preußischen Finanzminister und den Herrn Minister für Volkswohlfahrt. 30. August 1927" (GStA PK I. HA Rep. 151 IC Nr. 12228), 1–3.

75 Ibid., 4–5.

76 Backhaus, "Wohnungswesen," *Zentralblatt der Bauverwaltung* 48, no. 17 (25 April 1928): 280.

77 Deutsche Wohnstätten-Hypothekenbank A.-G., "Geschäftsbericht über das Geschäftsjahr 1928" (Berlin1929) (GStA PK I. HA Rep. 120 A XV MHG Nr. 341), 5.

78 Deutsche Bau- und Bodenbank A.-G., "Geschäftsbericht über das Geschäftsjahr 1928," 7.

79 Ibid., 8.

80 "Das Zwischenkreditgeschäft der Bau- und Bodenbank," *Magazin der Wirtschaft*, 5, no. 19 (7 March 1929): 334 (GStA PK I. HA Rep. 120 A XV Nr. 184).

81 Rudolf Wissell, "Entwurf eines Gesetzes über die Bereitstellung von Kredit zur Förderung des Kleinwohnungsbaues (Baukreditgesetz 1929)," in *Nr. 15 Reichsrat Tagung 1929* (GStA PK I. HA Rep. 120 A XV MHG Nr. 184), 2; Michael Schneider, "Rudolf Wissell (1869–1962)," *Vierteljahresschrift für Sozialrecht* 6, no. 1/2 (1978): 176–181.

82 Der Preußische Minister für Volkswohlfahrt, "Brief zu samtliche Herren Regierungspräsidenten, u. A. 19. Februar 1929" (GStA PK I. HA Rep. 151 IC Nr. 12264), 12VS.
83 Deutsche Wohnstätten-Hypothekenbank A.-G. and Preussische Landespfandbriefanstalt, "Brief zu den Herrn Reichsarbeitsminister. 24. Februar 1930" (GStA PK I. HA Rep. 120 A XV MHG Nr. 183 Bd. 4), 2VS; Meyer, "Brief zu den Preußisches Ministerium für Volkswohlfahrt Herrn Ministerialrat Kayser. 25. Februar 1930" (GStA PK I. HA Rep. 120 A XV MHG Nr. 183 Bd. 4), 3VS/1.
84 Sigrist, *Das Buch vom Bauen*, 155–6.
85 Ibid.
86 Adolf Maier, "Brief zu den Herrn Minister für Volkswohlfahrt. 8. September 1923" (GStA PK I. HA Rep. 191 Nr. 102), 222VS/1; Der Oberpräsident der Provinz Brandenburg und von Berlin, "Brief zu den Herrn Minister für Volkswohlfahrt. 8. September 1923" (GStA PK I. HA Rep. 191 Nr. 85).
87 Der Bund Deutscher Architekten – Hauptverwaltung, "Brief zu den Minister für Volkswohlfahrt. 11. August 1923" (GStA PK I. HA Rep. 191 Nr. 102), 281.
88 Cornelius Gurlitt and Freie Deutsche Akademie des Städtebaues, "Gutachten über die Grundzüge für die Aufstellung eines Gesetzes zur Aufstellung und Durchführung von Siedlungs- u. Bebauungspläne (Fluchtliniensplâne). 8. Oktober 1923" (GStA PK I. HA Rep. 191 Nr. 102), 290VS. "Bemerkungen zu den Grundzügen für die Aufstellung eines Gesetzes zur Aufstellung und Durchführung von Siediungs- und Bebauungsplänen (Fluchtlinienpläne)" (GStA PK I. HA Rep. 191 Nr. 85), 292VS/1–295RS/8.
89 Robert L. Nelson, "From Manitoba to the Memel," *Social History* 35, no. 4 (2010): 439–40.
90 Max Stolt and Gesellschaft zur Förderung der inneren Kolonisation, "Brief zu den Reichsarbeitsminister. 21. April 1920" (GStA PK I. HA Rep. 151 IC Nr. 12418.1), 1VS–2VS.
91 David T. Murphy, "'A Sum of the Most Wonderful Things,'" *History of European Ideas* 25, no. 3 (1999): 122.
92 Bernhard Dietz, "Countryside-versus-City in European Thought," *European Legacy* 13, no. 7 (2008): 803.
93 Zeithen and John, "Land Settlement the City of Berlin-Lichtenberg in Mahlsdorf in Berlin" (LAB A Rep. 251-06 Nr. 2), 1; Ellen L. Evans, "Adam Stegerwald and the Role of the Christian Trade Unions in the Weimar Republic," *Catholic Historical Review* 59, no. 4 (1974): 609–10.

94 Max Klesse, "Mehr sozialistische Bevölkerungspolitik!," *Sozialistische Monatshefte* 34, no. 4 (4 April 1928): 314.
95 Gustav Langen, "Die Besiedlungen des Vorlandes von Berlin," *Zentralblatt der Bauverwaltung* 51, no. 53/54 (23 December 1931): 779.
96 Martin Pfannschmidt and Alexander Schwab, "Städtebaufragen," *Zentralblatt der Bauverwaltung* 51, no. 26 (24 June 1931): 393.
97 Bernard Marchand and Joëlle Salomon Cavin, "Anti-Urban Ideologies and Planning in France and Switzerland," *Planning Perspectives* 22, no. 1 (2007): 33–4, 40–5.
98 Philipp August Rappaport, "'Statistische Beziehung zwischen Mensch und Fläche,'" *Städtebau-Baupolitik* 5, no. 9 (1931): 432.
99 Marco Giorgio Bevilacqua, "Alexander Klein and the *Existenzminimum*," *Nexus Network Journal* 13, no. 2 (2011): 297–8.
100 Alexander Klein, "Wirtschaftliche Grundrissbildung und Raumgestaltung," *Wasmuths Monatshefte für Baukunst* 15, no. 11/12 (1931): 539–41.
101 Roman Heiligenthal, "Deutsche Bauausstellung Berlin 1931," *Zentralblatt der Bauverwaltung* 51, no. 48 (19 November 1931): 697.
102 Ernst Runge, "Grundsätzliches zum Problem der Erweiterung Gross-Berlins (Eine städtebauliche, kommunal- und finanzpolitische Studie)" (Dissertation zur Erlangung der Würde eines Doktor-Ingenieurs der Technischen Hochschule zu Berlin, Technischen Hochschule zu Berlin, 1930), 7.
103 Langen, "Die Besiedlungen des Vorlandes von Berlin," 780.
104 Ibid., 781.
105 Jörg Thierfelder, "Fritz Elsas," in *Zeugen des Widerstands*, ed. Joachim Mehlhausen, 91–110 (Tübingen: Mohr Siebeck, 1998).
106 Fritz Elsas, "Das Wirtschaftsleben der Großstädte," *Magazin der Wirtschaft* 6, no. 24 (13 June 1930): 1123.
107 Pfannschmidt and Schwab, "Städtebaufragen," 393.
108 Peter Scott, "The State, Internal Migration, and the Growth of New Industrial Communities in Inter-War Britain," *English Historical Review* 115, no. 461 (2000): 329, 333.
109 Stovall, "French Communism and Suburban Development," 441.
110 Leberecht Migge, "Weltstadt-Grün," *Städtebau* 25, no. 5 (1930): 241.
111 Theodor Nußbaum, "Weltstadtgrün," *Städtebau* 26, no. 1 (1931): 41–2.
112 Eve Rosenhaft, *Beating the Fascists? The German Communists and Political Violence, 1929–1933* (Cambridge: Cambridge University Press, 1983), 16; Homann and Scarpa, "Martin Wagner, the Trades Union Movement and Housing Construction," 61.
113 Sigrist, *Das Buch vom Bauen*, 174.

114 Ibid., 175.
115 Ibid., 178, 180.
116 Ibid., 103–4.
117 Ibid., 107–9.
118 Leberecht Migge, "Kommunale Siedlung als Mittel zur Wiederherstellung Selbstverwaltung," *Zeitschrift für Kommunalwirtschaft und Kommunalpolitik* 11, no. 9 (1921): 346–7.
119 Abroteles Eleutheropulos, "Gesellschaft und Staat," *Zeitschrift für die gesamte Staatswissenschaft* 76, no. 1 (1922): 169. See also Gerhard Kessler, "Staat und Gesellschaft," *Zeitschrift für gesamte Staatswissenschaft* 82, no. 2 (1927): 225–34.
120 Eleutheropulos, "Gesellschaft und Staat," 171.
121 Kurt Wolzendorf, "Der reine Staat," *Zeitschrift für gesamte Staatswissenschaft* 75, no. 1/2 (1921): 199.
122 Ibid., 200, 209, 226–8.
123 Ibid., 202.
124 Neumann, "Change in the Function of Law in Modern Society," 62.
125 Cited as R. Dietz, *Gesetz für Ordnung der nationalen Arbeit*, 4th ed. (Munich, 1936); in ibid., 62–3. Neumann notes that while this concept was institutionalized during the National Socialist period, it already existed in the Weimar Republic and derives from Gierke's jurisprudence.
126 Otto Kirchheimer, "Decree Powers and Constitutional Law in France under the Third Republic," *American Political Science Review* 34, no. 6 (1940): 1104–7.
127 Josef Eimermann, "Sparsamkeit im Personaletat," *Kommunale Praxis*, 5 March 1921, 197.
128 Magistrat Deputation für das Ernährungswesen, "Brief zu den Magistrat (Generalbüro). 27. Oktober 1921" (LAB A Rep. 001-02 Nr. 646 Bd. 1), 16VS/1.
129 Der Minister für Volkswohlfahrt, "An die Herren Regierungspräsidenten, den Herrn Polizeipräsidenten in Berlin und den Herrn Verbandspräsidenten des Siedlungsverbandes Ruhrkohlenbezirke in Essen. 11 Februar 1921" (GStA PK I. HA Rep. 191 Nr. 44 Bd. 6), 172VS.
130 Martin Wagner, "American versus German City Planning," *Journal of Land Use & Public Utility Economics* 22, no. 4 (1946): 329. For similar sentiments, see also Emil Lang, "Was ist Stadtbaukunst?," *Stadtbaukunst*, no. 1 (1 April 1921): 6.
131 Heiligenthal believed that the first task of statistical analysis is to "gain a picture of population growth by comparing the census results." Roman Friedrich Heiligenthal, "Die Statistik im Dienste der Stadterweiterung" (Vereinigten Friedrichs-Universität Halle Wittenberg, 1921), 5.

132 Heiligenthal, "Probleme des Generalsiedlungsplans," 256.

133 Ursula von Petz, "The Environmental Transformation of the Ruhr," in *City, Country Empire*, ed. Dorsey Kurkpatrick and Jeffry M. Diefendorf (Pittsburgh: University of Pittsburgh Press, 2005), 52–64.

134 Wagner, "American versus German City Planning," 132.

135 Andreas Splanemann, "Bewährung und Begrenzung der Berliner Demokratie," in *Beiträge zur Geschichte der Berliner Demokratie, 1919–1933/1945–1985*, ed. Otto Büsch (Berlin: Colloquium Verlag, 1988), 4.

136 Ibid., 9.

137 Gustav Böß, "Interkommunalen Ausschußes über die Vorbereitungen zur Bildung von Groß-Berlin. 26. Mai 1920" (LAB A Rep. 001-02 Nr. 656), 2VS/1–6VS/5.

138 "Brief zu den Herrn Oberpräsident von Berlin. 1. März 1923" (LAB E Rep. 200-24 Böß Nr. 19), 48VS/3.

139 "Brief zu den Preußischen Landtag (16) Ausschuss" (LAB E Rep. 200-24 Nr. 19), 1RS/2–2VS/3.

140 Gustav Böß, Lange, and Herrmann, "Bericht über die 2. Sitzung der Magistratskommission zur Vorberatung des Entwurfs eines Abänderungsgesetzes zum Gesetz Groß-Berlin. 4. Mai 1922" (LAB E Rep. 200-24 Böß Nr. 19), 22VS/5.

141 Gustav Böß, Lange, and Herrmann, "Bericht über die 1. Sitzung der Magistratskommission zur Vorberatung des Entwurfs eines Abänderungs-Gesetzes zum Gesetz Groß-Berlin. 25. April 1922" (LAB E Rep. 200-24 Böß Nr. 19), 20VS/1–20RS/2.

142 Böß, Lange, and Herrmann, "Bericht über die 2. Sitzung der Magistratskommission zur Vorberatung des Entwurfs eines Abänderungsgesetzes zum Gesetz Groß-Berlin. 4. Mai 1922.," 22RS/6.

143 D. Gordan, "Mit anliegendem Schreiben an die Städtischen Gaswerke gemäß dem Beschluß der gemischten Deputation. 27. Mai 1920" (LAB A Rep. 001-02 Nr. 657), 1VS/1–1RS/2.

144 Böß, Lange, and Herrmann, "Bericht über die 1. Sitzung der Magistratskommission zur Vorberatung des Entwurfs eines Abänderungs-Gesetzes zum Gesetz Groß-Berlin. 25. April 1922," 20VS/1–20RS/2.

145 Gustav Böß, "Zum Ausgemeindung Spandaus aus Berlin. 7. XI. [1923]" (LAB E Rep. 200-24 Böß Nr. 19), 63RS/2–64RS/4.

146 Ibid., 64VS/3–64RS/4.

147 Ibid., 65VS/5–66VS/7.

148 Böß, "Brief zu den Herrn Oberpräsident von Berlin. 1. März 1923," 47RS/2.

149 Gustav Böß, "Brief zu den Herrn Oberpräsidenten von Berlin. 19. Mai 1922" (LAB E Rep. 200-24 Böß Nr. 19), 30VS/9, 35VS/19, 36RS/22; Böß, "Brief zu den Herrn Oberpräsident von Berlin. 1. März 1923," 48VS/3.

150 Rudischhauser, "Die parlamentarischen Debatten über die Sozialpolitik der neuen Stadtgemeinde Berlin," 70–83.

151 Rosenhaft, *Beating the Fascists?*, 9.

152 Dietz, "Countryside-versus-City in European Thought," 801–2.

153 Timothy Scott Brown, "The SA in the Radical Imagination of the Long Weimar Republic," *Central European History* 46, no. 2 (2013): 240–1; Anders G. Kjøstvedt, "The Dynamics of Mobilisation," *Politics, Religion & Ideology* 14, no. 3 (2013): 338–54.

154 Alexander Wilde, "Republikfeindschaft in der Berliner Bevölkerung und der Wandel der kommunal Selbstverwaltung um 1931," in *Beiträge zur Geschichte der Berliner Demokratie, 1919–1933/1945–1985*, ed. Otto Büsch and Felix Escher (Berlin: Colloquium Verlag, 1988), 112–13.

155 Stephan Malinowski, "Politische Skandale als Zerrspiegel der Demokratie," *Jahrbuch für Antisemitismusforschung* 5 (1996): 48–9.

156 Ibid., 56–9.

157 Harold James, "Municipal Finance in the Weimar Republic," in *The State and Social Change in Germany, 1880–1980*, ed. W. Robert Lee and Eve Rosenhaft (New York: Berg, 1990), 235–6.

158 Malinowski, "Politische Skandale als Zerrspiegel der Demokratie," 56–9.

159 Christian Goeschel, "The Criminal Underworld in Weimar and Nazi Berlin," *History Workshop Journal* 75, no. 1 (2013): 61–2. For more on the perception of criminals and criminality, see Daniel Siemens, "Explaining Crime Berlin Newspapers and the Construction of the Criminal in Weimar Germany," *Journal of European Studies* 39, no. 3 (2009): 336–52.

160 Elsas, "Das Wirtschaftsleben der Großstädte," 1123.

161 Hermann Kranold, "Die Selbstverwaltung im Staatswesen," *Sozialistische Monatshefte* 38, no. 11 (1932): 917–18, 923.

162 Runge, "Grundsätzliches zum Problem der Erweiterung Gross-Berlins," 13, 8.

163 [Theodor] von Pistorius, "Reichs-, Staats- und Gemeindefinanzen," *Zeitschrift für die gesamte Staatswissenschaft* 88, no. 3 (1930): 545.

164 Kranold, "Die Selbstverwaltung im Staatswesen," 922.

165 James, "Municipal Finance in the Weimar Republic," 236–7.

166 Kranold, "Die Selbstverwaltung im Staatswesen," 922.

167 James, "Municipal Finance in the Weimar Republic," 235–6.

168 Carl Schmitt, *Hugo Preuß* (Tübingen: Mohr, 1930), 5.

169 Ibid., 6.

170 Neumann, "Change in the Function of Law in Modern Society," 62.
171 Schmitt, *Hugo Preuß*, 9.
172 Ibid., 10–12.

6. The Organic Machine

1 Martin Mächler, "Die Grossstadt und der Städtebau," *Sozialistische Monatshefte* 28, no. 9 (1922): 408.
2 Sonne, *Representing the State*, 123.
3 Molly Loberg, "The Streetscape of Economic Crisis," *Journal of Modern History* 85, no. 2 (2013): 367.
4 Paul Ashton, "'This Villa Life,'" *Planning Perspectives* 25, no. 4 (2010): 457–83.
5 Vera F. Rezende, "Brazilian City Planners, American City Planning? New Perspectives on Urban Planning in Rio De Janeiro, 1930–1945," *Planning Perspectives* 25, no. 4 (2010): 505, 509.
6 Mauro F. Guillén, "Modernism without Modernity," *Latin American Research Review* 39, no. 2 (2004): 27.
7 Chris Godden, "Observers, Commentators, and Persuaders: British Interwar Economists as Public Intellectuals," *History of Political Economy* 45, no. 1 (2013): 42.
8 Manfredo Tafuri, "Sozialpolitik and the City in Weimar Germany," in *The Sphere and the Labyrinth* (Cambridge, MA: MIT Press, 1987), 203.
9 Feldman, *Great Disorder*, 239–40.
10 David Abraham, *The Collapse of the Weimar Republic* (New York: Holmes & Meier, 1986), 30.
11 Ruck, "Der Wohnungsbau," 94.
12 Michael Drupp, "Gemeinnützige Bauvereine im Wohnungswesen der Weimarer Republik," In *Die Weimarer Republik als Wohlfahrtsstaat*, ed. Werner Abelshauser (Stuttgart: F. Steiner, 1987), 124–6.
13 Scott, "Marketing Mass Home Ownership," 5–6; Leon Bettendorf and Erik Buyst, "Rent Control and Virtual Prices," *Journal of Economic History* 57, no. 3 (1997): 658.
14 Jill Lewis, "Red Vienna," *European History Quarterly* 13, no. 3 (1983): 339–40.
15 Wagner, "Wohnungswirtschaft-Finanzwirtschaft," 266.
16 Wisso Weiß, "Die Sozialisierung des Wohnungswesens unter besonderer Berücksichtigung der Verhältnisse in Deutschland und Oesterreich" (Ruprecht-Karls-Universität zu Heidelberg, 1930), 11.
17 Ibid., 13.
18 Robert Sachs, "Öffentliche Bodenpolitik gegen private Bodenspekulation," *Die Arbeit* 7, no. 5 (1930): 306.

19 Weiß, "Die Sozialisierung des Wohnungswesens," 38–9.
20 Ibid., 40.
21 Lotte Abrahamsohn, "Der öffentliche Einfluss auf den Berliner Wohungsbau" (Hamburg: Hamburgischen Universität, 1933), 5–6.
22 Wohnungsverband Groß Berlin, "An den Herrn Ministerpräsidenten Braun. 13. April 1920" (GStA PK I. HA Rep. 151 IC Nr. 12418.1). Valentiner, "Sitzung der Preußischen Staatsregierung (Staatsministerium) 20. April 1920" (GStA PK I. HA Rep. 151 IC Nr. 12418.1).
23 Vorst. Heimann, "Antrag der Stadtv. Dr. Weyl und Genossen – Vorlage 392," in *Auszug aus dem amtlichen stenographischen Bericht über die Sitzung der Stadtverordneten-Versammlung am 28. April 1920* (LAB A Rep. 000-02-01 Nr. 2378); Wermuth and Magistrat, "Nr.787 Vorlage," in *Auszug aus dem Sitzungs-Protokolle der Stadtverordenten-Versammlung. Verhandelt Berlin, den 19ten Oktober 1920 in der Sitzung der Stadtverordneten-Versammlung* (LAB A Rep. 000-02-01 Nr. 2378); "Nr. 787," in *Auszug aus dem Sitzungs-Protokolle der Stadtverordenten-Versammlung. Verhandelt Berlin, den 19ten Oktober 1920 in der Sitzung der Stadtverordneten-Versammlung* (LAB A Rep. 000-02-01 Nr. 1863), 16VS.
24 Stein, Zisseler, and Wohnungsausschusses, "Brief zu den Verfassunggebende Deutsche Nationalversammlung. Eingabe des Deutschen Wohnungsausschusses. 27. April 1920," 1VS.
25 Ibid., 5VS.
26 Joseph Stübben, "Wohnungsnot, Mietsteuer und freie Wirtschaft" (GStA PK I. HA Rep. 151 IC Nr. 12418.1).
27 Peter Marcuse, "The Housing Policy of Social Democracy," in *The Austrian Socialist Experiment*, ed. Anson Rabinbach (Boulder, CO: Westview, 1985), 202–3.
28 Gustav Brumby, *Groß-Berliner Wohnungsnotrecht* (Berlin: Franz Vahlen, 1921), 5–7, 9.
29 Der Vorstand das Bund Deutscher Architekten Landesbezirk Brandenburg, "Brief zu den Preußische Finanz-Ministerium. 30. November 1923" (GStA PK I. HA Rep. 151 IC Nr. 12254), 70VS/1.
30 Martina Sönnichsen, "Leistungsverwaltung in der ersten Berliner Demokratie Stadtplanung, Siedlungswesen und Wohnungsbau der Reichhauptstadt in der Amtzeit Martin Wagners 1926–1930," in *Beiträge zur Geschichte der Berliner Demokratie, 1919–1933/1945–1985*, ed. Otto Büsch and Felix Escher (Berlin: Colloquium Verlag, 1988), 85–106.
31 William T. Ham, "The German Building Guilds," *Quarterly Journal of Economics* 43, no. 2 (February 1929): 283–90.

32 Annemarie Jaeffi, "Hufeisensiedlung Britz," in *Vier Berliner Siedlungen der Weimarer Republik*, ed. Norbert Huse (Berlin: Argon, 1987), 124; Ludovica Scarpa, "Das Großsiedlungs-Modell," in *Vier Berliner Siedlungen der Weimarer Republik*, ed. Norbert Huse (Berlin: Argon, 1987), 21; Ham, "German Building Guilds," 283–90.

33 Sönnichsen, "Bewährung und Begrenzung der Berliner Demokratie," 85–106.

34 Ham, "German Building Guilds," 279.

35 Deutsche Bau- und Bodenbank A.-G., "Die Entwicklung der Deutschen Bauwirtschaft im zweiten Halbjahr 1929" (Berlin1930) (GStA PK I. HA Rep. 120 A XV MHG Nr. 337), 3.

36 Ibid., 4.

37 Ibid., 6.

38 Ibid., 12–13.

39 Ibid., 14–17, 20.

40 Kurt Bloch, "Die Wohnungsnot und ihre Bekämpfung," *Die Arbeit*, no. 1 (1928): 21.

41 Ibid., 22.

42 James, "Municipal Finance in the Weimar Republic."

43 Ludwig Hilberseimer, "Berlin und seine Bauprobleme," *Sozialistische Monatshefte* 34, no. 12 (17 December 1928): 1074; von Saldern, "Social Rationalization of Living and Housework," 77.

44 Hilberseimer, "Berlin und seine Bauprobleme," 1075.

45 Marcuse, "Housing Policy of Social Democracy," 213.

46 Ibid., 214.

47 Ferdinand Falk, "Verewigte Wohnungsnot," *Die Arbeit*, no. 8 (1931): 606–8.

48 Abrahamsohn, "Der öffentliche Einfluss auf den Berliner Wohungsbau," 8.

49 Ibid., 14.

50 H. Krüger, "Siedlungsfragen," *Die Arbeit* 9, no. 11 (1932): 674.

51 Das Preußische Staatsministerium, Otto Braun, and Heinrich Hirtsiefer, "Nr. 209. Entwurf eines Städtebaugesetzes. 11. Juni 1926," in *Preußischer Staatsrat 1926* (GStA PK I. HA Rep. 191 Nr. 67), 123RS/39.

52 Patricia L. Garside, "'Unhealthy Areas,'" *Planning Perspectives* 3, no. 1 (1988): 24–5, 30.

53 Deutscher Bund Heimatschutz et al., "Brief zu den Herrn Minister für Volkswohlfahrt. 1. November 1925" (GStA PK I. HA Rep. 191 Nr. 95), 200VS/1.

54 Carl Johannes Fuchs, "Brief zu den Herrn Minister für Volkswohlfahrt. 1. November 1925" (GStA PK I. HA Rep. 191 Nr. 95), 204VS/1.

55 Ibid., 205VS/3.

56 Karl von Mangoldt and Siedlungswissenschaftliche Arbeitsgemeinschaft, "Brief zu den Herrn Minister für Volkswohlfahrt. November 1925" (GStA PK I. HA Rep. 191 Nr. 95), 155VS/3–155RS/4, 156RS/6.

57 Otto Albrecht, "Deutsche Kleingartenpolitik " *Die Arbeit* 1, no. 3 (1924): 168–9.

58 Angestellte und Arbeiter Berlin. Reichswohnungsfürsorge- A.-G. für Beamte et al., "Vertrag. 12. Juli 1924" (LAB A Rep. 251-06 LIGA Nr. 2), 1–6. On 18 October 1927 Georg Haberland wrote an open letter to Stadtbaurat Martin Wagner expressing his frustration with Wagner. He believed that Wagner's non-profit housing association was a conflict of interest with his role as Stadtbaurat. Georg Haberland, "Offener Brief an Stadtbaurat Dr. Wagner. 18. Oktober 1927" (LAB A Rep. 001-02 Nr. 84), 135VS/1.

59 Heinrich Keller, "Brief zu den Herrn Minister für Volkswohlfahrt. 1. November 1925" (GStA PK I. HA Rep. 191 Nr. 95), 209VS/1.

60 von Mangoldt and Siedlungswissenschaftliche Arbeitsgemeinschaft, "Brief zu den Herrn Minister für Volkswohlfahrt. November 1925," 155VS/3–155RS/4, 156RS/6.

61 Konstanze Sylva Domhardt, "From the 'Functional City' to the 'Heart of the City,'" in *Greening the City*, ed. Sonja Dumpelmann and Dorothee Brantz (Charlottesville: University of Virginia Press, 2011), 133–4.

62 Paul Ferdinand Schmidt, "Probleme der Weltstadt Berlin," *Sozialistische Monatshefte* 35, no. 2 (18 February 1929): 137.

63 von Saldern, "Social Rationalization of Living and Housework," 79–80.

64 Heinrich de Fries, "Einführung," *Der Städtebau* 17, no. 1/2 (1920): 2. Martin Mächler agreed: the proletarian quarters had little green space and few spaces to bathe, but most importantly the housing structures were a "deceptive sham façade" on a "tower high, airless, lightless, monotonous gray cave dwellings or residential boxes" that "pile up the proletariat." Martin Mächler, "Das Siedelungsproblem," *Sozialistische Monatshefte* 27, no. 4 (1921): 184–5.

65 Heinrich de Fries, "Industriebaukunst," *Wasmuths Monatshefte für Baukunst und Städtebau* 5, no. 5/6 (1920): 127–8.

66 Leonardo Benevolo, *History of Modern Architecture*, 6th ed. (Cambridge, MA: MIT Press, 1999), 2:440; von Saldern, "'Instead of Cathedrals," 93.

67 Ernst Schuster, "Typisierung als Wirtschaftsorganisation," *Weltwirtschaftliches Archiv* 19 (1923): 429–33. Schuster added to Ford's automobile for the masses as the example of quantifying and "de-individualizing" effects of typification, "Stinnes-ification" i.e. vertically and horizontally integrated corporations or cartels with a powerful and prominent chief executive.

68 von Mangoldt and Siedlungswissenschaftliche Arbeitsgemeinschaft, "Brief zu den Herrn Minister für Volkswohlfahrt. November 1925," 164RS/22.
69 Ruttmann, "Berlin: Die Sinfonie der Großstadt"; Simmel, "Metropolis and Mental Life."
70 Robert Atkinson, "Deutsche Baukunst der Gegenwart," *Wasmuths Monatshefte für Baukunst* 12, no. 8 (1928): 340.
71 Mary Nolan, *Visions of Modernity* (New York: Oxford University Press, 1994), 206.
72 Eve Blau, *The Architecture of Red Vienna, 1919–1934* (Cambridge, MA: MIT Press, 1999), 169. See the original here: Otto Neurath, "Städtebau und Proletariat," *Der Kampf* 17, no. 6 (1924): 237–42.
73 von Saldern, "Social Rationalization of Living and Housework," 79–80.
74 Susan R. Henderson, "Housing the Single Woman," *Journal of the Society of Architectural Historians* 68, no. 3 (2009): 360.
75 Nolan, *Visions of Modernity*, 206–7; von Saldern, "Social Rationalization of Living and Housework," 81; Leif Jerram, "Kitchen Sink Dramas," *Cultural Geographies* 13, no. 4 (2006): 545; Susan R. Henderson, *Building Culture* (New York: Peter Lang Publishing, 2013), 147.
76 von Saldern, "'Instead of Cathedrals,'" 100–1, 105–10.
77 Jerram, "Kitchen Sink Dramas," 548.
78 For similar arguments see Richard Pommer, "Some Architectural Ideologies after the Fall," *Art Journal* 40, no. 1/2 (1980): 354; Alan Colquhoun, "Postmodernism and Structuralism: A Retrospective Glance," *Assemblage*, no. 5 (1988): 9.
79 Cited as: Irene M. Witte, *Heim und Technik in Amerika* (Berlin: VDI-Verlag, GmbH, 1928), 48–9; in Nolan, *Visions of Modernity*, 211–12; see also von Saldern, "Social Rationalization of Living and Housework," 83.
80 Nolan, *Visions of Modernity*, 215. Nolan, importantly, cautions against romanticizing the unrationalized home.
81 von Saldern, "Social Rationalization of Living and Housework," 73.
82 Anson Rabinbach, *The Crisis of Austrian Socialism* (Chicago: University of Chicago Press, 1983), 28.
83 Gustav Lampmann, "Reichsbauforschung," *Zentralblatt der Bauverwaltung* 48, no. 7 (15 February 1928): 100–1.
84 Walter Curt Behrendt, "Vom neuen Bauen," *Zentralblatt der Bauverwaltung* 48, no. 41 (10 October 1928): 660.
85 Eric Paul Mumford, *The CIAM Discourse on Urbanism, 1928–1960* (Cambridge, MA: MIT Press, 2000), 10–12.
86 Hugo Häring, "Neues Bauen," *Moderne Bauformen* 27, no. 9 (1928): 329–30.

87 Roger Ginsburger, "Architektur – Kunst – Technische Schönheit," *Moderne Bauformen* 30, no. 6 (1931): 265.

88 Peter Meyer, "Vom neuen Bauen," *Zentralblatt der Bauverwaltung* 49, no. 26 (26 June 1929): 413.

89 Werner Hegemann, "Neue Baukunst und Wohnungspolitk," *Wasmuths Monatshefte für Baukunst* 13, no. 1 (1929): 1–2.

90 von Saldern, "'Instead of Cathedrals,'" 103.

91 Walter Gropius, "Groß-Siedlungen," *Zentralblatt der Bauverwaltung* 50, no. 12 (26 March 1930): 233.

92 Ibid., 240. For a similar study, see Heinrich de Fries, "'Die Einrichtung der Kleinwohnung,'" *Moderne Bauformen* 29, no. 6 (1930): 267–9.

93 Walter Gropius, "Flach-, Mittel- oder Hochbau," *Moderne Bauformen* 30, no. 7 (1931): 321.

94 Ibid.

95 Klaus-Peter Kloß, *Siedlungen der 20er Jahre* (Berlin: Haude & Spenersche Verlagsbuchhandlung, 1982), 16–27.

96 Ibid., 29–41.

97 Blau, *Architecture of Red Vienna*, 7.

98 Marcuse, "Housing Policy of Social Democracy," 214.

99 Rabinbach, *Crisis of Austrian Socialism*, 61–2.

100 Blau, *Architecture of Red Vienna*, 7–8.

101 Ibid., 6.

102 Deutscher Bund Heimatschutz, "Brief zu den Herrn Oberregierungsrat W. C. Behrendt, Ministerium für Volkswohlfahrt. 5. Dezember 1925" (GStA PK I. HA Rep. 191 Nr. 95), 198VS/3.

103 Keller, "Brief zu den Herrn Minister für Volkswohlfahrt. 1. November 1925," 210VS/3–210RS/4, 211RS/6; Otto, "Modem Environment and Historical Continuity," 151–3.

104 Berg, "Hochhäuser im Stadtbild," *Wasmuths Monatshefte für Baukunst* 6, no. 4/5 (1921): 101–3.

105 Martin Mächler, "On the Skyscraper Problem [1921]," in *Metropolis Berlin*, ed. David Frisby and Iain Boyd Whyte (Berkeley: University of California Press, 2012), 330.

106 Atkinson, "Deutsche Baukunst der Gegenwart," 339.

107 Walter Curt Behrendt, "Wolkenkratzer, Luxusbauten und Wohnungsnot," *Kommunale Praxis*, 26 February 1921, 173.

108 Werner Hegemann, Martin Wagner, and Heinrich Mendelsohn, "Soll Berlin Wolkenkratzer Bauen," *Wasmuths Monatshefte für Baukunst* 12, no. 6 (1928): 288.

109 Ibid.

110 Ibid., 286–7.

111 Werner Hegemann and Charles du Vinage, "Hochhaus Friedrichstrasse," *Städtebau* 25, no. 4 (1930): 192.

112 Hegemann, Wagner, and Mendelsohn, "Soll Berlin Wolkenkratzer Bauen," 288; Siegfried Kracauer came to a similar conclusion in "On Skyscrapers [1921]," in *Metropolis Berlin*, ed. David Frisby and Iain Boyd Whyte, 326–9 (Berkeley: University of California Press, 2012).

113 Hegemann and du Vinage, "Hochhaus Friedrichstrasse," 192.

114 Cornelius Gurlitt, "Der Platz der Republik und der Wallotbau," ibid., no. 7: 340; Fritz Höger, "Ein Hochhaus beim Reichstag sehr wohl möglich!" ibid.; Werner Hegemann, "Turmhaus am Reichstag?!," *Städtebau* 25, no. 2 (1930): 98–9; Gustav Lampmann, "Zweiter Wettbewerb zur Reichstag-Erweiterung," *Zentralblatt der Bauverwaltung* 49, no. 50 (11 December 1929): 811.

115 Gurlitt, "Der Platz der Republik und der Wallotbau," *Städtebau* 25, no. 7 (1930): 341.

116 Bruno Taut, "Der Reichstagerweiterung in ihrer Beziehung zum Platz der Republik," *Zentralblatt der Bauverwaltung* 50, no. 5 (5 February 1930): 109.

117 Hegemann, "Turmhaus am Reichstag?!," 101–2.

118 Max Berg, "Der Platz der Republik in Berlin," *Zentralblatt der Bauverwaltung* 50, no. 9 (5 March 1930): 186–7.

119 Hugo Häring, "Die Baukunst und das Wettbewerbswesen," *Sozialistische Monatshefte* 35, no. 4 (15 April 1929): 316; Gurlitt, "Der Platz der Republik und der Wallotbau," 340.

120 Taut, "Der Reichstagerweiterung in ihrer Beziehung zum Platz der Republik," 109.

121 Häring, "Die Baukunst und das Wettbewerbswesen," 313.

122 Ibid., 314. For more on the effect of juries on avant-garde architecture, see Gurlitt, "Der Platz der Republik und der Wallotbau," 340.

123 Fritz Höger, "Ein Hochhaus beim Reichstag sehr wohl möglich!" *Städtebau* 25, no. 7 (1930): 344.

124 Berg, "Der Platz der Republik in Berlin," 186.

125 Ibid., 185.

126 Ibid., 186; Sonne, "Berlin," 198–200.

127 Leo Adler, "Wettbewerb für den Erweiterungsbau des Reichstages in Berlin," *Wasmuths Monatshefte für Baukunst* 12, no. 2 (1928): 78.

128 Gustav Lampmann, "Wettbewerb zur Erweiterung des Reichstagsgebäudes," *Zentralblatt der Bauverwaltung* 48, no. 5 (1 February 1928): 65.

129 Sonne, "Berlin," 198–200.

130 Berg, "Der Platz der Republik in Berlin," 185; Sonne, "Berlin," 198–200.

131 "Berlin," 200.

132 Deutscher Wirtschaftsbund für das Baugewerbe, "Brief zu das Preußische Ministerium für Volkswohlfahrt. 22. April 1924" (GStA PK I. HA Rep. 191 Nr. 85), 283VS; ibid.

133 Preußischer Landesverband der Haus- und Grundbesitzerverein e. V., "Brief zu das Preußische Ministerium für Volkswohlfahrt. 30. Oktober 1925" (GStA PK I. HA Rep. 191 Nr. 95), 285VS / 1.

134 Ibid., 285RS/2–286RS/4.

135 Ibid., 300RS/12, 302RS/16, quoted text from 300RS/12.

136 "Stellungnahme des Preußischen Landesverband der Haus- und Grundbesitzerverein e. V. zu dem Entwurf eines Städtebaugesetzes. 16. Februar 1926" (GStA PK I. HA Rep. 191 Nr. 96), 59VS/1–60VS/2, quoted text from 59VS/1.

137 Landesausschuß der preußischen Industrie und Handelskammern, "Brief zu den Preußischen Staatsrat. 16. Juni 1926" (GStA PK I. HA Rep. 191 Nr. 97), 3VS/1–4VS/3.

138 Franz von Mendelssohn and Landesausschuß der preußischen Industrie und Handelskammern, "Brief zu den Preußischen Landtag. 10 November 1926" (GStA PK I. HA Rep. 191 Nr. 98), 3/1–2.

139 von Mangoldt and Siedlungswissenschaftliche Arbeitsgemeinschaft, "Brief zu den Herrn Minister für Volkswohlfahrt. November 1925," 159VS/11.

140 Ibid., 160VS/13–160VS/14.

141 Ibid., 155VS/3–155RS/4, 156RS/6.

142 Bruno Möhring and Paul Fischer, "Brief zu den Herrn Minister für Volkswohlfarht. 27. Mai 1925" (GStA PK I. HA Rep. 191 Nr. 95), 174VS/1–176VS/3, quoted text from 174VS/1–175VS/2. The Free Academy's line-by-line response was submitted the next day and was written by Fischer, Lehweß, and Heiligenthal. Freie Deutsche Akademie des Städtebaues, "Bemerkungen zum Entwurf eines Stadtebaues" (GStA PK I. HA Rep. 191 Nr. 95), 142VS/1.

143 Deutscher Bund Heimatschutz et al., "Brief zu den Herrn Minister für Volkswohlfahrt. 1. November 1925," 200VS/1.

144 Keller, "Brief zu den Herrn Minister für Volkswohlfahrt. 1. November 1925," 209VS/1.

145 Fuchs, "Brief zu den Herrn Minister für Volkswohlfahrt. 1. November 1925," 208VS/9.

146 Ibid., 204RS/2.

147 Preußischen Städtetag, "Stellungnahme des Preußischen Städtages zum Entwurf eines preußischen Städtebaugesetzes. 11. Januar 1926" (GStA PK I. HA Rep. 191 Nr. 96).

148 Der Vorstand der Preußischer Städtetag, "Brief zu den Preußischen Staatsrat. 26. Juni 1926" (GStA PK I. HA Rep. 191 Nr. 97), 13VS/1.

149 Hermann Ehlgötz, "Brief zu das Wohlfahrtsministerium. 28. September 1929" (GStA PK I. HA Rep. 191 Nr. 105), 194VS/6–195VS/7; [Hans] von Meibom and [Franz] Czeminski, "Preußischer Staatsrat 1929 Mündlicher Bericht wird von dem Gemeinde und dem Wirtschafts-Ausschuss erstattet werden über den Entwurf eines Städtebaugesetzes. 19. Juni 1929" (GStA PK I. HA Rep. 191 Nr. 105), 91RS/2.

150 However, as Peter Scott has argued, in the case of Britain, owner-occupied suburban housing for the working class reduced birthrates. Peter Scott, "Did Owner-Occupation Lead to Smaller Families for Interwar Working-Class Households?," *Economic History Review* 61, no. 1 (2008): 122.

151 Fuchs, "Brief zu den Herrn Minister für Volkswohlfahrt. 1. November 1925," 204VS/1.

152 von Mangoldt and Siedlungswissenschaftliche Arbeitsgemeinschaft, "Brief zu den Herrn Minister für Volkswohlfahrt. November 1925," 155VS/3–155RS/4, 156RS/6.

153 [Otto] Braun and [Heinrich] Hirtsiefer, "Entwurf eines Städtebaugesetzes," in *Nr. 48 Preußischer Staatsrat 1929. 8. März 1929* (GStA PK I. HA Rep. 191 Nr. 108), 8RS/32–13VS/49.

154 [Martin] Wagner, "Brief zu den Herrn Minister für Volkswohlfahrt. 3. Mai 1929" (GStA PK I. HA Rep. 191 Nr. 105), 146VS/1; [Wilhelm] Arntz et al., "Die unterzeichneten Städtebauer … 3. Mai 1929" (GStA PK I. HA Rep. 191 Nr. 105), 148VS/1–49VS/2; Ehlgötz, "Brief zu das Wohlfahrtsministerium. 28. September 1929," 194VS/6–95VS/7.

155 von Meibom and Czeminski, "Preußischer Staatsrat 1929 Mündlicher Bericht wird von dem Gemeinde und dem Wirtschafts-Ausschuss erstattet werden über den Entwurf eines Städtebaugesetzes. 19. Juni 1929," 91VS/1–91RS/2.

156 Bund Deutscher Architekten, "Brief zu den Preußischen Herrn Minister für Volkswohlfahrt. 28 November 1929" (GStA PK I. HA Rep. 191 Nr. 107), 40VS/1.

157 Flinsch, "Brief zu den Ausschuss zur Vorberatung Entwurfs eines Städtebaugesetzes. 5. Januar 1930" (GStA PK I. HA Rep. 191 Nr. 107), 55VS/1–56VS/2.

158 Ibid., 57VS/3–58VS/4.

159 Ehlgötz, "Brief zu das Wohlfahrtsministerium. 28. September 1929," 194VS/6–195VS/7.

160 Arntz et al., "Die unterzeichneten Städtebauer … 3. Mai 1929," 148VS/1–149VS/2.

161 von Meibom and Czeminski, "Preußischer Staatsrat 1929 Mündlicher Bericht wird von dem Gemeinde und dem Wirtschafts-Ausschuss erstattet werden über den Entwurf eines Städtebaugesetzes. 19. Juni 1929," 91RS/2; Preußischen Städtetag, "Brief zu den Preußischen Herrn Minister für Volkswohlfahrt. 30 September 1929" (GStA PK I. HA Rep. 191 Nr. 107).
162 Schmidt, "Probleme der Weltstadt Berlin," 140.
163 Runge, "Grundsätzliches zum Problem der Erweiterung Gross-Berlins," 5.
164 Hellmut Delius, "Städtebau und Landesplanung," *Zentralblatt der Bauverwaltung* 50, no. 16 (1930): 306–7.
165 Gustav Langen, "Die Besiedlungen des Vorlandes von Berlin," ibid.51, no. 53/54 (1931): 780.
166 Hellmut Delius, "Städtebau und Landesplanung," *Zentralblatt der Bauverwaltung* 50, no. 16 (23 April 1930): 308.
167 Brandt, "Landesplanung," *Zentralblatt der Bauverwaltung* 48, no. 7 (1928): 97–8.
168 Henderson, *Building Culture*, 97.
169 Bernhard Harms, "Strukturwandlungen der deutschen Volkswirtschaft (Deutsche Wirtschafts-Enquete)," *Weltwirtschaftliches Archiv* 24 (1926): 263; Hans Bayer, "Strukturwandlungen der deutschen Volkswirtschaft," *Zeitschrift für Nationalokonomie* 1, no. 3 (1930): 448.
170 Roderich von Ungern-Sternberg, "Rationalisierung der deutschen Industriewirtschaft," *Sozialistische Monatshefte* 37, no. 3 (1931): 252.
171 Friedrich Olk, "Vor dem zweiten Abschnitt der deutschen Rationalisierung," *Die Arbeit* 7, no. 3 (1930): 156.
172 Ibid., 157.
173 Ibid., 159.
174 Cited as Walter Gropius, *Idee und Aufbau des staatlichen Bauhauses Weimar* (Munich: Bauhausverlag, 1923), [no page numbers given]; in Benevolo, *History of Modern Architecture*, 2, 421.
175 Colquhoun, "Criticism and Self-Criticism in German Modernism," 29–30.
176 Cited as Walter Gropius, "Der baugeist der neuen Volksgemeinde," in *Die Glocke* 10 (1924/5): 324; in Nike Bätzner, "Housing Projects of the 1920s," in *City of Architecture of the City*, ed. Thorsten Scheer, Josef Paul Kleihues, and Paul Kahlfeldt (Berlin: Nicolai, 2000), 150; Behrendt offers a similar summary in Walter Curt Behrendt, *The Victory of the New Building Style [1927]*, ed., trans. Harry Francis Mallgrave (Los Angeles: Getty Research Institute, 2000), 107. Those involved with housing production in France embraced a very similar inclusion of technological possibility in the

building industry. Robert Weddle, "Housing and Technological Reform in Interwar France," *Journal of Architectural Education* 54, no. 3 (2006): 167–75.

177 "Krisis der Siedlungspolitik," *Wasmuths Monatshefte für Baukunst und Städtebau* 5, no. 3/4 (1920): 124–5.

178 Joseph Brix, "Brief zu den Herrn Minister für Volkswohlfahrt. 8. Januar 1929" (GStA PK I. HA Rep. 191 Nr. 103), 159VS/1–160VS/2.

179 Mächler, "Die Grossstadt und der Städtebau," 408.

180 Mächler, "Das Siedelungsproblem," 182–5.

181 Martin Mächler, "Zum deutschen Neubau," *Sozialistische Monatshefte* 29, no. 10 (1923): 610–14.

182 Ludwig Hilberseimer, "Vom städtebaulichen Problem der Großstadt," *Sozialistische Monatshefte* 29, no. 6 (1923): 352.

183 Ibid.

184 Ibid., 353.

185 Pier Vittorio Aureli, "Architecture for Barbarians," *AA Files*, no. 63 (2011): 3–18.

186 Hilberseimer, "Vom städtebaulichen Problem der Großstadt," 354–7.

187 Henryk Grossmann, "Marx, Classical Economics, and the Problem of Dynamics [1940]," *International Journal of Political Economy* 36, no. 2 (2007): 45.

188 Postone, *Time, Labor, and Social Domination*, 286–306.

189 Sigrist, *Das Buch vom Bauen*, 60–3.

190 Ibid., 62–3.

191 Ibid., 124.

192 Adolf Behne, "Form und Klassenkampf," *Sozialistische Monatshefte* 37, no. 4 (13 April 1931): 363.

193 Ibid.; Loos, "Ornament and Crime."

194 Sigrist, *Das Buch vom Bauen*, 205–6.

195 Ibid., 211.

196 Ibid., 9.

197 Ibid., 124–5.

198 Ibid., 107–8.

199 Ibid., 107–9.

200 Ibid., 84.

201 Ibid.

202 Behne, "Form und Klassenkampf," 364.

203 Siegfried Kracauer, "Deutsche Bauausstellung Vorläufige Bemerkungen," in *Berliner Nebeneinander*, ed. Andreas Volk (Zürich: Epocha, 1996), 117.

204 Ibid., 117–18.

205 Franz Löwitsch, "Die Idee Berlin," *Städtebau-Baupolitik* 5, no. 9 (1931): 423, 426.

206 Adolf Behne, "Deutsche Bauausstellung Berlin 1931: Abteilung 'Die Wohnung unserer Zeit,'" *Zentralblatt der Bauverwaltung* 51, no. 49/50 (1931): 733–4; von Saldern, "'Instead of Cathedrals,'" 100.

207 Josef Gantner, "Deutsche Bauausstellung Berlin 1931: Abteilung 'Das Bauwerk unserer Zeit,'" *Zentralblatt der Bauverwaltung* 51, no. 49/50 (1931): 725.

208 Colquhoun, "Criticism and Self-Criticism in German Modernism," 30–1.

Conclusion: The Corporate City and a New Regime of Accumulation

1 Herbert Marcuse, "Some Implications of Modern Technology," in *The Essential Frankfurt School Reader*, ed. Andrew Arato and Eike Gebhardt (New York: Continuum, 1982), 160.

2 For more on this term, see the introduction to this book.

3 Early versions of this argument include works by Dunayevskaya and Marcuse: Raya Dunayevskaya, "Teaching of Economics in the Soviet Union," *American Economic Review* 34, no. 3 (1944): 501–30; Dunayevskaya, "A New Revision of Marxian Economics," *American Economic Review* 34, no. 3 (1944): 531–7; Herbert Marcuse, *Soviet Marxism* (New York: Columbia University Press, 1958). Attempts to reintroduce economics and capitalism into studies of the USSR include Stephen A. Resnick and Richard D. Wolff, *Class Theory and History* (New York: Routledge, 2002).

4 Andrew Sloin and Oscar Sanchez-Sibony, "Economy and Power in the Soviet Union, 1917–39," *Kritika: Explorations in Russian and Eurasian History* 15, no. 1 (2014): 7–22.

5 Oscar Sanchez-Sibony, *Red Globalization* (Cambridge: Cambridge University Press, 2014).

6 Jake Werner, "Global Fordism in 1950s Urban China," *Frontiers of History in China* 7, no. 3 (2012): 415–41.

7 Jeffry M. Diefendorf, "Planning for the Mark Brandenburg and for Prague during the Third Reich," *Planning Perspectives* 26, no. 1 (2011): 91–103.

8 Paul B. Jaskot, "Anti-Semitic Policy in Albert Speer's Plans for the Rebuilding of Berlin," *Art Bulletin* 78, no. 4 (1996): 622–3.

9 Ibid., 626–7.

10 Sophie B. Roberts, "Anti-Semitism and Municipal Government in Interwar French Colonial Algeria," *Journal of North African Studies* 17, no. 5 (2012): 822.

11 Ibid., 829–31.

12 Richard Parks, "The Jewish Quarters of Interwar Paris and Tunis," *Jewish Social Studies: History, Culture, Society* 17, no. 1 (2010): 67–9.

13 Rosemary Wakeman, "Nostalgic Modernism and the Invention of Paris in the Twentieth Century," *French Historical Studies* 27, no. 1 (2004): 116–17.
14 Garside, "'Unhealthy Areas'"; Caitríona Beaumont, "'Where to Park the Pram'?" *Women's History Review* 22, no. 1 (2013): 76.
15 Beaumont, "'Where to Park the Pram,'" 77; John Sheail, "Interwar Planning in Britain," *Journal of Urban History* 11, no. 3 (1985): 348–50.
16 Eric Mumford, "CIAM Urbanism after the Athens Charter," *Planning Perspectives* 7, no. 4 (1992): 392–5.
17 Ibid., 395–6.
18 Eric Mumford, "CIAM and the Communist Bloc, 1928–59," *Journal of Architecture* 14, no. 2 (2009): 239–45.
19 Armin Grünbacher, "Cold-War Economics," *Central European History* 45, no. 4 (2012): 703–4.
20 Jeffry M. Diefendorf, "Reconstructing Devastated Cities," *Journal of Urban Design* 14, no. 3 (2009): 381.
21 Eli Rubin, "Amnesiopolis," *Central European History* 47, no. 2 (2014): 342.
22 Ibid., 335–6.
23 Ibid., 344.
24 Nicholas Bullock, "Developing Prototypes for France's Mass Housing Programme, 1949–53," *Planning Perspectives* 22, no. 1 (2007): 6–7.
25 Ibid., 8.
26 Nicole Rudolph, "'Who Should Be the Author of a Dwelling?'" *Gender & History* 21, no. 3 (2009): 541–2.
27 Bullock, "Developing Prototypes for France's Mass Housing Programme," 23–5.
28 Christine Varga-Harris, "Homemaking and the Aesthetic and Moral Perimeters of the Soviet Home during the Khrushchev Era," *Journal of Social History* 41, no. 3 (2008): 561.
29 Ibid., 564–7.
30 Heather D. DeHaan, *Stalinist City Planning* (Toronto: University of Toronto Press, 2013), 70–1.

Bibliography

Abraham, David. *The Collapse of the Weimar Republic*. New York: Holmes & Meier, 1986.

Abrahamsohn, Lotte. "Der öffentliche Einfluss auf den Berliner Wohnungsbau." Hamburg: Hamburgischen Universität, 1933.

Adam, Thomas. "Heinrich Pudor: Lebensreformer, Antisemit und Verleger." In *Das bewegte Buch*, edited by Mark Lehmstedt and Andreas Herzog, 183–96. Wiesbaden: Harrassowitz in Kommission, 1999.

Adickes, Franz. "Vortrage von Oberbürgermeister D. Adickes in Frankfurt a.M." In *Die sozialen Aufgaben der deutschen Städte*, edited by Franz Adickes and Gustav Otto Beutler, 3–90. Leipzig: Druncker und Humbolt, 1903.

Adler, Leo. "Wettbewerb für den Erweiterungsbau des Reichstages in Berlin." *Wasmuths Monatshefte für Baukunst* 12, no. 2 (1928): 78.

Adorno, Theodor W. "Functionalism Today." *Oppositions*, no. 17 (1979): 30–41.

– "Nachwort zur 'Berliner Kindheit um neunzehnhundert.'" In *Über Walter Benjamin*, edited by Rolf Tiedemann, 74–8. Frankfurt am Main: Suhrkamp Verlag, 1990.

– "Society [1963]." In *Critical Theory and Society*, edited by Stephen Eric Bronner and Douglas Kellner, 267–76. New York: Routledge, 1989.

– "Veblen's Attack on Culture." Translated by Samuel Weber and Shierry Weber. In *Prisms*, 73–95. Cambridge, MA: MIT Press, 1997.

Akın, Yiğit. "War, Women, and the State." *Journal of Women's History* 26, no. 3 (2014): 12–35.

Albers, Gerd. *Zur Entwicklung der Stadtplanung in Europa*. Braunschweig: Vieweg, 1997.

Albrecht, Otto. "Deutsche Kleingartenpolitik." *Die Arbeit* 1, no. 3 (1924): 168–76.

Alexander-Katz, Paul. *Über Preußisches Fluchtlinienrecht*. Berlin: Wilhelm Ernst & Sohn, 1908.

"Allgemeine Städtebau-Ausstellung in Berlin, vom 1. Mai bis 15. Juni 1910." *Der Städtebau* 7, no. 6 (1910): 61–2.

"Allgemeine Städtebau-Ausstellung Berlin 1910." *Deutsche Bauzeitung* 44, no. 1/2 (5 January 1910): 3–6.

Altvater, Elmar. "Fordist and Post-Fordist International Division of Labor and Monetary Regimes." In *Pathways to Industrialization and Regional Development*, edited by Michael Storper and Allen J. Scott, 21–45. London: Routledge, 1992.

Arminius [Gräfin Adelheid zu Dohna-Poninska]. *Die Großstädte in ihrer Wohnungsnoth und die Grundlagen einer durchgreifenden Abhilfe*. Leipzig: Duncker & Humblot, 1874.

Arnold, Anthony J. "'A Paradise for Profiteers'?" *Accounting History Review* 24, no. 2/3 (2014): 61–81.

Ascher, Abraham. "'Radical' Imperalists within German Social Democracy, 1912–1918." *Political Science Quarterly* 76, no. 4 (1961): 555–75.

Ashton, Paul. "'This Villa Life.'" *Planning Perspectives* 25, no. 4 (2010): 457–83.

Assmann, Gustav. "Die Wohnungsnoth in Berlin: Ein Vertrag gehalten im Architekten-Verein zu Berlin." *Zeitschrift für Bauwesen* 23, no. 3/5 (1873): 111–30.

Atkinson, Robert. "Deutsche Baukunst der Gegenwart." *Wasmuths Monatshefte für Baukunst* 12, no. 8 (1928): 339–44.

Aureli, Pier Vittorio. "Architecture for Barbarians." *AA Files*, no. 63 (2011): 3–18.

Baar, Lothar. "Probleme der industriellen Revolution in großstädtischen Industriezentren." In *Wirtschafts- und sozialgeschichtliche Probleme der frühen Industrialisierung*, edited by Wolfram Fischer, 529–42. Berlin: Colloquium Verlag, 1968.

Backhaus. "Wohnungswesen." *Zentralblatt der Bauverwaltung* 48, no. 17 (25 April 1928): 280–1.

Bader, Karl Siegfried. "Gierke, Otto Friedrich von." In *Neue Deutsche Biographie*, edited by Der Historischen Kommission bei der Bayerischen Akademie der Wissenschaft, 374–5. Berlin: Duncker & Humblot, 1964.

Balderston, Theo. "German Banking between the Wars." *Business History Review* 65, no. 3 (1991): 554–605.

Bartschat, Johannes. "Das Problem des Grunewaldes [1]." *Der Städtebau* 5, no. 9 (1908): 122–4.

Bätzner, Nike. "Housing Projects of the 1920s." In *City of Architecture of the City*, edited by Thorsten Scheer, Josef Paul Kleihues, and Paul Kahlfeldt, 149–60. Berlin: Nicolai, 2000.

Baumeister, Reinhard. *Stadt-Erweiterungen in technischer, baupolizeilicher, und wirthschaftlicher Beziehung*. Berlin: Ernst & Korn, 1876.

Bayer, Hans. "Strukturwandlungen der deutschen Volkswirtschaft." *Zeitschrift für Nationalökonomie* 1, no. 3 (1930): 448–60.

Beaumont, Caitríona. "'Where to Park the Pram'?" *Women's History Review* 22, no. 1 (2013): 75–96.

Behne, Adolf. "Deutsche Bauausstellung Berlin 1931: Abteilung 'Die Wohnung unserer Zeit.'" *Zentralblatt der Bauverwaltung* 51, no. 49/50 (25 November 1931): 733–5.

– "Form und Klassenkampf." *Sozialistische Monatshefte* 37, no. 4 (13 April 1931): 362–5.

Behrendt, Walter Curt. *Die einheitliche Blockfront als Bauelement im Stadtbau.* Berlin: Bruno Cassirer Verlag, 1912.

– *The Victory of the New Building Style [1927].* Edited and translated by Harry Francis Mallgrave. Los Angeles: Getty Research Institute, 2000.

– "Vom neuen Bauen." *Zentralblatt der Bauverwaltung* 48, no. 41 (10 October 1928): 657–62.

– "Wolkenkratzer, Luxusbauten und Wohnungsnot." *Kommunale Praxis,* 26 February 1921, 173–6.

Behrens, Peter, and Heinrich de Fries. *Vom Sparsamen Bauen.* Berlin: Verlag der Bauwelt, 1918.

Benevolo, Leonardo. *History of Modern Architecture.* 2 vols. Cambridge, MA: MIT Press, 1999.

Benjamin, Walter. "Paris: Capital of the Nineteenth Century." *New Left Review* 1, no. 48 (1968): 77–88.

Berg, Max. "Der Platz der Republik in Berlin." *Zentralblatt der Bauverwaltung* 50, no. 9 (5 March 1930): 185–8.

Berg. "Hochhäuser im Stadtbild." *Wasmuths Monatshefte für Baukunst* 6, no. 4/5 (1921): 101–20.

Berger. "Dückerung des Schöneberger Regenauslasses unter der Untergrundbahn am Nollendorfplatz in Berlin." *Zentralblatt der Bauverwaltung* 37, no. 71/2 (1, 5 September 1917): 449–52, 453–6.

Bergmann, Klaus. *Agrarromantik und Großstadtfeindschaft.* Meisenheim a. Glan: Verlag Anton Hain, 1970.

Bernet, Claus. "The 'Hobrecht Plan' (1862) and Berlin's Urban Structure." *Urban History* 31, no. 3 (2004): 400–19.

Bernhardt, Christoph. "At the Limits of the European Sanitary City: Water-Related Environmental Inequalities in Berlin-Brandenburg, 1900–1939." In *Environmental and Social Justice in the City: Historical Perspectives,* edited by Geneviève Massard-Guilbaud and Richard Rodger 155–69. Cambridge: White Horse, 2011.

Bernstein, Eduard. *Die Geschichte der Berliner Arbeiter-Bewegung.* 3 vols. Berlin: Buchhandlung Vorwärts (Hans Weber), 1910.

–, ed. *Fünfzehn Jahre Berliner Arbeiterbewegung unter dem gemeinen Recht*. 3 vols. Berlin: Buchhandlung Vorwärts (Hans Weber), 1910.

Besgen, Fritz. "Die Wirkung der Eingemeindung auf Polizeiverordnungen nach preußischem Rechte." Leipzig: Universität Leipzig, 1909.

Bessel, Richard. "Mobilizing German Society for War." In *Great War, Total War*, edited by Roger Chickering and Stig Förster, 437–52. Cambridge: Cambridge University Press, 2000.

Bettendorf, Leon, and Erik Buyst. "Rent Control and Virtual Prices." *Journal of Economic History* 57, no. 3 (1997): 654–73.

Beuster, F. *Groß-Berlin nach dem Kriege*. Berlin: Carl Henmanns Verlag, 1918.

Bevilacqua, Marco Giorgio. "Alexander Klein and the *Existenzminimum*." *Nexus Network Journal* 13, no. 2 (2011): 297–313.

Blackbourn, David. "The Discreet Charm of the Bourgeoisie." In *The Peculiarities of German History*, by David Blackbourn and Geoff Eley, 159–292. Oxford: Oxford University Press, 1984.

Blau, Eve. *The Architecture of Red Vienna, 1919–1934*. Cambridge, MA: MIT Press, 1999.

Bloch, Joseph. "Der Krieg und die Sozialdemokratie." *Sozialistische Monatshefte* 20, no. 16 (1914): 1023–7.

Bloch, Kurt. "Die Wohnungsnot und ihre Bekämpfung." *Die Arbeit*, no. 1 (1928): 20–7.

Blum, Matthias. "Government Decisions before and during the First World War and the Living Standards in Germany during a Drastic Natural Experiment." *Explorations in Economic History* 48, no. 4 (2011): 556–7.

– "War, Food Rationing, and Socioeconomic Inequality in Germany during the First World War." *Economic History Review* 66, no. 4 (2013): 1063–83.

Blum, Otto. "Zur Verkehrspolitik der Großstädte, mit besonderer Berücksichtigung der Berliner Verhältnisse." *Zeitschrift der Vereines Deutscher Ingenieure* 52, no. 27 (4 July 1908): 1083–97.

Borght, Richard van der, and Paul Lippert. *Grundzüge der Sozialpolitik*. Vol. 15. Leipzig: C.L. Hirschfeld, 1904.

Bornhak, Conrad. *Verwaltungsrechtliches im Städtebau*. Berlin: Wilhelm Ernst & Sohn, 1908.

"Boston: 1915, Exhibition." *Art and Progress* 1, no. 1 (1909): 22.

Boyer, John W. *Culture and Political Crisis in Vienna*. Chicago: University of Chicago Press, 1995.

– *Political Radicalism in Late Imperial Vienna*. Chicago: University of Chicago Press, 1981.

Brandt. "Landesplanung." *Zentralblatt der Bauverwaltung* 48, no. 7 (1928): 97–100.

Brenner, Neil. "Globalisation as Reterritorialisation." *Urban Studies* 36, no. 3 (1999): 431–51.

– "Urban Theory without an Outside." In *Implosions/Explosions*, edited by Neil Brenner, 14–35. Berlin: Jovis, 2013.

Brentano, Lujo. *Die Arbeiterwohnungsfrage in den Städten mit besonderer Berücksichtigung Münchens*. Munich: M. Riegersche Universitäts-Buchhandlung, 1909.

– *Die Schrecken des überwiegenden Industriestaats*. Berlin: L. Simion, 1901.

Bresciani-Turroni, Costantino. *The Economics of Inflation*. Edited and translated by Millicent E. Sayers. London: G. Allen & Unwin, 1937.

Bridenbaugh, Carl. *Cities in the Wilderness*. 2nd ed. New York: Alfred A. Knopf, 1955.

Brix, Joseph. *Aufgaben und Ziele des Städtebau*. Berlin: Wilhelm Ernst & Sohn, 1908.

– *Aus der Geschichte des Städtebaues in den letzten 100 Jahren*. Berlin: Wilhelm Ernst & Sohn, 1912. Serial.

Brix, Joseph, Felix Genzmer, and Hochbahngesellschaft in Berlin. "Preisgekrönt mit der Hälfte des Zusammengelegten I. und II. Preises: Kennwort: 'Denk an Künftig.'" In *Wettbewerb Groß-Berlin, 1910: Die preisgekrönten Entwürfe mit Erläuterungsberichten*. Berlin: Ernst Wasmuth A.-G., 1911.

Broué, Pierre. *The German Revolution, 1917–1923*. Edited and translated by John Archer. Leiden: Brill, 2005.

Brown, Timothy Scott. "The SA in the Radical Imagination of the Long Weimar Republic." *Central European History* 46, no. 2 (2013): 238–74.

Bruch, Ernst. "Berlin's bauliche Zukunft und der Bebauungsplan." *Deutsche Bauzeitung* 4, no. 9, 10, 12, 13, 15, 16, 19, 20, 21, 23, 24 and 25 (1870): 69–71, 77–80, 93–5, 101–4, 121–2, 129–30, 151–4, 159–63, 167–8, 183–6, 191–3, 199–201.

Brühl, Ludwig, Kurt Gordan, and Walter Lebermann. *Zweckverbandsgesetz für Groß-Berlin vom 19. Juli 1911*. Berlin: J. Guttentag Verlagbuchhandlung, 1912.

Brumby, Gustav. *Groß-Berliner Wohnungsnotrecht*. Berlin: Franz Vahlen, 1921.

Bullock, Nicholas. "Developing Prototypes for France's Mass Housing Programme, 1949–53." *Planning Perspectives* 22, no. 1 (2007): 5–28.

Burgess, Ernst W. "The Growth of the City." In *The City*, edited by Robert Park, Ernst W. Burgess, and Roderick McKenzie, 47–62. Chicago: University of Chicago Press, 1967.

Burnham, Daniel Hudson, Edward H. Bennett, and Charles Moore. *Plan of Chicago*. Chicago: Commercial Club, 1909.

Büsch, Otto. *Geschichte der Berliner Kommunalwirtschaft in der Weimarer Epoche*. Berlin: De Gruyter, 1960.

Caldwell, Peter C. *Popular Sovereignty and the Crisis of German Constitutional Law*. Durham, NC: Duke University Press, 1997.

Capuzzo, Paolo. "The Defeat of Planning." *Planning Perspectives* 13, no. 1 (2010): 23–51.

Chickering, Roger. *Imperial Germany and the Great War, 1914–1918*. Cambridge: Cambridge University Press, 1998.

Childers, Thomas. "Interest and Ideology." In *Die Nachwirkungen der Inflation auf die deutsche Geschichte, 1924–1933*, edited by Gerald D. Feldman and Elisabeth Müller-Luckner, 1–20. Munich: R. Oldenbourg, 1985.

"Chronik: Wettbewerb Groß-Berlin." *Berliner Architekturwelt* 11, no. 8 (1909): 318.

City Club of Chicago. *The Railway Terminal Problem of Chicago*. Chicago: City Club of Chicago, 1913.

Clifford, Jim. "The River Lea in West Ham." In *Urban Rivers*, edited by Stéphane Castonguay and Matthew Evenden, 34–56. Pittsburgh: University of Pittsburgh Press, 2012.

Collins, Christiane Crasemann. *Werner Hegemann and the Search for Universal Urbanism*. New York: W.W. Norton, 2005.

Colquhoun, Alan. "Criticism and Self-Criticism in German Modernism." *AA Files*, no. 28 (1994): 26–33.

– "Postmodernism and Structuralism." *Assemblage*, no. 5 (1988): 6–15.

Cronon, William. *Nature's Metropolis*. New York: W.W. Norton, 1991.

Damaschke, Adolf. *Die Bodenreform*. Berlin: Buchverlag der "Hilfe," 1907.

– *Geschichte der Nationalökonomie*. Jena: Gustav Fischer, 1913.

"Das Zwischenkreditgeschäft der Bau- und Bodenbank." *Magazin der Wirtschaft* 5, no. 19 (7 March 1929): 334.

Davis, Belinda. "Food Scarcity and the Empowerment of the Female Consumer in World War I Berlin." In *The Sex of Things*, edited by Victoria De Grazia and Ellen Furlough, 287–310. Berkeley: University of California Press, 1996.

– *Home Fires Burning*. Chapel Hill: University of North Carolina Press, 2000.

de Fries, Heinrich. "'Die Einrichtung der Kleinwohnung.'" *Moderne Bauformen* 29, no. 6 (1930): 267– 9.

– "Einführung." *Der Städtebau* 17, no. 1/2 (1920): 2.

– "Industriebaukunst." *Wasmuths Monatshefte für Baukunst und Städtebau* 5, no. 5/6 (1920): 127–90.

De Gasperi, Mikael. "Liberalism in the Economic Thought of Costantino Bresciani-Turroni." In *Issues in Economic Thought*, edited by Miguel-Ángel Galindo Martín and Cristina Nardi Spiller, 57–69. New York: Nova Science Publishers, 2010.

DeHaan, Heather D. *Stalinist City Planning*. Toronto: University of Toronto Press, 2013.

Dekker, Erwin. "The Intellectual Networks of Otto Neurath." *European Studies* 32, no. 1 (2014): 103–21.

Delano, F.A. "The Chicago Plan, with Particular Reference to the Railway Terminal Problem." *Journal of Political Economy* 21, no. 9 (1913): 819–31.

Delius, Hellmut. "Städtebau und Landesplanung." *Zentralblatt der Bauverwaltung* 50, no. 16 (23 April 1930): 306–8.

Dennis, Richard. "The Geography of Victorian Values." *Journal of Historical Geography* 15, no. 1 (1989): 40–54.

Diefendorf, Jeffry M. "Planning for the Mark Brandenburg and for Prague during the Third Reich." *Planning Perspectives* 26, no. 1 (2011): 91–103.

– "Reconstructing Devastated Cities." *Journal of Urban Design* 14, no. 3 (2009): 377–97.

Dietrich, Richard. *Lebeweltnächte der Friedrichstadt*. Berlin: Hermann Seemann Nachfolger, GmbH, 1907.

Dietz, Bernhard. "Countryside-versus-City in European Thought." *European Legacy* 13, no. 7 (2008): 801–14.

Dietz, R. *Gesetz für Ordnung der nationalen Arbeit*, 4th ed. Munich, 1936.

"Die wirtschaftliche Tätigkeit der Gemeinden." *Zeitschrift für Kommunalwirtschaft* 20, no. 2 (25 January 1930): 103–14.

Dilworth, Richardson. "Urban Infrastructure Politics and Metropolitan Growth." *Public Works Management & Policy* 6, no. 3 (2002): 200–14.

Dittmar, Hermann. "Das Recht der Eingemeindung in Preußen." Universität zu Rostock, 1908.

Domhardt, Konstanze Sylva. "From the 'Functional City' to the 'Heart of the City.'" In *Greening the City*, edited by Sonja Dumpelmann and Dorothee Brantz, 133–56. Charlottesville: University of Virginia Press, 2011.

Dove, Heinrich. "Berlin." In *Verfassung und Verwaltungsorganisation der Städte*, edited by Vereins für Sozialpolitik, 95–154. Leipzig: Duncker & Humblot, 1906.

Drupp, Michael. "Gemeinnützige Bauvereine im Wohnungswesen der Weimarer Republik." In *Die Weimarer Republik als Wohlfahrtsstaat*, edited by Werner Abelshauser, 124–46. Stuttgart: F. Steiner, 1987.

Du Camp, Maxime. *Paris; ses organes, ses fonctions et sa vie dans la seconde moitié du XIXe siècle*. 6 vols. Paris: Hachette, 1869–75.

Duempelmann, Sonja. "Creating Order with Nature." *Planning Perspectives* 24, no. 2 (2009): 143–73.

Dunayevskaya, Raya. "A New Revision of Marxian Economics." *American Economic Review* 34, no. 3 (1944): 531–7.

– "Teaching of Economics in the Soviet Union." *American Economic Review* 34, no. 3 (1944): 501–30.

Dunlavy, Colleen A. *Politics and Industrialization: Early Railroads in the United States and Prussia*. Princeton, NJ: Princeton University Press, 1994.

Eberstadt, Rudolf. *Die Spekulation im neuzeitlichen Städtebau*. Jena: Gustav Fischer, 1907.

– *Handbuch des Wohnungswesens und der Wohnungsfrage*. Jena: Fischer, 1909.

Eberstadt, Rudolf, Bruno Möhring, and Richard Petersen. "Preisgekrönt mit dem III. Preise: Kennwort: 'Et in Terra Pax.'" In *Wettbewerb Groß-Berlin, 1910*. Berlin: Ernst Wasmuth A.-G., 1911.

Edel, Edmund. *Neu-Berlin*. 51 vols. Berlin: Hermann Seemann Nachfolger, GmbH, 1908.

Eimermann, Josef. "Sparsamkeit im Personaletat." *Kommunale Praxis*, 5 March 1921, 197–200.

Eiselen, Fritz. "Die Lösung der Verkehrsfragen im Wettbewerb Groß-Berlin." *Deutsche Bauzeitung: Beilage für Wettbewerbe* 44, no. 50, 52, 55, 58, 59 (22 June 1910): 385–92, 401–3, 435–8, 449–54, 461–5.

Eleutheropulos, Abroteles. "Gesellschaft und Staat." *Zeitschrift für die gesamte Staatswissenschaft* 76, no. 1 (1922): 169–78.

Eley, Geoff. "The British Model and the German Road." In *The Peculiarities of German History*, by David Blackbourn and Geoff Eley, 39–158. Oxford: Oxford University Press, 1984.

Elkart. "Vorschlage zur Umgestaltung der Wohnungswirtschaft: Vortrag im B.D.A. gehalten." *Zeitschrift für Bauwesen* 74, no. 1/3 (Hochbauabteilung) (1924): 18–21.

Elsas, Fritz. "Das Wirtschaftsleben der Großstädte." *Magazin der Wirtschaft* 6, no. 24 (13 June 1930): 1121–4.

Endell, August. *Die Schönheit der großen Stadt*. Stuttgart: Strecker & Schröder, 1908.

Engels, Frederick. *The Housing Question* [in English]. Moscow: Progress Publishers, 1970.

Erbe, Michael. "Berlin im Kaiserreich (1871–1918)." In *Geschichte Berlins*, edited by Wolfgang Ribbe, 691–796. Munich: C.H. Beck, 1987.

Escher, Felix. *Berlin und sein Umland: Zur Genese der Berliner Stadtlandschaft bis zum Beginn des 20. Jahrhundert*. Berlin: Colloquium Verlag, 1985.

Eulenburg, Franz. "Die sozialen Wirkungen der Währungsverhältnisse." *Jahrbücher für Nationalökonomie und Statistik* 67, no. 6 (1924): 748–94.

Evans, Ellen L. "Adam Stegerwald and the Role of the Christian Trade Unions in the Weimar Republic." *Catholic Historical Review* 59, no. 4 (1974): 602–26.

Falk, Ferdinand. "Verewigte Wohnungsnot." *Die Arbeit*, no. 8 (1931): 606–19.

Faure, Alain. "Local Life in Working-Class Paris at the End of the Nineteenth Century." *Journal of Urban History* 32, no. 5 (2006): 761–72.

Fehl, Gerhard. "Camillo Sitte als 'Volkserzieher.'" In *Städtebau um die Jahrhundertwende*, edited by Gordon Emanuel Cherry and Gerhard Fehl, 172–221. Cologne: Dt. Gemeindeverlag, 1980.

Feldman, Gerald D. *Army, Industry, and Labor in Germany, 1914–1918*. Princeton, NJ: Princeton University Press, 1966.

– *The Great Disorder*. New York: Oxford University Press, 1993.

Ferguson, Eliza. "The Cosmos of the Paris Apartment." *Journal of Urban History* 37, no. 1 (2011): 59–67.

Ferguson, Niall. "Constraints and Room for Manoeuvre in the German Inflation of the Early 1920s." *Economic History Review* 49, no. 4 (1996): 635–66.

Feuth, Ludwig. "Das Problem der Entwickelung Groß Berlins." *Sozialistische Monatshefte* 15, no. 11 (1909): 722–6.

– "Eine neue Etappe der Waldverwüstung." *Sozialistische Monatshefte* 15, no. 8 (1909): 508–13.

Fishman, Robert L. "American Suburbs/English Suburbs." *Journal of Urban History* 13, no. 3 (1987): 237–51.

Flesch, Karl. "Referaten: Verhandlungen des Vereins für Socialpolitik über die Verfassung und Verwaltungsorganisation der Städte." In *Schriften des Vereins für Socialpolitik: Verhandlungen der Generalversammulung in Magdeburg, 30. September, 1. und 2. Oktober 1907*, edited by Verein für Socialpolitik, 215–32. Leipzig: Duncker & Humblot, 1908.

Forsell, Håkan. *Property, Tenancy and Urban Growth in Stockholm and Berlin, 1860–1920*. Aldershot, Hampshire, UK: Ashgate, 2006.

Foucault, Michel. "Governmentality." In *The Foucault Effect*, edited by Graham Burchell, Colin Gordon, and Peter Miller, 87–104. Chicago: University of Chicago Press, 1991.

Frank, Albert. "Die Eingemeindung von Vororten in Städte." Jurist-Doktor, Juristenfakultät der Universität Rostock, 1908.

Freestone, Robert. "Reconciling Beauty and Utility in Early City Planning." *Journal of Urban History* 37, no. 2 (2011): 256–77.

Friedell, Egon. *Ecce Poeta [1912]*. Zürich: Diogenes, 1992.

Fritzsche, Peter. *Reading Berlin 1900*. Cambridge, MA: Harvard University Press, 1996.

– "Vagabond in the Fugitive City." *Journal of Contemporary History* 29, no. 3 (July 1994): 385–402.

Fuchs, Carl Johannes. *Zur Wohnungsfrage*. Leipzig: Duncker & Humbolt, 1904.

Gans, Herbert J. *The Urban Villagers: Group and Class in the Life of Italian-Americans*. New York: Free Press of Glencoe, 1962.

Gantner, Josef. "Deutsche Bauausstellung Berlin 1931: Abteilung 'Das Bauwerk unserer Zeit.'" *Zentralblatt der Bauverwaltung* 51, no. 49/50 (25 November 1931): 725–6.

Garb, Margaret. "Race, Housing, and Burnham's Plan." *Journal of Planning History* 10, no. 2 (2011): 99–113.

Garside, Patricia L. "'Unhealthy Areas.'" *Planning Perspectives* 3, no. 1 (1988): 24–46.

Gaumitz, Paul. "Die künftigen Aufgaben unserer Wohnungsämter." In *Probleme der Neuen Stadt Berlin*, edited by Hans Bennert and Erwin Stein, 277–84. Berlin-Friednau: Deutscher Kommunal-Verlag GmbH, 1926.

Geiger, Ludwig. *Geschichte der Juden in Berlin*. Berlin: J. Guttentag, 1871.

Geissler, Otto. "Fabrik- und Industrieviertel." *Der Städtebau* 3, no. 4/5 (1906): 51–3, 61–4.

Genzmer, Felix. *Die Ausstattung von Straßen und Plätzen*. Berlin: Wilhelm Ernst & Sohn, 1910.

– *Die Gestaltung des Straßen- und Platzraumes*. Berlin: Wilhelm Ernst & Sohn, 1909.

Gierke, Otto. *Die Genossenschaftstheorie und die deutsche Rechtsprechung*. Berlin: Weidmannsche Buchhandlung, 1887.

– *Das deutsche Genossenschaftsrecht*. Vol. 1. Berlin: Weidmannsche Buchhandlung, 1868.

Gingrich, Simone, Getrud Haidvogl, and Fridolin Krausmann. "The Danube and Vienna." *Regional Environmental Change* 12, no. 2 (2012): 283–94.

Ginsburger, Roger. "Architektur – Kunst – Technische Schönheit." *Moderne Bauformen* 30, no. 6 (1931): 265–8.

Girard, Louis. *La politique des travaux publics du Second Empire*. Paris: A. Colin, 1952.

Gneist, Rudolf. *Berliner Zustände*. Berlin: Bessersche Buchhandlung, 1849.

– *Der Rechtsstaat*. Berlin: J. Springer, 1872.

– *Verwaltung, Justiz, Rechtsweg*. Berlin: J. Springer, 1869.

Godden, Chris. "Observers, Commentators, and Persuaders: British Interwar Economists as Public Intellectuals." *History of Political Economy* 45, no. 1 (2013): 38–67.

Goecke, Theodor. "Allgemeine Städtebau-Ausstellung Berlin 1910." *Der Städtebau* 7, no. 7/8 (1910): 73–92.

– "Von den Beziehungen der Zonenbauordnung zum Bebauungsplane." *Der Städtebau* 2, no. 1 (1905): 2–5.

Goeschel, Christian. "The Criminal Underworld in Weimar and Nazi Berlin." *History Workshop Journal* 75, no. 1 (2013): 58–80.

Goetz, Edward G. "The Audacity of Hope VI." *Cities* 35 (2013): 342–8.

Gordon, Ian Richard, and Tony Travers. "London." *City, Culture and Society* 1, no. 2 (2010): 49–55.
Gray, Marion W. "Government by Property Owners." *Journal of Modern History* 48, no. 1 (1976): 71–121.
– "Prussia in Transition." *Transactions of the American Philosophical Society* 76, no. 1 (1986): 1–175.
Greve, J. "Die Verkehr auf dem Wasserstraßen Berlins im Jahre 1906." *Zentralblatt der Bauverwaltung* 27, no. 37 (1907): 251–2.
Gropius, Walter. "Flach-, Mittel- oder Hochbau." *Moderne Bauformen* 30, no. 7 (1931): 321–8.
– "Groß-Siedlungen." *Zentralblatt der Bauverwaltung* 50, no. 12 (26 March 1930): 233–40.
– *Idee und Aufbau des staatlichen Bauhauses Weimar*. Munich: Bauhausverlag, 1923.
Grossmann, Henryk. "Marx, Classical Economics, and the Problem of Dynamics [1940]." *International Journal of Political Economy* 36, no. 2 (2007): 6–83.
Grünbacher, Armin. "Cold-War Economics." *Central European History* 45, no. 4 (2012): 697–716.
Grzywatz, Berthold. *Stadt, Bürgertum und Staat im 19. Jahrhundert*. Berlin: Duncker & Humblot, 2003.
Guillén, Mauro F. "Modernism without Modernity." *Latin American Research Review* 39, no. 2 (2004): 6–34.
Guradze, Hans. "Der Einfluß der Eingemeindung auf die Bevölkerungsbewegung der Großstädte." *Jahrbücher für Nationalökonomie und Statistik* 90, no. 5 (1908): 628–32.
Gurlitt, Cornelius. "Der Platz der Republik und der Wallotbau." *Städtebau* 25, no. 7 (1930): 340–3.
Haberland, Georg. *Der Einfluss des Privatkapitals auf die bauliche Entwicklung Gross-Berlins*. Berlin: Carl Heymanns Verlag, 1913.
– *Groß-Berlin*. Berlin: L. Simion Nf., 1904.
Hachtmann, Rüdiger, and Adelheid von Saldern. "Gesellschaft am Fließband." *Zeithistorische Forschungen* 6, no. 2 (2009): 186–208.
Hadley, Elaine. *Living Liberalism*. Chicago: University of Chicago Press, 2010.
Haidvogl, Getrud. "The Channelization of the Danube and Urban Spatial Development in Vienna in the Nineteenth and Early Twentieth Centuries." In *Urban Rivers*, edited by Stéphane Castonguay and Matthew Evenden, 113–29. Pittsburgh: University of Pittsburgh Press, 2012.
Hall, Peter. "Metropolis 1890–1940." In *Metropolis, 1890–1940*, edited by Anthony Sutcliffe, 19–66. Chicago: University of Chicago Press, 1984.

Ham, William T. "The German Building Guilds." *Quarterly Journal of Economics* 43, no. 2 (February 1929): 278–302.

Hamburger, Ludwig. *Denkschrift über die Beziehungen zwischen Berlin und seinen Nachbarorten*. Berlin: W. & S. Loewenthal, 1903.

Hammer, B. "Moderne Stadtgründung." *Der Städtebau* 12, no. 1 (1915): 9–11.

Handlin, Oscar. "The Modern City as a Field of Historical Study." In *The Historian and the City*, edited by Oscar Handlin and John Burchard, 1–26. Cambridge, MA: MIT Press and Harvard University Press, 1963.

Haney, David H. "Leberecht Migge's 'Green Manifesto.'" *Landscape Journal* 26, no. 2 (2007): 201–18.

Hardtwig, Wolfgang. "Großstadt und Bürgerlichkeit in der politischen Ordnung des Kaiserreichs." *Historische Zeitschrift: Beihefte* 12 (1990): 19–64.

Häring, Hugo. "Die Baukunst und das Wettbewerbswesen." *Sozialistische Monatshefte* 35, no. 4 (15 April 1929): 313–16.

– "Neues Bauen." *Moderne Bauformen* 27, no. 9 (1928): 329–76.

Harms, Bernhard. "Strukturwandlungen der deutschen Volkswirtschaft (Deutsche Wirtschafts-Enquete)." *Weltwirtschaftliches Archiv* 24 (1926): 259–73.

Harris, Richard, and Robert Lewis. "The Geography of North American Cities and Suburbs, 1900–1950." *Journal of Urban History* 27, no. 3 (2001): 262–92.

Harris, Richard. "The Rise of Filtering Down: The American Housing Market Transformed, 1915–1929." *Social Science History* 37, no. 4 (2013): 515–49.

Harvey, David. *The Condition of Postmodernity: An Enquiry into the Origins of Cultural Change*. Cambridge, MA: Basil Blackwell, 1989.

– *Paris: Capital of Modernity*. New York: Routledge, 2003.

– "The Spatial Fix: Hegel, von Thunen, and Marx." *Antipode* 13, no. 3 (1981): 1–12.

Havestadt & Contag, Otto Blum, and Bruno Schmitz. "Preisgekrönt mit dem IV. Preise: Kennwort: 'Wo ein Wille, da ein Weg.'" In *Wettbewerb Groß-Berlin, 1910: die preisgekrönten Entwürfe mit Erläuterungsberichten*. Berlin: Ernst Wasmuth A.-G., 1911.

Healy, Maureen. *Vienna and the Fall of the Habsburg Empire*. Cambridge: Cambridge University Press, 2004.

Heap, Chad. *Slumming*. Chicago: University of Chicago Press, 2009.

Heath, Andrew. "'Every Man His Own Landlord.'" *Journal of Urban History* 38, no. 6 (2012): 1003–20.

Hegemann, Hans Werner. "Die neue Bebauungsplan für Chicago." *Deutsche Bauzeitung* 44, no. 40 (18 May 1910): 303–7.

Hegemann, Werner. "Einleitung. Rückblick." In *Der Städtebau nach den Ergebnissen der Allgemeinen Städtbau-Ausstellung in Berlin, nebst einem*

Anhang: Die internationale Städtebau-Ausstellung in Düsseldorf, edited by Werner Hegemann, 7–113. Berlin: Ernst Wasmuth A.-G., 1911.
– "Neue Baukunst und Wohnungspolitk." *Wasmuths Monatshefte für Baukunst* 13, no. 1 (1929): 1–6.
– "Turmhaus am Reichstag?!" *Städtebau* 25, no. 2 (1930): 97–104.
Hegemann, Werner, and Charles du Vinage. "Hochhaus Friedrichstrasse." *Städtebau* 25, no. 4 (1930): 191–5.
Hegemann, Werner, Martin Wagner, and Heinrich Mendelsohn. "Soll Berlin Wolkenkratzer Bauen." *Wasmuths Monatshefte für Baukunst* 12, no. 6 (1928): 286–9.
Heiligenthal, Roman. "Deutsche Bauausstellung Berlin 1931." *Zentralblatt der Bauverwaltung* 51, no. 48 (19 November 1931): 685–712.
– "Die Statistik im Dienste der Stadterweiterung." Vereinigten Friedrichs-Universität Halle Wittenberg, 1921.
– "Probleme des Generalsiedlungsplans." In *Probleme der Neuen Stadt Berlin*, edited by Hans Bennert and Erwin Stein, 254–61. Berlin-Friednau: Deutscher Kommunal-Verlag GmbH, 1926.
Heinrich, Gerd. "Hauptstadtraum und Miltärstaat." In *Stadt und militärische Anlagen*, edited by Akademie für Raumforschung und Landesplanung, 237–50. Hannover: Hermann Schroedel Verlag, 1977.
Henderson, Susan R. *Building Culture*. New York: Peter Lang Publishing, 2013.
– "Housing the Single Woman." *Journal of the Society of Architectural Historians* 68, no. 3 (2009): 358–77.
Henrici, Karl. "Gedanken über das moderne Städte-Bausystem." *Deutsche Bauzeitung* 25, no. 14, 15 (18, 21 February 1891): 81–3, 86–8, 90–1.
Herkner, Heinrich. *Die sociale Reform als Gebot des wirtschaftlichen Fortschrittes*. Leipzig: Duncker & Humblot, 1891.
Herwig, Holger H. "Through the Looking Glass." *Historian* 77, no. 2 (2015): 290–314.
Herzfeld, Hans, ed. *Berlin und die Provinz Brandenburg im 19. und 20. Jahrhundert*. Edited by Hans Herzfeld. Berlin: Walter de Gruyter, 1968.
Herzfeld, Hans. *Demokratie und Selbstverwaltung in der Weimarer Epoche*. Stuttgart: Kohlhammer, 1957.
– , ed. *Geschichte von Brandenburg und Berlin*. Vol. 3. Berlin: Walter de Gruyter, 1968.
Heusler, Andreas. *Der Ursprung der deutschen Stadtverfassung*. Weimar: Hermann Böhlau, 1872.
Hewitson, Mark. "The *Kaiserreich* in Question: Constitutional Crisis in Germany before the First World War." *Journal of Modern History* 73, no. 4 (2001): 725–80.

Hewitt, Lucy E. "The Civic Survey of Greater London." *Journal of Historical Geography* 38, no. 3 (2012): 247–62.

– "Towards a Greater Urban Geography." *Planning Perspectives* 26, no. 4 (2011): 551–68.

Hilberseimer, Ludwig. "Berlin und seine Bauprobleme." *Sozialistische Monatshefte* 34, no. 12 (17 December 1928): 1074–8.

– "Vom städtebaulichen Problem der Großstadt." *Sozialistische Monatshefte* 29, no. 6 (1923): 352–7.

Hillen, Barbara. *Scholz, Ernst August Gustav*. Berlin: Duncker & Humblot, 2007.

Hirsch, Julius. "Der Kettenhandel in wirtschaftlicher Darstellung." In *Der Kettenhandel als Kriegserscheinung*, edited by Volkswirtschaftlichen Abteilung des Kriegsernährungsamts, 1–30. Berlin: Verlag der Beiträge zur Kriegswirtschaft (Reimar Hobbing), 1916.

Hirschberg, Ernst. *Bilder aus der Berliner Statistik*. Berlin: Leonhard Simion Nf., 1904.

– *Die Wohnungsfrage und die Eingemeindung der Berliner Vororte*. Volkswirtschaftliche Zeitfragen, Vorträge und Abhandlungen 27, no. 4 (1905).

Hirschberg. "Wege der Wohnungsfürsorge." *Kommunale Praxis*, 3 May 1919, 272–4.

Hofer, Dirk Henning. *Karl Konrad Werner Wedemeyer (1870–1934)*. Frankfurt am Main: Peter Lang, 2009.

Hofmann, Albert. "Groß-Berlin, sein Verhältnis zur modernen Großstadtbewegung und der Wettbewerb zur Erlangung eines Grundplanes für städtebauliche Entwicklung Berlins und seiner Vororte im zwanzigsten Jahrhundert." *Deutsche Bauzeitung: Beilage für Wettbewerbe* 44, no. 37 (7 May 1910): 281–7.

– "Groß-Berlin, sein Verhältnis zur modernen Großstadtbewegung und der Wettbewerb zur Erlangung eines Grundplanes für die städtebauliche Entwicklung Berlins und seiner Vororte im zwanzigsten Jahrhundert." *Deutschen Bauzeitung: Beilage für Wettbewerbe* 44, no. 42 (25 May 1910): 325–8.

– "Groß-Berlin, sein Verhältnis zur modernen Großstadtbewegung und der Wettbewerb zur Erlangung eines Grundplanes für die städtebauliche Entwicklung Berlins und seiner Vororte im zwanzigsten Jahrhundert [1]." *Deutsche Bauzeitung: Beilage für Wettbewerbe* 44, no. 25 (26 March 1910): 169–76.

Hofmann, Wolfgang. "Der Verkehr beim Wettbewerb Groß-Berlin 1908/10: Am Beispiel von Hermann Jansens Beitrag." In *Stadt und Verkehr im Industriezeitalter*, edited by Horst Matzerath, 203–30. Cologne: Böhlau Verlag, 1996.

– "Die Entwicklung der kommunalen Selbstverwaltung von 1848 bis 1918." In *Grundlagen und Kommunalverfassung*, edited by Thomas Mann and Günter Püttner, 73–92. Berlin: Springer-Verlag, 2007.

– "Wachsen Berlins im Industriezeitalter." In *Probleme des Städtewesens im industriellen Zeitalter*, edited by Helmut Jäger, 159–77. Cologne: Böhlau Verlag, 1978.

Höger, Fritz. "Ein Hochhaus beim Reichstag sehr wohl möglich!" *Städtebau* 25, no. 7 (1930): 344.

Holtfrerich, Carl-Ludwig. *The German Inflation, 1914–1923*. Berlin: De Gruyter, 1986.

Homann, Klaus, and Ludovica Scarpa. "Martin Wagner, the Trades Union Movement and Housing Construction in Berlin in the First Half of the Nineteen Twenties." *Architectural Design* 53, no. 11/12 (1983): 58–61.

Home, Robert. "Peri-Urban Informal Housing Development in Victorian England." *Planning Perspectives* 25, no. 3 (2010): 365–73.

Horkheimer, Max. "The End of Reason [1941]." In *The Essential Frankfurt School*, edited by Andrew Arato and Eike Gebhardt, 26–48. New York: Continuum, 1982.

Hoskins, William George. *Industry, Trade and People in Exeter, 1688–1800*. Manchester: Manchester University Press, 1935.

Howard, N.P. "The Social and Political Consequences of the Allied Food Blockade of Germany, 1918–19." *German History* 11, no. 2 (1993): 161–88.

Hughes, Michael L. *Paying for the German Inflation*. Chapel Hill: University of North Carolina Press, 1988.

Imort, Michael. "A Sylvan People." In *Germany's Nature*, edited by Thomas M. Lekan and Thomas Zeller, 55–81. New Brunswick, NJ: Rutgers University Press, 2005.

Institut für Marxismus-Leninismus beim ZK der SED. *Dokumente und Materialen zur Geschichte der deutschen Arbeiterbewegung*. East Berlin: Dietz, 1958.

Jaeffi, Annemarie. "Hufeisensiedlung Britz." In *Vier Berliner Siedlungen der Weimarer Republik*, edited by Norbert Huse, 110–36. Berlin: Argon, 1987.

Jaffé, Edgar. *Volkswirtschaft und Krieg*. Tübingen: J.C.B. Mohr (P. Siebeck), 1915.

James, Harold. *The German Slump*. Oxford: Clarendon, 1986.

– "Municipal Finance in the Weimar Republic." In *The State and Social Change in Germany, 1880–1980*, edited by W. Robert Lee and Eve Rosenhaft, 228–53. New York: Berg, 1990.

– *The Reichsbank and Public Finance in Germany, 1924–1933*. Frankfurt am Main: F. Knapp, 1985.

Jansen, Hermann. "Preisgekrönt mit der Hälfte des Zusammengelegten I. und II. Preises: Kennwort: 'In den Grenzen der Möglichkeit.'" In *Wettbewerb*

Groß-Berlin, 1910; die preisgekrönten entwürfe mit erläuterungsberichten. Berlin: Ernst Wasmuth A.-G., 1911.

Jarzombek, Mark. "Joseph August Lux." *Journal of the Society of Architectural Historians* 63, no. 2 (2004): 202–19.

– "The 'Kunstgewerbe,' the 'Werkbund,' and the Aesthetics of Culture in the Wilhelmine Period." *Journal of the Society of Architectural Historians* 53, no. 1 (1994): 7–19.

Jaskot, Paul B. "Anti-Semitic Policy in Albert Speer's Plans for the Rebuilding of Berlin." *Art Bulletin* 78, no. 4 (1996): 622–32.

Jerram, Leif. "Kitchen Sink Dramas." *Cultural Geographies* 13, no. 4 (2006): 538–56.

– *Streetlife*. Oxford: Oxford University Press, 2011.

Johansen, Anja. *Soldiers as Police*. Aldershot, UK: Ashgate, 2005.

John, Michael. "The Peculiarities of the German State." *Past and Present*, no. 119 (1988): 105–31.

Jones, Gareth Stedman. "Society and Politics at the Beginning of the World Economy." *Cambridge Journal of Economics* 1, no. 1 (1977): 77–92.

Jones, Larry Eugene. "In the Shadow of Stabilization." In *Die Nachwirkungen der Inflation auf die deutsche Geschichte, 1924–1933*, edited by Gerald D. Feldman and Elisabeth Müller-Luckner, 21–41. Munich: R. Oldenbourg, 1985.

Kaeber, Ernst. *Berlin im Weltkriege*. Berlin: Crowissch, 1921.

– "Böß, Gustav August Johann Heinrich." In *Neue Deutsche Biographie*, edited by Der Historischen Kommission bei der Bayerischen Akademie der Wissenschaft, 408–9. Berlin: Duncker & Humblot, 1955.

– "The Metropolis as Home." In *Metropolis Berlin: 1880–1940*, edited by David Frisby and Iain Boyd Whyte, 337–40. Berkeley: University of California Press, 2012.

Kafkoula, Kiki. "On Garden-City Lines." *Planning Perspectives* 28, no. 2 (2013): 171–98.

Kahan, Michael B. "The Risk of Cholera and the Reform of Urban Space." *Geographical Review* 103, no. 4 (2013): 517–36.

Keller, Karl, and Philipp Nitze. *Gross-Berlins bauliche Zukunft*. Berlin: Renaissance-Verlag Ribert Federn, 1910.

Kerbs, Diethart. "Alexander Schwab (1887–1943)." *Internationale wissenschaftliche Korrespondenz zur Geschichte der deutschen Arbeiterbewegung* 41, no. 4 (2005): 487–95.

Kessler, Gerhard. "Staat und Gesellschaft." *Zeitschrift für gesamte Staatswissenschaft* 82, no. 2 (1927): 225–34.

Kirchheimer, Otto. "Decree Powers and Constitutional Law in France under the Third Republic." *American Political Science Review* 34, no. 6 (1940): 1104–23.

– "The Socialist and Bolshevik Theory of the State [1928]." In *Politics, Law, and Social Change*, edited by Frederic Burin and Kurt L. Shell, 3–21. New York: Columbia University Press, 1969.

Kjøstvedt, Anders G. "The Dynamics of Mobilisation." *Politics, Religion & Ideology* 14, no. 3 (2013): 338–54.

Klein, Alexander. "Wirtschaftliche Grundrissbildung und Raumgestaltung." *Wasmuths Monatshefte für Baukunst* 15, no. 11/12 (1931): 539–41.

Klesse, Max. "Mehr sozialistische Bevölkerungspolitik!" *Sozialistische Monatshefte* 34, no. 4 (4 April 1928): 314–19.

Kling, Samuel. "Wide Boulevards, Narrow Visions." *Journal of Planning History* 12, no. 3 (2013): 245–68.

Kloß, Klaus-Peter. *Siedlungen der 20er Jahre.* Berlin: Haude & Spenersche Verlagsbuchhandlung, 1982.

Kocka, Jürgen. "Class Formation, Interest Articulation, and Public Policy: The Origins of the German White-Collar Class in the Late Nineteenth and Early Twentieth Centuries." In *Organizing Interests in Western Europe*, edited by Suzanne Berger, 63–82. Cambridge: Cambridge University Press, 1981.

– "Family and Bureaucracy in German Industrial Management, 1850–1914." *Business History Review* 45, no. 2 (1971): 133–56.

– "Organisierter Kapitalismus oder Staatsmonopolistischer Kapitalismus?" In *Organisierter Kapitalismus*, edited by Heinrich August Winkler, 19–35. Göttingen: Vandenhoeck & Ruprecht, 1974.

Köhn, Theodor. *Wie ist die Schaffung von Groß-Berlin durchführbar?* Berlin: Carl Heymanns Verlag, 1907.

Köllmann, Wolfgang. "The Process of Urbanization in Germany at the Height of the Industrialization Period." *Journal of Contemporary History* 4, no. 3 (1969): 59–76.

Kötschke, Hermann. *Die Berliner Waldverwüstung*. Berlin: Ansiedlungsverein, 1910.

Kracauer, Siegfried. "Deutsche Bauausstellung Vorläufige Bemerkungen." In *Berliner Nebeneinander*, edited by Andreas Volk, 117–21. Zurich: Epocha, 1996.

– "On Skyscrapers [1921]." In *Metropolis Berlin: 1880–1940*, edited by David Frisby and Iain Boyd Whyte, 326–9. Berkeley: University of California Press, 2012.

Kranold, Hermann. "Die Selbstverwaltung im Staatswesen." *Sozialistische Monatshefte* 38, no. 11 (1932): 917–23.

Krause, Friedrich. "Der Westhafen von Berlin." *Zentralblatt der Bauverwaltung* 43, no. 69/70–71/72 (1923): 409–14, 421–9.

"Krisis der Siedlungspolitik." *Wasmuths Monatshefte für Baukunst und Städtebau* 5, no. 3/4 (1920): 124–6.

Krüger, H. "Siedlungsfragen." *Die Arbeit* 9, no. 11 (1932): 673–83.

Kuhfahl, Gustav Adolf. "Verfassung und Verwaltung der deutschen Städte." In *Die deutschen Städte*, edited by Robert Wuttke, 1–22. Leipzig: Friedrich Brandstetter, 1903.

Kutzsch, Gerhard. "Kirschner, Martin." In *Neue Deutsche Biographie*, 11:675. Berlin: Duncker & Humblot, 1977.

Laband, Paul. *Das Staatsrecht des deutschen Reiches*. 4 vols. Tübingen: J.C.B. Mohr (Paul Seibeck), 1901.

Ladd, Brian. "Urban Aesthetics and the Discovery of the Urban Fabric in Turn-of-the-Century Germany." *Planning Perspectives* 2, no. 3 (1987): 270–86.

– *Urban Planning and Civic Order in Germany, 1860–1914*. Cambridge, MA: Harvard University Press, 1990.

Lampard, Eric E. "American Historians and the Study of Urbanization." *American Historical Review* 67, no. 1 (1961): 49–61.

– "The History of Cities in Economically Advanced Areas." *Economic Development and Cultural Change* 3, no. 2 (1955): 81–136.

– "The Urbanizing World." In *The Victorian City*, edited by Harold James Dyos and Michael Wolff, 3–57. London: Routledge & Kegan Paul, 1973.

Lampmann, Gustav. "Reichsbauforschung." *Zentralblatt der Bauverwaltung* 48, no. 7 (15 February 1928): 100–2.

– "Wettbewerb zur Erweiterung des Reichstagsgebäudes." *Zentralblatt der Bauverwaltung* 48, no. 5 (1 February 1928): 65–70.

– "Zweiter Wettbewerb zur Reichstag-Erweiterung." *Zentralblatt der Bauverwaltung* 49, no. 50 (11 December 1929): 811–15.

Lang, Emil. "Was ist Stadtbaukunst?" *Stadtbaukunst* 1, no. 1 (1 April 1921): 2–6.

Lang, Fritz. *Metropolis*. Berlin: Erich Pommer, 1927.

Langen, Gustav. "Die Besiedlungen des Vorlandes von Berlin." *Zentralblatt der Bauverwaltung* 51, no. 53/54 (23 December 1931): 779–81.

Langewiesche, Dieter. *Liberalism in Germany*. Translated and edited by Christiane Banerji. Princeton, NJ: Princeton University Press, 2000.

Lawrence, Jon, Martin Dean, and Jean-Louis Robert. "The Outbreak of War and the Urban Economy." *Economic History Review* 65, no. 3 (August 1992): 564–93.

Le Corbusier. *Toward an Architecture [1924]*. Los Angeles: Getty Research Institute, 2007.

Lees, Andrew. "Berlin and Modern Urbanity in German Discourse, 1845–1945." *Journal of Urban History* 17, no. 2 (February 1991): 153–80.

– *Cities Perceived*. Manchester: Manchester University Press, 1985.

Lefebvre, Henri. *The Production of Space*. Oxford: Blackwell, 1991.

– *The Urban Revolution [1970]*. Edited and translated by Robert Bononno. Minneapolis: University of Minnesota Press, 2003.

Lehweß, Walter. "Bruno Möhring." *Zentralblatt der Bauverwaltung* 49, no. 16 (17 April 1929): 260–1.

– "Die Ergebnisse des Wettbewerbs um einen Bebauungsplan für Groß-Berlin und die Allgemeine Städtebauausstellung in Berlin." *Zentralblatt der Bauverwaltung* 30, no. 41 (21 May 1910): 273–6.

– "Felix Genzmer." *Zentralblatt der Bauverwaltung* 49, no. 33 (14 August 1929): 536.

– "Vom Wettbewerb Gross-Berlin." *Tägliche Rundschau, Berlin*, 4 March 1910.

Leidig, Eugen. *Preußisches Stadtrecht*. Berlin: Siemenroth & Worms, 1891.

Lensch, Paul. "Die Neugestaltung der Wirtschaftsordnung." In *Die Arbeiterschaft im neuen Deutschland*, edited by Friedrich Wilhelm Karl Thimme and Carl Legien, 139–47. Leipzig: S. Hirzel, 1915.

Lewinnek, Elaine. "Better Than a Bank for a Poor Man? Home Financing Strategies in Early Chicago." *Journal of Urban History* 32, no. 2 (2006): 274–301.

Lewis, Jill. "Red Vienna." *European History Quarterly* 13, no. 3 (1983): 335–55.

Lewis, Robert, and Richard Walker. "Beyond the Crabgrass Frontier." *Journal of Historical Geography* 27, no. 1 (2001): 3–19.

Liang, Hsi-Huey. "The Berlin Police and the Weimar Republic." *Journal of Contemporary History* 4, no. 4 (1969): 157–72.

Liebknecht, Karl. *Militarism and Anti-Militarism*. New York: Howard Fertig, 1969.

Lindemann, Carl Hugo. *Die deutsche Städteverwaltung*. Stuttgart: J.H.W. Dietz nachf., 1906.

– "Die städtische Grundrente und ihre Bekämpfung." *Socialistische Monatshefte* 9, no. 3 (1905): 248–58.

– "Probleme des Munizipalsozialismus." *Sozialistische Monatshefte* 14, no. 8 (1910): 508–13.

– "Selbstverwaltung und Gemeinde in Preussen." *Sozialistische Monatshefte* 11, no. 11 (1907): 918–24.

– "Selbstverwaltung und staatliche Bureaukratie." *Sozialistische Monatshefte* 12, no. 18/19 (1908): 1181–5.

– "Unsere Forderungen an die Communen." *Socialistische Monatshefte* 6, no. 6 437–447 (1902).

– "Wohnungsstatistik." In *Verhandlungen des Vereins für Socialpolitik über die Wohnungsfrage und die Handelspolitik: Deutschland und Österreich*, edited by Carl Johannes Fuchs and Vereins für Socialpolitik, 261–384. Leipzig: Duncker & Humblot, 1901.

– "Zur Kritik der socialdemokratischen Communalprogramme." *Sozialistische Monatshefte* 6, no. 4 (1902): 277–88.

Linke, Felix. "Das Berliner Verkehrsproblem." *Sozialistische Monatshefte* 14/16, no. 25 (1910): 1619–26.

– "Die neue Architektur." *Sozialistische Monatshefte* 20, no. 17 (1914): 1133–9.

Llorca-Jaña, Manuel. "Shaping Globalization." *Business History Review* 88, no. 3 (2014): 469–95.

Loberg, Molly. "The Streetscape of Economic Crisis." *Journal of Modern History* 85, no. 2 (2013): 364–402.

Locke, John. "Second Treatise." In *Two Treatises of Government and a Letter Concerning Toleration*, edited by Ian Shapiro, 100–10. New Haven, CT: Yale University Press, 2003.

Loesche, Wilhelm. "Berlin North." In *Metropolis Berlin*, edited by David Frisby and Iain Boyd Whyte, 16–17. Berkeley: University of California Press, 2012.

Lohmeyer, Hans. "Groß-Berlin: Grundlage zu einem Gesetz betreffend Bildung einer Gesamtgemeinde." *Kommunale Praxis*, 25 January 1919, 33–9.

Löhr, Isabella, and Roland Wenzlhuemer, eds. *The Nation State and Beyond*. New York: Springer Verlag, 2013.

Long, Christopher. "The Origins and Context of Adolf Loos's 'Ornament and Crime.'" *Journal of the Society of Architectural Historians* 68, no. 2 (2009): 200–23.

Loos, Adolf. "Ornament and Crime [1908]." Translated by Michael Mitchell. In *Ornament and Crime*, edited by Adolf Opel, 167–76. Riverside, CA: Ariadne, 1998.

Löwitsch, Franz. "Die Idee Berlin." *Städtebau-Baupolitik* 5, no. 9 (1931): 423–8.

Lukács, Georg. "Reification and the Consciousness of the Proletariat." In *History and Class Consciousness: Studies in Marxist Dialectics*, 83–222. Cambridge, MA: MIT Press, 1971.

Lux, Joseph August. *Die moderne Wohnung und ihre Ausstattung*. Vienna: Wiener Verlag, 1905.

Lyon, John B. *Out of Place*. New York: Bloomsbury Academic, 2013.

Mächler, Martin. "Das Siedelungsproblem." *Sozialistische Monatshefte* 27, no. 4 (1921): 182–7.

– "Die Grossstadt und der Städtebau." *Sozialistische Monatshefte* 28, no. 9 (1922): 408–11.

– "On the Skyscraper Problem [1921]." In *Metropolis Berlin*, edited by David Frisby and Iain Boyd Whyte, 329–32. Berkeley: University of California Press, 2012.

– "Zum deutschen Neubau." *Sozialistische Monatshefte* 29, no. 10 (1923): 610–15.

Maciuika, John. "Wilhelmine Precedents for the Bauhaus." In *Bauhaus Culture*, edited by Kathleen James-Chakraborty, 1–25. Minneapolis: University of Minnesota Press, 2006.

Mackowsky, [Hans]. "Die geschichtliche Entwicklung des Stadtplanes." *Der Städtebau* 5, no. 3, 4, 5 (1908): 29–30, 45–6, 73–7.

Magistrat der Stadt Berlin, ed. *Bericht über die Gemeinde-Verwaltung der Stadt Berlin in den Verwaltungs-Jahren 1906 bis 1910 mit Abildung, Plan und Graphischen Darstellungen*. 3 vols. Berlin: R. Boll, 1912.

Maier, Charles S. *Recasting Bourgeois Europe*. 2nd ed. Princeton, NJ: Princeton University Press, 1988.

– "Strukturen kapitalistischer Stabilität in den zwanziger Jahren." In *Organisierter Kapitalismus*, edited by Heinrich August Winkler, 195–213. Göttingen: Vandenhoeck & Ruprecht, 1974.

Malinowski, Stephan. "Politische Skandale als Zerrspiegel der Demokratie." *Jahrbuch für Antisemitismusforschung* 5 (1996): 46–65.

Mangoldt, Karl von. "Zur Einführung." In *Gross-Berlins bauliche Zukunft*, edited by Karl Keller and Philipp Nitze, 5–9. Berlin: Renaissance-Verlag Ribert Federn, 1910.

Marchand, Bernard, and Joëlle Salomon Cavin. "Anti-Urban Ideologies and Planning in France and Switzerland." *Planning Perspectives* 22, no. 1 (2007): 29–53.

Marcuse, Herbert. "The Affirmative Character of Culture." Translated by Jeremy J. Shapiro. In *Negations*, 65–98. London: Mayfly Books, 2009.

– "Some Implications of Modern Technology." In *The Essential Frankfurt School Reader*, edited by Andrew Arato and Eike Gebhardt, 138–62, nn180–2. New York: Continuum, 1982.

– *Soviet Marxism*. New York: Columbia University Press, 1958.

Marcuse, Peter. "The Grid as City Plan: New York City and *Laissez-Faire* Planning in the Nineteenth Century." *Planning Perspectives* 2, no. 3 (1987): 287–310.

– "The Housing Policy of Social Democracy." In *The Austrian Socialist Experiment*, edited by Anson Rabinbach, 201–21. Boulder, CO: Westview, 1985.

Marquardt, Frederick D. "A Working Class in Berlin in the 1840s?" In *Sozialgeschichte Heute: Festschrift für Hans Rosenberg zum 70. Geburtstag*, edited by Hans Ulrich Wehler, 191–210. Göttigen: Vandenhoeck & Ruprecht, 1974.

Marx, Karl. *Capital: A Critique of Political Economy*. Translated by David Fernbach. 3 vols. London: Penguin Books in association with New Left Review, 1991.

– *Capital: A Critique of Political Economy*. Edited and translated by Ben Fowkes. 3 vols. Harmondsworth, UK: Penguin Books in association with New Left Review, 1976.

– "Letter to Friedrich Adolph Sorge: June 21, 1881." Translated by Dona Torr. In *Karl Marx and Friedrich Engels: Correspondence, 1846–1895: A Selection with Commentary Notes*, 394–6. New York: International Publishers, 1942.

– *The Poverty of Philosophy: Answer to the "Philosophy of Poverty" by M. Proudhon*. Peking: Foreign Languages, 1978.

– "Theses on Feuerbach [1845]." In *The Marx-Engels Reader*, edited by Robert C. Tucker, 143–5. New York: W.W. Norton, 1978.

Matzerath, Horst. "Städtwachstum und Eingemeindungen im 19. Jahrhundert." In *Die deutsche Stadt im Industriezeitalter*, edited by Jürgen Reulecke, 67–89. Wuppertal: Peter Hammer, 1978.

Mauro, Paolo, Nathan Sussman, and Yishay Yafeh. *Emerging Markets and Financial Globalization*. Oxford: Oxford University Press, 2006.

McCarthy, Michael P. "Chicago Businessmen and the Burnham Plan." *Journal of the Illinois State Historical Society* 63, no. 3 (1970): 228–56.

McKelvey, Blake. "American Urban History Today." *American Historical Review* 57, no. 4 (1952): 919–29.

McNeil, William C. *American Money and the Weimar Republic*. New York: Columbia University Press, 1986.

Metzler, Tobias. "Secularization and Pluralism: Urban Jewish Cultures in Early Twentieth-Century Berlin." *Journal of Urban History* 37, no. 6 (2011): 871–96.

Meyer, Dora. "Das öffentliche Leben in Berlin im Jahr vor der Märzrevolution." *Schriften des Vereins für die Geschichte Berlins* 46 (1912): 1–116.

Meyer, Peter. "Vom neuen Bauen." *Zentralblatt der Bauverwaltung* 49, no. 26 (26 June 1929): 413–14.

Migge, Leberecht. "Das grüne Manifest [1918]." In *Der soziale Garten*, 7–15. Berlin: Gebr. Mann, 1999.

– "Kommunale Siedlung als Mittel zur Wiederherstellung Selbstverwaltung." *Zeitschrift für Kommunalwirtschaft und Kommunalpolitik* 11, no. 9 (1921): 346–50.

– "Weltstadt-Grün." *Städtebau* 25, no. 5 (1930): 241–8.

Millward, Robert. "Urban Government, Finance and Public Health in Victorian Britain." In *Urban Governance: Britain and Beyond since 1750*, edited by Richard H. Trainor and Robert Morris, 47–68. Burlington, VT: Ashgate, 2000.

Moch, Leslie Page, and Rachel G. Fuchs. "Getting Along." *French Historical Studies* 18, no. 1 (1993): 34–49.

Moga, Steven T. "Marginal Lands and Suburban Nature." *Journal of Planning History* 8, no. 4 (2009): 308–29.

Mombert, Paul. *Die deutschen Stadtgemeinden und ihre Arbeiter*. Vol. 50. Stuttgart: J.G. Cotta'sche Buchhandlung Nachfolger, 1902.

Moore, James R. "Liberalism and the Politics of Suburbia." *Urban History* 30, no. 2 (2003): 225–50.

Moravánszky, Ákos. "The Optical Construction of Urban Space." *Journal of Architecture* 17, no. 5 (2012): 655–66.

Mullin, John Robert. "Ideology, Planning Theory and the German City in the Inter-War Years: Part I." *Town Planning Review* 53, no. 2 (1982): 115–30.

Mumford, Eric. "CIAM and the Communist Bloc, 1928–59." *Journal of Architecture* 14, no. 2 (2009): 237–54.

– *The CIAM Discourse on Urbanism, 1928–1960*. Cambridge, MA: MIT Press, 2000.

– "CIAM Urbanism after the Athens Charter." *Planning Perspectives* 7, no. 4 (1992): 391–417.

Murphy, David T. "'A Sum of the Most Wonderful Things.'" *History of European Ideas* 25, no. 3 (1999): 121–33.

Nelson, Robert L. "From Manitoba to the Memel." *Social History* 35, no. 4 (2010): 439–57.

Neumann, Franz L. "The Change in the Function of Law in Modern Society." Translated by Klaus Knorr. In *The Democratic and the Authoritarian State*, edited by Herbert Marcuse. 22–68. Glencoe, IL: Free Press, 1957.

– "Types of Natural Law." *Studies in Philosophy and Social Science [Zeitschrift für Sozialforschung]* 8, no. 3 (1939/40): 338–61.

Neurath, Otto. "Die Naturalwirtschaftslehre und der Naturalkalkül in ihren Beziehungen zur Kriegswirtschaftslehre [1916]." In *Durch die Kriegswirtschaft zur Naturalwirtschaft*, 174–82. Munich: Callwey, 1919.

– "The Economic Order of the Future and the Economic Sciences." Translated by Christoph Schmidt-Petri and Thomas E. Uebel. In *Otto Neurath Economic Writings Selections 1904–1945*, edited by Thomas E. Uebel and Robert Cohen, 241–61. New York: Springer, 2005.

– "Economics in Kind, Calculation in Kind and Their Relation to War Economics." Translated by Christoph Schmidt-Petri and Thomas E. Uebel. In *Otto Neurath Economic Writings Selections 1904–1945*, edited by Thomas E. Uebel and Robert Cohen, 299–311. New York: Springer, 2005.

– "Städtebau und Proletariat." *Der Kampf* 17, no. 6 (1924): 237–42.

– "The Conceptual Structure of Economic Theory and Its Foundations [1917]." In *Otto Neurath Economic Writings Selections 1904–1945*, edited by Thomas E. Uebel and Robert Cohen, 312–41. New York: Springer, 2005.

Nolan, Mary. *Visions of Modernity*. New York: Oxford University Press, 1994.

Nußbaum, Theodor. "Weltstadtgrün." *Städtebau* 26, no. 1 (1931): 41–8.

Nyhart, Lynn K. *Modern Nature*. Chicago: University of Chicago Press, 2009.

O'Connell, James C. "How Metropolitan Parks Shaped Greater Boston, 1893–1945." In *Remaking Boston*, edited by Anthony N. Penna and Conrad Edick Wright, 168–98. Pittsburgh: University of Pittsburgh Press, 2009.

Oettingen, Wolfgang von. *Berlin*. Leipzig: Klinkhardt & Biermann, 1907.

Olk, Friedrich. "Vor dem zweiten Abschnitt der deutschen Rationalisierung." *Die Arbeit* 7, no. 3 (1930): 156–60.

Olmsted, Frederick Law, and J. James R. Croes. "Document No. 72 of the Board of the Department of Public Parks ... [1876]." In *Landscape into Cityscape*, edited by Albert Fein, 349–75. Ithaca, NY: Cornell University Press, 1968.

Olsen, Donald J. *The Growth of Victorian London*. New York: Holmes & Meier, 1976.

Ostwald, Hans. *Berliner Kaffeehäuser*. 51 vols. Berlin: Hermann Seemann Nachfolger, GmbH, 1905.

Otter, Chris. "Making Liberalism Durable." *Social History* 27, no. 1 (2002): 1–15.

Otto, Christian. "Modem Environment and Historical Continuity." *Art Journal* 43, no. 2 (1983): 148–57.

Palmer, Thomas C., Jr. "City Makes Filene's Site a Landmark." *Boston Globe*, 10 May 2006.

Palmowski, Jan. "Liberalism and Local Government in Late Nineteenth-Century Germany and England." *Historical Journal* 45, no. 2 (2002): 381–409.

– "The Politics of the 'Unpolitical German.'" *Historical Journal* 42, no. 3 (1999): 675–704.

Parks, Richard. "The Jewish Quarters of Interwar Paris and Tunis." *Jewish Social Studies: History, Culture, Society* 17, no. 1 (2010): 67–87.

Patterson, Gordon. "Race and Anti-Semitism in the Life and Work of Egon Friedell." *Jahrbuch des Instituts für deutsche Geschichte* 10 (1981): 319–39.

Pepper, Simon, and Peter Richmond. "Homes Unfit for Heroes." *Town Planning Review* 90, no. 2 (2009): 143–71.

Petersen, Richard. *Die Verkehrsaufgaben des Verbandes Groß-Berlin*. Berlin: C. Heymann, 1911.

Peus, Heinrich. "Der Sozialismus und der sogenannte Kriegssozialismus." *Sozialistische Monatshefte* 23, no. 4 (1917): 190–4.

Pfannschmidt, Martin, and Alexander Schwab. "Städtebaufragen." *Zentralblatt der Bauverwaltung* 51, no. 26 (24 June 1931): 393–9.

Pfeifer, Hermann. "Kontrast und Rhythmus im Städtebau." *Der Städtebau* 1, no. 7 (1904): 97–9.

Phimister, Ian. "Late Nineteenth-Century Globalization: London and Lomagundi Perspectives on Mining Speculation in Southern Africa, 1894–1904," *Journal of Global History* 10, no. 1 (2015): 27–52.

Pierce, Bessie Louise. *A History of Chicago*. 3 vols. New York: A.A. Knopf, 1937–57.

Pohle, Ludwig. "Der Kampf um die Wohnungsfrage I." *Zeitschrift für Socialwissenschaft* 8, no. 11 (1905): 679–700.

– "Der Kampf um die Wohnungsfrage II." *Zeitschrift für Socialwissenschaft* 8, no. 12 (1905): 759–81.

Pöhls, Joachim. "Tägliche Rundschau (1881–1933)." In *Deutsche Zeitungen des 17. bis 20. Jahrhunderts*, edited by Heinz-Dietrich Fischer, 349–63. Pullach bei München: Verlag Dokumentation, 1972.

Poling, Kristin. "Shantytowns and Pioneers beyond the City Wall." *Central European History* 47, no. 2 (2014): 245–74.

Pommer, Richard. "Some Architectural Ideologies after the Fall." *Art Journal* 40, no. 1/2 (1980): 353–61.

Pooley, Colin G. "Housing for the Poorest Poor." *Journal of Historical Geography* 11, no. 1 (1985): 70–88.

Postone, Moishe. "Anti-Semitism and National Socialism." In "Germans and Jews," special issue, *New Germans Critique* 19 (Winter 1980): 97–115.

– "The Holocaust and the Trajectory of the Twentieth Century." In *Catastrophe and Meaning*, edited by Moishe Postone and Eric L. Santner, 81–114. Chicago: University of Chicago Press, 2003.

– "Theorizing the Contemporary World." In *History and Heteronomy*, edited by Viren Murthy and Yasuo Kobayashi, 85–109. Tokyo: University of Tokyo Center for Philosophy, 2009.

– *Time, Labor, and Social Domination*. Cambridge: Cambridge University Press, 1993.

Preuß, Hugo. *Das städtische Amtsrecht in Preußen*. Berlin: Georg Reimer, 1902.

– *Das Völkerrecht im Dienste des Wirthschaftslebens*. Berlin: Leonhard Simion, 1891.

– *Entwicklungsgeschichte der Deutschen Städteverfassung*. Vol. 1. Leipzig: B.G. Teubner, 1906.

– *Gemeinde, Staat, Reich als Gebietskörperschaften*. Berlin: J. Springer, 1889.

– "Sozialpolitik im Berliner Verkehr." In *Fragen der kommunalen Sozialpolitik in Groß-Berlin*, edited by Gesellschaft für soziale Reform Ortsgruppe Berlin, 1–26. Jena: Gustav Fischer, 1911.

Pudor, Heinrich. "Der Volkspark von Groß-Berlin." *Der Städtebau* 7, no. 2 (1910): 21–2.

Purseigle, Pierre. "The First World War and the Transformations of the State." *International Affairs* 90, no. 2 (2014): 249–64.

Queis, Martin. *Begriff und Wirkung der Eingemeindung nach preußischem Verwaltungsrecht*. Greifswald: J. Abel, 1913.

Rabinbach, Anson. *The Crisis of Austrian Socialism*. Chicago: University of Chicago Press, 1983.

Rappaport, Philipp August. "'Statistische Beziehung zwischen Mensch und Fläche.'" *Städtebau-Baupolitik* 5, no. 9 (1931): 432.

Rathenau, Walther. *Zur Kritik der Zeit*. Berlin: S. Fischer Verlag, 1912.

– *Zur Mechnanik des Geistes*. Berlin: Fischer Verlag, 1913.

Resnick, Stephen A., and Richard D. Wolff. *Class Theory and History*. New York: Routledge, 2002.

Retzlaff, Rebecca C. "The Illinois Forest Preserve District Act of 1913 and the Emergence of Metropolitan Park System Planning in the USA." *Planning Perspectives* 25, no. 4 (2010): 433–55.

Rezende, Vera F. "Brazilian City Planners, American City Planning? New Perspectives on Urban Planning in Rio De Janeiro, 1930–1945," *Planning Perspectives* 25, no. 4 (2010): 505–13.

Richter, Günter. "Zwischen Revolution und Reichsgründung (1848–1871)." In *Geschichte Berlins*, edited by Wolfgang Ribbe, 605–90. Munich: C.H. Beck, 1987.

Riehl, Wilhelm Heinrich. *Land und Leute*. Stuttgart: J.G. Cotta'scher Verlag, 1856.

Ritschl, Albrecht. "The Pity of Peace." In *The Economics of World War I*, edited by S.N. Broadberry and Mark Harrison, 41–77. Cambridge: Cambridge University Press, 2005.

Roack, Victor. "Groß-Berlin Siedlungs- und Wohnungsfrage." *Kommunale Praxis*, 21 September 1918, 593–8.

– "Mieterlend in Groß-Berlin." *Kommunale Praxis*, 30 March 1918, 193–6.

Roberts, Sophie B. "Anti-Semitism and Municipal Government in Interwar French Colonial Algeria." *Journal of North African Studies* 17, no. 5 (2012): 821–37.

Rodenstein, Marianne. *Mehr Licht, mehr Luft: Gesundheitskonzepte im Städtebau seit 1750*. Frankfurt/Main: Campus, 1988.

Rodriguez Lores, Juan. "Stadtentwicklung und sozialer Wohnungsbau: die Anfänge in Europa." *Die Alte Stadt* 23, no. 2 (1996): 176–97.

Roessler, Gustav von. "Zur Bauart deutscher Städte (I–II)." *Deutsche Bauzeitung* 8. The complete article is serialized in three issues no. 39, 41, and 101 (1874): 153–4, 162–5, 402–5.

Rosenhaft, Eve. *Beating the Fascists? The German Communists and Political Violence, 1929–1933*. Cambridge: Cambridge University Press, 1983.

Roth, Guenther. "Edgar Jaffé and Else von Richthofen in the Mirror of Newly Found Letters." *Max Weber Studies* 10, no. 2 (2010): 151–88.

Rubin, Eli. "Amnesiopolis." *Central European History* 47, no. 2 (2014): 334–74.

– "From the Grünen Wiesen to Urban Space: Berlin, Expansion, and the Longue Durée." *Central European History* 47, no. 2 (2014): 221–44.

Ruck, Michael. "Der Wohnungsbau: Schnittpunkt von Sozial- und Wirtschaftspolitik." In *Die Weimarer Republik als Wohlfahrtsstaat*, edited by Werner Abelshauser, 91–123. Stuttgart: F. Steiner, 1987.

Rudischhauser, Sabine. "Die parlamentarischen Debatten über die Sozialpolitik der neuen Stadtgemeinde Berlin in der ersten Stadtverordnetenversammlung 1920/21." In *Beiträge zur Geschichte der Berliner Demokratie, 1919–1933/1945–1985*, edited by Otto Büsch and Felix Escher, 45–84. Berlin: Colloquium Verlag, 1988.

Rudolph, Nicole. "'Who Should Be the Author of a Dwelling?'" *Gender & History* 21, no. 3 (2009): 541–59.

Runge, Ernst. "Grundsätzliches zum Problem der Erweiterung Gross-Berlins (Eine städtebauliche, kommunal- und finanzpolitische Studie)." Dissertation zur Erlangung der Würde eines Doktor-Ingenieurs der Technischen Hochschule zu Berlin, Technischen Hochschule zu Berlin, 1930.

Ruttmann, Walter. *Berlin*. 1:01:52. Berlin: Deutsche Vereins-Film, 1927.

Sachs, Robert. "Öffentliche Bodenpolitik gegen private Bodenspekulation." *Die Arbeit* 7, no. 5 (1930): 306–12.

Sanchez-Sibony, Oscar. *Red Globalization*. Cambridge: Cambridge University Press, 2014.

Sass, Konrad. *Die Bauklassen der Bauordnung für die Berliner Vororte*. Berlin: A. Seydel, 1906.

Sassen, Saskia. *The Global City*. Princeton, NJ: Princeton University Press, 1991.

Scarpa, Ludovica. "Das Großsiedlungs-Modell." In *Vier Berliner Siedlungen der Weimarer Republik*, edited by Norbert Huse, 21–6. Berlin: Argon, 1987.

Scheffler, Karl. *Berlin*. Berlin-Westend: Erich Reiss Verlag, 1910.

– *Die Architektur der Großstadt*. Berlin: Gebr. Mann, 1998.

Schlesinger, Arthur M., Sr. "The City in American History." *Mississippi Valley Historical Review* 27, no. 1 (1940): 43–66.

– *The Rise of the City, 1878–1898*. New York: Macmillan, 1933.

Schliepmann, Hans. "Der Krieg und die Baukunst." *Berliner Architekturwelt* 17, no. 9 (1915): 319–58.

– "Verbesserung Großstädtischer Bauordnung." *Berliner Architekturwelt* 20, no. 11/12 (1918): 253–302.

Schmidt, Paul Ferdinand. "Probleme der Weltstadt Berlin." *Sozialistische Monatshefte* 35, no. 2 (18 February 1929): 136–40.

Schmitt, Carl. *Hugo Preuß*. Tübingen: Mohr, 1930.

Schmitthenner, Paul. "Die Siedlung Plaue bei Brandenburg a. H." *Wasmuths Monatshefte für Baukunst* 4, no. 5/6 (1920): 161–81.

Schneider, Michael. "Rudolf Wissell (1869–1962)." *Vierteljahresschrift für Sozialrecht* 6, no. 1/2 (1978): 165–82.

Scholz, Ernst. "Die moderne Stadtverwaltung [1]." *Zeitschrift für Kommunalwirtschaft und Kommunalpolitik*, no. 1 (11 January 1913): 2–3.

– "Die moderne Stadtverwaltung [2]." *Zeitschrift für Kommunalwirtschaft und Kommunalpolitik*, no. 2 (25 January 1913): 30–1.

– "Die moderne Stadtverwaltung [15]." *Zeitschrift für Kommunalwirtschaft und Kommunalpolitik*, no. 22 (25 November 1913): 673–75.

Scholz, Robert. "Die Auswirkungen der Inflation auf das Sozial- und Wohlfahrtswesen der neuen Stadtgemeinde Berlin." In *Konsequenzen der Inflation*, edited by Gerald D. Feldman, Carl-Ludwig Holtfrerich, Gerhard A. Ritter, and Peter-Christian Witt, 45–78. Berlin: Colloquium Verlag, 1989.

Schorske, Carl E. *Fin-de-siècle Vienna*. New York: Vintage Books, 1981.

Schraepler, Ernst. "Berlin als Zentrale der deutschen sozialistischen Arbeiterbewegung." In *Berlin im Europa der Neuzeit*, edited by Wolfgang Ribbe and Jürgen Schmädeke, 155–64. Berlin: Walter de Gruyter, 1990.

Schröder, Wilhelm. "Das Projekt des Zwangszweckverbands für Gross Berlin." *Sozialistische Monatshefte* 15/17, no. 3 (1911): 187–93.

Schultz. "Zur Wohnungsfrage: II. Wohnungsbau nach dem Kriege." *Kommunale Praxis* 5 October 1918, 630–33.

Schultze-Naumburg, Paul. *Städtebau*. Vol. 4. Munich: Callwey, 1909.

Schuster, Ernst. "Typisierung als Wirtschaftsorganisation." *Weltwirtschaftliches Archiv* 19 (1923): 429–38.

Schwartz, Frederic J. "Commodity Signs." *Journal of Design History* 9, no. 3 (1996): 153–84.

Schwartz, Robert M. "Rail Transport, Agrarian Crisis, and the Restructuring of Agriculture: France and Great Britain Confront Globalization, 1860–1900." *Social Science History* 34, no. 2 (2010): 229–55.

Schwebel, Oskar. *Geschichte der Stadt Berlin*. 2 vols. Berlin: Brachvogel & Ranft, 1888.

Schwenke, Wilhelm. "Brix, Joseph." In *Neue Deutsche Biographie*, 2:618. Berlin: Duncker & Humblot, 1955.

Schwippe, Heinrich Johannes. "Öffentlicher Personen-Nahverkehr, Stadtentwicklung und Dezentralisierung: Berlin 1860–1910." In *Stadt und Verkehr im Industriezeitalter*, edited by Horst Matzerath, 161–202. Cologne: Böhlau Verlag, 1996.

Scott, James C. *Seeing like a State*. New Haven, CT: Yale University Press, 1998.

Scott, Joan Wallach. "A Statistical Representation of Work." In *Gender and the Politics of History*, 113–38. New York: Columbia University Press, 1999.

Scott, Peter. "Did Owner-Occupation Lead to Smaller Families for Interwar Working-Class Households?" *Economic History Review* 61, no. 1 (2008): 99–124.

– "Marketing Mass Home Ownership and the Creation of the Modern Working-Class Consumer in Inter-War Britain." *Business History* 50, no. 1 (2008): 4–25.

– "The State, Internal Migration, and the Growth of New Industrial Communities in Inter-War Britain." *English Historical Review* 115, no. 461 (2000): 329–53.

Sewell, William H., Jr. "Connecting Capitalism to the French Revolution." *Critical Historical Studies* 1, no. 1 (2014): 5–46.

– "Refiguring the 'Social' in Social Science." In *Logics of History*, 318–73. Chicago: University of Chicago Press, 2005.

Sheail, John. "Interwar Planning in Britain." *Journal of Urban History* 11, no. 3 (1985): 335–51.

Sheehan, James J. "Liberalism and the City in Nineteenth-Century Germany." *Past and Present* 51, no. 1 (1971): 116–37.

Siemens, Daniel. "Explaining Crime: Berlin Newspapers and the Construction of the Criminal in Weimar Germany." *Journal of European Studies* 39, no. 3 (2009): 336–52.

Sigrist, Albert. *Das Buch vom Bauen*. Berlin: Der Bucherkreis GmbH, 1930.

Simmel, Georg. "Individual and Society in Eighteenth and Nineteenth Century Views of Life." Translated by Kurt H. Wolff. In *The Sociology of Georg Simmel*, edited by Kurt H. Wolff, 58–84. Glencoe, IL: Free Press, 1950.

– "The Metropolis and Mental Life." In *Metropolis*, edited by Philip Kasinitz, 30–45. New York: New York University Press, 1995.

Sitte, Camillo *Der Städtebau nach seinen künstlerischen Grundsätzen*. Vienna: Graeser; Teubner, 1909.

Skalweit, August. *Die Viehhandelsverbände in der deutschen Kriegswirtschaft*. Vol. 10. Berlin: Verlag der Beiträge zur Kriegswirtschaft (Reimar Hobbing), 1917.

Sloin, Andrew, and Oscar Sanchez-Sibony. "Economy and Power in the Soviet Union, 1917–39." *Kritika: Explorations in Russian and Eurasian History* 15, no. 1 (2014): 7–22.

Smith, Adam. *An Inquiry into the Nature and Causes of the Wealth of Nations [1776]*. Chicago: University of Chicago Press, 1976.

Smith, Carl S. *The Plan of Chicago: Daniel Burnham and the Remaking of the American City*. Chicago: University of Chicago Press, 2006.

Smith, Neil. "Homeless/Global: Scaling Places." In *Mapping the Futures*, edited by Jon Bird, Barry Curtis, Tim Putnam, and Lisa Tickner, 87–119. London: Routledge, 1993.

Sollman, W. "Kleinhaus oder Mehrfamilienhaus." *Kommunale Praxis*, 8 June 1918, 353–6.

Sombart, Werner. "Vienna [1907]." In *Metropolis Berlin: 1880–1940*, edited by David Frisby and Iain Boyd Whyte, 31–3. Berkeley: University of California Press, 2012.

Sonne, Wolfgang. "Berlin." In *Planning Twentieth-Century Capital Cities*, edited by David L.A. Gordon, 196–213. London: Routledge, 2006.

– "Dwelling in the Metropolis." *Progress in Planning* 72, no. 2 (2009): 53–149.

– "'The Entire City Shall Be Planned as a Work of Art'." *Zeitschrift für Kunstgeschichte* 66, no. 2 (2003): 207–36.

– *Representing the State*. Munich: Prestel, 2003.
– "Specific Intentions, General Realities." *Planning Perspectives* 19, no. 3 (2004): 283–310.
– "'Stadtbaukunst' als Konzept: ein internationales Phänomen um 1910." *Informationen zur modernen Stadtgeschichte* 6, no. 1 (2010): 14–27.

Sönnichsen, Martina. "Leistungsverwaltung in der ersten Berliner Demokratie Stadtplanung, Siedlungswesen und Wohnungsbau der Reichhauptstadt in der Amtzeit Martin Wagners 1926–1930." In *Beiträge zur Geschichte der Berliner Demokratie, 1919–1933/1945–1985*, edited by Otto Büsch and Felix Escher, 85–106. Berlin: Colloquium Verlag, 1988.

Spartakus in Grün an dem der rote sterben soll. "Das grüne Manifest." *Die Tat* 10, no. 12 (1919): 912–19.

Splanemann, Andreas. "Bewährung und Begrenzung der Berliner Demokratie." In *Beiträge zur Geschichte der Berliner Demokratie, 1919–1933/1945–1985*, edited by Otto Büsch. 3–44. Berlin: Colloquium Verlag, 1988.

Städte-Ordnung für die sechs östlichen Provinzen der Preußischen Monarchie: Vom 30. Mai 1853. Berlin: Carl Salewski, 1853.

Stargardt, Nicholas. *The German Idea of Militarism*. Cambridge: Cambridge University Press, 1994.

Stein, Mary Beth. "Wilhelm Heinrich Riehl and the Scientific-Literary Formation of 'Volkskunde.'" *German Studies Review* 24, no. 3 (2001): 487–512.

Steinbrucker, Franz. "Wohnungsmangel und Wohungselend." *Der Städtebau* 12, no. 12 (1915): 114–16.

Stolberg-Wernigerode, Otto zu. "Endell, Ernst Moritz August." In *Neue Deutsche Biographie*, 4:490–1. Berlin: Duncker & Humblot, 1959.

Stolleis, Michael. *Public Law in Germany, 1800–1914*. Translated and edited by Pamela Beil. New York: Berghahn, 2001.

Storper, Michael Charles, and Allen John Scott. "The Wealth of Regions." *Futures* 27, no. 5 (1995): 505–26.

Stovall, Tyler. "The Consumers' War: Paris, 1914–1918." *French Historical Studies* 31, no. 2 (2008): 293–325.
– "French Communism and Suburban Development." *Journal of Contemporary History* 24, no. 3 (July 1989): 437–60.

Streckfuss, Adolf. *500 Jahre Berliner Geschichte*. 2 vols. Berlin: Albert Goldschmidt, 1886.

Stübben, Josef. *Der Städtebau [1890]*. Vol. 9. Stuttgart: Alfred Kröner Verlag, 1907.
– "Otto March." *Zentralblatt der Bauverwaltung* 33, no. 29 (12 April 1913): 199–200.
– "Ueber einige Fragen der Städtebaukunst." *Deutsche Bauzeitung* 25, no. 21, 25 (14 and 28 March 1891): 122–8, 150–5.

Sutcliffe, Anthony. "Introduction." In *The Rise of Modern Urban Planning, 1800–1914*, edited by Anthony Sutcliffe, 1–10. New York: St Martin's, 1980.

Sweeney, Dennis. *Work, Race, and the Emergence of Radical Right Corporatism in Imperial Germany*. Ann Arbor: University of Michigan Press, 2009.

Tafuri, Manfredo. "Sozialpolitik and the City in Weimar Germany." In *The Sphere and the Labyrinth*, 197–233. Cambridge, MA: MIT Press, 1987.

Takáts, Elek. "Der Verband Groß-Berlin vom 19. Juli 1911 bis 1. Okt. 1920 seine wirtschaftlichen Aufgaben und Leistungen insbesondere im Verkehrs- und Siedungswesen." Universität Koln, 1933.

Taut, Bruno. "Das Problem des Opernbaus." *Sozialistische Monatshefte* 20, no. 6 (1914): 355–7.

– "Der Reichstagerweiterung in ihrer Beziehung zum Platz der Republik." *Zentralblatt der Bauverwaltung* 50, no. 5 (5 February 1930): 109–16.

– *Die Auflösung der Städte*. Hagen in West Erschienen im Folkwang, 1920.

Thienel, Ingrid. "Industrialisierung und Städtewachstum." In *Untersuchungen zur Geschichte der frühen Industrialisierung vornehmlich im Wirtschaftsraum Berlin/Brandenburg*, edited by Otto Büsch, 107–50. Berlin: Colloquium Verlag, 1971.

– *Städtewachstum im Industrialisierungsprozess des 19. Jahrhunderts: Das Berliner Beispiel*. Berlin: Walter de Gruyter, 1973.

Thierfelder, Jörg. "Fritz Elsas." In *Zeugen des Widerstands*, edited by Joachim Mehlhausen, 91–110. Tübingen: Mohr Siebeck, 1998.

Thieß, Karl. "Höchstpreispolitik." In *Die Preisbildung im Kriege*, edited by Volkwirtschaftlichen Abteilung des Kriegsernährungsamts, 5–33. Berlin: Verlag der Beiträge zur Kriegswirtschaft (Reimar Hobbing), 1916.

Tooze, Adam, and Ted Fertik. "The World Economy and the Great War." *Geschichte und Gesellschaft* 40, no. 2 (2014): 214–38.

Totomjanz, Vakhan Fomich. *Über die wirtschaftlichen Aufgaben der städtischen Verwaltung*. Vol. 84. Leipzig: Felix Dietrich, 1906.

Twain, Mark. "The German Chicago." In *Metropolis Berlin, 1880–1940*, edited by Iain Boyd Whyte and David Frisby, 17–18. Berkeley: University of California Press, 2012.

Umbach, Maiken. "A Tale of Second Cities: Autonomy, Culture, and the Law in Hamburg and Barcelona in the Late Nineteenth Century." *American Historical Review* 110, no. 3 (2005): 659–92.

van Ballegooijen, Jan, and Roberto Rocco. "The Ideologies of Informality." *Third World Quarterly* 34, no. 10 (2013): 1794–1810.

Varga-Harris, Christine. "Homemaking and the Aesthetic and Moral Perimeters of the Soviet Home during the Khrushchev Era." *Journal of Social History* 41, no. 3 (2008): 561–89.

Vereinigung Berliner Architekten, and Architekten-Verein zu Berlin. *Anregungen zur Erlangung eines Grundplanes für die städtebauliche Entwicklung von Groß-Berlin*. Berlin: E. Wasmuth A.-G., 1907.

Voigt, Andreas, and Paul Geldner. *Kleinhaus und Mietkaserne*. Berlin: J. Springer, 1905.

Voigt, Wolfgang. "Schmitthenner, Paul." *Neue Deutsche Biographie* 23 (2007): 246–8.

Volkov, Shulamit. *The Rise of Popular Antimodernism in Germany*. Princeton, NJ: Princeton University Press, 1978.

von Blume, Wilhelm. "Autonomie Körperschaften." In *Handbuch der Politik*, edited by Paul Laband, Adolf Wach, Adolf Wagner, Georg Jellinek, Karl Lamprecht, Franz von Liszt, Georg von Schanz, and Fritz Berolzheimer, 219–24. Berlin: Dr Walther Rothschild, 1912.

von Carstenn-Lichterfelde, Johann Anton Wilhelm. *Die Schenkung des Terrains zu Gross-Lichterfelde an den Preussischen Militaer-Fiskus zum Bau der Central Kadetten-Anstalt*. Berlin: E. Staude, 1890.

– *Die zukünftige Entwicklung Berlins*. Berlin, 1892.

von Dincklage[-Campe], F[riedrich] Freiherr. "Das militärische Berlin." In *Groß-Berlin: Bilder von der Ausstellungsstadt*, edited by Albert Kühnemann and Richard Schott, 155–64, 183–7. Berlin: W. Pauli's Nachfolge, 1896.

von Kessel, Gustav. "Berlin in a State of War." In *Metropolis Berlin, 1880–1940*, edited by Iain Boyd Whyte and David Frisby, 279–80. Berkeley: University of California Press, 2012.

von Möller, Ernst. *Preussisches Stadtrecht*. Breslau: W. Clar, 1864.

von Petz, Ursula. "The Environmental Transformation of the Ruhr." In *City, Country, Empire*, edited by Dorsey Kurkpatrick and Jeffry M. Diefendorf, 52–76. Pittsburgh: University of Pittsburgh Press, 2005.

von Pistorius, [Theodor]. "Reichs-, Staats- und Gemeindefinanzen." *Zeitschrift für die gesamte Staatswissenschaft* 88, no. 3 (1930): 545–79.

von Saldern, Adelheid. "Gesellschaft und Lebensgestaltung Soziolkuturelle Streiflicher." In *Geschichte des Wohnens: 1918–1945*, edited by Gert Kähler, 47–182. Stuttgart: Deutsche Verlags-Anstalt, 1996.

– "'Instead of Cathedrals, Dwelling Machines.'" Translated by Bruce Little. In *The Challenge of Modernity*, 93–114. Ann Arbor: University of Michigan Press, 2002.

– "Social Rationalization of Living and Housework in Germany and the United States in the 1920s." *History of the Family* 2, no. 1 (1997): 73–97.

von Ungern-Sternberg, Roderich. "Rationalisierung der deutschen Industriewirtschaft." *Sozialistische Monatshefte* 37, no. 3 (1931): 250–5.

von Wiese, Leopold. "Liberalismus und Demokratismus in ihren Zusammenhängen und Gegensätzen." *Zeitschrift für Politik* 9 (1916): 407–25.

Vurpillat, J. Taylor. "Empire, Industry, and Globalization." *History Compass* 12, no. 6 (2014): 531–40.

Wagemann, Ines. "Möhring, Bruno." In *Neue Deutsche Biographie*, edited by Der Historischen Kommission bei der Bayerischen Akademie der Wissenschaft, 621–2. Berlin: Duncker & Humblot, 1994.

Wagner, Martin. "American versus German City Planning." *Journal of Land Use & Public Utility Economics* 22, no. 4 (1946): 321–38.

– "Baukostenverbilligung im Kleinwohnungsbau." In *Ein Programm für die Ubergangswirtschaft in Wohnungswesen*, edited by Deutscher Verein für Wohnungsreform, 69–83. Berlin: F. Siemenroth, 1918.

– "Die Sanierung der Mietskasernen." In *Die Wohnungs- und Siedlungsfrage nach dem Kriege*, edited by Carl Johannes Fuchs, 398–406. Stuttgart: W. Meyer-Ilschen, 1918.

– *Gemeinwirtschaft im Wohnungswesen*. Kiel: Vollbehr & Riepen, 1920.

– "Mehr Organisation im städtischen Siedlungswesen." *Preußisches Verwaltungs-Blatt* 36, no. 50 (1915): 808–10.

– *Neue Wege zum Kleinwohnungsbau: ein Programm der Selbsthilfe*. Vol. 2. Berlin: Vorwärts-Buchdruckerei, 1924.

– *Städtische Freiflachenpolitik*. Vol. 11 der neuen Folge der Schriften der Zentralstelle für Arbeiter-Wohlfahrtseinrichtungen. Berlin: Carl Heymanns Verlag, 1915.

– "Wohnungswirtschaft-Finanzwirtschaft." *Kommunale Praxis*, 20 March 1920, 265–70.

Wakeman, Rosemary. "Nostalgic Modernism and the Invention of Paris in the Twentieth Century." *French Historical Studies* 27, no. 1 (2004): 115–44.

Walker, Richard. "Industry Builds the City." *Journal of Historical Geography* 27, no. 1 (2001): 36–57.

Ward, David. "Environs and Neighbours in the 'Two Nations': Residential Differentiation in Mid-Nineteenth-Century Leeds," *Journal of Historical Geography* 6, no. 2 (1980): 133–62.

Warner, Sam Bass. "If All the World Were Philadelphia." *American Historical Review* 74, no. 1 (1968): 26–43.

Webb, Steven Benjamin. "Government Revenue and Spending in Germany, 1919 to 1923." In *The Adaptation to Inflation*, edited by Gerald D. Feldman, Carl-Ludwig Holtfrerich, Gerhard A. Ritter, and Peter-Christian Witt, 46–82. Berlin: W. de Gruyter, 1986.

Weber, Adolf. *Boden und Wohnung*. Leipzig: Verlag von Duncker & Humbolt, 1908.

– *Die Großstadt und ihre sozialen Probleme*. Leipzig: Verlag von Quelle & Meyer, 1908.

Weber, Alfred. *Theory of the Location of Industries [1909]*. Edited and translated by Carl Joachim Friedrich. Chicago: University of Chicago Press, 1929.

– *Ueber den Standort der Industrien [1909]*. 2nd ed. Tübingen: J.C.B. Mohr, 1922.

Weddle, Robert. "Housing and Technological Reform in Interwar France." *Journal of Architectural Education* 54, no. 3 (2006): 167–75.

Wehler, Hans Ulrich. "Der Aufstieg des Organisierten Kapitalismus und Interventionsstaates in Deutschland." In *Organisierter Kapitalismus*, edited by Heinrich August Winkler, 36–57. Göttingen: Vandenhoeck & Ruprecht, 1974.

Weiß, Wisso. "Die Sozialisierung des Wohnungswesens unter besonderer Berücksichtigung der Verhältnisse in Deutschland und Oesterreich." Ruprecht-Karls-Universität zu Heidelberg, 1930.

Wells, Christopher. "Rebuilding the City, Leaving It Behind." *Journal of Transport History* 35, no. 2 (2014): 183–99.

Welzbacher, Christian. "Schultze-Naumburg, Paul Eduard." In *Neue Deutsche Biographie*, 23:709–11. Berlin: Duncker & Humblot, 2007.

Werner, Jake. "Global Fordism in 1950s Urban China." *Frontiers of History in China* 7, no. 3 (2012): 415–41.

Wernigerode, Alfred Baron a. "Der Haus- und Grundbesitzer in Preussens Städten einst und jetzt (unter Berücksichtung von Steins Städteordnung)." Vereinigten Friedrichs-Universität Halle-Wittenberg, 1911.

Wilde, Alexander. "Republikfeindschaft in der Berliner Bevölkerung und der Wandel der kommunal Selbstverwaltung um 1931." In *Beiträge zur Geschichte der Berliner Demokratie, 1919–1933/1945–1985*, edited by Otto Büsch and Felix Escher. 107–42. Berlin: Colloquium Verlag, 1988.

Williams, John Alexander. "'The Chords of the German Soul Are Tuned to Nature.'" *Central European History* 29, no. 3 (1996): 339–84.

Wilson, Jeffrey K. *The German Forest, 1871–1914*. Toronto: University of Toronto Press, 2012.

Winkler, Heinrich August. "Einleitende Bemerkungen zu Hilferdings Theorie des Organisierten Kapitalismus." In *Organisierter Kapitalismus*, edited by Helmut Berding, Jürgen Kocka, Hans-Christoph Schröder, and Hans Ulrich Wehler, 9–18. Göttingen: Vandenhoeck & Ruprecht, 1974.

Wirckau, Edgar. "Das preußische Zweckverbandsgesetz vom 19. Juli 1911." Königlichen Universität Marburg, 1913.

Witte, Irene M. *Heim und Technik in Amerika*. Berlin: VDI-Verlag, GmbH, 1928.

Wittling, Gernot. "Zivil-militärische Beziehungen im Spannungsfeld von Residenz und entstehendem großstädtischen Industriezentrum." In *Stadt und Militär 1815–1914*, edited by Bernhard Sicken, 215–42. Paderborn: Ferdinand Schöningh, 1998.

Wolzendorf, Kurt. "Der reine Staat." *Zeitschrift für gesamte Staatswissenschaft* 75, no. 1/2 (1921): 199–229.

Woodson-Boulton, Amy. *Transformative Beauty*. Stanford, CA: Stanford University Press, 2012.

Wutztky, Emil. "Städtebau, Siedlung, Wohnung." In *Probleme der Neuen Stadt Berlin*, edited by Hans Bennert and Erwin Stein, 239–43. Berlin-Friednau: Deutscher Kommunal-Verlag GmbH, 1926.

Wygodzinski, W[illy]. *Wandlungen der deutschen Volkswirtschaft im neunzehnten Jahrhundert*. Cologne: M. Du Mont-Schauberg'schen Buchhandlung, 1907.

Yaney, George L. *The World of the Manager*. New York: P. Lang, 1994.

Yates, Alexia. "Selling Paris." *Enterprise and Society* 13, no. 4 (2012): 773–89.

Yelling, J.A. "The Selection of Sites for Slum Clearance in London, 1875–1888." *Journal of Historical Geography* 7, no. 2 (1981): 155–65.

Zerfaß, Julius. "Die Gartenstadtfrage und das Großstädische Wohnungsproblem." *Kommunale Praxis* 18, no. 29 (20 July 1918): 449–53.

Zhong, Weimin. "The Roles of Tea and Opium in Early Economic Globalization." *Frontiers of History in China* 5, no. 1 (2010): 86–105.

Ziethen, Oskar. "Wald- und Wiesengürtel für Groß-Berlin." In *Fragen der kommunalen Sozialpolitik in Groß-Berlin*, edited by Gesellschaft für soziale Reform Ortsgruppe Berlin, 38–62. Jena: Gustav Fischer, 1912.

Zimmermann, Max Georg. *Künstlerische Lehren aus der Geschichte des Städtebaus*. Berlin: Wilhelm Ernst & Sohn, 1909.

Zippel, Martin. "Untersuchungen zur Militärgeschichte der Reichshauptstadt Berlin von 1871 bis 1945." Geschichte, Westfälischen Wilhelms-Universität, 1981.

Index

German and European Studies

General Editor: Jennifer J. Jenkins

1 Emanuel Adler, Beverly Crawford, Federica Bicchi, and Rafaella Del Sarto, *The Convergence of Civilizations: Constructing a Mediterranean Region*
2 James Retallack, *The German Right, 1860–1920: Political Limits of the Authoritarian Imagination*
3 Silvija Jestrovic, *Theatre of Estrangement: Theory, Practice, Ideology*
4 Susan Gross Solomon, ed., *Doing Medicine Together: Germany and Russia between the Wars*
5 Laurence McFalls, ed., *Max Weber's 'Objectivity' Revisited*
6 Robin Ostow, ed., *(Re)Visualizing National History: Museums and National Identities in Europe in the New Millennium*
7 David Blackbourn and James Retallack, eds., *Localism, Landscape, and the Ambiguities of Place: German-Speaking Central Europe, 1860–1930*
8 John Zilcosky, ed., *Writing Travel: The Poetics and Politics of the Modern Journey*
9 Angelica Fenner, *Race under Reconstruction in German Cinema: Robert Stemmle's Toxi*
10 Martina Kessel and Patrick Merziger, eds., *The Politics of Humour in the Twentieth Century: Inclusion, Exclusion, and Communities of Laughter*
11 Jeffrey K. Wilson, *The German Forest: Nature, Identity, and the Contestation of a National Symbol, 1871–1914*
12 David G. John, *Bennewitz, Goethe,* Faust: *German and Intercultural Stagings*

13 Jennifer Ruth Hosek, *Sun, Sex, and Socialism: Cuba in the German Imaginary*
14 Steven M. Schroeder, *To Forget It All and Begin Again: Reconciliation in Occupied Germany, 1944–1954*
15 Kenneth S. Calhoon, *Affecting Grace: Theatre, Subject, and the Shakespearean Paradox in German Literature from Lessing to Kleist*
16 Martina Kolb, *Nietzsche, Freud, Benn, and the Azure Spell of Liguria*
17 Hoi-eun Kim, *Doctors of Empire: Medical and Cultural Encounters between Imperial Germany and Meiji Japan*
18 J. Laurence Hare, *Excavating Nations: Archaeology, Museums, and the German-Danish Borderlands*
19 Jacques Kornberg, *Pope Pius XII's Dilemma: Facing Atrocities and Genocide in World War II*
20 Patrick O'Neill, *Transforming Kafka: Translation Effects*
21 John K. Noyes, *Herder: Aesthetics against Imperialism*
22 James Retallack, *Germany's Second Reich: Portraits and Pathways*
23 Laurie Marhoefer, *Sex and the Weimar Republic: German Homosexual Emancipation and the Rise of the Nazis*
24 Bettina Brandt and Daniel Purdy, eds. *China and the German Enlightenment*
25 Michael Hau. *Performance Anxiety: Sport and Work in Germany from the Empire to Nazism*
26 Celia Applegate, *The Necessity of Music: Variations on a German Theme*
27 Richard J. Golsan and Sarah M. Misemer, eds. *The Trial That Never Ends: Hannah Arendt's* Eichmann in Jerusalem *in Retrospect*
28 Lynne Taylor, *In the Children's Best Interests: Unaccompanied Children in American-Occupied Germany, 1945–1952*
29 Jennifer A. Miller, *Turkish Guest Workers in Germany: Hidden Lives and Contested Borders, 1960s to 1980s*
30 Amy Carney, *Marriage and Fatherhood in the Nazi SS*
31 Michael E. O'Sullivan, *Disruptive Power: Catholic Women, Miracles, and Politics in Modern Germany, 1918–1965*
32 Gabriel N. Finder and Alexander V. Prusin, *Justice behind the Iron Curtain: Nazis on Trial in Communist Poland*
33 Parker Daly Everett, *Urban Transformations: From Liberalism to Corporatism in Greater Berlin, 1871–1933*
34 Melissa Kravetz, *Women Doctors in Weimar and Nazi Germany: Maternalism, Eugenics, and Professional Identity*

www.ingramcontent.com/pod-product-compliance
Lightning Source LLC
LaVergne TN
LVHW090147080826
844660LV00013B/707/J

* 9 7 8 1 4 4 2 6 5 0 5 3 4 *